What others are saying about this book:

"This book is a must for those considering publishing as a business, for writers who want to investigate self-publishing, and is eminently useful for its new and old ideas to those who have already begun to do it. A fine and handy guide by a fine and successful publisher." — *Small Press Review*.

"Never before has this reviewer seen such accurate, concise information covering all the aspects of self-publishing as will be found in this helpful book." — Naples, Florida, *Daily News*.

"Poynter is at his best when discussing such specifics as starting one's own publishing house; dealing with printers; establishing discount, credit and return policies; promoting, advertising and selling a book; and order fulfillment." — *Publishers Weekly*.

"Self-publishers: This how-to book and encyclopedia will be your most important investment. The subject matter is succinctly stated, well-organized with excellent illustrations, and particularly notable are the sections on how to gather and refine material for any nonfiction book, no matter who publishes it." — *Teacher-Writer*.

"A handy, concise and informative sourcebook . . . Expertly organized and chock full of hard facts, helpful hints, and pertinent illustrations . . . Recommended for all libraries . . . ." — *The Southeastern Librarian*.

"The most comprehensive, readable, and informative book about self-publishing on the market today. None better. **If you can afford to buy only one book on self-publishing, buy this book. It is indispensable.**" — John Kremer, *Self-Publishing Book Review*.

"*The Self-Publishing Manual* is by far the best on the market, and a fabulous addition to my library. More than that, it is a handbook, an encyclopedia, a friend, a companion, and a labor of love." — Paul E. Harris, Jr., Soccer For Americans, Inc.

The Self-Publishing Manual
The guide that has launched thousands of books

The Self-Publishing Manual
How to Write, Print and Sell Your Own Book

Dan Poynter

Ninth Edition, Revised

Para Publishing, Santa Barbara, California

The Self-Publishing Manual
How to Write, Print and Sell Your Own Book

By Dan Poynter

Published by:

Para Publishing
Post Office Box 8206
Santa Barbara, CA 93118-8206 U.S.A.

Copyright © 1979, 1984, 1986, 1989, 1991, 1993, 1995 and 1996
by Dan Poynter
First Printing 1979
Second Printing 1980, revised
Third Printing 1984, completely revised
Fourth Printing 1986, revised
Fifth Printing 1989, completely revised
Sixth Printing 1991, revised
Seventh Printing 1993, revised
Eighth Printing 1995, completely revised
Ninth Printing 1996, revised
Printed in the United States of America

Library of Congress Cataloging-in-Publication Data
Poynter, Dan
   The self-publishing manual : how to write, print and sell your
own book / by Dan Poynter. — 9th ed.
      p.   cm.
   Includes bibliographical references and index.
   ISBN 1-56860-018-6 (pbk.)
   1. Self-publishing—United States.   I. Title.
   2. Desktop Publishing—Computer publishing, etc.
   3. Publishers and Publishing—Handbooks, manuals, etc.
   4. Printing, Practical—Handbooks, manuals, etc.
   5. Authorship—Handbooks, manuals, etc.
Z285.5.P69   1996
070.5'93—dc20   95-33712
                                                CIP

Table of Contents

About The Author

Dan Poynter fell into publishing. He spent eight years researching a labor of love. Realizing no publisher would be interested in a technical treatise on the parachute, he went directly to a printer and "self-published." The book sold, the orders poured in and he suddenly found he was a publisher himself.

In 1973, he became interested in a new aviation sport, couldn't find a book on the subject, so he sat down and wrote one. After four months of writing and intense research which took him from coast to coast, he delivered the manuscript to the printer. So far, *Hang Gliding* has sold over 130,000 copies—a "best seller!"

Continuing to write, Dan produced 70 books and revisions, of which some have been translated into Spanish, Japanese, Russian and German. Over the years, Dan has developed a system of writing which makes it all so easy and fun. His books are loaded with facts and figures and contain detailed inside information. They are always up-to-date because he revises them before going back to press. Dan has sold over a million of his books, including several best-sellers, for millions of dollars in sales. Many of his books sell at the rate of a steady 10,000 copies per year, every year.

For many years, Dan ran Para Publishing all by himself. In fact, he was often billed as the *world's largest one-person publishing company*. As a one-man show, an author-publisher who handled all the writing, publishing and promotion, office management and shipping himself, Dan is in the best position to advise a first-time self-publishing author who is on a limited budget.

Today, Dan has staff, a number of products (books, reports, tapes, seminars, etc.) and a large plant. He travels extensively and in 1994, he skydived into the North Pole from a Russian transport plane at 10,000 feet. When you have your own business and control your own product, you can pursue your dreams.

Dan was prompted to write this book because so many publishers wanted to know his secret to selling so many books. Now he is revealing to you the secrets of writing, printing and selling your book—the good life of self-publishing.

Acknowledgment

I have not attempted to cite in the text all the authorities and sources consulted in the preparation of this manual. To do so would require more space than is available. The list would include departments of the federal government, libraries, industrial institutions, periodicals and many individuals.

Scores of people contributed to the earlier editions of this manual. Information and illustrations have been contributed to this edition by Bill Alarid, Judy Appelbaum, Walter Becker, James Scott Bell, Jerry Buchanan, Gordon Burgett, Judy Byers, Dawson Church, Dave Dunn, Robbie Fanning, Alan Gadney, Barbara Gaughen, Peggy Glenn, Bill Harrison, Don Hausrath, Jerry Jenkins, Andrew Linick, John Kremer, John McHugh, Jan Nathan, Chris Nolt, Ralcigh Pinskey, Tag Powell, Ed Rigsbee, Joe Sabah, Ellen Searby, Ted Thomas, Jan Venolia and Liz Zelandais.

I sincerely thank all these fine people. I know they are as proud of the part they have played in the development of "entrepreneurial publishing" as they are of their contribution to this work.

Copy editing by Nancy Capelle
Book design and typography by Cirrus Design
Cover by Robert Howard

Warning—Disclaimer

This book is designed to provide information in regard to the subject matter covered. It is sold with the understanding that the publisher and author are not engaged in rendering legal, accounting or other professional services. If legal or other expert assistance is required, the services of a competent professional should be sought.

It is not the purpose of this manual to reprint all the information that is otherwise available to the author and/or publisher, but to complement, amplify and supplement other texts. You are urged to read all the available material, learn as much as possible about self-publishing and to tailor the information to your individual needs. For more information, see the many references in the Appendix.

Self-publishing is not a get-rich-quick scheme. Anyone who decides to write and publish a book must expect to invest a lot of time and effort. For many people, self-publishing is more lucrative than selling manuscripts to another publisher, and many have built solid, growing, rewarding businesses.

Every effort has been made to make this manual as complete and as accurate as possible. However, there **may be mistakes** both typographical and in content. Therefore, this text should be used only as a general guide and not as the ultimate source of writing/publishing information. Furthermore, this manual contains information on writing/publishing only up to the printing date.

The purpose of this manual is to educate and entertain. The author and Para Publishing shall have neither liability nor responsibility to any person or entity with respect to any loss or damage caused, or alleged to be caused, directly or indirectly by the information contained in this book.

If you do not wish to be bound by the above, you may return this book to the publisher for a full refund.

Chapter One

Your Publishing Options

Why You Should Consider Self-Publishing

Everyone wants to "write a book." Most people have the ability, some have the drive, but few have the organization. Therefore, the greatest need is for a simple system, a "road map." The basic organizational plan in this book will not only provide you with direction, it will promote drive and expose ability no one thought existed.

Magazines devoted to businesspeople, sales reps and opportunity seekers are littered with full-page advertisements featuring people with fabulous offers. Usually these people discovered a successful system of business in sales, real estate or mail order, and, for a price, they are willing to let the reader in on their secret. To distribute this information, they have written a book. Upon close inspection, one often finds that the author is making more money from the book than from the revealed original enterprise. The irony is that purchasers get the wrong information; what the reader needs is a book on how to write a book.

Writing a book is easy! If you can voice an opinion and think logically, you can write a book. If you can *say* it, you can *write* it. Most people have to work for a living and, therefore, can spend only a few minutes of each day on their book. Consequently, they can't keep the whole manuscript in their head. When overwhelmed and confused, it is easy to quit the project. The solution is to break up the manuscript into many small easy-to-attack chunks (and never start at page one, where the hill looks steepest). Then concentrate on one section at a time and do a thorough job on each one.

People want to know "how to" and "where to," and they will pay well to find it. The information industry, the production and distribution of ideas and information as opposed to goods and services, now amounts to over one-half of the gross national product. There is money in information. To see how this market is being tapped by books, check the best seller lists in the back of *Publishers Weekly, USA Today, The Wall Street Journal* or *The New York Times*.

Your best sources for this salable information are from your own experience, plus research. Write what you know. Whether you already have a completed manuscript, have a great idea for one, or need help in locating a suitable subject, this book will point the way.

Since poetry and fiction are very difficult to sell and, even when sold, have a short sales life, we will concern ourselves with nonfiction. Writing nonfiction doesn't require any great literary style; it is simply a matter of producing well-researched, reorganized, updated and, most important, repackaged information. Some of the recommendations here may be applied to fiction, just as the chapters on publishing,

---

The number one reason any professional writes is to pay the bills. This isn't the Lawn Tennis Association, where you play for the thrill of it. — Jimmy Breslin

promotion and the mail order business may be taken separately and used elsewhere. However, all the recommendations are written toward, and for, the reader who wishes to become an author or an author-publisher of useful information.

The prestige enjoyed by the published author is unparalleled in our society. A book can bring recognition, wealth and an acceleration in one's career. People have always held books in high regard, possibly because in past centuries they were very expensive and were, therefore, purchased only by the rich. Even 150 years ago, many people could not read or write. To be an author then was to be an "educated" person.

Many enterprising people are using books to establish themselves in "the ultimate business." Usually starting with a series of nonpaying magazine articles, they develop a name and make themselves visible. Then they expand the series of articles into a book. Now with their credibility established, they operate seminars in their field of expertise, command high speaking fees and issue a high-priced business advice newsletter. From there, they teach a course in the local college and become a consultant, advising large corporations and commenting on legal briefs for lawyers. They find they are in great demand. People want their information or simply want them around. Clubs and corporations fly them in to consult, because it is cheaper than sending all their people to the expert.

This "dream product" is the packaging and marketing of information. Starting with a field you know, then researching it further and putting it on paper will establish you as an expert. Then your expert standing can be pyramided with interviews, articles, TV appearances, talks at local clubs, etc. Of course most of this activity will promote your book sales.

> *If you don't make the dust, you eat the dust.*

In turn, all this publicity not only sells books, but opens more doors and produces more invitations leading to more opportunities to prove your expert status and make even more money for yourself. People seek experts whose opinions, advice and ideas are quoted in the media. Becoming an expert does not require a great education or a college degree. You can become an expert in one small particular area if you are willing to go to the library, read up on it and write down the important elements.

A book is like a new product design, similar to an invention but usually much, much better. A patent on a device or process runs only 17 years whereas a copyright runs for the author's life plus 50 years. Patents cost thousands of dollars to secure and normally require a lot of legal help. By contrast, a copyright may be filed by the author with a simple two-page form and $20; there is no waiting period. Once you write a book, it is yours. You have a monopoly and there is no direct competition.

Many people work hard at a job for 40 years and have nothing to show for it but memories and pay stubs. Some take their knowledge and write a book; the result is a tangible product for all to see. A book lasts forever like a painting or a sculpture, but there are many copies of the book, not just one. Whereas a sculpture can only be admired by a limited number of persons at any one time in the place where it is displayed, books come in multiple copies for all the world to use and admire simultaneously.

The next secret is to cut out the middlemen by by-passing the commercial publishers to produce and sell the book yourself. You can take the author's royalty and the publisher's profit. You get all the rewards because you are both of them. Now, in addition to achieving the wealth and prestige of a published author, you have propelled yourself into your

People can be divided into three groups: those who make things happen, those who watch things happen and those who wonder what happened. — John W. Newbern

own lucrative business: a publishing house. This shortcut not only makes you more money (why share it?), it saves you the frustration, trouble and time required to sell your manuscript to a publisher. You know the subject and market better than some distant corporation anyway.

Publishing doesn't mean purchasing a printing press to actually put the ink on the paper yourself. Nearly all publishers leave the production to an experienced book printer.

In addition to the writing and publishing of your book, you will want to investigate its distribution. Today, more books are sold through the mail than through bookstores. In fact, books are the leading mail order product. One-third of all these books are in the "how-to" category. Mail order is considered one of the best ways for the beginner with no previous business experience to start a venture of his or her own. Selling books by mail is a good, solid day-to-day business opportunity. Your book will be sold in bookstores, but you will sell even more books through the mail.

Mail order is not only the simplest way to distribute books, it is an ideal way to build a second income or a new life. You don't have to give up your job, there is little overhead, there are tax breaks, you work for yourself and the business can be operated anywhere: you need only be near a post office. No one knows about your age, education, race or sex; your opportunities are indeed equal.

Direct mail marketing is like fishing. You throw out a line by promoting your products and you find out almost immediately if you have made a sale. Every day is like Christmas; opening envelopes and finding checks is great fun.

Initially, you will warehouse your books in a closet or your garage, and will slip them into padded bags for mail-

---

You cannot avoid making decisions. Every time you fail to act on a question, you have, in effect, made a decision to do nothing.

ing. It is quite easy, and starting out is not expensive or time-consuming.

Your writing/publishing/mail order company is actually combining three profitable fields and concentrating on only the best parts of each. A business of your own is the great American dream and it is still an attainable possibility. In your own business, you make the decisions to meet only those challenges you find interesting. This is not "goofing off," it is making more effective use of your time; "working smarter, not harder." After all, there are only 24 hours in a day and only one day at a time for each of us. You have to concentrate on the good areas if you are to prosper.

Running your own enterprise will provide you with many satisfying advantages. You should earn more money because you are working for yourself rather than splitting your efforts with someone else. You have job security and never have to worry about a surprise pink slip. If you keep your regular job and "moonlight" your own enterprise as recreation, it will always be there as a fall-back position should you need it. You start at the top, not the bottom, in your own company, and you work at your own pace and schedule. You will meet interesting people because, as an author and publishing executive, you will be sought out by them.

In your own small business, you may work when and where you wish; you do not have to go to where the job is. You can work 'til dawn, sleep 'til noon, rush off to Hawaii without asking permission: This is flexibility not available to the clock punchers.

Before you charge into literary battle to attack your key-board, you may wish to review Chapter Twelve. It describes

> *I guess every normal writer has a desire to give birth to a book someday—to become, in fact, an author. Books are . . . a chance at immortality.*
> — Margaret Bennett in *Publishers Weekly*

how your life will change once you become a published author. You may like to know what you are getting into.

Being an author-publisher sounds like a good life, and it can be. Working for yourself requires organization and discipline, but work doesn't seem so hard when you are counting your own money. To help you understand what is ahead, here are some definitions and some background on the book publishing industry.

"Publish" means to prepare and issue material for public distribution or sale or "to place before the public." The book doesn't have to be beautiful, it doesn't even have to sell, it needs only to be issued. Salability will depend upon the content and the packaging.

A **"Publisher"** is the one who puts up the money, the one who takes the risk. He or she has the book printed and then distributes it hoping to make back more money than has been spent to produce it. The publisher may be a big New York firm or a first-time author, but he or she is always the "investor."

A **"Book"** by international standards is a publication with at least 49 pages, not counting the covers. The U.S. Postal Service will accept publications with eight or more pages for "book rate" postage. Books should not be confused with pamphlets, which have less than 49 pages, or periodicals. Magazines and newspapers are examples of periodicals. They are published regularly and usually carry advertising.

The book publishing industry in the U.S. consists of some 53,000 firms (up from 3,000 in 1970) by R. R. Bowker's count, but there are many thousands more publishers who do not bother to apply for a listing. Altogether, they publish some 120,000 titles every year. About 100 pub-

> . . . writing. It was a private thing that I could do. I could just send it out and see what it did. If someone laughed, I could stand up and say, "I did that."
> — Erma Bombeck in The Writer

lishers are considered to be the big firms, and most of them are located in New York City. Eight thousand new publishing companies are established each year. Sales amount to $18 billion per year for the over 1,066,000 active titles listed in *Books in Print* (BIP).

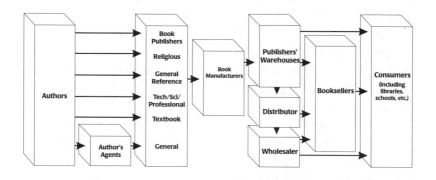

How books get from writer to reader

Your choices. An author who wishes to get into print has many choices. You may approach a large New York general publisher or a medium-sized niche publisher. You may work with an agent, use a book packager, deal with a "vanity" press or publish yourself. We will discuss each of your choices here, and you will probably decide to self-publish. As you expand your list of titles and take in other authors, you may graduate to the ranks of the medium-sized publisher. You could, one day, even become a major conventional publisher. Here are the choices.

— **The big publishing firms** are like department stores; they have something for everyone. They publish in many different fields and concentrate on books that anticipate audiences in the millions. Recently these large publishers have grown even bigger by acquiring other publishing companies. A look at the numbers in big publishing will help us to better understand their problems.

It has been estimated that some 350,000 book-length manuscripts are written each year. Many of the larger publishers receive 10,000 unsolicited manuscripts annually. Reading manuscripts takes an enormous amount of editorial time, and a very high percentage of the submissions do not fit the publisher's line; they are a waste of editorial time.

The 12,000 bookstores in the United States don't have the space to display all the 147,000 titles published each year, so they concentrate on the books that move the best in their neighborhoods. Consequently, most publishers figure that even after selecting the best manuscripts and pouring in the promotion money, only three books of ten will sell well, four will break even and three will be losers. Only 10% of the New York-published books earn out their advance.

Ever wonder why all the books in the store have very recent copyright dates? They are seldom more than a year old because the store replaces them so fast. Shelf space is expensive and in short supply. The books either sell or they go back. If one title doesn't move, it is replaced by another.

Large publishers have three selling seasons per year. They keep books alive for four months and then replace them. Most initial print runs are for 5,000 books. Then the title remains "in print" (available for sale) for maybe a year. If the book sells out quickly, it is reprinted and the publisher dumps in more promotion money. If the book does not catch on, it is pulled off the market and "remaindered" (sold off very cheaply) to make room for new titles.

The financial demands cause the publisher to be terribly objective about the line. To many publishers, in fact, a book is just a book. If they already cover a subject, they won't be interested in a new manuscript on the same topic. They already serve that interest and do not care that your version might be better. Many big publishers are not interested in whether it is a good book; all they want to know is whether it will sell. Therefore, they concentrate on authors with good track records, or Hollywood and political personalities who can move a book with their name. Only occasionally will they accept a well-written manuscript by an unknown, and then it must be on a topic with a ready and massive audience. A published writer has a much better chance of selling than an unpublished one, regardless of the quality of the work.

Publishers, like most business people, seem to follow the "80-20 principle." That is, they spend 80% of their effort on the top 20% of their books. The remaining 20% of their time goes to the bottom 80% of their line. Most books have to sell themselves to induce the publisher to allocate more promotion money.

> There is a story about one author who sent her relatives around to bookstores to buy up every copy of her new book. The sudden spurt in sales excited the publisher, who increased the ad budget. The increase in promotion produced greater sales and her book became a success.

The author will get a royalty from the large publisher of 6% to 10% of the net (what the publisher receives), usually on a sliding scale, and the economics here are not encouraging. For example, a print run of 5,000 copies of a book selling for $20 could gross $100,000 at retail, but an 8% royalty on the net (most books are sold at wholesale) may come to $3,200. That isn't enough money to pay for all the time spent at the computer. The chances of selling more than 5,000 copies are highly remote because, after a few months, the publisher takes the book out of print. In fact, the publisher will probably sell less than the amount printed, because some books will be used for promotion while others will be returned by the bookstores, unsold.

If your manuscript is a blockbuster with potential sales in the millions, you may need a big publisher; and they certainly want you. They will take care of all the printing and distributing and you can have your royalty checks sent to you in Bimini.

> *I hope you get as much pleasure reading my book as I got spending the money you paid me for it.*

Your publisher will put up the money, have the book produced and use sales reps to get it into bookstores but they will not promote the book. The author must do it. The problem is that most first-time authors think the publisher will do the promotion. Once they figure out that nothing is being done, it is too late, the book is no longer new (it has a quickly-ticking copyright date in it) and is being remaindered. Then they also discover, to their dismay, that their contract provides that they must submit their next two manuscripts to this same publisher.

The big publishing houses provide a needed service, but for many first-time authors they are unapproachable. Once in, the author doesn't get the best deal and getting out may be difficult. To begin with, the publisher may sit on the manuscript for many months before rejecting it. Then once accepted, they often chop it up editorially and change the title; you lose artistic control of your book.

All these changes might be acceptable if the big commercial publishers were great financial successes. They aren't, or at least they haven't been so far. One publishing house even admits it would have made more money last year if it had vacated its New York office and rented out the floor space.

The publishing industry attracts lovely, creative people who find their rewards in its non-material aspects. They often come from tax-supported academic or library communities; they have never been marketing-oriented. In fact, the editorial function in most publishing houses jealously guards its independence so it won't be "corrupted" by the marketing department. This leads editors into the greatest trap in publishing: producing titles which "should be published" but do not sell. When a book fails to earn back its investment, the publishing house calls it a "prestige" book and justifies its production as a public service.

One person in the sales department has to love your book, or it's gone. — Charles Oviatt, McGraw-Hill

Many of the people working in the big firms know the editing-marketing approach is wrong (or that losing money is not what business is all about), and they are frustrated by it. But no matter how many seminars they attend or books they read, they can't move their companies out of their rut.

In the big firms, salaries are too low to attract highly motivated marketing people. Without better marketing, the companies can't afford to pay more. It is a vicious circle, and there has been little effort to reverse it.

The answer is for the marketing department to select the manuscripts they feel they can sell and to confine the editors' work to editing.

But there is a brighter side for the small publisher who understands who his or her readers are and where they can be found. Since the old-line big *department store-like* publishers only know how to sell through bookstores, there is a lot of room left for the smaller *boutique-like* publishing house and self-publisher.

Be careful if you hang around with people from the book industry. Learn, but don't let their ways rub off. Study the big New York publishing firms, but don't copy them. You can do a lot better.

— **The medium-sized "niche" publishers** are the smaller and newer firms which specialize in serving individual technical fields, particular geographic regions or other niche markets (business books, hiking books, boating books, etc.). Some of these publishers are very small, while others are fairly large, but the most successful ones concentrate on a single subject area.

The owners and staff are usually *participants* in their books' subject matter. For example, those who publish parachute books do it with a sense of mission—because they like to jump out of airplanes. Participants know their subject

> *A little publishing house may surface with one or two books—how-to, self-help, pop psychology—and start a trend.*
> — Patricia Holt, Book Editor, *San Francisco Chronicle*

matter and where to find their reader/buyer, because they join the same associations, read the same magazines and attend the same conventions.

The secret to effective book distribution is to make the title available in places with a high concentration of (your) potential buyers. When a specialized publisher takes on your book, they can plug it right into their distribution system. For example, while some parachute books would be sold in bookstores, over 90% would be sold through parachute stores, skydiving catalogs, jump schools and through the U.S. Parachute Association for resale to its members. Usually three or four calls to major dealers can sell enough books to pay the printing bill—before the book is even printed!

Some writers may think a large New York publisher is more prestigious, but a small to medium-sized publisher will usually sell more books. Remember, most book buyers are interested in the subject matter of the book and want to know if the author is a credible person. No one ever asks who the publisher is.

Contacting a publisher. If you decide you want your book published by someone else, the secret is to match the manuscript to the publisher. To find the right publisher, check your own bookshelf. Go to your nearby larger public library and consult the shelves where your book will be. Then see *Books In Print*, a multi-volumed reference listing all the books that are currently available for sale. Look for smaller publishers who do good work. Then look up their addresses in the last volume. When you contact a specialized publisher, you will often get through to the top person. They know what you are talking about and they are always very helpful. They will be able to tell you instantly whether the proposed book will fit into their line.

> *I'll be damned if I'll do my publishers' job for them. If I had wanted to become a hustler, I would have hit the streets long ago. I am a creative artist—I know it sounds pretentious, but that's what I am. I am no businessman or salesman.* — From an article by Rebekah Jordan in *Publishers Weekly*.

Book publishers are helpful and friendly. No two books are alike. It is a rarity that two books on the same subject are published in the same year. Consequently, publishers do not feel threatened by other publishers. In fact, publishers often promote other books and each other. This is why when you contact a publisher and they determine that your manuscript is not for them, they are eager to recommend another publisher. They know of lots of other publishing companies and most relish being able to help you and the other publisher get together.

— **Vanity or subsidy publishers** produce around 6,000 titles each year; some twenty firms produce about 70% of all the subsidized books. Subsidy publishers offer regular publishing services, but the author invests the money. Under a typical arrangement, the author pays the full publishing (more than just printing bill) costs, receives 40% of the retail price of the books sold and 80% of the subsidiary rights, if sold. Many vanity publishers will charge you $10,000 to $30,000 to publish your book depending upon its length.

The vanity publisher claims he will furnish all the regular publishing services including promotion and distribution. All this might not be so bad if they had a good track record for delivery. But according to *Writer's Digest*, vanity publishers usually do not deliver the promotion they promise, and the books rarely return one-quarter of the author's investment.

The ads reading "To the author . . ." or "Manuscripts wanted by . . ." easily catch the eye of the writer with a book-length manuscript. Vanity presses almost always accept a manuscript for publication and usually do so with a glowing review letter. They don't make any promises regarding sales and usually the book sells fewer than 100 copies. The vanity publisher doesn't have to sell any books because the author has already paid him for his work. Therefore, subsidy

> *Small publishing is exhibiting robust health, while the traditional industry is ailing.* — Paul D. Doebler

publishers are interested in manufacturing the book, not in editing, promotion, sales or distribution. Since they are paid to publish, they are really selling printing contracts, not books. They are simply taking a fee to print unedited manuscripts.

Since binding is expensive, the subsidy publisher often binds a few hundred copies; the rest of the sheets remain unbound unless needed. The "advertising" promised in the contract normally turns out to be only a "tombstone" ad listing many titles in the *New York Times*. Sales from this feeble promotion are very rare.

The review copies sent to columnists by a subsidy publisher usually go straight into the circular file. The reviewer's time is valuable, and they do not like vanity presses because they know that so little attention was paid to the editing of the book. Further, they realize there will be little promotional effort and that the book will not be available to readers in the stores. The name of the vanity publisher on the spine of the book is a kiss of death.

One major vanity press lost a large class-action suit a few years ago, but they are still advertising in the *Yellow Pages*. Before considering a subsidy or vanity publisher, send for *Should You Pay to Have it Published* (*Writer's Digest,* 1507 Dana Avenue, Cincinnati, OH 45207).

— **Book packagers** are graphic arts shops that specialize in the production of books. They will edit the manuscript, design the book, set the type and lay out the pages. When the book is printed, it is delivered to you. Book packagers (or producers) do not invest in books, they do not promote books and they do not store or ship books. They only put them together.

Book producers serve publishers who have more projects than they can handle in-house. They are a good alternative for the busy beginning self-publisher. To find a book pro-

> *Legitimate publishers don't have to look for business.*
> — L.M. Hasselstrom

ducer, see the Publishers Marketing Association newsletter (see the Appendix) and *Literary Market Place.*

— **Literary agents** match manuscripts with the right publisher and negotiate the contract; most new material comes to big publishers through them. The agent has to serve the publisher well, for if he or she submits an inappropriate or poor manuscript, the publisher will never offer another appointment. Therefore, agents like sure bets, too, and many are reluctant to even consider an unpublished writer. Their normal commission is 15%.

For the author, the agent will make manuscript suggestions, negotiate the contract and try to sell the book to one of his or her many contacts; the agent will exploit all possible avenues. If your manuscript is a winner, it is wise to have professional management. Some authors feel it is best to contract with an agent based in New York; he or she will have closer contacts and can deal in person.

According to *Literary Agent's Marketplace,* about 40% of the book agents will not read manuscripts by unpublished authors, and a good 15% will not even answer query letters from them. Of those agents who will read the manuscript of an unpublished author, 80% will charge for the service. Eighty percent of the agents will not represent professional books; 93% will not touch reference works; 99% will not handle technical books; 98% will not represent regional books, satire, musicals and other specialized manuscripts. While most agents will handle novel-length fiction, only 20% are willing to take on either novelettes or short stories, and only 2% have a special interest in literature or quality fiction.

On the fringe, there are several "agents" who charge a "reading fee" and then pay students to read and critique the manuscript. They make their money on these fees, not from placing the manuscripts. For a list of literary agents, see *Fic-*

Vanity publishing is to legitimate publishing as loansharking is to banking. — Martin J. Baron

tion Writer's Market, Literary Agents Marketplace and *Literary Market Place.*

— **Self-publishing** is where the author by-passes all the middlemen, deals directly with the printer and then handles the marketing and distribution. If you publish yourself, you will make more money, get to press sooner and keep control of your book. You will invest your time as well as your money, but the reward is greater; you will get it all.

Self-publishing is not new. In fact, it has solid early American roots; it is almost a tradition. Well-known self-publishers include Mark Twain, Zane Grey, Upton Sinclair, Carl Sandburg, James Joyce, D.H. Lawrence, Ezra Pound, Edgar Rice Burroughs, Stephen Crane, Mary Baker Eddy, George Bernard Shaw, Edgar Allen Poe, Rudyard Kipling, Henry David Thoreau, Walt Whitman, Robert Ringer, Spencer Johnson, Richard Bolles, Richard Nixon and many, many more. These people were self-publishers, though today the vanity presses claim their books were "subsidy" published.

Years ago, some authors elected to go their own way after being turned down by regular publishers, but today most self-publishers make an educated decision to take control of their book—usually after reading this book.

Do self-publishers ever sell many books? Here are some numbers (at last count): *What Color is Your Parachute*, 4.3 million; *Fifty Simple Things You Can Do to Save the Earth*, 3.5 million; *How to Keep Your Volkswagen Alive*, 2.2 million; *Leadership Secrets of Attila the Hun*, over half a million and *Final Exit*, over half a million copies. These authors took control and made it big.

Self-publishing is not difficult. In fact, it may even be easier than dealing with a publisher. The job of the publish-

> *I was thrilled at the cooperation of agents, but was a little alarmed when I found, more than once, a rejection letter from the first recipient in the manuscript.* — Ruth Nodkins Nathan in *Publishers Weekly*

ing manager is not to perform every task, but to see that every task gets done. The self-publisher deals directly with the printer and handles as many of the editing, proofing, promotion and distribution jobs as he or she can. What they can't do, they farm out. Therefore, self-publishing may take on many forms depending on the author's interests, assets and abilities. It allows you to concentrate on those areas you find most challenging.

Properly planned, there is little monetary risk in self-publishing. If you follow the plan, the only variable is the subject of the book. Unlike poetry and fiction, most nonfiction topics sell easily. In fact, many authors publish themselves because this method provides the best return on their labor in the long run. Because the big publisher only tries a book for a few months and then lets sales dictate its fate (reprint or remainder), the first year is most important. The self-publisher, on the other hand, uses the first year to build a solid market for a future of sustained sales. While a big publisher may sell only 5,000 copies total, the self-publisher can often count on 5,000 or more each year, year after year.

Is There a Book Inside You? has a self-paced quiz to help you decide between a large publisher, a medium-sized niche publisher, an agent, a book producer, a vanity press and self-publishing.

Here are eight good reasons to self-publish:

1. To make more money. Why accept 6% to 10% in royalties when you can have 35%? You know your subject and you know the people in the field. Certainly you know better than some distant publisher who might buy your book. While the trade publisher may have some good contacts, he doesn't know the market as well as you, and he isn't going to expend as much promo-

---

I can't understand why a person will take a year or two to write a novel when he can easily buy one for a few dollars.
— Fred Allen

tional effort. Ask yourself this question: Will the trade publisher be able to sell four times as many books as I can?

2. Speed. Most publishers work on an 18-month production cycle. Can you wait that long to get into print? Will you miss your market? The 1 1/2 years doesn't even begin until *after* the contract negotiations and contract signing. Publication could be three years away! Why waste valuable time shipping your manuscript around to see if there is a publisher out there who likes it? Richard Nixon self-published *Real Peace* in 1983 because he felt his message was urgent; he couldn't wait for a publisher's machinery to grind out the book.

   Typically, bookstores buy the first book on a popular subject. Later books may be better, but the buyer will pass on them since the store already has the subject "covered."

3. To keep control of your book. According to *Writer's Digest*, 60% of the big publishers do not give the author final approval on copy editing. Twenty-three percent never give the author the right to select the title, 20% do not consult the author on the jacket design and 36% rarely involve the author in the book's promotion.

   The big New York trade publishers may have more promotional connections than you, but with a stable of books to push, your effort may get lost in the shuffle. The big publishers are good at getting books into bookstores but they fail miserably at approaching other outlets. Give the book to someone who has a personal interest in it—the author.

4. No one will read your manuscript. Many publishers receive more than 100 unsolicited manuscripts for consideration each day. They do not have time to unwrap, review, rewrap and ship

all these submissions, so they return them un-opened. Unless you are a movie star, noted politician or have a recognizable name, it is nearly impossible to attract a publisher. Many publishers work with their existing stable of authors and accept new authors only through agents.

5. Self-publishing is good business. There are more tax advantages for an author-publisher than there are for just authors.

6. Self-publishing will help you to think like a publisher. You will learn the industry and will have a better understanding of the big picture. A book is a product of one's self. An analogy may be drawn with giving birth. The author naturally feels that his book is terrific and that it would sell better if only his publisher would dump in more promotion money. He is very protective about his book (ever try to tell a mother her child is ugly?). The publisher answers that he is not anxious to dump more money into a book that isn't selling. So, if the author self-publishes, he gains a better understanding of the arguments on both sides. It is his money and his choice.

7. You will gain self-confidence and self-esteem. You will be proud to be the author of a book. Compare this to pleading with people to read your manuscript.

8. Finally—you may have no other choice. There are more manuscripts than can be read. Most publishers don't have time to even look at your manuscript.

The appearance of the finished book took two whole years from acceptance to publication, and I'm a better writer now than I was then. — Pam Conrad

The greatest problem facing the smaller and newer publisher today is finding a system for *managing the excitement*. Nonfiction book publishers produce valuable information that our customers willingly buy because it is going to save them time and money. We send out review copies, make direct mail solicitations and circulate news releases on our books—and our customers respond. That is exciting! Publishing is an easy business, a profitable business and a fun business. The publishing business is truly *excitement driven*.

Should you self-publish? Would-be author-publishers should be cautioned that self-publishing is not for everyone. Writing is an *art,* while publishing is a *business*, and many people are unable to do both well. If you are a lovely, creative flower who is repelled by the "crass commercialism" of selling one's own product, you should stick to the creative side and let someone else handle the business end. On the other hand, some people are terribly independent. They will not be happy with the performance of any publisher, no matter how much time and effort are spent creating and promoting the book. These people should save the publisher from all this grief by making their own decisions. You must understand all the alternatives so that you can make an intelligent, educated choice.

Selling out. Many self-publishers find that once they have proven their books with good sales, they are approached by the big publishing houses with offers to print a new edition. If you decide to sell out to a large publisher, see the *Selling Out* discussion in Chapter Eight.

The future. Packaged information is becoming increasingly specialized. More and more books are being printed in smaller quantities. The information in books is going out of date faster. Books are being produced more rapidly. Comput-

If you would be thrilled by watching the galloping advance of a major glacier, you'd be ecstatic watching changes in publishing. — John D. MacDonald in *InfoWorld*

erized equipment is being used to write, edit, lay out and print books. The customer wants more condensed information fast.

The chapters which follow describe in detail an alternative route to traditional publishing. This route will enable you to get your book into print at minimum cost.

This book could be your "second chance." It will show you the way to publication, fame, extra income—a new life.

Obviously your success cannot be guaranteed, but many people are doing very well in the writing/publishing business. This isn't a get-rich-quick scheme; there is work involved. While you are working for yourself, at your own pace, it is still work. You won't get rich overnight. Building a sound business venture takes several years.

The secret is to invest your labor. Your time is precious. Like gold, there is a finite quantity. You have only 24 hours of time each day. You may use your time in several ways: You may throw it away, sell it or invest it. You can waste your valuable time in front of the television set; time is easy to "lose." Most people punch in at the clock, go to work and get a check. They trade their labor for money on a one-for-one basis. If you don't punch in, you don't get paid. How much better it is to invest your time in a book which will sell and generate income while you are away doing something else. Your labor becomes an investment which pays dividends for years while you are playing, or working on another investment.

Don't throw away your time; invest it. It is up to you.

Chapter Two

Writing Your Book

How to Generate Salable Material

Where are your talents and what do you want to do? Do you enjoy writing, or do you want to be a published author without the "pain" of writing? Analyze yourself. Do you want to write, publish or sell books, any combination of these activities, or even all three? Here we will cover all three to help you make an educated choice. First we will cover how to get your thoughts on paper. Then we will discuss both sides of publishing: as seen by the author and as seen by the publisher.

Picking a subject is the first step. Sitting there waiting for inspiration is called "writer's block." You cannot write about a subject until you select it. So, do not waste time thinking about what to write. Consider the four elements necessary for producing good nonfiction:

1. The subject is interesting to you.

2. You have the necessary expertise, and the information is available.

3. The subject is of interest to others and is, therefore, salable.

4. The subject matter is tightly focused.

The book should be on a subject in which you are interested and in which you are an expert or would like to become an expert. You have spent years working at, specializing in, and learning something, and there are thousands of
people out there willing to pay good money to get the inside
information on it. Write what you know! If you select your
hobby, there are a number of advantages: You know what
has been written in the past, you have the contacts for gathering more information and your further participation in that
hobby will become tax deductible.

If you need help evaluating your project, contact author-
publisher Gordon Burgett. He will read your manuscript and
make recommendations on market targeting, manuscript re-
work (if necessary), publishing and marketing. Call him at
(805) 937-8711.

At Para Publishing, we specialize in coaching nonfiction
book publishers to sell more books. We do not claim to have
any expertise in magazine publishing, newsletter publishing, fiction or poetry. Fiction and poetry are much more difficult to sell than nonfiction books. Some of our programs,
ideas, leads and resources will work for creative literature,
but that is not our specialty.

Fiction v. Nonfiction. There is a difference between entertainment and information, known as fiction and nonfiction. Every nonfiction book is unique. The buyer interested
in the subject of raising llamas is not necessarily a good
prospect for a book on skydiving or waste-water treatment.
Fiction, on the other hand, is related to all other fiction in its
category. A reader who buys one mystery is a prime candidate for another mystery. Consequently, fiction must compete for people's time. People must choose not only between
reading this book of fiction and reading other books but between reading this book and engaging in other forms of en-

tertainment, such as going to a movie or walking on the beach. Nonfiction does not compete for time. Nonfiction is information that people buy because it will save them time or money. It is much easier to convince people to buy non-fiction than fiction.

Consequently, the unknown poet or fiction writer is at the same point as the unknown painter or musician.

Fiction. It is possible to sell fiction, or at least some people are doing it, but it isn't easy. Dorothy Bryant, a novelist in Berkeley, California, publishes and promotes what she writes. She calls her publishing company Ata Books. You might be able to sell your fiction if you consider the market first. Stories tailored to a specific geographic area might sell well locally.

Very generally speaking, a large New York publisher will do a better job on fiction, while you will do a better job yourself with nonfiction.

For a list of fiction publishers, see *Fiction Writers* at your public library.

Poetry is even more difficult to sell. Since we receive so many requests for information, we have assembled an Instant Report titled *Publishing Fiction and Poetry*. It is on Para Publishing's Fax-On-Demand system; request Document 606. The price is $4.95. See the Appendix.

Nonfiction. The subject of a book, not the name of the publisher or the comments of a reviewer, is what sells it. Every new national craze requires how-to books. According to *Newsweek,* there are over 1,300 books on fitness and health currently in print. Do not be discouraged if your subject has already been covered. That just proves someone else thought it was important. Using your own experience and the latest information, you can do it better. The subjects with the best sales potential are how-to's, money, health, self-improve-

---

To avoid writer's block, do not sit waiting for inspiration, get out and search for a subject.

ment, hobbies, sex and psychological well-being. Find a need and fill it.

One specialized book that sold for years was *Hang Gliding,* by this author; it went through the press ten times for 130,000 copies in print.

Anticipate reader interest and pick a subject which will sell on its own, even if the buyer has never heard of the book.

Regional guidebooks are easier to write and market, since both the information and the distribution are local. Tourist guides, restaurant guides and historical books are a good way to get started in publishing.

You do not have to be an expert—yet. If you are new to a subject, you could produce a better book than an old hand, because you are better able to understand and relate to the reader-novice. You know what his reactions and needs are, as well as what he is thinking. Once you are finished researching and writing, you too will be an expert.

There may be more money publishing your information in short monographs than in longer books. Timely monographs usually command a higher price, can be published in shorter runs and take less time to produce. Do not overlook well-researched short reports.

Now, to obtain a manuscript, you have the choice of buying it from others or writing it yourself (are you an author or a writer?). In this chapter, we will discuss the many possibilities—only one has to be right for you. If one possibility "clicks," you are on your way. First we will cover how to write material yourself, and then we will show you how to obtain some or all the material from others.

Write it yourself. Creating your own material is easy if you have a system; all it takes is organization and discipline. Following the system outlined below, creating copy becomes

> *There are three rules for writing the novel. Unfortunately, no one knows what they are.* — Somerset Maugham

challenging fun and allows you to see the progress you are making, which is encouraging. While this method may be of some help in writing fiction, it has been developed specifically for nonfiction.

While writing a book is not difficult, it is not for the lazy. Like AA or a diet, you will have to change your lifestyle. This means waking up one morning and making a decision: to do it now. To get into the system and develop good habits will provide you with a sense of purpose and a feeling of accomplishment. Once you have selected a topic, only the decision to go stands between you and the finished book.

Time or lack of it is the most frequently heard excuse. But somehow we always find the time for those things most important to us. We just put them first. Often we can fit in an hour of writing time each day by completing our other chores faster. One way is to get up one hour earlier each day. This is perfect scheduling, as the house is quiet, the telephone does not ring, and most writers find the early morning to be their most creative and productive time. But you must put this hour first and not let anything interfere with it. Once you gather momentum in your project, you will find arising early will be easy; you won't even miss that hour of sleep.

Set up a writing area in a spare room or a corner of the living room. Keep all your writing materials and research tools there. Your creative writing time is precious; do not waste it trying to get started.

Write your back-cover copy before you write your book in order to set your sights on your objective. The back cover of your book is important sales space; use it wisely. List benefits, quote experts and write copy that will convince the browsers they need this book.

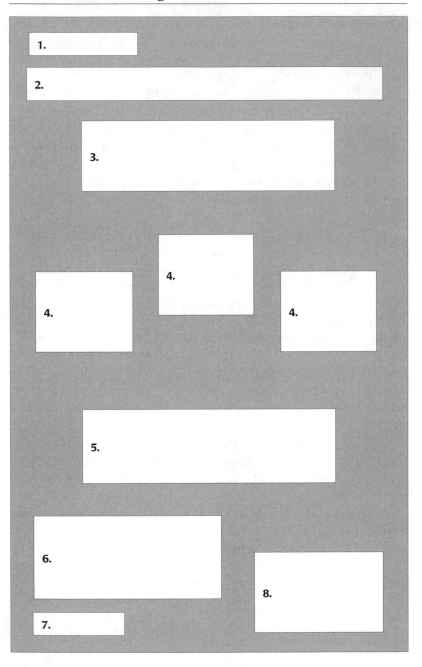

Back Cover Worksheet

Use your computer to draft your back cover following the paint-by-the-numbers outline. Draft a paragraph on each of the following:

1. **Category.** Check the shelves in the bookstores where your book will be displayed. Note the categories on the books and the shelves. Listing the category on the back cover of your book will insure your book is easy to find—because the bookshop personnel will place it on the right shelf.

2. First you need an arresting **headline** addressed to potential buyers, so they can relate to the book and find themselves in it. For example: The back-cover copy of *Choices, A Teen Woman's Journal for Self-Awareness and Personal Planning,* starts off: *A book that every mother, grandmother, aunt, and mentor will want to give to the teenage women in their lives.* The buyer of this book is not the teenager but the adult, so the headline is directed toward the adult.

3. **Sales copy.** Concisely state what the book is about. What will the reader gain by reading this book? The back cover of *The Self-Publishing Manual* recommends that all authors read the book even if they do not plan to self-publish. Your sales copy should promise health, wealth, entertainment or a better life. Stress benefits. Promise to make readers better at what they do. Many books use:

You will learn:
- (benefit)
- (benefit)
- (benefit)
- (benefit)

> *There are three rules to successful writing: 1. Have something to say, 2. Know how to say it, and 3. Be able to sell it.*
> — David Hellyer

4. **Testimonials and endorsements.** Dream up three different endorsements from people you would like to quote. If *"This book changed my life.— Colin Powell,"* would look good, try it. Use *names* or *titles* recognizable in your field—sources that might impress potential buyers.

5. Make the **author** look like the ultimate authority on the subject.

6. End with a **sales closer** in bold type. Ask the browser to buy the book.

7. **Price.** Bookstores like a price on the back cover. Pick a price for your book and be realistic. See the discussion on book pricing.

8. **Bar code** with International Standard Book Number. The bar code on a book identifies the ISBN, which in turn identifies the publisher, title, author and edition (hardcover, etc.). Make room for, but do not worry about, the bar code and ISBN just now.

The back-cover copy will help you to focus on who your audience is and what they want, so you will be able to slant the book to their needs. You are making promises. Now all you have to do is to deliver on all your promises.

Unfortunately, most nonfiction books are written without a specific market in mind, and since the book does not provide what the potential buyers want, it does not sell. Do not ignore other markets, though. If you have an instruction book aimed at students of flying schools and the bookstores pick it up, so much the better. But the bookstore sales are the frosting, not the cake. The more markets the book may be fitted into, the better its chances of success.

> *The how-to article is to writing as McDonald's is to restaurants; it enjoys no epicurean status. Nevertheless, McDonalds advertises "billions and billions sold," a point the writer might keep in mind.* — Leonard S. Bernstein

Research is simply reading, making notes, condensing and rearranging the gathered pertinent information. The importance of the library cannot be over-emphasized. All research must begin there, and most of the required information will be found within its walls. The first library visit will be to determine whether the subject has already been beaten to death. If not, then on to the book.

Ask the reference librarian for Bowker's *Books in Print,* which lists all books currently available by subject, title and author. Make a list of those books you would like to read. Research the library's card file to see which books may be obtained there. The others you may purchase at your local bookstore or by writing directly to the publisher; addresses are listed in the back of *Books in Print.* You will find that some of the books listed in *BIP* never went to press. And remember that this is probably not the only library in town. Try the local college, too; it will have different types of books. Research the *Reader's Guide to Periodical Literature,* which lists magazine articles on every subject. Also see the *Business Periodicals Index.* The telephone books will help you find firms offering materials and services. Look for newspaper indexes such as *The Wall Street Journal Index.* There are at least three directories listing thousands of associations. The associations are sources of information, and many have their own special-interest magazine. Ask the librarian to see the periodical directories and the newsletter directories. Then look for periodicals in the field you are researching.

> *The writer does the most who gives his reader the most knowledge and takes from him the least time.*
> — Sydney Smith

> *Faulty research is like a faulty septic tank. Sooner or later the evidence will surface and become embarrassing.*
> — Rex Alan Smith

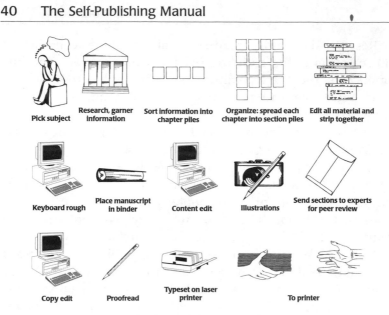

The flow of the manuscript

Be a detective. When you run out of leads, ask the librarian. Libraries carry hundreds of indexes, listings and source books. Gather everything ever written on your subject. Load yourself up with so much material you will have to decide what to leave out. Overdo it, and you will be proud of the result, secure in the knowledge that you have covered the subject completely.

Check out those books and magazines you can. With those restricted to the reference room, use the photocopy machine to record longer pieces. Take a couple of floppies with you and download useful electronic files. Where you wish to use photos and drawings of material with expired copyrights, use a plain-paper photocopier for the drawings and use a camera to reshoot the photos (more on this later). But even where the copyright has not expired, make a photocopy of valuable illustrations to guide you in your research.

> *The ideal best seller would be about a quiche-eating cat with thin thighs.*

After exhausting the library of its information, there are many other sources. Write for *U.S. Government Books* to the Superintendent of Documents, U.S. Government Printing Office (USGPO), Washington, DC 20402. This is a monthly catalog of government publications. Many of these pamphlets are also available at U.S. Government bookstores in the larger cities. Check the white pages. The Bureau of the Census can provide you with sales and revenue data and much other information on virtually any industry. For ordering information on the *Census Catalog & Guide*, write Public Information Office, Bureau of the Census, Department of Commerce, Washington, DC 20233. The National Technical Information Service maintains abstracts and data bases in 28 technical areas. Write for a copy of their *Published Search Master Catalog* to: National Technical Information Service (NTIS), Department of Commerce, 5285 Port Royal Road, Springfield, VA 22161.

Need more facts, figures and material for your book? Contact an editorial researcher. See *Literary Market Place*.

For more information on your field of study, there are interviews with the experts you uncover in your research. You may write or call them. Use your computer/modem to search distant data bases for information.

You want your readers to know about all the books, tapes, software and other references available on your subject. As an author and opinion molder, you should not have to buy these resources. Ask for "checking copies." Now that you are researching, you are a member of the print media and will be able to attend a lot of related events free. Use your new business card to get a press pass, media packet and preferential treatment.

Copyright is the subject which most interests potential authors. They want to know how to protect their precious

> *Professionals sell, then write, while amateurs write, then try to sell.* — Gordon Burgett

material from others and to know how much they, themselves, may steal.

A copyright covers exact printed words, not ideas or thoughts, so you are safe if you just do not copy word-for-word. The copyright law was completely overhauled in 1978, and it will be many years before every aspect of it has been interpreted by the courts. The courts seem to deal with each case individually, when determining infringement. One test has been whether the original work is any less salable once it has competition from an alleged infringer.

Copying ideas is research, copying words is plagiarism. Make it a personal rule never to copy any three words in a row. If your book is not recognizable as being a copy, you should be safe. Since 1978, copyright protection runs for the life of the author plus 50 years.

If you find material that you wish to use as is, contact the author for permission. Your letter might go like this:

Permission to reprint material

Dear _____:

I am writing a book tentatively titled *Parachuting, The Skydiver's Handbook.* I would like your permission to include the excerpts as outlined below in any and all editions of the book, as well as in advertisements and promotion, non-exclusively, throughout the world.

In exchange for your permission, you will be listed in the Acknowledgments and will be sent a copy of the book. I hope you will agree to our giving your book greater exposure.

For your convenience, here is a self-addressed, stamped envelope and a duplicate copy of this letter for your records.

Sincerely,

Material to be reprinted:

Title and author:

Copyright date and holder: _____

Page:_____ , Line:_____ To page:_____ , Line:_____.

Permission granted by:_____

Permission letter

Many documents are not copyrighted. If you want to find out whether some material is protected under either the current or pre-1978 law, the Copyright Office will conduct a search for you. Send them as much information as possible, such as the author, title, publisher and publication date. The easiest way is to photocopy the title page and copyright page of the book. They charge for the time, and they should be able to make two searches per hour. See the Copyright Office's Circular 22, "How to investigate the Copyright Status of a Work." Contact the Copyright Office at Tel: (202) 707-9100 to get a copy.

Government and military publications are in the public domain. Even if they weren't, they would probably be covered by the Freedom of Information Act. If you really need a piece of material, military or civilian, ask for permission. It is safer and cheaper than hiring a lawyer later to prove you have a right to it.

Your copyrighted material is valuable property, or it may be so one day. File copyright forms on all those magazine articles you don't get paid for. You may need an article for inclusion in a book someday, and the expenditure on fees will justify to the IRS that you really are in the word business.

If you are asked for permission to reprint some of your work, you might consider a limit of a section or two and stipulate that an editor's note indicate that it was used with your permission and came from your book. This will show once again that you are an expert and is good publicity for the original work. A copyright on your book is not only for protection. It is prestigious; it shows you are a professional. Copyright is discussed in several places in this book. See the Index. For more information on copyrights, see the discussion in *Writer's Market* and read *A Business Guide to Copyright*

> *Writing is one of mankind's most important endeavors, the primary vehicle by which man leaves his mark.*
> — James Warren in *Writer's Yearbook*

Law by Woody Young, and the other copyright references listed in the Appendix.

Organize your material with the "pilot system." Start by drawing up a preliminary table of contents; just divide your message into 10 or 12 chapters. Then sort all your research material and "pile it" as required. Decide on your chapter titles and, using scissors, tape and staples, sort all this photocopied material into the applicable chapter piles. During your library research, you must have written down a number of interesting observations and many of your own experiences. Add your own notes to the piles.

Now spread out the individual chapters. They will probably completely fill the living room. Pick an interesting pile, any one, not necessarily the first, and go through it, underlining important points and writing in your additional comments. Write out longer thoughts on a tablet and file them in order in the pile.

This floor spread will enable you to see the whole interrelated project, lending excitement and encouragement—a great incentive. Move the piles around to insure a good, logical flow of thought and to avoid duplication of copy. Condense the material by discarding unnecessary and duplicate material.

This use of other information from other sources is not plagiarizing, it is research. Your notes insure that you will not leave out any important points. However, you will be entertained as you compare what other authors say about the same item. The similarities are often remarkably coincidental, sometimes to the point of including the same words and phraseology. This experience also emphasizes the importance of being accurate. Your work will be researched by others in the future.

As you read what others say on a particular point, your memory will be jogged. You will have additional points, a clearer explanation or an illustrative story. Where you disagree with another author, you can always say, "Some people believe . . ." and then tell it your way. You have the advantage of the most recent information, since you came last.

Carry paper and pen with you at all times, especially when driving, running or engaging in any solo activity. This is a time to think, create, compose; this is when there is no one around to break your train of thought. Some authors keep a writing tablet in their car and compose while commuting. When you are confined, captive, isolated, you have nothing else to do but create. Make use of any available time. A lot of good material develops while attending dull meetings.

Some people like to work with a small pocket tape recorder, but remember that someone must transcribe this noise onto paper. It all depends on what you are used to, how you perform best. If you often dictate letters and have a secretary to transcribe your tapes, this may be the most comfortable and most efficient method for you.

When a particularly original thought or creative approach hits you, write it down or you will lose it. Keep on thinking and keep on note-taking. Add your thoughts and major pieces to the piles. As you go along, draw up a list of questions as they come to mind, so that you will remember to follow up on them for answers.

Strip your notes by cutting, sorting and taping. Paste the strips together with Magic transparent tape. Write on the tape and the paper when adding notes.

Keyboard (or dictate) from the pasted strips. With practice you will learn to think, create and compose at the computer. Write as you speak; relax and be clear. Do not worry about punctuation, grammar or style. You will edit the work later, and it is always easier to edit than it is to create. Right now, all you want to do is to get your thoughts and research material onto the hard disk. Make notes where you are considering illustrations.

> *Writing from notes is not plagiarism but solid, thorough research and an efficient system made possible by Xerox. There is nothing new in the universe. Practically every nonfiction book is simply a re-packaging of existing and new material.*

A computer allows you to lay out your pages as you go along. Use a format 4" wide by 7" long so you can get a good feel for the look of the book and its length.

Do not start your writing with Chapter One—to do so makes book writing look like an impossible mountain climb—and it is hard to get started. Select the chapter pile that looks the smallest, easiest or most fun. It may simply be the most interesting, but it is sure to go the fastest. Once you have drafted it, take the next most interesting chapter and so on. Soon you will be past the half-way mark and the going will be downhill. You will be encouraged and will gather momentum. Using this approach, you will probably find you are writing the first chapter last. This is as it should be, as the first chapter is usually introductory in nature, and you cannot know where you are going until you have been there. Many authors wind up rewriting and re-slanting the first chapter because they wrote it first.

Do not be concerned with what goes into the computer the first time around. The important thing is to get it down. Often these first impressions are the best; they are complete, natural and believable. Later you will go through the draft, making corrections, additions and deletions.

Read the whole section of pasted-together notes to grasp the overall theme. Then boil it down and use your own words. Think about the section and how you might explain the basic message better. Can't you say it more clearly with fewer words? Do not just write from the paper strips sentence by sentence; that method approaches plagiarism. For organization, list the main points and rearrange the pieces. If you are having trouble with a section, arrange it as best you can and then sleep on it. If you still cannot bring it all together with a few well-chosen sentences, you may have to call another expert for his or her explanation of the subject matter.

As you keyboard the rough first draft, and later as you review it, you will decide whole paragraphs are misplaced and belong elsewhere. Using a computer, it is an easy matter to move material.

If you lack a certain piece of information, a number or fact, leave a blank space, put a note in the text to remind you and go on. Do not lose momentum. Some authors use "***" as asterisks are easy to find visually or with a computer search. Similarly, if you find yourself repeating material, make a note with three asterisks so you may compare it with the other material later.

Keyboard one complete section at a time if possible. One chapter at a time is better, and the whole book straight through is the best way to go. Most beginning authors must work at other jobs and are able to devote only a short period each day to their writing. But the more time you can put into each piece of the book, the better, as there will be greater continuity, less duplication and clearer organization. If you can only do a small section at a time, try arranging the pieces in the evening, reviewing them in the early morning, thinking about them while commuting, etc., and then come home to type it all up.

On the other hand, if you can, take two weeks off from work, shut out all distractions and become totally involved in the manuscript. Do not pick up the mail or answer the telephone. Eat when hungry, sleep when tired and forget the clock except as a gauge of your pace. Keep up the pressure and keep on keyboarding. Pace yourself at, say, one chapter per day. You should not have to force yourself to write, but you will need organization and discipline. After a couple of books, you will find yourself making very few major changes in your original draft. In fact, using a computer, you will alter type styles for body type, boldface, italics and captions as you go along.

Writing from notes is much easier than composing from thin air. Thin air produces writer's block. Incidentally, many writers say the hum of a computer—knowing the electricity is on—prompts them to work.

> *Don't use "I," the perpendicular pronoun.*

Do not throw out your materials once your draft is typed. Put them in a cardboard carton. Someone may ask where you found a particular piece of information and you may wish to trace it. Traceability is especially important with photographs and artwork.

Writing style. Before writing a magazine article, always read one or more editions of the magazine thoroughly to absorb the style. Reading the magazine will help you to subconsciously adapt to that magazine's way of writing. The same technique may be used in writing a book by reading a couple of chapters of a book by a writer you admire.

Writing is a communication art. You should not try to impress. Write as you speak, avoiding big words where small ones will do. Most people regularly use only 800 to 1,000 of the some 26,000 English words available to them. Use simple sentences, and be precise in your selection of words. Vary sentence and paragraph length, and favor the shorter ones. Try to leave yourself out of the copy; avoid the word "I."

Use action nouns and verbs. Help the reader draw a mental picture by introducing sight, sound, smell, touch and taste to your copy. Be precise by avoiding superlatives and overuse of adverbs and adjectives. Study newspaper writing, and place the words you wish to emphasize at the beginning of the sentence. The important sentence should start the paragraph, and the main paragraph should head the chapter.

Relax, talk on paper, be yourself. Explain each section in your own words, as you would to help a friend who is new to the subject. Do not use contractions in your writing as you do in your speech, as they're (there is one now) more difficult to read. "Which" and "that" can usually be left out to the benefit of the sentence. Keep your writing short. You are paying for the words, so edit out the junk.

> *There's nothing to writing. All you have to do is sit down at the computer and open up a vein.* — Red Smith

Writing is hard work; it is an intellectual and emotional workout. Some authors enjoy the discipline it requires, but more have a greater appreciation for the reward of the results.

Like a speech, every paragraph of your book should have a beginning, a middle and an end. Each paragraph should tie in with both the preceding and following paragraphs (good transitions). The first sentence of the paragraph is called the "topic sentence"—stay with one subject per paragraph.

Be a professional and give the readers their money's worth. Your material will be used by others in coming years and you will be quoted. If you are accurate and correct now, you won't be embarrassed later by the written legend you have created. As a published author, you have the responsibility of being a recognized expert. Use proper terms; don't start a new language. Steer away from highly technical expressions; you will only turn off your reader.

> In the early 1970s, hang gliding was a hot new subject. It was the rebirth of aviation, using a wing made in the sail industry, whose participants were kids off the streets. The terms for flying and parts of the glider could have come from the aviation community, the sail industry or popular (new) jargon could have been used. Obviously aviation terms were in order. This was impressed upon the early book and magazine writers; aviation terms were used almost exclusively, and this usage aided the introduction of hang gliding into the community of sport aviation.

One technique for educating your readers in the correct terms is to use the proper term and then follow it with the more popular word or explanation in parentheses. Educating the reader as you progress through the book is preferable to making readers wade through a glossary in the Appendix.

Anticipate trends to keep your work up to date. Use nonsexist terms.

Book length. Aim for 130 to 280 typeset pages in a 5.5" x 8.5" book. Your book should have enough heft to command its price but not be so big as to be intimidating. If you have less than 130 pages, add some resources to the Appendix. See the Appendix of this book as an example. The most expensive part of a book is the paper. If your book is 800 pages long, you will have to price it out of sight for most buyers.

Do not get wrapped up in book length. Concentrate on quality, not quantity.

You are finished when the manuscript is 99% complete and 100% accurate. Do not wait for one more photo, one more statistic, one more piece of information. Get your book to press and to your buying public. Hopefully, you will sell out in a few months, make corrections, add some updated material and return to the press with a "revised edition."

Help is available to those who still cannot write even after learning the tricks mentioned above.

If you still cannot get your thoughts on paper, try the **team approach.** There are a lot of writers out there—people who love to put good thoughts into words. Look for a moonlighting newspaper reporter. They are trained to listen and put your thoughts down accurately. Once they have your material written out, you may edit the work for rewriting. The reporter may even wind up doing a feature story on you, and his or her media contacts are invaluable.

> Joe Karbo sold millions of dollars' worth of *Lazy Man's Way to Riches*, and while he "authored" the book, he did not write it. He gathered his original thoughts and material and hired a writer to put it all on paper.

Perhaps you can get your thoughts down on paper but all that good information does not read very well. What you need is an editor, someone who can take your information and put energy into it.

> Doctor Hartbrodt wrote a medical book about a common disease. The manuscript contained a lot of solid, helpful information but was hard to read. He contacted writers' groups, editorial services and secretarial services through the *Yellow Pages* and located four people who were willing to help. He gave each a copy of the first chapter

---

You don't really believe Lee Iacocca wrote those two best sellers all by himself?

---

and asked them to edit a couple of sample pages and to quote their fee. Some editors only want to dot "i's" and cross "t's" while others want to do complete rewrites. Using this method, he was able to compare their work and select the work he wanted, the editor he liked most and the best per-page price.

Many big-name authors cannot type or spell, so they hire people who can. To contact people in the "word game," go to libraries, public relations firms, advertising agencies, or college English departments. Check the *Yellow Pages* under "Writing" and see the *Writer's Digest Yearbook*. See the editorial services listed in *Literary Market Place* and see the directory published by the Freelance Editorial Association, Tel: (617) 729-8164. There are a lot of people out there who will be happy to work for you at a reasonable rate. You have the knowledge of the subject, and a writer knows how to put your thoughts on paper. The big winner is the reader/book buyer who receives good information, expressed well.

Make sure your contract has a "work for hire" clause, or you may not own what you have hired the person to write. For an explanation and a sample contract, see *Is There a Book Inside You?*

Many people who are not professional writers get into print. If they cannot pick up the skills, they ask for help. You can, too.

— Commissioned writing. Many of the more successful book houses approach publishing from a hard-nosed marketing position. They know what they have been able to sell in the past, and they often stay in their field of expertise by assigning writers to produce more of these "commissioned books." Once you decide on an area of concentration, you too may approach others to write for you, by paying cash outright or using modest royalty advances as an inducement. The accounting is easier and the arrangement is often more cost effective when you pay outright for material rather than paying royalties. Flat fees for shorter books are often around $5,000, half on assignment and half on acceptance. These books may be wrapped up in less than 60 days by moonlighting advertising copywriters.

— **Author submissions.** Another source of material is the traditional one of unsolicited author submissions. If you are concentrating on a certain interest area and selling books to a select market, you are also in contact with those people best qualified to generate new material for you. Once you publish something they like, they will come to you. Many people have always cherished the dream of becoming an author, and they will seek you out once they recognize your publishing success.

Of course, you can always wait for manuscripts in your interest area to come to you, but you will save time and a lot of useless manuscript reading by issuing one-paragraph outlines of books you need to round out your list. Send them to writing magazines such as *Writer's Digest*. Also fill out a form for a listing in *Writer's Market*. Make it easy for qualified writers to find you.

— **Co-authorship.** If you have a book you want to do yourself, but recognize that you lack the required technical expertise, consider co-authorship. Find an expert in the field to write part of it while you write the other part, and then each of you can edit the other's material. This approach has many advantages, including the endorsement of an expert, more credibility for the book and another body to send on the promotional tour. The disadvantages are smaller royalties, extra accounting and author hand-holding.

— **Ghost writers.** Lee Iacocca did not write those two best sellers by himself. Iacocca is the author (it is his material), but he is not the writer. He does not have time to write. If you do not have the time or inclination to write but you do have material recorded in articles, on tape, etc., you might hire a ghostwriter to put it all on paper. See *Is There a Book Inside You?* for details.

This author shared the responsibilities for the *Frisbee Players' Handbook* with disc expert Mark Danna. Danna wrote the throwing and catching chapters, while Poynter wrote on history, record attempts and competition and assembled the Appendix. Poynter came up with the unique package and marketing idea but did not have enough expertise or credibility as a Frisbee player. Mark Danna rounded out the team well.

Spouses without experience outside the home may choose to co-author a book with their partner on their area of expertise. A project like this gets both of them published, provides them with a common project (which may do great things for the marriage) and elevates their job stature.

— **Republishing articles.** Many author-publishers have gone the easy route by simply editing the material of others. Deeply interested in a subject, area they have thoroughly researched a subject, only to find that many fine experts have already written good material on several aspects of it. The collection of these articles, one per chapter, formed a book. To pursue this course, contact each author for permission to use his material, and ask him to go over a photocopy to update it with any new information or changed views. This makes your chapter better than the original article. If the chapter must be shortened, ask the author to do it. This is faster and easier than doing it yourself and then negotiating your changes with him.

If, for example, you are deeply involved in the sport of parachuting, you might contact the national association and their magazine about gathering like articles which have appeared over the years and republishing them in a series of booklets. Booklet Number One might consist of all the best articles on student training. Your primary market would be the members of the association: You would sell them through the organization's "store" and via mail order by advertising in their magazine. Thus, the association is providing both the material and the customers. As an editor, you simply repackage the information.

— **Out-of-print books.** Sometimes you can find good books which large publishers have let go out of print. Normally, the copyright has reverted to the author. These authors are usually thrilled to have a new publisher put their books back into print. Often the original page negatives can be purchased from the publisher for a few hundred dollars, so the book does not even have to be typeset. See the Bowker directory *Books Out Of Print*, available at your library. For an article on buying the rights to, and reprinting, out-of-print books, send a self-addressed, stamped envelope to George Van Patten, 4204 SE Ogden Street, Portland, OR 97206, Tel: (503) 775-3815.

> Bill Kaysing discovered an out-of-copyright book called *Thermal Springs of the World*. He abstracted just the data on hot springs in the western U.S., added some original comments and reprinted it as *Great Hot Springs of the West*. Review copies sent to several major magazines resulted in an entire column of flattering coverage in *Sunset*. Some 3,000 copies were sold in a little over a year.

— **Translations** offer another source of material and are a royalty consideration. A good translator is a highly skilled artist who issues a product which does not read like a word-for-word translation. He or she will spend hours searching for the single right word or phrase to convey the original meaning. Translators must not only be bilingual, they must be good writers, too. There may be some 1,200 literary translators in the U.S., but few are very good. To find a translator, write the American Translators Association, 1735 Jefferson Davis Highway, #903, Arlington, VA 22202-3413, Tel: (703) 412-1500; Fax: (703) 412-1501. The going rate is $30 or less per 1,000 words, so few can make a living at translating. Citing their creative input, some translators are now requesting royalties, but few have been successful so far. The English language rights to foreign language books are rarely expensive, so this is another interesting source of material.

Negotiating and contracting with authors. The object of an author-publisher contract is to clarify thinking and positions by laying out all the details on the table and arriving at a mutually beneficial agreement. There will never be a second book if one side takes unfair advantage of the other; it pays to keep the future in mind. Small publishers should not offer less than the industry norm unless they will be

---

The publisher is financing the author on the one end and the bookstore's inventory at the other. — Sol Stein, President of Stein and Day

satisfied with just one book per author, and there is no need to offer more.

Each contract will be a little different, but you can start with a standard one. For sample contracts with explanations, see *Publishing Agreements* by Charles Clark. For sample contracts, ready to load into your computer, see *Publishing Contracts on Disk*. See the Appendix. It is easier to edit (contracts) than it is to create.

First-time authors will be eager to become published and may not be terribly concerned about the contract initially. Many creative people are not business- or commercially oriented. It is imperative that contract negotiation and signing be taken care of first. Rough draft the contract and ask the author whether it is generally acceptable. If he or she has made any other commitments, such as for some subsidiary rights, this information must be added into the contract. Include a work schedule and a clause allowing you to cancel if he or she fails to meet deadlines; always keep the pressure on writers to perform. See *Is There a Book Inside You?*

Unless you have a narrow field of interest or the writer has very strong feelings about a particular area, you will want a contract which includes all possible territories and rights. Once you have published the basic book, you will want to entertain the possibilities of translations to other languages or co-publishing in other English-speaking markets. (However, unless the market is quite large, it will be more economical to ship your own print run in "direct sacks of prints.") Then there are book club adoptions, film rights, magazine excerpts, newspaper serializations and the mass-market paperback rights. You will also want to sell through bookstores, other types of stores, through the mail, to associations, etc. Your promotion will rub off on all areas, so take advantage of it by taking complete control of the manuscript. Remember that people who write contracts slant them their way. Take control. Use *Publishing Contracts on Disk* to provide your own contract.

Advances against royalties depend on the proposed selling price, projected print run and sales potential of the book. The advance seals the deal, which is an important legal consideration while it puts pressure on the author and the publisher to perform. The advance makes the author feel accepted and has great psychological value; it does not have to be large to work as an incentive.

Advances generally range from $100 to $5,000, and small publishers often keep them low. A good rule of thumb is to offer an advance equal to the projected first year royalties. One way to create an incentive, or at least make the author feel morally obligated, is to make progress payments. One-third may be paid on signing the contract, one-third when the writer submits the first draft and one-third when he or she completes the proofreading. Advances are paid against royalties; they are not in addition to this percentage. Ordinarily, advances are nonrefundable; the author keeps them even if he or she fails to deliver the manuscript. This is another good reason to protect your investment with progress payments.

Advances work both ways. Authors demand high advances from publishers in order to commit the publisher to the book. The publisher, with a lot invested in a book, has to bring it to market quickly and market it well. The advance is the publisher's gamble. The author keeps it even if the book fails to sell and generate enough royalties to cover the advance. Some authors with little faith in their manuscript or the publisher will, therefore, request larger advances.

Flat fees or royalties. Should contributors get a percentage of the book or be paid a flat fee? Obviously flat fees are simpler, and they are occasionally cheaper. An illustrator creating a major portion of the book should get royalties, while someone doing basic research, keyboarding or contributing a drawing should be paid a set fee. Everyone must understand

> *I just sat down and started all by myself. It never occurred to me that I couldn't do it as well as anyone.*
> — Barbara Tuchman

clearly what is in it for him. If you require a few drawings, go to a graphic artist and have them drawn to order. Then pay the bill and be done with it. The artist deserves a piece of the action no more than the person does who painted your car before you sold it. One exception is a children's book, where the illustrations are considered to be equally as important as the text.

The royalty formula, traditionally, has been to pay the author 10% of the **list** (cover) **price** for each hardcover book sold through regular channels, such as book wholesalers, bookstores and libraries. Remember that after discounting the book to dealers, this amounts to 15% to 20% of the selling price. Graduated royalties for the hardcover edition might be 10% of the list price on the first 5,000 books sold, 12.5% on the next 5,000 and 15% on sales over 10,000. Often softcover authors command 7% for the first 12,000 sold and 9% above that number.

A few years ago, most publishers changed their terms by offering authors 6% to 10% of the **net** on books. They amended their contracts with some generous-sounding wording such as "We will pay you 6% of the net receipts." The problem is that most of the books are sold at wholesale prices. Further, the accounting required is a heavy burden, and this is another expense to be considered. A percentage of the list price is preferable, as it is easy to calculate.

Royalties for college texts range from 10% to 18%, while those for heavily illustrated elementary and secondary school texts run from 4% to 10%. Royalties for children's books range between 10% and 15%, to be split between the author and illustrator. mass-market paperback publishers usually pay 4% to 7.5%, but they print in much greater quantities.

Most contracts call for the author and publisher to split the subsidiary rights (films, book clubs, etc.) 50-50. Many of the big publishers barely break even on the book itself and hope to make their money on the subsidiary rights.

Lay out the binder. Now that you are generating copy, you need a place to store it. Find a large three-ring binder (3") and add divider cards corresponding to the chapters you have selected. Punch and insert the rough-draft pages as you complete them. As the piles come off the floor, cross the desk and flow through the computer into the binder, you will gain a great feeling of accomplishment.

You will be further encouraged by setting up the front matter of the book. Soon you will have a partial manuscript, the book will be taking shape and you will have something tangible to carry around. This makes you feel proud and gives you the flexibility to proof and improve your manuscript away from home.

Write your name and address in the front of the binder with a note that it is a valuable manuscript. You do not want to misplace and lose your future book.

And carry that binder with you everywhere you go. Busy people often have trouble finding the time to return to their desk and "the book." With the binder system, the book is always with you. As you go through the day and find a minute here and there, open the binder—to any section—and write in your changes, notes and comments. Periodically enter your changes into the computer and print out new pages. The binder is an anti-procrastination crutch, and it works.

With the binder under your arm, the book will be continually in your thoughts. Your work and your manuscript will improve.

> Ed Rigsbee agreed the binder was helping him stay on his project, but he also found an added benefit: His wife became much more supportive of the project once she saw the tangible evidence.

With your binder in one place and your hard disk in another, you will not have to worry about the financial and emotional disaster of losing your work in a fire.

Parts of a book. Most books are divided into three main parts: preliminary pages or *front matter*, the *text* and the *back matter*. We will discuss each of them in order, so you can add a sheet for each to the binder with as much information as you have so far. It is not necessary to have all the pages mentioned or even to place them in any given order, but it is recommended that convention be followed unless you have a good, specific reason to stray. Set up these sections as best you can, so the book will begin to take shape. You will make additions and revisions to the binder later.

There are two pages to each sheet or leaf of paper. The *verso* pages are on the left-hand side and are even numbered while the *recto* pages are the opposite.

The front matter is that material placed at the beginning of the book. It includes everything up to the beginning of Chapter One.

— **End papers** may be plain or printed, are usually of heavier paper, and are glued to the inside front and back covers of a hardbound (casebound) book. End papers dress up the book and hold it together.

— **Testimonials,** endorsements and excerpts from reviews are being seen more and more on the first page of softcover books. This is important sales space.

— **The bastard title** or half title is usually the first printed page of a book and is more often found in hardbound books than in paperbacks. It contains only the title and is a right-hand page. Until the later 1800s, books were usually sold without covers—so the buyer could have all his books bound in the same style for a matching library. The bastard title page was just a wrapper for the text. It was often removed before binding.

— **The frontispiece** is a photograph or *plate* usually found on a left-hand page facing the title page. Before modern printing machinery, illustrations were expensive, and the frontispiece had the only picture in the book. Often the frontispiece was an engraving of the author. Today this page is left blank or used to list other books by the same author.

— **The title page** is on the right-hand side and lists the full title and subtitle of the book. This page may also include the name of the author or editor, the publisher, whether this is an original or revised edition, location of the publisher and the date.

> *No man but a blockhead ever wrote except for money.*
> — Samuel Johnson

Choosing a title. Spend some time on your title. Title testing has shown a good one will sell some 15% more books. In some cases, the title made the book go. In any case, your potential buyer may not recognize a bad title as being for him or her.

Start with a short, catchy and descriptive title, and add a lengthy, explanatory subtitle. The first word of the title should be the same as the subject to make the book easy to find. The book will be listed in Bowker's *Books In Print* by title, author and subject. If the title and subject are the same, you have doubled your exposure. Most other directories list only titles in alphabetic order; position your book where it can be found.

Book listings in *BIP* include only the title, not a description of the contents, so get more mileage with a subtitle to tell what the book is about. For example, *COMPUTER SELECTION GUIDE, Choosing the Right Hardware & Software: Business-Professional-Personal* is listed under the most common heading, "computers," while the rest of the title and subtitle tell what the book is about.

Many self-published books are sold by mail order, and to be marketed they must be advertised. Here the title must grab the attention of the reader and make him a promise, such as: "Buy this book and make a million dollars." Test proposed titles out on your friends and acquaintances.

Good book titles are your best teaser copy, whether they are selling the book from a magazine advertisement or the bookstore shelf. Brainstorm the title and come up with a good "one-liner" which tells a complete and compelling story. The title is perhaps the single most important piece of promotional copy you will draft for the book.

— **The copyright page** or *title page verso* is on the reverse of the title page and is the most important page in the book. Proofread it a dozen times! Here you print the copyright notice, show the printing history (number of printings and revisions), list the Library of Congress Catalog number, the ISBN, the Library of Congress Cataloging-in-Publication

Data, name and address of the publisher (you) and *printed in the United States of America* (to avoid export complications).

Those who know the book trade will turn to the copyright page first when picking up a book. Next to the cover, this page is the most important in selling a book to the trade, so make it look professional. You want to look like a big-time publisher, not a kitchen-based word shop.

Each time you revise the book, it is worthwhile to restrip and reshoot the copyright page in order to add, for example, *Second Printing, revised, 1996*, as this lets the potential purchaser know the book is up-to-date. Most big publishers do not make any changes to the copyright page and print a string of numbers on it instead. You will note: "10 9 8 7 6 5 4 3 2 1," which indicates to the trained eye that this is the first edition. On reprinting it, they will opaque out the "1" on the photographic negative. Actually, many big publishers will print the full number of books they think they can sell. They never expect to go back to press.

— **The dedication page** usually contains a short statement, if one is made at all, but some authors like to praise their parents—presumably without whose help, *the author would not have been possible*. It is not likely that anyone other than the person mentioned will care about the dedication. This right-hand page was used historically by writers to acknowledge their patrons: the persons or institutions that supported them during the writing.

— **The epigraph page** contains a pertinent quotation which sets the tone of the book. Using a separate page for an epigraph is sometimes a nice touch but often is a waste of space.

— **The table of contents** should start on the right-hand side. This page will include the chapter numbers, chapter titles and beginning page numbers. You can leave these page numbers blank for now. They will be filled in when the

> *Publishing is an active life while writing is a quiet life.*
> — Linda Meyer

book is formatted. Remember, when buying technical, professional or how-to books, most people turn immediately to the table of contents to check the coverage. Use some imagination when drafting your chapter titles—make them descriptive.

— **A list of illustrations** is in order if the book is heavily illustrated, has many important tables or if it is a picture-type book. Most books do not need this list.

— **The foreword** is positioned on the right-hand side and is a pitch for the book by someone other than the author. Try to get an expert in your field to contribute a foreword. It is very prestigious when a person with a recognizable name or a recognizable title is connected with your book. Contact one of the peer reviewers (described later in this chapter) about writing your foreword. Help them by writing it yourself to show them what you are looking for. Experts are busy people, and it is always easier for them to edit than to create.

It is doubtful that many people read the foreword, but they will notice who wrote it; most readers turn directly to the action. You may wish to note "Foreword by . . . " on the cover if that big name will help sell books.

If you include a foreword, note the correct spelling; it is not "forward."

— **The preface** is written by the author and tells why and how he or she wrote the book. It gets about as much attention from the reader as a foreword and appears on the right-hand side. If you have an important message and want to be sure the reader receives it, put it in Chapter One, not in the preface or introduction.

— **Acknowledgments** are a great sales tool. List everyone who helped you in preparation of your manuscript. People love to see their name in print, and each will become a disciple spreading the word on your great contribution to literature. On this blank sheet in your binder, add names of contributors as you encounter them so that you don't forget anyone.

— **The introduction** was covered above in the discussion of the preface.

— **The list of abbreviations** is only required in some very technical books.

— **The repeated bastard title** is next, is optional and is a waste of space in most books.

— **Disclaimers** are showing up in more and more books today. Lawsuits are an unfortunate fact of life in the United States, and while disclaimers are not absolute protection against them, the warning can't hurt.

Paraphrase the Disclaimer in this book and do not leave the last sentence out. Judges have ruled you must provide buyers with an alternative if they refuse to be bound by your disclaimer.

Obviously, if all the front matter pages listed above were included in your book, you would have a large number of pages already. You do not need all these pages, and it is recommended that you do away with most, except the title page, copyright page, table of contents, acknowledgments, about the author and disclaimer. Check over several other books for layout, especially old hardbound books which followed convention.

The text of the book is the meaty part on which the front matter and back matter hang. This is the second or main section.

Start your book off with an *action chapter*. Like the introductory part of a speech, Chapter One should arouse the reader and whet his or her appetite. Too many authors want to start from the *beginning* and put a boring history chapter first. The reader wants to know "where to" and "how to." Do not lose the reader in the first chapter.

— **Divisions** are sometimes made in long books with distinct but related sections. Their title pages contain the

I love being a writer. What I can't stand is the paperwork.
— Peter De Vries

name and number of the section, and their reverse sides are usually blank.

— **Chapter titles** should reveal the subject of the chapter to aid the reader in finding what he or she wants. The reader may be skimming the book in a store, pending possible purchase, or may be referring back to something he or she read. In either case, you want the description to be as clear as possible.

— **The subhead** is a secondary heading or title, usually set in less prominent type than the main heading, to divide the entries under a subject. Subheads can contribute a logical progression, aid in finding needed material and help to break up long chapters.

— **Footnotes** are not needed except in technical publications. If your book will be used as a research tool, readers may want the footnotes so they can follow up on the material. Where footnotes must be used, some people recommend they be placed at the end of the chapter or in the appendix. Placing extensive footnotes at the bottom of the page can make for some short pages and tedious reading.

— **The afterword** is sometimes seen in manuals. Often it is a personal message from the author to the reader, wishing the best of luck and/or requesting suggestions for improvement.

The back matter is reference material, such as the glossary, resources and index, placed at the back of the book. It is less expensive to revise lists at the end of the book when reprinting; avoid printing lists subject to change in the text.

— **The appendix** contains important lists and other resources; it may be composed of several sections. A book with a large appendix often becomes a valuable reference. It is permissible to set this reference material in smaller type.

— **The glossary** is an alphabetically arranged dictionary of terms peculiar to the subject of the book. Some authors like to save space and simplify use by combining the glossary and the index.

— **The bibliography** lists the reference material or sources used in writing the book.

— **The addendum** has brief, subsequent additional data. It is printed as part of the book or on a loose sheet.

— **Errata** are errors discovered after printing. The list is printed on a separate sheet and may be pasted in or loose.

— **Author's notes** come next and include additional information in chapter order.

— **Colophon** is Greek for *finishing touch,* and it details the production facts by listing the type style, designer, typesetter, printer, kind of paper, etc. The colophon is not as common as it once was but is still found today in special *labor of love*-type publications.

— **The index** aids the reader in locating specific information in the pages and is particularly important in reference works. Many librarians will not purchase books without indexes, so plan on an index.

Assembling the index is not hard if you build it with your word processing program. Simply read through your typeset manuscript and list the key words and the pages. List all the main headings, subheadings and key words, double post two-word listings ("ripcord housing" and "housing, ripcord"), and cross-reference different terms. Format the page in two columns, and set the type in ragged-right alignment. Then use your computer to autosort it.

Indexing software is available, and there are professional indexers. The index must be revised every time the book is updated because the page numbers change.

— **Order blank.** The last page of the book should contain an order blank; place it on a left-hand page—facing out. Some readers will want to purchase a copy for a friend, while others may want a copy for themselves after seeing your book at a friend's home or in the library. Make ordering easy for them by listing the full price including sales tax (if applicable) and shipping. This order blank system works.

There are books of which the backs and covers are by far the best parts. — Charles Dickens

Several orders "on the coupon" are received for *The Self-Publishing Manual* each week.

Make a page for each of the sections listed above that you wish to include, and fill in as much information as you now have. Keep adding (with a pencil) to your manuscript in the binder as you progress. The collected information does not have to be neat or in order; the important thing is that now you have a place to store your material. As you add pages, as the book fills up, you will have more work to carry as you venture away from home. When you find a few idle moments, open the binder and revise a section, bit by bit.

Editing your manuscript is where you cut, rearrange and add material. Go through the manuscript section by section and clean it up. Tighten your writing, change words, cut out those which fail to add to your message. Revise and improve.

Photos and drawings are easily indicated in the manuscript with page and position numbers. The second photo on page 40 would be marked "40-B," for example. Mark the location both in the manuscript and on the back of the photo or drawing. Mark the photo near its edge, and do not press too hard; you may push through to damage the photo. Incidentally, it is sometimes necessary to indicate which end of the photo goes up, if it is not obvious to someone not familiar with the subject. Type the captions into the manuscript under the photo position number. Make photocopies or contact prints of the photos and paste them into the manuscript (set the copy machine on "light"). This will make the draft clearer to you, your peer reviewers and the copy editor. Never paste in the photos themselves; they are hard to get off and could be damaged.

Typesetting. Most books today are typeset with computer-driven laser printers. Ordinarily, the money saved on traditional typesetting will pay for the equipment. See our Special Report *Book Production: Composition, Layout, Editing, Design, Getting it Ready For Printing*, listed in the Appendix.

Proofreading has to be done again and again. You will proof your manuscript for content and style, you will proof it for punctuation and grammar, and then you will proof the book as it makes its way through the various stages of production.

The secret to good material is **peer review.** Smart nonfiction authors take each chapter of their nearly complete manuscript and send it off to at least four experts on that chapter's subject. They enclose a cover letter that goes something like this: "You are an expert in this subject and I value your opinion. Please make your changes, additions and comments with a red pen. You may comment on anything—even punctuation, grammar and style, but I am really interested in content. I want to make sure I have not left anything out and have not said anything that is wrong. Be brutal, I can take it. I would not ask for your input if I did not want and need it."

Send the chapters to the highest-placed, most important opinion molders and mover/shakers in your association or industry. They will love to be included, and a single 15-page chapter will not overwhelm them.

What you get back is terribly valuable: They add two more items to your list; they cross out whole paragraphs, saying, "We aren't doing that any more." They cross out that part you thought was cute but was really embarrassingly stupid; they sometimes even correct punctuation, grammar and style.

Enclose an SASE (self-addressed, stamped envelope) with the chapter you send for peer review and 95% will reply within ten days. When the corrections arrive, spread them out on your desk by chapter and go through them page by page to make corrections in your computer. Evaluate each suggestion. Did they find a mistake? Did they misunderstand what you were trying to say? Are they behind the times?

When your book comes out, you don't have to wait for your readers' reaction, "for the other shoe to drop," because you know the book is right. After all, it has been reviewed and accepted by the best—the opinion molders in your field. There is another valuable reason for peer review: You have more than a dozen important people telling everyone about your book—and how they helped you with it.

Ken Blanchard, co-author of *The One Minute Manager*, says, "I don't write my books, my friends write them for me." He explains that he jots down some ideas and sends them off to friends for comment. They send back lots of good ideas which he then puts into his manuscript. Ken is being very generous, of course, and what he is describing is "peer review."

There will be a lot of proofing. The manuscript must be proofed and marked before final typing, the final draft has to be proofed for the typesetter, the set type or "boards" have to be proofed and the blueline prints of the book signatures have to be proofed. You will have some errors anyway, but without careful proofreading, you will have more. Being familiar with your own writing style, you will find it difficult to catch all your own errors. Now is the time to hire a professional wordsmith to proof your copy.

> There is an interesting story about a professor who wanted to publish an errorless book. He brought it out in loose computer printout form and offered his students 10 cents for each error they could find during the term. They found quite a few. Then he corrected the copy and ran off another set. This time he offered the new class 25 cents per error. They searched harder and found fewer. By the fourth time around at $1 per error, only a very few errors turned up and the professor was satisfied. Incidentally, this game also proved to be an effective way to encourage the class to read the required text thoroughly.

Proof well. Get it right the first time. "What you (don't) see is what you get." There is no practical way to take ink off paper.

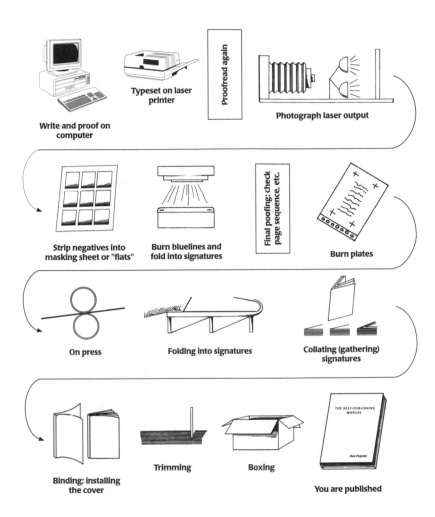

The printing process

The printer will take your typeset pages, photograph them, make negatives and paste the negatives into "flats." Then he will shoot a blueline proof for your review. Bluelines are large folded blueprints which are assembled into signatures just like the proposed book. They enable the printer to make sure the pages are in order and that everything is in place. This is your last chance to proofread. Check especially the page numbering, sentence continuation from one page to the next, the chapter page numbers in the table of contents, chapters beginning on a right-hand page, proper insertion of the illustrations (right side up?) and captions, the numbers on the copyright page, the ISBN and bar code on the cover, etc. Most important, hold the pages up to the light to check registration. The blocks of text and page numbers should be superimposed. Do not proof bluelines outdoors; the sun will turn them solid blue—fast.

Compare the bluelines with your typeset pages. Use "PE" (printer's error) next to your correction in the manuscript where the printer made the mistake, so you will not be charged for the change. If the change is your fault, it is called an "author's alteration," and they cost. Use a red pen to mark the proofs, so your notes cannot be missed. Write in small corrections, but type out and paste in large ones. To change even punctuation at this point, it is necessary to reset the entire line, paste it on the board, reshoot the negative, strip it into the flat and reshoot the blueline. Expensive! If you delete or add words, entire pages may have to be reset, and this may affect more than one page. It may be necessary to reset the rest of the chapter.

No matter how carefully you proofread, some errors will always show up in the final printed book. Do not be too concerned; resign yourself to this event and make the corrections in the next printing.

Keep a "correction copy" of the book near your desk, and pencil in changes as they come to your attention. Then when you are ready to reprint, you will be ready to go.

PROOFREADER'S MARKS

ℒ delete; take it out	ꜱ.ᴄ. or ꜱᴍ.ᴄᴀᴘ set in small capitals (SMALL CAPITALS)
⌒ close up; print as one word	ℓc set in lowercase (lowercase)
ℒ deleta and close up	ital set in italic (*italic*)
∧ or ⟩ or ⋏ caret; insert here (something)	rom set in roman (roman)
# insert a space	bf set in boldface (**boldface**)
eg # space evenly where indicated	= or -/ or ⌒ or /ℳ/ hyphen
stet let marked text stand as set	⅟ or en or /N/ en dash (1965-72)
tr transpose change/order the /	⅟ or em or /M/ em — or long — dash
/ used to separate two or more marks and often as a concluding stroke at the end of an insertion	∨ superscript or superior (∛ as in r²)
	∧ subscript or inferior (∧ as in H₂O)
⌐ ⌊set farther to the left	◇ or ✕ centered (◇ for a centered dot in p · q)
⌐set⌋ farther to the right	⅄ comma
⌒ set æ or fl as ligatures æ or fl	⅋ apostrophe
= straighten alignment	⊙ period
‖ ‖ straighten or allign	; or ;/ semicolon
✗ imperfect or broken character	: or ⊙ colon
⬚ indent or insert em quad space	ᶺ ᶹ or ∀ ∧ quotation marks
¶ begin a new paragraph	(/) parentheses
ⓢⓟ spell out (set 5 lbs. as five pounds)	⌊/⌋ brackets
cap set in capitals (CAPITALS)	ok/? query to author: has this been set as intended?

A complete set of proofreader's marks can be found in your dictionary under "Proofreader's Marks."

Proofreader's marks are standardized to enable you to communicate clearly with your typesetter and printer. A complete set of marks can be found in your dictionary under "Proofreader's Marks." Stick to the standard marks. If you make up your own, you will only confuse those who must understand them. Use these marks throughout the editing/proofreading process.

Artwork consists of *line work* and *halftones*. Line work is a clean black on white drawing without any shading. Line drawings may be pasted directly onto the laser-output sheets. Enlarge or reduce them with a photocopy machine.

Halftones are made from photographs, or drawings with shading, by taking a photograph of them through a screen. You will notice the result, using a magnifying glass to look closely at a printed photograph. A screened photograph is composed of many tiny dots of various sizes (shading). This takes camera work, and you will be charged for each shot. Camera charges are a start-up cost; the cost of an individual photo, when spread over the entire print run, is very small. It is foolish to be cheap at this point.

If you need line work and cannot draw, you can hire a commercial artist. Most typesetters have illustrators on their staff, or know some, and they usually work inexpensively. Your typesetter or printer may also have a large file of "clip art," and you may find something there you can use. These are commercially provided drawings on a large variety of subjects that may be used without permission. Many people lift art from reprints of old Sears catalogs and other publications whose copyright has expired. Depending on your subject, you may be able to clip drawings from certain military and government publications which are in the public domain.

Photographs, rarely seen in fiction, are almost a requirement in nonfiction, especially how-to books. The most successful how-to books are those that manage to integrate words and pictures into an attractive teaching tool. Unless you are writing an art-type book, you will use black and white rather than the more expensive color. Color requires four trips through the press, plus pre-press "color separations." The best photos are large (they become sharper when reduced), glossy, black and whites with a lot of contrast. Color photos and slides may be reproduced in black and white, but they tend to be muddy. Photographs which have already been printed once may be pasted in directly or reduced and rescreened, but the results are not as good as with an original glossy photo. When in doubt about the suitability of a photo, ask your printer. Occasionally the screening improves the photo.

Cameras. You will want to get a good camera with attachments and buy a book on how to use it. There are many types of cameras, but the most popular and versatile is the single-lens reflex. Many used models and accessories are available at your discount photo shop, and they have good resale value. If you are shooting fast-moving people or objects, you may need a camera with automatic features and/or motor drive. (Aircraft mounts may dictate motor drives and a

Life is too short for reading inferior books. — James Bryce

remote firing device, too.) Do not overlook the new zoom lenses which make framing faster and easier.

Using the camera. As you compile your manuscript, make a photo list so you will know what pictures you need. Then set out with your gear to take them. Try to frame your shots on the object, person or activity you are trying to show; avoid distracting clutter. For good black and white contrast, avoid tonal shades. Put people in your photos. If you are showing a number of pieces of equipment which are better modeled, such as parachutes, invite as many different people as possible to wear them. You can bet that each model will buy a copy of the book. When taking still shots of people, make them smile. Get their teeth in the picture. Most people do not know how to pose for a photo and complain that they do not photograph well. Catch them smiling and they will love you for it. Try to capture action in your photos, make them move. Seek the unusual, tell a story, look for human interest, shoot from a different angle. Then have your film processed by a custom photo lab. Do not send it out through your supermarket. Slide processing is easy, but in black and white processing the enlarger must be focused.

Handle negatives and photographs carefully; you have a lot invested in them. Keep them clean, and mail them flat between cardboard sheets. When you wish the typesetter or printer to crop a print, do not take out the scissors; draw crop marks on the edges. If a photo needs retouching, such as to remove an extraneous object like your camera bag, let the graphic artist do it. Do not use paper clips. When writing on the back, use a fine-point felt-tip pen, concentrate on the edge and do not push down too hard. Make sure the ink is dry before restacking the photos, and to be safe, put pieces of plain paper between them. For more information on cameras and photography, see the discussion in *Writer's Market.*

Photo release forms are advisable, particularly for pictures of minors. Permission might cost $20 to $500, but normally your subjects are just tickled to be in the book. A news photo does not require a release unless it is used in an advertisement. Permission fees are normally paid to the subject by the author upon publication. For an example of a photo release form, see *Publishing Contracts on Disk*. See the Appendix.

> Often you will overlook getting permission, and occasionally a subject will ask about his rights. The best way to handle this is to tell him that you are about to go back to press with a revised printing and, while it will cost you to replace the photo, you can take him out. I have yet to hear of a subject who wanted to be deleted from a book.

Other photo sources. Freelancers with a stock of photos will sell them for a few dollars each, or you can have them custom shot for $5 to $20 per photo. Photo syndicates are in the business of selling stock photos. The chamber of commerce, private firms, trade associations and some governmental agencies have public relations departments that provide photos as part of their function. Libraries and museums sometimes have photo files. Photos from old books with expired copyrights are easily copied with your camera. Just carry the book over to the light, lay it out flat and snap a photo. These photos of photos come out very nicely. When covering an event, make contact with the other photographers and get their cards. They may have just what you need. Picture sources are listed in *World Photography Sources, Writer's Market* and *Literary Market Place*. Ask for them at your library.

Mailing the laser printout. Enclose both the laser output and the illustrations in plastic bags and pack them in a sturdy cardboard carton. The post office does offer a special manuscript rate (same as book rate), but most authors prefer United Parcel Service because the service is good and the parcel must be signed for on the receiving end. A couple of

---

In this work, when it shall be found that much is omitted, let it not be forgotten that much likewise is performed.
— Dr. Samuel Johnson upon completion of his dictionary, 1755

extra dollars now are well worth the expense. Be sure the carton contains your complete return address.

Always keep a copy of the manuscript. This is to protect you if the original is lost in shipment or by the printer, and it is your ready reference when the printer calls with questions.

Writing a book can be easy if you have a system. With the organization outlined here, a decision to go and some discipline, you will start a whole new rewarding life.

Dan's first book took eight years to produce. He worked on this labor of love without guidance or direction. The huge, steady-selling manual on parachutes became the foundation upon which he built his publishing company. His second book was a study guide for an obscure parachuting rating; it sold better than expected.

In 1973, he became interested in the new sport of hang gliding. Unable to find any information at the library, he wrote the first book on the subject. He foresaw a trend and cashed in on it; the book has sold 130,000 copies over ten years. Total writing time: two months.

By this time, he had developed a writing formula. His fourth book took less than 30 days from idea and decision, until he delivered the boards to the printer. And most of this time was used in waiting for answers to his many letters requesting information. The first draft took only five days.

From there he concentrated on several high-priced, low-cost course pamphlets, turning out most within a week. His ninth book took all of two weeks to first-draft, and it was typed "clean." Very few editing changes had to be made to the original copy.

Using a word processor, Dan took 31 days to write, edit and typeset a book on computers. The actual time spent working on the book was just 18 3/4 days. Lately, his books have been longer and have required more time, but Dan still produces manuscripts efficiently. Writing a book is easy if you know the formula.

Today, as always, if a talented author remains unpublished and unnoticed, the fault is the author's. — Bill Henderson

Before going on to Chapter Three, turn to "Your Book's Calendar" at the beginning of the Appendix. You might also like to skim Chapter Twelve. Before you start, it is nice to know where you are going. For more information on publishing choices and self-evaluated quizzes to help you make a decision, see *Is There a Book Inside You?* It is listed in the order blank at the end of this book.

The last thing one discovers in writing a book is what to put first. — Blaise Pascal

Chapter Three

Starting Your Own Publishing Company

Forming your own publishing company is not difficult, and many of the requirements may be postponed until you are ready to send your manuscript off to the printer. But you do need a system and must get into the habit of using it. This is, after all, a business.

Having a business is just good business. Tax laws favor business. Businesses get to deduct goods and services which the wage earner must pay for with after-tax dollars. If you don't have a business, you don't get to deduct very much.

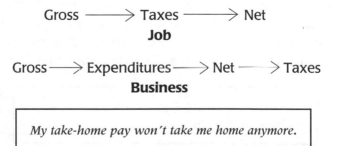

Gross ———> Taxes ———> Net
Job

Gross ——> Expenditures ——> Net —— > Taxes
Business

My take-home pay won't take me home anymore.

If you own a business, a lot of what you are already buying becomes deductible (car, dues, subscriptions, travel, etc.).

There are three forms of business: sole proprietorship, partnership and corporation, and each choice has advantages and disadvantages which you will have to weigh. You do not have to make the choice right now. If you do not file for corporation status, you will be operating as a sole proprietorship anyway. All you have to do is say, "I am a business" and file a Schedule C with your tax return. Here are a few things to keep in mind while you are concentrating on your most important project: your manuscript.

— As a **sole proprietor,** what the business earns is yours to keep; what the business borrows is money you owe.

In a sole proprietorship you have the choice of keeping your financial records on a modified *cash basis* or an *accrual basis.* The cash system is easier to understand, allows you to defer more income and requires less bookkeeping, which makes more sense for a small business. You may always switch to accrual when you grow larger. Once you use the accrual system, however, you cannot switch back to cash and you must get IRS permission to make any switch.

— Many business consultants discourage the formation of **partnerships,** as their success rate is not much better than that of marriages—for a lot of the same reasons. It is a rare pair who complement each other well enough to divide the work so that both are happy. If two or more people want to form a company, they should consider a corporation.

— **In a corporation,** you are an employee, not the company itself. This means more accounting, payroll taxes, paperwork, annual meetings with published minutes, more taxes and annual registration fees. Incorporation may lend

> *If you ain't the lead dog, the scenery never changes.*
> — John G. Russell

an air of permanence, but it can also saddle you with unwanted paperwork, meetings and legal bills.

Corporations are separate legal "beings" and can be sued, but their stockholders cannot normally be touched. A sole proprietor does not have the protection of this "limited liability" and could lose his home and other possessions if he lost in a legal action. There is more to consider in publishing than just the debts of the business. Keeping some of these problems in mind and considering your book's subject, talk to other people around you in small businesses and to your accountant and attorney. Also see the legal discussion later in this chapter.

Publications. When your manuscript is near completion and you have a "product," you will want to concentrate on the business end of publishing to get it printed and off to market. The Small Business Administration (SBA) has many free publications, and some sold at a slight charge, which should help you. Write SBA, Washington, DC 20416 and request a *Directory of Business Development Publications*. The SBA also provides a toll-free answer desk to provide information on free counseling, prebusiness workshops and other SBA services. Call (800) 827-5722.

It is strongly recommended that you subscribe to *Publishers Weekly* magazine. It will teach you about the publishing trade, provide many stimulating ideas and generate enthusiasm. Purchase a copy of *Literary Market Place*; it is *the* resource of the book industry. I used to recommend referring to it in the library whenever it was needed, but it has become too important for just occasional use. Check accounting and business books, such as Bernard Kamoroff's *Small Time Operator*. Purchase a copy of *The Business Planning Guide* by David H. Bangs. See the Appendix. Your writing references such as

Most successful people are not working for the money. They're working for the rewards . . . the satisfaction . . . the challenge of it . . . to win. — Michael J. Cutino, Publisher, *Nightlife* magazine

dictionaries, thesauri and style manuals can be purchased inexpensively in used book stores.

SCORE is the Small Business Administration's volunteer network, the letters of which stand for "Service Corps of Retired Executives." These are retired men and women who will call on you to help with your problems. There is no charge for this service except for occasional out-of-pocket traveling expenses. There are several hundred SCORE chapters around the country. Call the SBA office nearest you to see if there is a nearby SCORE chapter. Look in the *White Pages* under "U.S. Small Business Administration." Tell them what you need, and they will find someone tailored to you and your business. Naturally, it is always best to get this advice before you get into trouble; do it sooner, not later.

PMA Mentoring Program. The Publishers Marketing Association has a volunteer network of coaches who are even more valuable than SCORE since they are all experienced publishers. Contact the PMA, Tel: (310) 372-2732.

Your company name will have to be selected before you go to press, so keep thinking about it. You could name it after yourself, say *Carolyn Porter Enterprises* or *Alan Gadney Publishing Co.*, but these choices do not make you look as big as a separate name. The use of "enterprises" is the sign of a rank beginner and gives the impression that you don't know yet what your company is going to do. If the business succeeds and one day you decide to sell out, the name will be sold with it. A good name will have more value. After all, what is the value of *Alan Gadney Publishing* without Alan Gadney? Looking big may be important when applying for credit from your vendors or asking a paper mill for samples. A separate company name will create the impression that you have a going business.

> Starting the company name with an "A" will place your company high in alphabetic listings. Peggy Glenn changed her *PiGi Publishing* to *Aames-Allen* to assure top billing in directories.

Foreign names can pose cataloging problems. Would you list "La Cumbre Publishing" under "L" or "C"? If people do not know where to catalog you or where to look for you, you may not be found, and you could lose business.

Geographical names can be limiting. Which makes you sound larger, East Weedpatch Press or North American Publishing? Which would you rather run, and what happens if you move to West Weedpatch?

To find a new name, one that isn't being used in the publishing industry, go to the library and look through *Books in Print, International Directory of Little Magazines and Small Presses* and your local telephone directory. Then ask the reference librarian for more directories. This search is fun, and you will note that the newer publishing companies have some pretty interesting names. As a new, little outfit, it does not hurt to have a handle that attracts attention. Pick a name that isn't being used by anyone else.

Do not select a name that has already been taken. You will receive some of their mail, some of their returns and calls from confused customers. No name is worth that hassle.

After you select a name for your new publishing company, you will probably be required to file it as a "fictitious business name" with your city or county and run a notice in a local newspaper. This notice is your way of letting the public know that you and the publishing company are the same person.

⌐⌐⌐ *Para Publishing*

Your logo is a graphic image, an easily recognizable symbol; it may consist of a drawing or just the company name in a distinctive style of type. If you can dream up something clever and easily recognizable, start putting it on all your letterhead, labels, business cards and brochures.

> *An entrepreneur spends 16 hours a day to avoid having to work for someone else for eight hours.* — James Healey

Your place of business will be your residence for a while. You will not need a lot of space to write, store or ship books initially. When you have several titles and need more space and employees, you may have to move out, but for now home has many advantages. "Home alone" (house, mobile home, camper, wherever you live) workers save on gasoline, cosmetics, clothes, additional rent, utilities and the headaches of a second property. And, as we will discuss later in this chapter, you can write off part of the household expenses on your tax return. Working at home requires some organization and discipline, but for many it is very comfortable working in this lower-stress atmosphere.

Forty million people in the U.S. work out of 35 million households; they can measure their commute with a yardstick. According to *The Wall Street Journal*, many states are now realizing that home-based businesses are more stable than large companies.

Before you begin sorting, shipping and selling books in your front room, quietly check the zoning ordinances. Local regulations may allow some types of business to be run from your home. Your business will be small at first, and as long as you don't have employees, and large trucks aren't pulling into the drive every few minutes, no one is likely to complain. Avoid walk-in traffic and refer to yourself as an "author" rather than a "publisher," and you shouldn't encounter any difficulty.

Working from your home should not be confused with "office in the home." The IRS has cracked down on the offices which are in addition to one's place of business. If you use one-half of your home for your business activities and do not have another office, you may deduct 50% of most of the house expenses, for example, mortgage or rent payments, electricity, heat, insurance and water.

If you are worried that a visiting vendor or client might not be favorably impressed with your home setup, make a lunch appointment in a restaurant. Actually, the visitor will probably envy you. Working out of your home is more comfortable, more efficient and cheaper.

P.O. box or street address. There are many good arguments for each one. Some people feel quite strongly that a street address is more effective in a mail order ad because the location reflects more substance and stability. But today, even the big firms are using boxes. This is probably the result of the high incidence of urban crime. There was a time when the mail was sacred and no crook would dare to touch it, but not anymore.

You can always rent a box from a private company such as Mail Boxes Etc., but make sure they are stable. If they go out of business or lose their lease, you will have to change a lot of stationery and you will lose a lot of mail order business. Incidentally, postal box leasing companies may no longer allow their customers to call their box a "suite" in Pennsylvania. In 1991, Attorney General Ernest D. Preate, Jr., said it is misleading to call a 5" x 3" cubbyhole an office.

Depending on your address ("1234 Northwest Whispering Valley Parkway, Suite 1701" or "Box 3"), a long street address could cost you more in classified ads where they charge by the word.

You will have to go to the post office regularly to ship books, so you might as well pick up your mail there, and with a box you will be able to pick up your mail a few hours earlier. Another advantage of a box is that you can maintain the same address even if you move a few blocks. Perhaps the most important reason to maintain a box is to keep your excited, loyal readers from dropping in at all hours to meet their author, who *must be interested in them and their project.*

Apply for a box now, and consider a larger one. In some areas boxes are in short supply, and there is quite a waiting list. It may take you months to get one. Write your name, your company name and the title of your book on the box registration card, so you will get your mail no matter how it

---

Profit is not a dirty word.

is addressed. Remember, all your stationery and business references need an address, so get a box now.

Your stationery is you. It should look nice, but you do not want to tie up a lot of money here. Windowed envelopes save time, as you only type the name and address once. Also order business cards and a rubber stamp with your company name and address.

Your telephone may be listed under your name and the company name. When business picks up, install a second line for outgoing calls. This way you won't be tying up your order line.

Buy a plain-paper fax and order a dedicated line for it. This means two telephone lines to start. Do not fool with fax/phone switches or *call waiting.* The fax is one of your most important communication and order-taking tools. Without a fax on a dedicated line, you will not appear to be running a real business.

Your computer is your most important piece of machinery; spend the money and get a good one. You are a "wordsmith" now and require the best word processing machine you can afford.

Your computer will speed up your writing, and it may be used for correspondence, mailing list maintenance, typesetting, order entry and bookkeeping. In fact, you will save enough on typesetting just one or two books to pay for the whole system.

The legal requirements of operating a business are covered in many parts of this book, just as you will encounter them in every facet of your daily publishing life. The following is what you need to run your business, but remember that most of this may be postponed until you are ready to go to press, move out of the house or hire employees. These tips, of course, are food for thought, not a substitute for legal counsel.

> *No one takes better care of your money than you do.*
> — Cliff Leonard in *License to Steal*

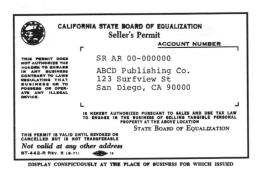

THE CITY OF SAN DIEGO
MUNICIPAL BUSINESS LICENSE

ABCD Publishing Co
123 Surfview Street
San Diego, CA 90000

123   Surfview Street

90000   sole proprietor

CALIFORNIA STATE BOARD OF EQUALIZATION
Seller's Permit

SR AR 00-000000
ABCD Publishing Co.
123 Surfview St
San Diego, CA 90000

Licenses

Interview a friend or acquaintance who has recently set up a small business in your community. They will be happy to tell you what happened to them, where to get various licenses, recommend an accountant, etc. In some areas you must register your business with local authorities, but not in all. Ask this same friend where to find the office. As a sole proprietorship, your business won't need a separate bank account, and until you hire employees, you will avoid Employer Identification Numbers (EIN) and special accounts.

Sales taxes. Most states have a sales tax. If your state does, you will be required to collect it ONLY on those books shipped to destinations within the state which are NOT for resale by another dealer. The sales tax is collected only once

We don't charge *sales tax here, we just* collect *it.*

at the retail level from the ultimate purchaser. As a commercial firm, you must either collect the sales tax, show by the shipping address on the invoice that the goods are going out of state, or claim to be selling the books to another dealer, such as a bookstore, "for resale." Many states will require you to maintain a file of customer resale numbers. Some dealers will list their resale number on purchase orders, but usually you have to send a standard resale number request card, available from your stationer, with the invoice. Type "for resale" on the invoice and record the resale number there if you have it.

FIRM NAME _____

I HEREBY CERTIFY,
That I hold valid seller's permit No. _____
issued pursuant to the Sales and Use Tax Law; that I am engaged in the business of selling

that the tangible personal property described herein which I shall purchase from: _____

will be resold by me in the form of tangible personal property; PROVIDED, however, that in the event any of such property is used for any purpose other than retention, demonstration, or display while holding it for sale in the regular course of business, it is understood that I am required by the Sales and Use Tax Law to report and pay for the tax, measured by the purchase price of such property.

Description of property to be purchase _____

Dated: _____ 19 _____ Signature _____

at _____ By and Title _____

Phone _____ Address _____

Example of a California resale number request card

In some states, shipping supplies, such as cartons and tape, are not subject to the sales tax. Other states exempt certain nonprofit or public institutions, such as libraries and schools.

Before you go to press, obtain your resale permit. Then if your books are printed in the same state, you won't have to pay sales tax when you pay the printing bill. Find the office in the telephone directory. In California it is called the *State Board of Equalization;* in Massachusetts it is the *Sales and Use Tax Bureau* of the *Department of Corporations and Taxation.* Check the posted resale permit at a nearby store; the name of the controlling agency will be on it.

When you apply for your resale license or resale permit, tell them you are just starting out as an author and hope to sell a few of your books. Tell them that most sales will be wholesale to bookstores or shipped out of state. This way you may be able to avoid giving them a deposit, and you may be allowed to report annually instead of quarterly, thus saving both money and paperwork. For example, in California, if you say your taxable sales (retail and within the state) might amount to more than $300 per month, you must place at least $100 on deposit with the Board of Equalization before you start. If you say you might be collecting over $12.50 per month in sales taxes, they will want you to fill out the forms and remit the taxes quarterly instead of annually. When you apply, the tax office will supply you with an explanatory sheet detailing your responsibilities for the sales tax in your state.

The law you must know as an author-publisher concerns copyright, defamation (libel), right of privacy, illegal reproduction and negligence. Briefly, copyrights work both ways: They protect your work from others and their work from you. Take pride, do your own original work and make it better. For a detailed explanation of the copyright, see Chapters Two and Five.

— **Defamation** is libel in the printed word and slander when spoken. *Black's Law Dictionary* defines defamation as: "the offense of injuring a person's character, fame or reputation by false and malicious statements." Libel may take the form of either words or pictures. The offense is in the "publication" of the matter, so you are not "covered" just because you read it somewhere else first. You are safe if the statement is true; this is the perfect defense, but check the source. The best advice is never to say anything nasty about anyone. You will need all the support you can get to sell your book. If you disagree with another authority, leave his or her name out and write: "Some people will argue . . ." or "Many authorities believe . . ." and then tear up their position with your view. If you don't like someone, the worst thing you can do to them is to leave them out of your book altogether.

Cover yourself and stay out of court; the legal game is expensive.

— **Right of privacy** is another area of law you may face. Unless part of a news event, a person has a right to keep his photo out of publications. Most people love to see their photo in a book and in fact are prime customers for the finished product, but if you suspect there may be a problem, have them sign a written release.

— **Illegal reproduction** covers the promoting of lotteries, financial schemes, fraudulent activities, printing of securities, reproducing postage stamps, etc. In other words, don't print money. If you are writing about these subjects, you probably already know about the problems, and the postal and other laws relating to them. If not, seek legal advice.

— **Negligence.** A reader could sue you, claiming your book misled him to his great damage. Incorporation will not shield you, as the plaintiff will sue both the author and publisher.

Warner recalled 115,000 copies of *First Love* when Dr. Ruth Westheimer and Dr. Nathan Kravetz mixed up the "safe" days for the rhythm method of birth control. Suits have been brought against the publishers of a diet book and a cookbook, but so far, the courts have sided with the publishers.

In most cases, the courts have not found books to be "products," so publishers are not strictly liable for their content; it must be proved the publisher knew or should have known of the inaccuracies. Books are not the reader's only source of information.

Today, many books contain disclaimers warning readers not to rely on the text.

Taxes are one place an author-publisher gets a big break. Not only are the costs of printing your book deductible, so are all the direct expenses incurred while writing and promoting it. If you are writing about your favorite hobby, you can deduct the expenses of pursuing it, too. For example, if you are writing on aviation, you can probably deduct flying lessons and trips to the national convention. There are sales and publicity tours, and you can even write off a portion of your home, its rent or mortgage, utilities, etc. Assuming you are already employed and Uncle Sam is withholding 30% or more from your weekly check, that amounts to thousands of dollars a year. The game is to see how much you can get back. How much did you pay to the IRS last year? Would you like to get a full refund? Getting money back is fun and rewarding. Of course, if your book is a great success, you will make more money and have to pay taxes on it. For complete details, get a copy of the *Small Business Tax Guide* from your nearest IRS office. Under "record keeping," below, we will list possible deductions.

Record keeping must be done from the beginning of your writing, because you cannot deduct what you do not have written down. Many small business people get themselves into a jam by coming up with a great business idea and then charging off pursuing it. At the end of the year they suddenly realize that they have forgotten to fill out forms or record expenses. At that point their only choice is to hire an accountant to straighten out the mess. Accountants charge much more for this sort of work, and they are rarely able to reconstruct the records completely or take all the deductions the business is entitled to take. The IRS is plugged into your bank, and when they notice that $50,000 went through your bank account, while you reported only $35,000, they will be contacting you with questions. You can't avoid the bank, as you have to cash all those checks which come in the mail for your book.

Dun & Bradstreet claims that 80% of all business failures are due to poor records. A University of Pittsburgh survey found that 40% of the retailers surveyed did not keep proper records. It is silly—no, tragic—because record keeping is easy with a simple system. As the business grows, you will

> *"High cash flow" is taking in lots of money but being unable to find any of it.*

also need financial information on your past in order to project the future properly.

Start right now. Get *Quicken* for your computer. It is an accounts payable program with a general ledger. Label the columns in the expense ledger (Category & Transfer List) as follows: meals (ME), lodging (LO), gas/lube/wash (GL), office supplies (OS), shipping & postage (SP), advertising (AD), entertainment (EN), transportation fares (AF), travel expenses (TR), cost of supplies & book printing (CS), dues & licenses (DL), subscriptions (SB), telephone (TL), electricity (EL), water (WA), mortgage/rent (MG), parking & tolls (PT), car repairs (CR), car tires & supplies (CS), refunds (RE) and miscellaneous (MI). For a detailed explanation of the items that fit into these columns, see the IRS publication *Small Business Tax Guide* mentioned above. Also see *Taxes For The Self-Employed*, an audiotape album by Noelle Allen, CPA. Contact Canyon View Institute, Tel: (408) 252-1367, for details.

The best way to get into the habit and to learn what is deductible is to list EVERY cent you spend the first year. Get receipts whenever possible, at the post office, for parking, tolls, meals, motels, etc.

You have already decided to carry pen and paper at all times to record your thoughts for your manuscript, so carry one more sheet for recording expenditures. Any money spent in the pursuit of income is deductible, so write down every cent. As you learn what is deductible, you will find that you become generous where an expenditure can be written off and stingy where it can't. This is good discipline and good business.

Keep an envelope in the car. Each day, as you get in and start the car, let the engine warm up a moment as you record the date, odometer reading and places you intend to go. Use the envelope to hold the receipts you acquire during the day. Start a new envelope every month.

You can't deduct it if you don't record it.

At the end of each month, use *Quicken* to post the *petit* cash expenses from your pocket notes and car envelope. If you are not sure what account an expenditure might go in, place it in miscellaneous. If you have a lot of expenses in a new area (e.g., building repair), set up a new account.

At the end of the year, total up the columns and take the ledger and totaled figures to your accountant. The accountant will do the rest, and the charge will be reasonable. You will be amazed at the size of your refund, and the accountant will compliment you on your work. Record keeping is so easy, and yet many people think there is some great mystery to accounting.

You don't even have to make money to claim deductions. You can claim a loss for at least three years in a row before the IRS questions whether you are a hobbyist rather than an author-publisher. Chrysler lost money for years and still took deductions. Keep good records, and you will be able to prove you are in business.

Raising the money you need to pay for the production and promotion of your book will take you into the world of finance, unless you have a lot of loose, ready cash lying about. Insufficient capitalization is one of the greatest problems facing most new businesses. Money won't come looking for you. You have to find it by selling yourself and your book. But the money is there; it is available.

According to *The Wall Street Journal*, most entrepreneurs spend their own money to start their business. Forty-eight percent rely on savings, 29% borrow from banks, 13% shake down their friends, 4% look for individual investors, less than 1% strike deals with venture capital firms or government agencies, and 5% are successful with other sources.

Do not expect the large national book printers to be interested in postponing the printing bill. They are printers, not publishers.

You're the living, breathing, embodiment of the American Dream—free enterprise division.

Do not take in partners on your book. Partners are rarely "silent." They want to know why the book is not selling better, why it is not in the airport bookstore, why you are spending money to attend a bookfair, etc. You will spend more time explaining the publishing business to your partner(s) than you will promoting the book.

In the beginning, you won't run up bills by hiring help or renting space, and you will even save some leisure time money by staying home to write, so you will not have any immediate needs for large sums of cash. Many people have more money than they need for necessities; they throw away their disposable income on frivolous purchases. Going without alcohol, cigarettes and nights out is not only healthier, but the time can be better spent writing your book.

Some people advise the use of "OPM" (other people's money) rather than your own. Then if your business goes bust and you lose all the borrowed funds, you still have your own money in reserve. But as you tuck your prized manuscript under your arm and venture off, you are going to find that locating OPM takes some searching.

— **The Small Business Administration** used to prohibit financial assistance to book publishers, bookstores, movie theaters, news operations and others. This was to avoid financing radicals who might publish seditious literature and writings and then file for bankruptcy, which would leave the taxpayers with a social problem and the bill for starting it. The "opinion molder" rule was overturned in mid-1994.

— **Banks** don't search for loan applicants in the publishing industry. They like "going" firms with upbeat balance sheets; like everyone else, they are in business to stay in business. Banks look on manuscripts/books as "speculative." Even armed with a detailed market research report on your product, you may find that you can't even get an appointment with the loan officer. A stack of books is not consid-

---

You know you have arrived when you do not have to check the balance before writing a check.

ered good collateral to a bank; if you defaulted, they would not know how to turn the books back into money. If you ask for money to go into business, the bank probably won't be interested.

Basically, there are two ways to borrow money from a bank. The first is the "term" loan, which is normally used to finance purchases such as a car. Term loans are paid back monthly and are usually limited to 36 months. The second is an ordinary signature loan with interest at the prime rate plus about 5%. A signature loan runs for a period of months and you pay it off at the due date. But while the loan is written for a stated period, it is common to pay just the interest and renew it. Many authors have been successful in acquiring money by leaving the manuscript at home and asking for a "vacation" loan.

> Bear Kamoroff found seven friends to participate in the first and second printings of his best-seller *Small Time Operator*. He reasoned: why be selfish; why not let your friends share in the project?

You may need collateral, perhaps a second mortgage. If you have enough real and personal property, you will be able to get the money on your signature alone. Don't think small; large amounts are often easier to borrow.

All banks are not the same; shop around not only for loans, but for checking account charges. Banks are not doing you any favors; you are doing them a favor by storing your money with them and paying interest to them. Stop in at several and pick up pamphlets on their checking account and loan policies. Take the brochures home and compare them. Do they charge for each check deposited? You will be receiving a lot of small checks, and any check charges will add up fast. Do they pay interest on checking accounts, and if so, what is the minimum required balance? Will they let you bank by mail, and will they pay the postage? Don't just think of your present needs; think of the future.

Incidentally, you may be better off working your new publishing company part-time initially. Then if it fails, at least you are not out of a job, too.

— **Altering your W-4 Form** is advocated by some people as a way to have the IRS lend your withheld taxes back to you. If you have a regular job, and a lot of money is being withheld from each paycheck, you may claim an exemption from withholding by making out a new W-4 form for your employer, early in the year. If you are in the 30% tax bracket, this is like getting a 50% raise. Of course, you must be serious about starting your business, keep good records and take deductions. Done correctly, you should be able to spend and deduct the formerly withheld money and "zero out" at tax time. Once you are working for yourself full-time, you will file estimated tax forms rather than W-4's.

— **Pre-publication specials** are often used to raise money. As the book goes to press, send out a brochure to all who might be interested in the book, and offer to pay the postage for a pre-publication order (but never discount a new book). Emphasize that the manuscript is complete and that the book is on the press. Tell them you won't cash their check until the book is shipped. Mention a shipping date, but give yourself an extra month or two. Make another special offer to dealers. Pre-publication sales sometimes bring in enough to pay the printing bill.

— **Selling stock** in your business is another way to raise money, but there are a lot of problems. You are not big enough to make it worth your while, so you should give money raising a great deal of thought before sharing the rewards of your work. If you can find someone who will risk an investment in your book, you can find one who will give you a straight loan at a good rate of interest where his risk is lower.

— **Royalty financing** is where an investor lends you money on a specific product in return for a royalty for every book sold. You do not have to give up any equity in your company, you do not have to pay any debt until money comes in from sales and there are no liabilities on your balance sheet. Limit the term to the first printing.

— **Grants** are available from many foundations for worthwhile publishing projects. Check your state arts agency, the National Endowment for the Arts, 1100 Pennsylvania Avenue NW, Washington, DC 20506 (government), Alicia Patterson Foundation (private), and see the listings in *Grants and Awards Available to Writers*. Additional listings may be found in *Literary Market Place, Corporate Fund Raising Directory* and the *National Fund Raising Directory*. There are several magazines for fund raisers. See listings in the Appendix and ask your reference librarian. Most of the grants and fellowships are for fiction and poetry. If your book qualifies, it can mean a large amount of money, but there is a lot of paperwork to go along with it.

— **Writers' colonies** often supply free room and board to support budding authors. Some have rigid rules limiting the length and number of stays. For a list, see *Writer's Market*.

— **Parents** will often lend on a book. They often have faith in their offspring and want to see your name on a book as much as you do. But if you do borrow from friends or relatives, make the same presentation to them that you would to a bank. Talk figures and do not get emotional. Then write a loan contract and pay them the 10% to 15% interest that you would pay the bank. Put the loan on a business basis and keep the friendship.

— **Other possibilities** include credit unions, retirement plans, the Veterans Administration (if appropriate) and the Farm Home Loan Association, which is said to be very liberal in its definition of a "farm community." Send $23.50 for *Money Sources for Small Business* by William M. Alarid, Puma Publishing Co., 1670 Coral Drive, Santa Maria, CA 93454. Shop around. All these suggestions for borrowing money assume you have a good salable product to begin with.

How much does it cost to publish? That is like asking how much a car costs. All books are different. If you are planning to print 3,000 copies of a 208-page, 5.5" x 8.5" softcover book with a few photographs, black ink on white

---

If you want your book to sell like a book, you'll have to make it look like a book.

paper with a four-color cover, the books will cost less than $1.75 each, so your printing bill will run a little over $5,000. Then there is typesetting, which most of us do on our laser printers, book cover design ($1,500), other pre-press expenses and trucking from the printer.

After the book is printed, it has to be promoted with book reviews, news releases and some direct mail advertising. Money will not be coming in right away. There is a lot of lead time for writing, printing and promotion, and the bookstores are notorious for being slow pay. For a book like the one described here, you should budget about $12,000 to get started.

A book with fewer photos, fewer pages and a one-color cover could run much less, but without a good-looking book and some promotion money, the book will not sell. For details, see the chapters on pricing and promotion.

On the first venture, the printer will probably want his money in installments: 1/3 to start, 1/3 when the plates are made and 1/3 on the completion of the printing. After a book or two, he will no doubt give you normal 30-day terms and want his money a month after he delivers the books to you. If he wants installments, agree to them and then request a "2% discount for cash." (2% of $5,000 is $100.)

Lean and mean. Run a streamlined, efficient operation. Do everything yourself and buy only those services you cannot perform. Avoid employees initially; they cost you time (management), money and paperwork. Print in small quantities to keep the inventory low. Once you have learned the business by doing every part of it yourself, farm out the repetitive and least enjoyable tasks. When contracting for services, remember that everyone is in business for himself first; you come second. The graphic artist, accountant and all the rest will try to sell you more than you need. They don't care about your business as much as you do, because they have less to lose. Be careful taking advice from someone who is trying to sell you something. If this is your first business, pick up a copy of *Working Solo* by Terri Lonier for just $14.95. Call (800) 222-SOLO.

Keep on top of costs. If you can save $1,000 per year by streamlining procedures and your net profit is normally 3%, the effect is the same as if you increased sales by $30,000.

Don't waste anything. Save the stamps from the incoming mail. Stamp collecting is big business, and years from now you may be able to sell them to stamp companies. Check the *Yellow Pages* and call several local stamp dealers for prices.

Machinery. As your publishing company grows, look for labor-saving machinery to multiply your efforts. Personal computers, photocopy machines, cordless telephones and postage meters will save you time. They are much better buys than an employee, and you will find that with depreciation, machines are not very expensive. As machinery accumulates, you will begin to understand the advantages of owning your own business.

The author has operated, and worked for, large firms but he opted to go it alone in 1969. It was 1983 before he decided to take on his first employee. In terms of both dollar volume and books sold, he was probably the world's largest one-person publishing company. Now Para Publishing is larger, but Dan has help.

Because he had committed himself to the luxury of a one-person enterprise, he had to operate efficiently. He concentrated on those areas which provided a maximum return on his investment of time and money: the highest profit and best results for the time and energy expended (invested).

Dan knows small business and small publishing inside out because he plays both roles: He sets policy as management and implements it as labor. Consequently, he has developed simple systems to handle every task.

Dan is a small businessman. His background is in marketing and mail order. He did not come from the publishing industry and, consequently, he doesn't make their mistakes.

Fortune assists the bold. — Virgil

We think that small presses and self-publishing individuals frequently precede the market because they can more easily become involved in a new trend at the conceptual level and can bypass a lot of the red tape that slows things down in larger houses. — Bob Speer of Southwest Book Services

Chapter Four

Printing Your Book

— The Printing Process
— Design of Books
— Book Materials

Here is what you can expect when your book enters the production stage. This explanation of the printing process is meant to be brief, and yet provide you with enough information to deal effectively with your printer. There are many excellent books on the printing trade. Also see our Special Reports *Book Production* (on pre-press: composition, layout, editing and design) and *Buying Book Printing*. See the Appendix.

Information packaging. Do not think of yourself as a book author or book publisher. You are an information provider. You might print your information in a series of magazine articles, put it on audio cassette tapes, present it at a seminar or print it in a book, or you might concentrate on one of them, such as the book, and spin off parts to other formats. Now the challenge is to decide how to package the information to make it salable. Some packages will bring in more money than others. People are paying good money for well-packaged information today. Some manuals cost $75.00, and seminars may run $600.00 per day. Obviously, the "package" must appear to be worth the asking price. It must be a professionally run seminar, a nicely printed book or an attractive article in a prestigious magazine.

We will begin by discussing how to package your material into a book. Toward the end of this chapter, we will discuss packaging your information on audiotape, videotape, computer disk and CD-ROM disc.

Printing processes. Almost all books are printed with the photo-offset process today. Your original copy will be *typeset* with a computer-driven laser printer or a computerized photocomposition machine. Your pasted-up "boards" will be photographed and the negatives will be "stripped" into a "flat." Then a bright light will be used to burn the thin printing plate through the flat. You may hear of other printing processes, such as letterpress, which is old, and gra-

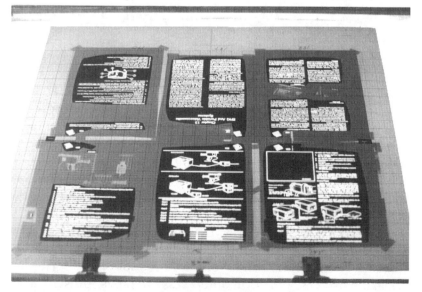

A stripped-in flat

vure, which is used for larger runs, but you will not use them. You may send your disk to the printer who will go directly to plates. This typesetting technique will also be described in this chapter.

Conversely, there are also some less expensive, short-run methods. Wire-stitched (stapled) booklets with up to about 60 5.5" x 8.5" pages can be reproduced very nicely on photocopy machines.

This book will concern itself with square-backed softcover and hardcover books, those you normally see in a bookstore. If you have a book-length manuscript, one which will fill a book of 100 pages or more, you will want a clean, sharp, professional-appearing product, one that will sell. You want a book you can be proud of, and you want it to be acceptable to the stores.

Time. You can figure on four to five weeks to print, bind and deliver your books to you, but the work may take longer if your printer can't do all the work in-house and has to farm some of it out. Hardbound books, for example, will take a couple of weeks more because they take longer to bind. Softcover reprints usually take about three weeks. Add two to six days to the above time estimates for trucking.

Thirty years ago, it took eight to ten weeks to produce a book. Now it takes just over a month, and most book printers are pushing for eight to ten days. Just like a fast-food restaurant, the object is to get the customer in, served and out as quickly as possible.

The composition and layout should take less than a week, if you do it yourself on a computer with a laser printer, and about five weeks if you give the work to a typesetter.

Book design. Go to a bookstore to search for a book you can use as a *model*. Look for books in your subject area. If you can't find a book in your subject area that you like for

> *A book should not just be something to read, it should be something to possess.* — Lee Collins

its look and feel, try other subject areas that would appeal to your intended audience. If your intended audience is used to hardcover books, select hardcover. If they need a larger format book, select 8.5" x 11". If this is a reference book, select Smyth sewn pages. Consider paper, binding, layout, everything. Buy that book and place it above your desk; it is your model. You will use it as a guide for typesetting, layout, printing and binding.

Book printers will produce an acceptable book, but that book will be boring unless you provide some direction. What usually happens is that the author-publisher spends a great deal of time on the text, and the manufacturing becomes an afterthought. The package design is left up to the printer. What we see today are many 5.5" x 8.5" softcover books that look the same. Printers can supply foldout pages, gold foil on the cover, die-cut jackets, embossed covers and many other things. All you have to do is ask, so find a book you like and use it as a model. Do not just leave book design to the printer.

Design your book to fit your customer. If this is a business book, it should be in hardcover with a dust jacket; if it is a professional book for doctors, lawyers or accountants, it should be hardcover without a dust jacket; if it is a children's book, it should be in four-color, hardcover and have a dust jacket. Give your customers what they want, expect and deserve.

If you need help with book design, see a book producer or book packager. These are graphic arts shops that specialize in books. See the Appendix.

Note that the chapters of a book start on a right-hand page. If this leaves you with a blank on the left, fill the space with a photograph. Never leave a blank page; fill it with something, even if it is just a page number. Books with blank pages sometimes are returned by buyers who think there is a manufacturing defect. Just supply the typesetter with a few extra photos and provide instructions to fill any blank pages with them.

Type may be set to *run around* illustrations, but it is simpler and cheaper to make a break in the text and insert the photo or drawing full-width, from margin to margin. The width of the text in this book is 4.125 inches, and most illustrations run margin to margin.

Running heads are lines of type which appear across the top of the book page. Usually the title of the book appears on the left-hand page, while the chapter title is on the right.

The folio is the page number. Folios may be placed in the top outside corner, bottom middle or even on the side. Usually, the folio is part of the running head. Traditionally, pages received Roman numerals in the front matter and Arabic numbers in the text, because the text was set separately and then the front matter was expanded or contracted to use up most of the pages in the signatures. Today, many publishers take a tip from the magazine companies and start the count, though not the numbering, from the title page. This makes the final page count higher and makes the purchaser feel he is getting more for his money. The argument goes: "I paid (the printer) for those pages, so I'm going to count them." See this book, for example.

If all publishers thought alike, all books might look alike.
Sometimes there is a good marketing reason to venture from the standard.
This book is die-cut, nestled into a disc and shrink-wrapped.

Standardize and save money. If you vary from the norm, the creativity will cost you sales. Occasionally variations can be justified, as in a die-cut, circular book on Frisbee play, but make sure the special work will contribute to the sales of the book. Remember, too, that libraries and bookstores have standardized shelving. You want your book to fit. Most short-run books are 5.5" x 8.5", perfect bound (glued) paperbacks, with or without photos and drawings, on a 50- or 60-pound paper stock. The cover is four-color on a 10-point C1S (coated one side) cover stock. Beyond this basic specification, a number of variations are possible.

Measurements. There are many standard book trim sizes, and you want to give your customer what they expect. If this is a cookbook or computer book that is usually in a wide format so it will open and lie flat, you must provide the same.

The conventional 5.5" x 8.5" size is suitable for both hardcover and soft; it is one of the most economical, fits a library shelf well and is by far the most popular. One hundred and twenty 5.5" x 8.5" pages make a much nicer book than sixty 8.5" x 11" pages. The only good reason to go oversize is if you have too much material. If you have large illustrations, such as charts, consider foldout pages. The printer can insert them between signatures; specify where you want the foldouts. If you have a lot of material (over 500 pages, for example) in the 5.5" x 8.5" measurement, select the 8.5" x 11" size.

Many web presses will not yield a full measurement. Instead of 5.5" x 8.5", the finished trim will be 5.375" x 8.375". If you want a full trim size, specify sheet-fed press.

Whatever size you select, make all your books measure the same in order to standardize your shipping bags and cartons. If some books are 5.5" x 8.5", while others are 8.5" x 11", they will still stack well together. If some are 6" x 9", you will have packaging problems.

Number of pages. You need eight pages to qualify for the post office's "book rate," 50 to get a Library of Congress Catalog Card number, 50 for a listing in Bowker's *Books in*

Print, and 100 pages to qualify for a listing in H.W. Wilson's *Cumulative Book Index*. Over 100 is psychologically good and will help to justify your price, so if you have just 90 pages, set the book in larger type, put more *leading* (space) between the lines, expand the Appendix or add some illustrations.

Your book will be printed on several very large sheets of paper which will be folded down into "signatures." (Originally, the person who sewed the pages together *signed* his work.) The number of book pages in each signature will depend on the size of your printer's press, but 32 is common. This means that 16 of the pages will be printed on one side of the sheet ("sixteen up"), and 16 will be printed on the other. Therefore, you will figure the pages in your book in multiples of 32.

To visualize this, take a sheet of paper and fold it in half four times. The folding results in 16 panels on each side of the sheet (16 up and 16 down) for a grand total of 32 pages in the signature. If your book comes out to 176 pages, it will have 5 signatures of 32 pages and one signature of 16. The last signature will be shot twice and run side by side, but the press will be stopped at half the count.

If your type is not set yet, roughly estimate your pages from your computer printout or figure the number from the word processor's character count. Many authors like to write their books in a 5.5" x 8.5" printout, so their manuscript looks closer to the finished page. The margins are set for a text block measurement of 4.125" x 7.125". Naturally, you will have to adjust your figures to compensate for the different type styles between your computer type and the type the book will be set in, if different.

Often we want to have a page count before we lay out the pages, so that we can quote the number in our advertising. In your brochures, refer to the page count as: "More than 150 pages"; you don't have to be exact, but people do like to know what they are paying for.

Poetry gets different treatment. Unless very short, each poem should have its own page.

Palatino   Helvetica

Palatino italic   *Helvetica* italic

Palatino bold   **Helvetica** bold

Palatino bold italic   ***Helvetica*** bold italic

Typefaces are many and varied. Your page layout program will have a selection. Pick a serif typeface such as New Century Schoolbook for the body copy and a sans serif font for headlines.

New Century Schoolbook

Four type factors affect legibility: type style (san serif is harder to read), type size, leading (rhymes with "heading" and is the space between the lines), and the column width (the human eye is trained to read narrow newspaper columns).

Times Roman

To give your book some variation, you may use *italics*, **boldface**, ***bold italic***, SMALL CAPS and larger sizes for chapter heads, captions, subheads and for lending emphasis.

Palatino

Here are some more type terms to make you sound as though you know what you are talking about. "Point size" is the height of a capital letter (and its mount), as in "10-pt. type." There are 72 points to the inch. "Pica" is the printer's standard measurement for the length of a line and the depth of a page. There are

Bookman

12 points to a pica and six picas to the inch. Therefore, 24 picas means a four-inch-wide column. "Leading" or slug is the space between the lines. Printers used to use a strip of lead, hence the name. If you have nine points of type plus two points of leading, the specification would be written out as "9/11."

Bookman

Nine on eleven is about as small as you should go for a legible book. Ten on twelve is very common, though children and older people with failing eyesight prefer 12 on 14. Most page layout programs will set your leading automatically unless you specify what you want.

Helvetica

Some computer programs put more type on a page than others, using the identical typeface, size, spacing and leading. It all depends on how the machine is programmed. Try to use the same machine for revisions.

AvantGarde

Do not venture too far from the common type styles, such as Times Roman, Palatino, Baskerville, Caledonia, Bookman and New Century Schoolbook. If you want your book to sell like a book, it has to look like a book.

Courier

Compare the various typefaces

6 Helvetica

7 Helvetica

8 Helvetica

8½ Helvetica

9 Helvetica

10 Helvetica

11 Helvetica

12 Helvetica

13 Helvetica

14 Helvetica

15 Helvetica

16 Helvetica

17 Helvetica

18 Helvetica

19 Helvetica

20 Helvetica

21 Helvetica

22 Helvetica

23 Helvetica

24 Helvetica

**Character heights are measured in "points."
There are 72 points to the inch.**

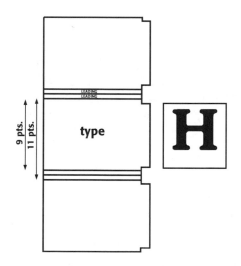

"Leading" is the space between the lines of type.

Headlines, such as chapter titles, are usually set in larger type. While text is usually set in a serif typeface such as Times-Roman or New Century Schoolbook, headlines are often set in a sans serif typeface such as Helvetica.

Illustrations will augment the text, enhance the appearance and aid the salability of the book. Don't be cheap with illustrations. Each one is very inexpensive when the cost is spread out over the entire print run of the book. If a photo or drawing will make the book more attractive, readable or useful to the buyer, include it.

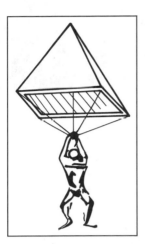

Line drawing

Extra lines were crowded into this line drawing to give it the appearance of shading.

**Photo printed
unscreened**

**Same photo
screened.
Study with a
magnifying glass
or loupe.**

Line art may consist of type, charts, sketches, etc. Drawings may be created on your computer or drawn separately and pasted in. If you draw your own artwork or have it done, use a fine-point felt-tip pen with black ink. Reductions and enlargements may be made on a photocopy machine.

Art may be taken from old magazines and books. If the copyright has expired, the art is in the public domain. Prior to January 1, 1978, copyright protection was for 28 years and was renewable for 28 years. The new law makes the original (pre-1978) copyright renewable for an additional 47 years, for a total of 75 years. Therefore, anything printed prior to 1919 is safe and anything in print before 1966 is probably safe. See Copyright Circular R99.

Now, the copyright is for the author's life plus 50 years.

Halftones must be made of any artwork, such as a photograph, which is not solid black-white. To make a halftone, the original photo is rephotographed through a screen. The resulting print is composed of dots of various sizes, and the eye blends the dots together into a continuous tone. Making a halftone of a photo, pencil drawing, watercolor, etc., costs $8 to $10 each.

Screens come in several values and are measured in dots per linear inch. The more dots, the crisper the printed halftone. Newspapers commonly use a 65- or 85-line screen (85 dots per inch), while books are commonly done in 120-, 133- or even 150-line. Black-and-white photographs screen best. Color prints reproduced in black and white tend to get muddy.

Photos taken from other magazines and books have already been screened and may be pasted right onto your laser-output pages. However, if they are to be enlarged or reduced, they must be rescreened, and this usually reduces the quality.

With both photos and drawings, reductions are preferable to enlargements. Reductions become sharper, while enlargements only magnify flaws, losing clarity.

Your photos will be inserted by the printer. Simply size the photos with a proportion wheel and leave space for them in the typeset text. Paste each photograph to a larger sheet of paper and list its page number. The first photograph on page 17 will be "17-A," for example. Use a red pen to write "17-A" on the blank space on your laser-output page.

Digital cameras may be used to capture images which you may then "drop" into your page layout program. This eliminates printed photographs and some work for the printer. The screened photograph comes out on the printer's film with the type.

Four-color printing should be used on covers but is normally too expensive for inside pages. To reproduce a color photo or slide, it is rephotographed (or laser scanned) four times, each time with a different colored filter over the lens. This produces four negatives consisting of the three primary colors (red, blue and yellow) plus black. The result is called a "four-color separation." Then the paper is run through the press four times, each time with one of the colors, and the color photo is re-created. Naturally, four-color printing is more expensive because of the additional camera work and press time. Always ask for a "color key" before your color pages are run through the press. When checking these four plastic color overlays, remember simply that the sky is blue, the grass is green, clouds are white, wood is brown, etc. What you see is what you get.

Transparencies usually produce the best covers. If you are taking photographs for the cover and have a choice, use slide film, not color print film.

With very few exceptions, covers must be four-color today. We live in a four-color world. Our magazines, television and newspapers are in color. Buyers for both chain and independent bookstores are looking for books with good package design that will inspire a purchase. Everyone buys a book by its cover. The ultimate purchaser reads the outside, but they do not read the book, prior to purchase. Sales reps take only (lighter-weight) covers when they visit the bookstores. Even the wholesalers say, "Please do not send the books; we only want to see the covers."

Paper is even more confusing than typefaces, and while you should know what to look for, you will need the guidance of your printer to make a final choice. Most book printers stock a few basic types of book paper which they buy in huge quantities. They can get almost any paper, but other types will be more expensive because they must be special-ordered in smaller lots. Basically, you have four general paper choices:

D DELTA LITHOGRAPH COMPANY

TEXT PAPER COMPARATIVE COST FINDER

Many of our customers are interested in cost comparisons of the various weights and shades of text papers. The reasons for this are varied; weight savings, bulking, shade preferences and others. The cost trade-offs involved are often significant in reaching a decision. This Text Paper Comparative Cost Finder will help in these decisions.

The use of this chart is very easy. Using 50# Delta White offset book rolled stock as the base, or 100%, compare the other shades and stocking to calculate the comparative prices.

For example, if you have an estimate based on 10,000 copies of a book printed on 60# White sheets and want to calculate the approximate savings if printed on 50# White rolls, compare the 50# rolls listed below to the 60# sheets, or 100 vs. 130. Paper savings on the job would be 30%.

Text paper costs run between 28% and 50% of the total printing costs, depending on total pages in the book and the quantity of books produced. Therefore, in the example given, the overall cost savings would probably be about 15% (50% of 30%).

These figures cannot be used to calculate exact figures. They are only intended to give you a guide in figuring the comparative costs and specifications for your book.

STOCK	AVAILABLE IN	COMPARABLE PERCENT
50# Delta	Rolls	100
50# Delta	Sheets	112
60# Delta	Rolls	115
60# Delta	Sheets	130
45# Delta	Rolls	92
45# Delta	Sheets	105
70# Delta	Sheets	185
30# Omega Book	Rolls	78
35# Alpha Workbook	Rolls	65
50# Theta Natural Text	Rolls	115
50# Theta Natural Text	Sheets	130
50# Litecoat Beta Book	Rolls	110
60# Pica Matte	Sheets	215
60# Kappa Coated Book	Sheets	195

Delta is the difference

Paper comparison chart

1. Newsprint: Inexpensive, but it looks cheap, it yellows quickly and the photo reproduction is poor.
2. Uncoated book stock: Looks good, photos OK. Most common.
3. Coated book stock (matte, coated or gloss): Looks great, photos great, more expensive.
4. Fancy textured papers: May be hard to print, especially photos. Expensive.

Unless you are doing an art book, an uncoated book stock is what you need. Your printer will probably suggest a 50-pound or 60-pound "white offset book."

Paper comes by the sheet (for that sheet-fed press) or the roll (cut into sheets after printing on the web press). There are many criteria which must be considered when selecting paper:

1. Weight is expressed in pounds per 500 sheets, but the measurements of the sheet vary according to the category to which the paper belongs. Sixty-pound cover stock and 60-pound book papers are not the same. For example: 16 lb. bond = 40 lb. book; 20 lb. bond = 50 lb. book; 24 lb. bond = 60 lb. book and 28 lb. bond = 70 lb. book. Cover stock is rated in point sizes with 10 point (10/1000 of an inch thick) being very common.

   Most books are printed on 50, 55 or 60 lb. stock. Generally, heavier paper is more expensive, though some of the newer light-weight papers, developed for combating postal rates, are even higher in price. If the paper is too thin, the book will look and feel "cheap," if it is too heavy, the book may not fold flat. In either case, you have wasted your money.

   In the metric system the weighing system is easier; all paper is simply weighed in grams per square meter of paper. There are no classifications.

2. Texture. Some highly textured paper does not accept ink well, especially halftones. Use a smooth paper such as "50 lb. white offset book."

3. Opacity. You don't want the type on the other side of the page to show through. Light-weight paper can be very opaque, especially when coated. Opacity may be tested by placing a printed sheet under the sample sheet to see how much type shows through.

4. Bulking factor is expressed in pages per inch (ppi). A 45 lb. paper may have a bulking factor of 640 pages per inch, while a 55 lb. stock might be 370 ppi. Heavier weight does not always mean thicker paper. Bulking depends on the fiber content of the paper and the milling process used; a high bulk may also be produced by whipping air into the paper during manufacture. Whipping produces a thicker paper without increasing weight. However, this fluffed-up paper allows ink to diffuse more, so halftones are not as crisp. PPI is measured by the even inch. Once you know the bulking factor of the paper you plan to use, you can calculate the width of the spine.

5. Grain in paper is similar to the grain in wood—it has a direction. Grain affects the way the text and cover lie. If the grain of the text is not parallel to the spine, the book will want to snap shut. Grain is also important if you plan to fold the paper, since it may fold better in one direction than another.

   If the cover grain is perpendicular to the spine, the cover will tend to curl or pop open. Sometimes the cover will even crack on the folds. The problem is that some automated book machinery trims the books cleaner when the grain is perpendicular to the spine than when it is parallel. When the grain is parallel, the trimmer may make small tears in the cover stock where it curves around the spine of the book. With such machinery, the choice is between cover curl and cover tear. See the discussion of cover coatings and "lay-flat" film.

6. Grade refers to the type of paper, be it writing grade, book, cover stock, envelope, gummed, blotting, chipboard, etc.

7. Coating is done with a clay-like material and produces a smooth, shiny finish. Since the ink dries on the surface of coated stock, rather than down in the fibers of the paper, the printed pages look crisper and cleaner. Coated stock, while more expensive, makes halftones look much better. It is essential for art books. Smooth finishes may also be produced by drawing the paper over a blade edge, or through calendering (a heat and pressure roller process). The result may be a duller finish which is easier on the eyes.

8. Acid-free paper lasts longer and should be used for books of long-term interest. Some printed products, such as newspapers and magazines, are made to be read and discarded. There is no need to save them. Sixty percent of the university presses (which sell primarily to libraries) and 21% of other publishers produce their hardcover books on acid-free paper. You may wish to specify acid-free paper.

9. Recycled paper is becoming more and more popular, but the price is still higher than for new paper. The price is expected to drop as more publishers use it. If you want to extend the life of the landfills, specify recycled paper.

If you attend one of the many publishing seminars, you will probably be advised to purchase your own paper and "save about 15%." This makes about as much sense as taking your own oil to the gas station when you want it changed. The printer won't be happy about losing his markup and will probably charge you a "handling fee." Or he may raise your price later, claiming the job was "hard to print." If you buy your own paper, you will have to pay for it sooner, will be faced with storage and transportation problems and might lose it all if the printer botches a press run. It is far safer to obtain several quotes on the finished product and let the printer worry about the materials. After all, what you want is the least hassle and best price. Incidentally, printers and paper salespeople continually use the same pressure tactic, claiming there will be a paper shortage soon. Expect it. For more information on paper, see the *Pocket Pal*, listed in the Appendix.

Ink comes in a lot of colors and types, too, but both you and your printer will probably want black. If you are doing something special, ask to see his ink color sample books and run some tests. Remember that inks are transparent. If you print a drawing in blue and then overprint part in red, that part will become purple. Similarly, if you print blue ink on yellow paper, the print will be green. Unless you are doing a special art-type book, you should stick to the traditional black ink on white paper.

Hardcover or softcover. Traditionally, publishers printed in hardcover at a high price and waited until sales dropped to come out with a cheaper softcover version. They might also publish a "library edition" with a supposedly reinforced hard cover, maybe an extra-fancy "deluxe edition" on special paper, with gold-stamped leather covers, and numbered and autographed. Then there might be a "large type" edition for both the elderly and visually impaired and, finally, an inexpensive "mass-market paperback" edition. But what has emerged more recently is the very popular "oversize paperback," also known as the quality, trade, large format, large size, special or higher-priced paperbacks. These softcover books fill the gap between the mass-market pocket-size book and the hardcover version. Today, more and more books are being published in a softcover edition *only*. Softcover books are printed on the same quality paper as the hardcover version. The differences are that the softcover edition is not normally sewn, has a thinner cover and usually does not have a jacket. Now your choice of covers is narrowed to the hardcover and the softcover.

Hardcover books are somewhat more expensive to produce and must carry a higher cover (list) price, and libraries used to prefer them. Today, however, libraries know how many times books can be lent out (about 18 for softcover) before they fall apart. If the price difference between the two is too great, it becomes less expensive to purchase copies of the softcover edition and replace them more often.

The question is, just how long do you want a book to last? What good is a computer book that is five years old, even if its condition is perfect? The package lasts, but the content is out-of-date. Better the library or retail purchaser pays a lower price for a softcover edition and replaces it in a year or two with a revised edition or another title. Some reference books, such as dictionaries, should be published with more durable hard covers, but even annual references, such as the telephone directory, stand up very well in softcover. Another argument for the softcover book is that their covers last longer than the jacket on a hardcover book.

Some reviewers still do not take softcover books seriously; they do not consider a title to be a real book unless it is published in hardcover.

It is usually less expensive to publish all the books in hardcover than to split the run. Hardcover will cost just 70 cents to 90 cents more per book than softcover, and you can usually charge some $50 more for the book. Give your customers what they expect. If this is a business book, they expect hardcover with a jacket. Most people still think hardcover books are fresher, newer and more important. If your major mission is to use your book as an introduction to your consulting, speaking or other work, consider hardcover. Hardcovers do make a nicer presentation than a softcover edition; you will be prouder of a hardcover book.

The cover of softcover books must be coated. Traditionally, this was done with varnish. The cover made another pass through the press filled with varnish instead of ink. Today, ultraviolet-set plastics and plastic laminates are more popular. The extra treatment on the cover protects it against scuffing during shipment and provides a shiny or wet look. The slight additional cost is easily justified, as fewer books are returned damaged.

The plastic laminate used to be a polyester or polypropylene, which was moistureproof. Since humidity could not enter the plastic-coated side, the cover would curl as the other side expanded. Now there is a "lay-flat" laminate made of nylon film which has very tiny holes. Always specify "lay-flat laminate."

Workbooks and lab manuals must be durable enough to resist the flexing produced by constant use. Good results have been attained with Smyth sewing and perfect binding. The cover material may be 12 pt. C1S (coated one side) with a lay-flat plastic laminate or a latex-impregnated thick paper such as Lexotone or Kivar.

The cover of your book has two purposes: to protect the contents and to be a selling tool: Book covers sell books. In the U.S., companies spend over $50 billion on product design and packaging. That huge sum is not for the products themselves or for the wrapper but just for the design of the wrapper. Good packaging sells soap, breakfast food, pantyhose—and books. A good spine, front cover and title say, "Pick me up." Good back-cover sales copy says, "Buy this book." Unfortunately, most authors put all their effort into the text; the cover becomes an afterthought. Meanwhile, most large publishers slap some type onto a plain background and call it a cover design.

According to *The Wall Street Journal*, the average bookstore browser who picks up a book spends eight seconds looking

> *You can't tell—but you can sell—a book by its cover.*
> — *The Wall Street Journal*

at the front cover and 15 seconds reading the back. And this assumes the spine stood out enough to catch her attention, enticing her to pick up the book in the first place. Every word on the outside of your book must be used to sell what is inside. In mass-market (small size, high volume) paperbacks, this "hype" consists of about 12 words on the front cover and 75 on the back. The blurbs use words like "stunning," "dazzling," "moving" and "tumultuous."

> Alan Gadney commissioned covers for three computer books he planned to write. He had the covers printed in four colors and made into dummy books for display at the ABA Book Fair in Dallas in 1983. His books were the talk of the show and he took a number of large orders. Covers must be important, as he had not yet written one word on the subject.

The cover should include the title, subtitle (helps to identify the subject), name of the author and a related photograph or drawing with impact. The print shouldn't be so fancy that it is hard to read at a glance. It is said that red attracts and sells best, and many cover designers like to use it. Visit a bookstore and check the section where your book will rest. Consider what colors are there and pick something contrasting and bright that will stick out. Color sells, and the money should be spent to send the cover through the press four times. For an action sport, an eye-catching color photo will sell more books than straight lines of type. The colors must contrast with each other. You will take black/white photographs of the cover for distribution with review copies. Darker colors may run together and look muddy when photographed in black and white.

Your cover must be bold, distinctive and intriguing enough to catch the eye and sell; it must stand out from the thousands of books around it. Important new information, such as a quote from a prestigious book review, may be

---

Catalog copy (is) designed for the people who will sell the book and the flap copy for those who will buy it.
— Hugh Rawson

printed on a sticker. Make the sticker a contrasting color, and apply it at an angle so it doesn't look printed on.

The design and production of a good book cover will cost about $1,500 for the complete mechanical (front, spine and back), ready for the printer. That may sound like a major portion of your book production budget, but it is worth it because book packaging is so important to the sale of the book. For a list of book cover designers, use Para Publishing's Fax-On-Demand system. See the Appendix.

The spine usually has the title, the name of the author and an eye-catching symbol. If it is a dog book, include the outline of a dog. The symbol may attract the buyer more easily than the printed word. If there is room, you may include the subtitle, but make sure the title is big enough to be legible. Traditionally, the name of the publisher was included on the spine, but in this case, you are the publisher and no one has heard of your company yet. Besides, people buy books by content or author, not by publisher. Beware of too much spine clutter. Your book will probably end up in the bookstore with only the spine showing from the shelf. Make the spine an eye-grabber.

The back-cover layout was covered in Chapter Two. Many back covers have a photo and biographical sketch of the author. If you are a well-known celebrity, put your photograph there; if you are not immediately recognizable, do not waste valuable selling space on an ego trip. Sometimes the back cover is used to promote other books by the author, but this valuable space shouldn't be wasted in this manner, either; mention your other titles inside. Use whatever will sell the book in that valuable back-cover territory. Make every word count on the front cover, spine and back cover.

After your title, your back cover is your most important selling tool. List the benefits, quote testimonials, tell why the author is an expert and explain how this book will improve the life of the reader. End with closing copy, the bar code and the price.

Different markets are used to looking for different things on book covers. Target your primary audience and then try to cater to as many other markets as possible.

Mass-market (smaller) paperbacks use a lot of color and "hype" because they have to compete with magazines for attention in supermarkets. It is assumed by some that these books are aimed at the less sophisticated people who don't frequent bookstores.

Mail order books don't have to be flashy, but their type must be large and clear to show up well in photographs in brochures and ads. The back covers don't show in the ads, so they are sometimes used to sell other books.

Trade books aimed at bookstores need a poster-like cover to aid in their sale. The back should also have a sales message, as it is the next place a potential customer will look after the cover.

Textbook covers must be much more conservative, or they will "turn off" the educators who make the purchasing decisions. Don't make wild claims.

Don't be confined by convention. The unorthodox cover may catch the eye better. Unless the cover is offensive, it will be the first step in selling the book. But look over other books you admire. Most follow the same pattern in layout. There must be a reason, and you can bet it isn't lack of Madison Avenue imagination.

If the cover is not doing its job, consider changing it when you go back to press for a second printing. Once the book is in print the first time, you will come up with a number of ideas for changes.

Ask your printer to send you the overruns on the covers. You might even ask to have a few hundred extra printed. He will take these covers off the line before they are scored, folded and installed on the texts. These covers are beautiful and look very nice framed. You will be proud to hang one on your wall, and you might like to send a flat cover to those who provided you with a lot of help, such as the cover designer. Commissioned representatives carry covers to the bookstores rather than heavy books, so your distributor may need 20 to 30 covers. Many publishers use covers to make public relations folders; they put all their sales information inside.

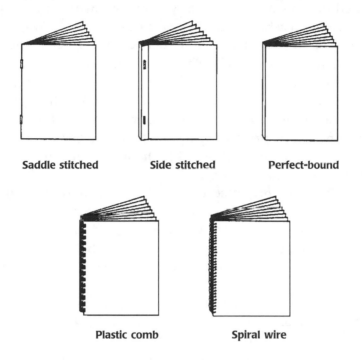

Saddle stitched   Side stitched   Perfect-bound

Plastic comb   Spiral wire

Binding is your book packaging, the final touch. Consider your market (to whom will you sell it?) and the expected usage (will it be read once or used as a manual?). Because of the expense of traditional hard binding, there may well be a cross between the hardcover and the paperback one day. In Japan, it is common to place a dust jacket on softcover books already. Give your buyers what they expect. If this is a higher-priced law book, select hardcover, but most nonfiction will be perfectly acceptable in softcover. The choices of bindings are many, and here are the most common types:

— *Perfect binding* is the standard glued-on cover you see on most paperbacks. The pages are folded into signatures, often of 32 pages each, stacked, roughened on the edge and then the cover is wrapped around and glued on. The greatest advantage, besides lower cost, is that perfect binding presents a squared-off spine on which the title and name of the author may be printed. A text of more than 50 pages is required for a square spine, and you might have to use a high-bulk paper to achieve a sufficient thickness.

If it is important that your perfect-bound book open to lie flat, specify "Otabind." This system leaves the cover stock free of the spine as it goes around to the back of the book, so the book flexes better when opened and will easily lie flat. Otabind is much better than comb or spiral binding, as the spine can be printed with the title of the book. Narrower gutter margins are possible with Otabind, which means you can get more type on a page.

— *Cloth binding* (case binding or hard binding) usually consists of Smyth sewing, or side stitching the individual signatures together. Then they are installed (and glued) between two hard paper boards. Case-bound books will accept a lot more flexing because they depend on thread, not glue, to retain the pages.

— *Wire stitches* are staples and may be used in binding paperback books. This is the least expensive way, and many highly automated printing plants are set up for it. Wire stitches may be "saddle stitched," where the staple is on the fold, or "side stitched," where the staple is driven through from the front to back cover. Saddle stitching will handle 80 pages (20 sheets) or less, depending on the thickness of the stock, because of the amount of paper "lost" in wrapping around the spine. On the other hand, side stitching may be used to bind even several hundred pages. Side stitched books won't open to lie flat, so this method shouldn't be used in manuals. Sometimes "Holland tape" is used to cover the staples, making the book more attractive. The "stitches" come from a roll of wire and are adjustable in length.

— *Spiral wire* binding will allow books, such as automotive manuals and cookbooks, to open and lie flat, but spiral looks cheap. Spiral-bound books do not sell well in bookstores because the title doesn't show, and libraries don't care for them. It is possible to spiral bind pages *inside* a heavy cover stock. Some computer manuals are bound this way. But spiral still costs more.

— *Plastic comb* binding allows the book to open and lie flat and is often used for mail order books directed at professionals, short-run academic texts and industry manuals. This system may be used on books up to 1.5 inches thick. Comb binding is relatively expensive but looks cheap, the pages tear out and comb bound books don't stack well, making shipping a chore.

— *Velo-Bind* is similar to side wire stitches but uses melted plastic rivets. This method is very strong and may be used to install either special Velo-Bind hardcovers or soft document covers. The books will not open to lie flat.

— *Cheshire* has an interesting hot-melt hard- and soft-cover binding machine, which is good for very short-run production.

— *Channel Bind* is used to install hard and soft covers on 8.5″ x 11″ paper. It is too expensive for producing a large run of books.

— *Binders* are sometimes used for very expensive manuals directed toward professionals. They have the usual advantages of a binder, but they are expensive, hard to ship and their pages tear out easily.

Typesetting is best done on your own computer. Using a word processing program (*Word For Windows* or *WordPerfect*), page layout program (*Pagemaker, Corel Ventura* or *QuarkXpress*) and a laser printer will give you complete control over the finished product, will be much faster and will save you a lot of money. See Chapter Eleven. For more information on book typesetting and layout, see our Special Report *Book Production*.

If you wish to have someone else typeset and lay out your book, see a book producer or book packager. These are graphic arts shops that specialize in books. For a list, use Para Publishing's Fax-On-Demand system. See the Appendix, 412.

Electronic pre-press. Most printers today will accept your book on disk. There is no reason to set the type on paper. The result is a sharper (higher resolution) type and some cost savings. Essentially, you set the type using a page layout program, run off laser (proof) sheets and submit both the hard copy and the disk to the printer. The printer will make negatives directly from the disk and use the hard copy as a checking proof. Ask your printer about electronic pre-press and request their requirements.

Print run. 3,000 is a good number for most first runs. Do not print more unless you have some presold, such as to a book club. Ask for two, maybe three, quantities so you will be able to see what a difference in price the various print runs make. Each printer has a different mix of machinery, so their quotations for various quantities will be quite different.

Short run. Occasionally, we need only a few copies of a book. If your print run will be 25 to 150 copies, investigate the Docutech Printing System. The Docutech is a duplex (both sides) printer which is toner-based (600 dpi) as opposed to ink-based like most printing presses. Check with local quick-print and photocopy shops. Some of the book printers also have a Docutech.

Selecting a book printer. Each printer is set up differently. Some specialize in case binding (hardcover), some in perfect binding (softcover) and some in saddle stitch (staples). Some are set up for very short runs (under 500), short runs (3,000 to 5,000), long runs (100,000), etc. Any item in your specifications varying from their system will drive up their costs and your quote. When they have to take a book off the line to shift it to the other side of the factory or send it out to a binder, costs go up. As a publisher, you don't have to learn printer capabilities and printing equipment. Just send out a request for quotation (RFQ), describing your book to all 40+ book printers. Take the lowest bid. If your next book has similar specifications, you will probably deal with the same printer. Once you establish a relationship with the printer, your costs will probably go down further because you require less hand-holding. But do send out RFQs from time to time to make sure your printer is still giving you a good price. See our Special Report *Buying Book Printing*. See the Appendix.

Beware of job printers soliciting book printing. The poor economy has affected the printing industry, too. Many printers are looking for new territory and are attracted to the big-ticket item: books. There are only about 40 genuine book printers in the U.S. These printers print only books, have set up streamlined operations, have specialized equipment, use teams to handle the pre-press functions and often run two and three shifts on their equipment. Their quality is consistently good—they don't have to spend time figuring out how to lay up the negatives in the flats so that the pages come out in the right order and right side up. They want to do a good job, and they have to; they can't suddenly decide to switch to printing posters or labels or business cards.

For best quality, lowest price and on-time service, stick with printers who print nothing but books. How can you tell? Just ask what they print. See the list in the Appendix.

Request for quotation. To calculate book production costs, send a request for quotation (RFQ) to a number of printers.

Request that all quotes for printing, halftones, reductions, etc., be made on a per-item and per-page basis. If your quotes are not figured this way, reduce them to these page/item figures yourself. Then when the book is finished and the exact number of pages, photos, etc., are known, both you and the printer, individually and objectively, will come up with the same figure for the bill.

Here is a sample Request For Quotation, or *RFQ*. To help you interpret it, specification examples and hints are in parentheses.

Request for Quotation

Please quote your best price and delivery in printing and binding the following book:

Identification

Title of book: (*Parachuting, The Skydiver's Handbook*)

Author: (Dan Poynter)

Specifications

Quantity: (3,000 and 5,000)

Number of pages including front and back matter: (352)

Trim size: (5.5 x 8.5)

Method of printing: (Offset: web press OK)

Copy: (Customer to provide laser output "boards")

Illustrations: (Seven halftones, no bleeds)

Cover: (Print sides 1 and 4 only. Customer to supply color separations)

Paper:

Text: (50# white offset book. Paper shall be recycled, acid-free and neutral pH.)

Cover: (12 pt. C1S. Cover shall be acid-free. Plus lay-flat film lamination.)

Ink:

Text: (Black throughout)

Cover: (Four colors)

Proofs: (Complete bluelines)

Binding: (Perfect—softbound)

Packaging: (Shrink-wrapped in twos and packed in a 275# burst test carton. Cartons shall be tightly packed and sealed and shall weigh no more than 40 lbs. each.)

Terms: (Net 30 days. Credit references available on request)
Deadline: (Please quote by   )

Your quote:
3,000: $
Overruns: $
Reprint of 3,000: $
5,000: $
Overruns: $
Reprint of 5,000: $
Price per halftone: $
Delivery charges: $
Discount for prompt payment:
Delivery time:
Other miscellaneous charges:

Remarks:
Signed:
For:
Date:
Quote valid for:
Are there any minor specification changes that will result in a lower price? Please explain.
Any item in this RFQ takes precedence over any industry convention. The boards, flats and all artwork shall be returned to the customer on completion of the job.

Solicit several printing quotes. You will find some bids to be three times higher than others. These price differences are amazing and make it obvious that it pays to shop around. Some printers are too big for you, some specialize in something other than books and some are too busy. You need a good printer who is hungry and specializes in "short-run" book printing.

If your state has an inventory tax, you might consider avoiding it by printing in another state and having the books shipped to you in small batches to avoid the date inventory must be taken. Shipping is not too expensive, as trucking companies give special rates for "bound books." Your printer may even be willing to drop-ship large quantities for you so you can ship direct to major customers.

Some publishers have found considerable savings on color processes outside the U.S. They may have color separations made in Singapore, printing done in Hong Kong, etc. For more information on foreign printing, see our Special Report *Buying Book Printing*; information is in the Appendix.

Request for quotations should be sent to the printers listed in the Appendix. Add two local print shops to this list. Simply make up an RFQ like the one pictured, make enough photocopies and mail them to all on your list. Don't send your RFQ to just a few; the inquiry will not result in enough comparative data. The only way you will know you are paying the best price is if you get quotes from all. Don't worry about their reception of a photocopied RFQ; printers are used to making competitive quotes. Adams, Delta, McNaughton & Gunn, Morgan, Multiprint and some others provide "printing pricers" to help you estimate your costs.

When the RFQs are returned, spread them out for comparison. Some printers will fill out your sheet, while others will use their own form. Make sure the quotes are "FOB destination," that trucking to you is figured in. You will probably find that the distant printers quote much lower prices even with the trucking costs.

Don't worry about hurting the feelings of your local printer. If his bid is not the lowest, show him the other bids. They are your excuse for not giving him the work. He will be interested in what the competition is quoting and will appreciate your openness.

Shrink-wrapping. Have the printer shrink-wrap your books in twos. Shrink-wrapping will protect your book by providing a moisture/dust barrier while preventing scuffing. If you shrink-wrap the books individually, the stores usually do not break the wrap, so the customer can't look inside and that usually results in a lost sale. If you wrap the books in larger increments, you may have to break the wrap for small orders, losing the benefits of the protective plastic. The best compromise is twos.

Print it yourself. You might even decide to acquire a press and do the printing yourself. Be forewarned, however, that unless you have a simple job and are willing to sacrifice quality, the press run should be left to the professional. You have to decide whether you want to be a writer, printer or to concentrate on sales. Some people gain great satisfaction doing the whole job themselves. Unless you can use the printing press regularly, your own printing won't be competitive in price.

Proofing. Always insist on blueline (or equivalent) proofs prior to printing. This is your last chance to check the printer's work prior to its going on the press.

Get it in writing. Get everything in writing. You are new to publishing, and what you assume may not be the same as what your printer assumes. Good faith, trust and friendship are fine until the bill arrives. Ask for samples and show him what you like, what you expect. Get a contract with the printer explaining exactly what each part of the job will cost. Then if you have two more photos than your estimate covered, you and he will arrive at the same added figure. Count the books you pick up, and get copies of the receiving slips. After the typesetting is done and you have an exact page count, ask for a new quote on the press run. You should be able to calculate it using the original quote, but it is best to avoid any possible misunderstanding.

Make sure your contract includes a clause which states: "Any item in this contract takes precedence over any industry convention." You aren't familiar with the printing industry and aren't interested in how business is normally done.

You simply want an attractive book and you want to know what it will cost.

Keep your artwork. Maintain a file with a couple of clean copies of the book and all your reproduction materials. If you need them again, and you do hope for many happy reprintings, you don't want to have to regenerate lost material.

Put all the artwork, photos, drawings, etc., into a large envelope. You want to be able to find them easily if you contract for a translation or other foreign edition. Keep the boards and negatives of all promotional material, such as brochures and order forms.

The art boards for the book are the publisher's property. Many job printers will tell you the large, thin metal printing plates, stripped-in negatives (flats) and boards belong to them, as "they are the product of the printer's craftsmanship." A printer who argues this simply wants to make sure you return to him for reprints. The plates are difficult to store, and printers usually throw them out. Many also discard the boards, keeping only the flats. You may take possession of the plates and flats if you reserve their ownership in the printing contract.

Fortunately, most book printers do not want to keep your flats and will even charge you for storage if they have not been reused or returned within three years.

You should store the laser-output pages for future revisions. Find a cool, dry, clean place; they are subject to yellowing. If you think you might like to switch printers for the revision, you can always specify in the contract that you want the flats back after printing. On the other hand, allowing the printer to store the flats while you keep the boards is good insurance. If one place burns to the ground, you won't lose everything. If you will want to make revisions when you go back to press, it is more valuable to have the boards than the flats.

When the books arrive from the printer, count the cartons. Compare the carton count with the number on the bill of lading. Sometimes books disappear in transit. Open random cartons and check for damage. If the books were loose in the carton, the top ones will be scuffed.

Do not stack cartons directly on top of each other. Overlapping them like bricks will provide a sturdier stack. Make sure the storage area is clean and dry and has a floor capable of supporting a great deal of weight.

Electronic formats. Since more and more information is being packaged in magnetic media format, they will be covered here at the end of the production chapter. After your book is published, consider pouring your information into other formats.

— **Audiotapes.** Audiotapes allow people to do two things at once, such as driving and learning. Many children's books are coming packaged with tapes now. For publishers, tapes mean high markup and low inventory costs; tapes may be reproduced in small quantities. See *Let Your Ideas Speak Out,* listed in the Appendix. For audio editing, reproduction, packaging and advice, call Judy Byers at Audio/Video Cassette Producers in Denver, Tel: (303) 751-1198; Fax: (303) 751-5655. Also see Bowker's *Audio Video Market Place.*

— **Videotapes.** Over 45 million households have a VCR and the number is increasing rapidly. For publishers, videotapes, like audiotapes, mean high markup and low inventory; tapes may be reproduced in small quantities. For more information on producing videotapes, get *Home Video: Producing For The Home Market* by Michael Weise, Tel: (818) 379-8799. For a directory of more than 40,000 available videos, get the *Video Source Book,* National Video Clearinghouse, 100 Lafayette Drive, Syosset, NY 11791.

— **Computer disks.** Certain products lend themselves to reproduction and distribution on disk. For example, Para Publishing has a product titled *Publishing Contracts on Disk.* There are 22 lengthy contracts on the disk, and some are over 12 pages of dense ten-point type. The disk format saves the buyer from typing the long contract, making it easily worth the low price. Perhaps you have a number of forms in your book that can be sold separately on disk.

Bowker's *Software Encyclopedia* lists 25,000 software packages in 800 different subject areas (see your library). *Data Sources* (20 Brace Road, Cherry Hill, NJ 08034, or at your library) is a three-volume guide to software companies and hardware manufacturers.

— **CD-ROM.** With an "authoring" program, you can format your text and illustrations for an electronic book on CD-ROM. Then your customers will be able to read your book on a computer screen, and you will be able to give them a lot more than text at much less cost to you.

One CD can hold over 660 MB. of text, animation, audio and motion pictures. For example, the *World Book Encyclopedia* CD contains the full text of the 22 volumes plus 4,700 full-screen photographs, illustrations, tables and maps. The CD version sells for $389 (non-discounted price) while the print version costs $849.

Many people have a CD-ROM player, and it is estimated that in 1994 over 90% of the computers sold came with a CD-ROM drive.

CD-ROMs in Print is available from the Meckler Corporation, 11 Ferry Drive, Westport, CT 06880. For the very latest in suggestions for the electronic book and CD-ROM output, see Para Publishing's Fax-On-Demand system. See the Appendix.

Para Publishing is a unique book business. It does not operate like a big traditional publisher, and it doesn't lose money. Dan Poynter lays out the following reasons for the success of his company:

1. Publish your own material. Do not waste your time on, or split the money with, other authors.

2. Perform every publishing and business function yourself. After your first book, farm out those tasks you do not wish to perform.

3. Operate as a sole proprietorship, not a corporation, and keep your books on a cash basis.

4. Do not mimic the big traditional New York publishers. Many are not making a sufficient return on their investment. Some of their procedures ex-

ist for a good reason, while others are just convention (also known as a rut). The trick is to know the difference.

5. If you cannot "find a need and fill it," then create a need and fill it. Decide on your market before you write the book, and write to that market.

6. Market your books like breakfast food, not like a film. This is not one-shot entertainment; go after a market share and keep selling that book year after year.

7. You will have to spend more time selling than you will writing. Concentrate on marketing rather than editorial functions.

8. Produce valuable information, aimed at a small target audience, and charge a fair price.

Whether you think you can or think you can't, you're right.
— Henry Ford

Chapter Five

Announcing Your Book

Telling the World You Are an Author and a Publisher

Getting Listed

Before you run off to promote your book to potential readers, you should announce it to the industry, the government and the world. In fact, some of these announcements must be made before you go to press. For a clear understanding of when each of the following should be done, see the Calendar at the beginning of the Appendix. Make your book and your company easy to find.

As you use this chapter, remember, if the people at some registration offices and directories reject your application, do not give up. Try to figure a way around their objection and file a new form. It is very doubtful they will remember your initial application rejection.

Since these people may not have a lot of confidence in publishers with a single title (who may never publish again), it is best to represent yourself as being larger. After all, this will not be your only book. Use different names for your company, publisher and author. "Burgett Publishing, Gordon Burgett Publisher and book by Gordon Burgett" is a sure tip-off that you are small and new.

Getting listed in all the right places is easy with the use of *Publishing Forms*, a collection of applications and information for the beginning publisher. See the Appendix. Names and numbers change as people and companies move. For a free current list of contacts, use our Fax-On-Demand system and request Document 112. See the Appendix for details.

An ISBN application

The International Standard Book Number (ISBN) is a worldwide identification system which has been in use since the late sixties. There is a different ISBN for each edition and each binding of every book, so the number's use avoids errors in identifying the books ordered, shipped, received, etc. Publishers are finding that with the increased use of computers in the book industry, this system has become an essential element in the distribution of their books.

A typical ISBN might be 0-915516-21-7. Here, the initial "0" or a "1" indicates a book originating in an English-speaking country. The "915516" identifies the publisher. The suffix "21" identifies this particular title and edition of the book, hardcover or softcover. The last number, "7," is a check digit, which is a mathematical function to make sure the rest of the numbers are correct, that they haven't been miscopied or transposed.

The ISBN is printed on the copyright page of the book and at the bottom of the back cover or jacket, above or below the bar code, in OCR-B typeface.

Contact the International Standard Book Numbering Agency, 121 Chanlon Road, New Providence, NJ 07974, Tel: (908) 665-6770, and request a "Title Output Information Request form" and a "User's Manual." There is a $115.00 charge for 20-day service; $165.00 for rush 72-hour service.

An ISBN logbook sheet

The ISBN people will send you a number and a log sheet for 10, 100 or 1,000 titles. If you get 10, your publisher identifier number will be seven digits long and your suffix will be just one digit. If it is 1,000, your publisher identifier will be five digits, leaving you with three in the suffix. The ISBN people will probably limit you to a block of ten numbers because you are new and because they are short of the

100-number series. They will send you a card bearing your ISBN publisher identifier and a logbook sheet with enough room for listing ten different book editions.

Once started in the system, you will assign each of your new titles an ISBN suffix yourself. You do not have to start at the beginning of the log. The only requirement is that each title, revision and binding have a different number. If you use the first number on the logbook sheet, the "00" will tip off those in the industry that this is a first book.

ISSN is for serials. Publications issued in parts, such as magazines, newspapers, annuals, directories, proceedings and any publication expected to continue indefinitely are called "serials." For more information on the ISSN, contact the Library of Congress, National Serials Data Program, Washington, DC 20540, Tel: (202) 707-6452.

R.R. Bowker. By now, you are probably finding there are a lot of agencies and offices catering to the book trade at 249 West 17th Street and 121 Chanlon Road. Bowker is a subsidiary of Reed Reference, which publishes many references and performs many services for the publishing industry. Bowker administers the ISBN and SAN programs, as well as publishing the magazines *Publishers Weekly, Library Journal* and *School Library Journal.* Bowker publishes reference books such as *Books in Print, American Book Publishing Record, Literary Market Place, Publishers Trade List Annual* and many more. Treat each Bowker office separately, as though it were in a different building, so your mail won't get misdirected or lost.

ISBN 0-915516-61-6

The Bar Code

Bar codes. The bar code on a book identifies the ISBN, which in turn identifies the publisher, title, author and edition (hardcover, etc.). The wholesalers, chains and other bookstores will not accept your book or audiotape without a bar code. If your book arrives at a wholesaler without a bar code, they will sticker one on and charge you for it.

You must have a bar code even if you think you won't be selling many books through bookstores. Some people will order your book through stores. And, if you do not have a bar code, your book will not appear to be mainstream. It will look like kitchen-table publishing, loving hands at home, not quite ready for real publishing. Without a bar code, your book does not look credible.

The bar code you want is the "Bookland EAN/13 with add on" bar code and it should be printed on the lower half of "cover 4" (the back cover) on hardcover and softcover books and on "cover 2" (the inside of the front cover) on mass-market paperback books. On mass-market paperbacks, the UPC bar code goes on the back cover. Cost of the UPC bar code starts at $300. To obtain a UPC, contact Uniform Code Council, 8163 Old Yankee Road, Dayton, OH 45458, Tel: (513) 435-3870.

On hardcover books, the price is printed on the top of the left-hand jacket flap.

The ISBN is printed above or below the bar code. Use the ISBN on invoices, catalogs, order forms, packing lists and the book itself.

Beginning from the left, the first three symbols (978) identify this as being a Bookland bar code, that the product is a book. The next nine digits (091551661) correspond to the ISBN (less the check digit at the end) for the book. The last figure is a bar code check digit. In the smaller price extension bar code to the right, the first digit indicates the type of currency, such as U.S. dollars. The next four digits indicate the retail price of the book.

Order a copy of *Machine-Readable Coding Guidelines for the U.S. Book Industry* ($7.50) from: The Book Industry Study Group, 160 Fifth Avenue, #604, New York, NY 10010, Tel:

(212) 929-1393. Or, you may be able to get a copy free from: GGX Associates, George Goldberg, 11 Middle Neck Road, Great Neck, NY 11021, Tel: (516) 487-6370.

Bar code/ISBN prints and negatives cost $10 to $30 and are available from a number of suppliers. Two of them are: FOTEL/GGX Associates, 11 Middle Neck Road, Great Neck, NY 11021, Tel: (800) 834-8088, and Precision Photography, Inc., 1150 North Tustin Avenue, Anaheim, CA 92807, Tel: (714) 632-9000. Assign an ISBN to your book, order a bar code negative and give it to your cover artist for incorporation into your back-cover design.

To order a bar code, call one of the above-mentioned suppliers and tell them you want a "Bookland EAN bar code with price extension." Specify the smaller one. Then provide the ISBN, price, name of the book and any other information (e.g., hardcover edition) you may need to identify the negative they will send you. The bar code negative will be delivered in a couple of days.

Standard address number. The SAN identifies each separate address of every firm in the book publishing industry—from publishers, to wholesalers, to libraries, to bookstores. SAN's sort out the billing and shipping addresses and help to determine which "Book Nook" an order is going to.

You may request a SAN when you apply for an ISBN. The seven-digit number should be printed on all purchase orders, invoices, etc.

Advanced Book Information is another Bowker service. By filling out their ABI form, your book will be listed in *Books in Print* and several other specialized directories. *Books in Print*, published in November of each year, is your most important directory.

Everyone in the industry turns to *BIP* first when looking for a particular book. This multi-volumed reference lists all available books by subject, title and author. Ask for it at the library and become familiar with this important work.

Contact the ABI Department, R. R. Bowker Co., 121 Chanlon Road, New Providence, NJ 07974, Tel: (908) 464-

The ABI form

6800 or (800) 521-8110, and request an ABI guidebook and five ABI forms. There is no charge.

Fill out the ABI form and return it to Bowker. They will use the information to list your book in *Books in Print, Subject Guide to Books in Print, Forthcoming Books* and several other reference books.

You should fill out an ABI form about six months before your book comes off the press, but don't be too anxious. On your first book, wait until you are about to ship your boards off to the printer. Some new publishers act prematurely; they list the book and then get delayed or never get into print. Your "publication date" will probably be six months away anyway, as discussed in Chapter Seven. Code your address on the ABI forms (see the discussion in Chapter Seven).

Always use the ABI guide sheet when filling out the ABI form. Some of the questions may mislead a person not familiar with publishing terminology.

Bowker will send you a computer-generated ABI checklist every other month to keep your listings up-to-date. This checklist must be returned every time, even if all the information is correct. Failure to return the checklist may result in your books or company being dropped from *Books in Print*.

Library of Congress Catalog Card Number. LC numbers appear on the copyright page of each book and are also included in the lists and reviews appearing in the leading journals of the book trade. The LC number differs from the ISBN in that one ISBN is assigned to each different *edition* of a work (hardcover, softcover, etc.); the LC number is assigned to the work itself, regardless of the number of bindings. Use of the number enables subscribers to the Library of Congress's catalog card service to order cards by number and thus eliminate the searching fee. About 20,000 libraries from all over the world subscribe to this service, and some order almost every cataloged book. Additionally, most of the books are listed in *The National Union Catalogue*, issued several times a year in four editions. Most public and private libraries subscribe to it.

The Library of Congress card number must be requested prior to the publication of the book, so that the number may be printed on the copyright page. They do not *preassign* numbers to books that are already in print, since it is too late to print the number in the book.

Catalog card numbers are preassigned only to books which the Library of Congress assumes will be added to library collections, or for which they anticipate substantial demand for LC printed cards. The types of material which the Library collects only in a very limited way, and for which catalog card numbers are generally not available, include: calendars, laboratory manuals, booklets of less than 50 pages, brochures, advertisements, bank publications designed for customers, blueprints, certain kinds of light fiction, privately printed books of poems, religious materials for students in Bible schools, catechisms, instructions in devotions, individual sermons and prayers, question and answer books, most elementary and secondary school textbooks, tests except for standard examinations, teachers' manuals, correspondence school lessons, translations from

English into foreign languages, picture books, comic strip and coloring books, diaries, log and appointment books, prospectuses and preliminary editions, workbooks, and vanity press publications. Since the people at the Library of Congress sometimes confuse self-publishing with vanity publishing, it is best to fill out the forms using different names for author, publisher, etc.

Library of Congress application Form 607-7

New publishers should write to the Library of Congress, Washington, DC 20540, and ask for "Procedures for Securing Preassigned Library of Congress Catalog Card Numbers" and their "Request for Preassignment of LCC Number" applications (Form 607-7). Their telephone number is (202) 707-6372.

The Library of Congress will send you your number typed on a 3" x 5" slip, giving the author, title, imprint and publication date. The catalog card number appears in the upper right-hand corner of the slip.

The first two digits of the LC number do not indicate the year of publication but the year in which the card number is preassigned. If you register after January first, your book will appear to be a year newer. Ever wonder why the dates on films are in Roman numerals?

The Library of Congress must be advised of all subsequent changes in titles, authors, etc., and cancellations. This notification is important, as it prevents duplication of numbers. A new number is not necessary when changes are made. Confirmations of changes will not be acknowledged unless requested by the publisher.

There is no charge for the preassignment of a card number. An advance complimentary copy of each publication must be sent to the CIP Office, Library of Congress, Washington, DC 20540. This copy is used for final cataloging, so that cards may be printed before the book is released. The CIP Office provides postage-free mailing labels for use in sending these advance publications. The book is only for checking, so send the less expensive, softcover edition.

The Copyright Office is operationally separate from the CIP Office, but the CIP and Catalog Card Number offices are the same. Catalog card numbers may be applied for per the above information or when applying for Cataloging-in-Publication Data.

Apply for your numbers and listings in this order: ISBN, LC number and then file the ABI form.

Cataloging In Publication (CIP) is a separate program which enables publishers to print Library of Congress cataloging information on the copyright page of their books. Because the data block is already printed in the book, librarians are able to process new titles for library users rapidly and economically. Printing the CIP data block on the copyright page of your book will make you look more established.

First you must be accepted into the program, and then you must request cataloging data for each new book. For information on the CIP program, write the CIP Office, Library of Congress, Washington, DC 20540, Tel: (202) 707-5000, and request: "Cataloging in Publication—Information for Participating Publishers" and some "Publisher's Response" forms. The CIP people are eager to help and can be reached at (202) 707-6372. They even provide postage-paid mailing labels for the materials you are expected to send back.

Here is a line-by-line explanation of the CIP data block:

1. **Library of Congress Cataloging-in-Publication Data**
2. Poynter, Daniel F.
3. Parachuting, The Skydiver's Handbook
4. 1, Parachuting. 2, Skydiving. I Title
5. GV 770P69 797.56 77-83469
6. ISBN 0-915516-16-0 Softcover
7. ISBN 0-915516-17-9 Hardcover

Typical CIP data block

1. The heading is made distinctive by setting in bold typeface.
2. The author's name
3. The title of the book
4. The LC subject headings
5. The "GV 770" is the LC classification number. The "P69" is keyed into the last name of the author, in this case "Poynter."

   The second number group is the Dewey Decimal Classification Number (see *The Dewey Decimal Classification and Relative Index*) and the last is the LC Card number.
6&7. The International Standard Book Numbers.

The CIP copy is taken from the *Anglo-American Cataloging Rules*, the *Library of Congress Subject Headings* (the big red book) and *the Dewey Decimal Classification*. See them at the Reference Desk at your public library.

Once you are accepted into the CIP program, you will send in information on each book prior to printing. Send photocopies of the front matter of your pasted-up boards and a filled out LCC Data sheet to the CIP Office. This enables them to select the proper classification numbers. They also like to have any other information you might have, such as a descriptive brochure on the book, a photocopy of your ABI form and a biographical sketch of the author. Within ten working days, the Office will send the CIP data and the catalog card number.

Sometimes titles mislead and the CIP Office does not catalog the book correctly. For example, is *What Color is Your Parachute?* about job hunting or skydiving? If your book is miscataloged in every library across the country, readers will never find it. Give the CIP people as much information on your new book as possible, and read their "Information For Participating Publishers" carefully. You may even supply suggested data. Pay particular attention to the "subject tracings" (line 4 above). How a book gets cataloged can be just as important as how it gets reviewed or advertised.

Form 607-6

To participate in the CIP program, you must be an established publisher, which is defined here as having already published three books. For your first three books, make up your own data block and apply to the Library of Congress for just an LC number. Ask a librarian to help you with the numbers or contact Quality Books. For just $30, a staff librarian at Quality Books will catalog your forthcoming title and send you a data block for your copyright page. Contact Quality Books for an application: 1003 West Pines, Oregon, IL 61061-9680, Tel: (815) 732-4450; Fax: (815) 732-4499.

Copyright may be registered before your manuscript is published, but, unless you are passing a lot of copies around for technical proofing and comment, you might just as well do as most publishers do: wait for books to come off the press. Your work is automatically copyright *protected* under common law because you created it; it just isn't copyright *registered* yet.

Write to the Register of Copyrights, Library of Congress, Washington, DC 20559, and request five copies of Form TX (for registering books) and copies of Circular 1, *Copyright Basics*, and Circular 2, *Publications of the Copyright Office*. Upon receipt, read over these publications and order any others you feel you need. The Copyright Office will also send you some business reply mailing labels so that you may send them the copyright form, your check and the books for registration.

Form TX

To register your copyright, follow these three steps:

1. Print the copyright notice on the copyright page (title page verso). The notice takes the following form: " © 1996 by Robert Howard." You may use the word "copyright," but the "©" says the same thing and is necessary for international protection. Also add "all rights reserved" and expand on this if you like. Check other books. The copyright notice must appear in *all* copies of the book to protect you, so double-check it and all the numbers on the copyright page every time you proof copy, boards, bluelines, etc.

   The copyright should be in the name of the owner. The owner may be the author, the publishing company or whoever created or paid for the work.

2. Publish the book. Check for the copyright notice before any of the books are distributed.

3. Register your claim with the Copyright Office within three months of the book coming off the press. To do this, send a completed Form TX, two copies of the "best edition" of the book and a fee of $20. The "best edition" would be the hardcover if both the hardbound and softbound came from the printer at the same time. However, since the hardbound edition often takes longer to produce, the softcover may be the "best edition" at the time of publication. If you enclose softcover copies with the Form TX, be sure to note that they were produced first.

The Copyright Office will add a registration number and date to the form and send you a photocopy containing a seal and the Registrar's signature.

The new copyright term is for the author's life plus 50 years. Your ownership of the book is now a valuable part of your estate, so be certain your copyrighted material is mentioned in your will.

Copyrights protect you like a patent, but they are cheaper and much easier to secure. Like a patent, however, you must always be on the lookout for infringers. The copyright protects your text, photographs, drawings, maps, everything in the book except the title.

The **Cumulative Book Index** is an international bibliography of new publications in the English language. All the bibliographical information necessary to identify a book is provided: full name of author, complete title, date of publication, edition, paging, price, publisher, International Standard Book Number and Library of Congress card number.

In addition to bibliographical information, the *Cumulative Book Index* also provides subject headings to describe the contents of the book. These headings can usually be determined by an examination of the table of contents and a reading of the preface; sometimes, a careful examination of the text is necessary. Books must have at least 100 pages and a minimum press run of 500 copies to be eligible for inclusion in the *Index*.

INFORMATION SLIP

Description of new book for FREE record in Cumulative Book Index, published by The H. W. Wilson Company, 950 University Ave., Bronx, N.Y. 10452

The Cumulative Book Index is published monthly.   A copy of the book or descriptive material will be appreciated.

Author ....
    (Full Name) (Please print)
Title ....
    (Verbatim)
....
Subject ....
Series and Number ....
Edition... ...... No. of vols........ Size.........No. of pages........... Illustrations............
Binding .... Retail price..........Date of publication ....
    (In your currency)   (Exact)
Name and Address of Publisher ....
    (From whom the book may be obtained)
For *IMPORTATIONS* the following additional information is *REQUIRED*: (a) Are you the sole U.S. agent for the book? .... (b) What is the U.S. publication date? .... (c) How many copies will be on hand in this country on the U.S. publication date? (or are on hand now)? ....

11-65—50M (2687)M.A.   Printed in U.S.A.

Cumulative Book Index Information Slip

A listing in the *Cumulative Book Index* gives your publication valuable publicity. Subscribers include most of the major libraries and booksellers around the world. No charge is made for a listing, but in order to record your book accurately, the H. W. Wilson Company needs a copy of the book. Wilson will also list your book in the *Vertical File Index*. Send books to: *Cumulative Book Index*, H. W. Wilson Co., 950 University Avenue, Bronx, NY 10452, Tel: (718) 588-8400. For more information on the *Vertical File Index*, use the same address.

Book Publishers in the United States and Canada is a directory in which you may have a free listing. For an application form, write Gale Research Company, Penobscot Building, Detroit, MI 48226-4093, Tel: (313) 961-2242.

Small Press Record of Books in Print is a special *Books in Print* for smaller publishers. Contact Dustbooks, P. O. Box 100-P, Paradise, CA 95967, Tel: (916) 877-6110, for an application.

International Directory of Little Magazines and Small Presses is another place you will want to list your new firm. Contact Dustbooks, P. O. Box 100-P, Paradise, CA 95967, Tel: (916) 877-6110, for an application.

Publishers Trade List Annual is another Bowker publication. It is a multi-volume collection of publishers' catalogs used by the publishing industry to announce books. For information and an ad rate card, contact R. R. Bowker Co., 121 Chanlon Road, New Providence, NJ 07974, Tel: (908) 464-6800 or (800) 521-8110.

Publishers, Distributors, Wholesalers of the United States. Contact R.R. Bowker Co., 121 Chanlon Road, New Providence, NJ 07974, Tel: (908) 464-6800 or (800) 521-8110.

Publishers' International Directory is published by the K. G. Saur Publishing Co. Contact Saur, 121 Chanlon Road, New Providence, NJ 07974, Tel: (908) 665-3576 or (908) 464-6800, for information and a questionnaire.

ABA Book Buyer's Handbook is used by bookstores to find your shipping, discount, STOP and returns policies. A listing of your company here will encourage STOP orders

(See Chapter Six). The ABA will include your company listing when you have been in business for one year and have published three books. Contact the American Booksellers Association, 560 White Plains Road, Tarrytown, NY 10591, Tel: (914) 631-7800 or (800) 637-0037, for an application.

The Book Buyer's Manual is published by the National Association of College Stores. For an application, contact them at NACS, P.O. Box 58, Oberlin, OH 44074, Tel: (216) 775-7777.

Literary Market Place is one of the most important reference books in the publishing industry. It lists every major publisher, publicity outlet and supplier. An inclusion here will help your customers and suppliers to find you. To be listed in this annual reference, you must publish at least three books a year. Send for an application form to *Literary Market Place*, 121 Chanlon Road, New Providence, NJ 07974, Tel: (908) 464-6800.

Writer's Market. A listing here means you want manuscript submissions from authors. For an application, contact *Writer's Market*, Writer's Digest Books, 1507 Dana Avenue, Cincinnati, OH 45207, Tel: (513) 531-2222.

Directories In Print will accept your book listing if it has an extensive appendix. Send for a form to Gale Research Company, Penobscot Building, Detroit, MI 48226-4094, Tel: (313) 961-2242. Visit the library and look for other directories that might list your book.

Contemporary Authors is a large reference book containing over 91,000 biographical sketches. Authors of technical and vanity press books are not eligible. Send for a form to *Contemporary Authors*, Gale Research Company, Penobscot Building, Detroit, MI 48226-4094, Tel: (313) 961-2242. Don't be modest; the more you write on the form, the more space you get in the book. After you fill out the application, make a few photocopies, so you will be ready when someone else asks for extensive biographical information. The listing is free.

Who's Who in U.S. Writers, Editors & Poets. For an application, contact December Press, Curt Johnson, 3093 Dato, Highland Park, IL 60035, Tel: (312) 432-6804.

Policies of Publishers: A Handbook for Order Librarians. Scarecrow Press, 52 Liberty Street, Metuchen, NJ 08840, Tel: (908) 548-8600.

Publishers Marketing Association (PMA) is an international association of more than 2,500 publishers who band together to promote their books in a cooperative manner. PMA holds educational seminars, buys and shares advertising space, makes cooperative mailings and operates booths at major book fairs. Local affiliates of PMA are located all over North America. Contact PMA, 2401 Pacific Coast Highway #102-P, Hermosa Beach, CA 90254, Tel: (310) 372-2732, for a sample newsletter and a membership application.

COSMEP is the international association of independent book and magazine publishers. The name Committee of Small Magazine Editors and Publishers is, however, misleading. They publish a very informative monthly newsletter, and membership will establish many valuable contacts. Contact COSMEP, P. O. Box 420703-P, San Francisco, CA 94101, Tel: (415) 922-9490, for a sample of the newsletter and a membership application.

Book Trade in Canada is the *LMP* of the Canadian book publishing industry. Contact Ampersand Communications Services, 5605 Scobie Crescent, Manotick, ON K4M 1B7, Canada, Tel: (613) 692-2080.

Canadian Books in Print is the *BIP* of the Canadian book publishing industry. Contact University of Toronto Press, 10 St. Mary Street, #700, Toronto, ON M4Y 2W8, Canada, Tel: (416) 978-2239.

Canadian Publishers Directory. Contact Key Publishers, 59 Front Street East, Toronto, ON M5E 1B3, Canada, Tel: (416) 364-3333.

New & Forthcoming Canadian Books. Contact Key Publishers, 59 Front Street East, Toronto, ON M5E 1B3, Canada, Tel: (416) 364-3333.

Forms. For a complete set of forms, including all those mentioned in this chapter, see the order blank on the last page of this book for *Publishing Forms.*

With listings in *Books in Print,* the *Small Press Record* and *Literary Market Place,* a membership in the Publishers Marketing Association and subscriptions to *Publishers Weekly, Small Press,* and *Writer's Digest,* you will begin to receive a lot of writing and publishing mail. See the listings in the Appendix.

The competition from the small presses, which have sprung up around the country, and which seem to be willing to take risks, has led some observers to conclude the New York publishing industry will eventually lose its primacy as the showcase for new talent and as the arbiter of literary taste. The rising cost of doing business in Manhattan, they argue, will force its firms to pursue only the most commercially promising manuscripts—blockbusters to sell through bookstore chains. — Richard Hartzell, *Wilson Library Bulletin*

A book is the only immortality. — Rufus Choate

Never skimp on your research. So-called writer's block is invariably the result of too little research. If you know enough, you won't have trouble filling as many pages as you want to. — Louise Purwin Zobel

Chapter Six

What is Your Book Worth?

Prices, Discounts, Terms, Collections and Returns

Book pricing is a complicated affair which strikes a compromise between a price high enough for the publisher to stay in business and low enough to overcome customer price resistance. There are, perhaps, three reasons people write books: reward (fame and/or fortune), love of writing and a desire to disseminate important material. While you may want to get the word out, your first book is usually for recognition, and once that is out of your system, the second is for money. Consequently, the author is likely to under-

> *Writing is like prostitution. First you do it for the love of it, then you do it for a few friends, and finally you do it for the money.* — Molière

price the first book but work with a very sharp pencil on the price of the next.

The list price of your book will not be easy to set. Many first-time author-publishers ask themselves whether they want maximum financial return or maximum distribution, feeling they can't have both. Usually they wind up with a price on the cover which is too low. As a result, many small publishers have warehouses full of books which they cannot afford to market effectively. Without a sufficient price, there is not enough money for promotion, and without promotion, the book will not sell. If the book fails to sell, there is no money for promotion, or even to pay the printing bill.

One major reason small publishers stay small is their failure to think objectively about pricing their books. Low prices make you work harder for less and limit your growth.

You must also consider that the price printed on the cover is not what you will receive for the book. Dealers require a percentage for their selling efforts. Your promotion costs, to let people know the book exists, are likely to be much higher than you originally anticipated—around 25% of the list price. Ten to 20 percent of the books may be shipped out as review copies, and 10% may come back from bookstores damaged. Discounts, advertising and returns take a big chunk out of the list price.

Books are becoming more and more expensive; visit a bookstore and compare prices. According to *Publishers Weekly*, the average prices for books in 1993, the latest year available, were as follows:

Hardcover (eliminating those special books priced over $81): $32.44, and this compares with $17.32 in 1977. Some more specific areas were: Business $37.36, Science $45.88, Sports & Recreation $31.67 and Travel $25.88. Hardcover fiction averaged $19.35.

Softcover: $19.24, and this compares with $5.93 in 1977. Business books averaged $21.71, Science $31.54, Sports & Recreation $15.40 and Travel $15.84. Softcover fiction averaged $13.59.

Mass-market paperback: $5.70, and this is up from $1.72 in 1977. Business books averaged $10.40, Science $7.86, Sports & Recreation $7.16 and Travel $10.56. Mass-market fiction averaged $4.78.

Some publishers like to test prices before deciding on them. There are times when a higher price will make a product seem more valuable and will make the book sell better. These publishers run identical ads, except for the price, and then check the returns. Mail order book buyers are said to be the least price-conscious of all.

In a how-to book, you are selling exclusive information, not entertainment or stacks of paper. Your book is unique. Like you, it is one of a kind. While a customer will not pay more than what he figures is a fair price, if your book is a good one and he wants it badly enough, he will pay what you ask. The selling price is not nearly so frightening to the buyer as it is to the author.

Underpricing a book to increase sales is often a very big mistake. In fact, it may even undermine the credibility of the book. And remember, price has a reverse impact when a book is purchased as a gift.

According to *Publishers Weekly*, women are more resistant to book prices than men. Women buy most of the books on cooking, health, diet and gardening, as well as fiction.

Here is a formula for pricing your book. You must look at price from the bottom up and from the top down.

— **Bottom up:** Books you intend to sell through bookstores and mail order should be priced at eight times "unit production cost," textbooks at five times. If you charge less, you won't have enough money to promote the book, because you must give away so much to the distribution network of distributors, wholesalers and bookstores. Promotion is also expensive, and it is normal to invest 20% to 30% of the

---

The book *How to Beat Inflation* has just gone from $9.95 to $14.95

gross back into letting the world know your book is available. Depending upon the subject matter and the size of the potential audience, we often send out more than 500 review copies to appropriate magazines, newsletters, newspaper columns and opinion molders. Reviews are the most effective and least expensive promotion you can do for your book.

We used to say "8X production costs," but today most publishers set their own type with computers, so there are few outsourced pre-press expenditures. Now we say eight times printing (and trucking).

The 8X formula does not fit every case; there may be a few exceptions. Consider your audience and the cost of reaching them. If you write a pictorial history of your town, and the Chamber of Commerce is buying all the books to give to tourists, your promotion and distribution costs will be much lower. For continuously-selling nonfiction aimed at a small target audience, you may be able to justify 7X. If 8X seems like a lot, you should know that audiovisual materials are often marked up 11X.

Direct mail. If you plan to sell your book through direct mail advertising, you will get the full price of the book by avoiding book trade discounts. However, your list price will have to be higher, not lower, because direct mail is so expensive. A direct mail offer will cost more than 40 cents each for bulk rate postage, envelope, cover letter, mailing house stuffing, etc. Your expected response may be 2% or less. Conventional direct mail industry wisdom says you can't profitably sell a book through direct mail advertising unless it is priced over $35.

—Top down: The price you put on your back cover, imbed in your bar code, put on the order blank on the last page of your book and list in all your promotion should be

> *Retail price should depend more upon the value the buyer places on the product than on cost to the producer.*
> — Leonard Shatzkin, author of *In Cold Type*

as much as the traffic will bear. Visit a bookstore and check other books like yours.

Yes, I know, your book has no competition; all authors feel their book is unique.

Look for other books on the same subject that would be purchased by the same type of person.

Yes, I know, your book is for everyone.

Look, I publish books on skydiving. I want everyone to jump—to have fun, to skydive safely and to come back, make more jumps, join the club, buy equipment and (hopefully) buy more books. But, I am realistic. I know skydiving is not for everyone. Just because you spent the last year pouring your heart, soul and credit limit into your tome, that does not mean everyone is interested enough to buy it and read it. Now, that said, what is the profile of the typical potential purchaser for your book?

Also look at the formats of those other books: hardcover, softcover, size, shape, color printing, etc.

You want to find out what your potential buyer is willing to spend. If you are selling to teenagers, your price will have to be low and the book in softcover. If yours is a business book, $29.95 and hardcover with a dust jacket may be right. If this is a professional book aimed at doctors or lawyers, a hardcover book without a jacket at $90 would not be out of line.

Please do not call and ask me how much you can charge for your book. For books on book promotion (such as *The Self-Publishing Manual*) and for books on parachutes (such as *The Parachute Manual*), I can make an educated guess. I do not know your field or your customers. I would have to visit a bookstore and check the shelves. You must do the same.

If you poll a bookstore manager on pricing, remember that lower prices will sell more books, so they will often advise a lower price.

Compare. Now, hopefully, your bottom-up price (8X) is lower than your top-down price. If there is an overlap, you will have to reformulate your book.

If the cover price is too high, you will price your book out of the market; if too low, the book will not be credible.

Potential buyers will think there is something wrong with it. If your book is priced too high for its class of buyer, it won't sell well; your potential customer will resist. If it is priced too low, you won't make enough to invest in further promotion.

Pricing the book any lower than 8X is courting financial disaster. If the projected list price seems too high, consider cutting out some of the copy or photographs, or selecting a smaller type and narrower leading (space between the lines) to get more material on each page. Check with your printer for ways to reduce costs. Now, if the customer still won't pay that much, you picked the wrong subject to write about.

You may price revised editions a bit higher. When updating a book and going back to press, there is an advantage: your book has been out there working for you. It has a reputation and can command more attention and more money. For example, a revised edition of *The Self-Publishing Manual* is a new book—with a track record.

Always charge X.95. It may seem old and silly, but $19.95 still seems a lot cheaper to the subconscious mind than $20, and there is no good argument for a mid-price like $19.50.

Raising the price. Recheck your costs at reprint time; you may wish to raise the cover price. If you do raise the price, remember to change your ads, brochures, etc., and send off a news release on the reprint to *Publishers Weekly*. (Every little mention helps.) To ease the blow on your better dealers, who have you listed in their catalogs, consider offering them a one-time buy on the new edition at the old price in order to protect their catalog listing. This offer will also generate quick cash to help you pay your printing bill.

ABI Form. If you have already sent in the ABI form, do not worry. You will receive a checking printout every couple

> *Retail price is established by the marketplace not by the cost of production.*
> — Jerrold Jenkins, The Jenkins Group

of months. Just write any changes in title, publication date or price on the sheet and return it to Bowker.

Price on cover. Your book must have a price on the cover—for three reasons.

1. If you do not print your price on the back cover of a softcover book or on the jacket flap of a hardcover book, the bookstores will sticker it. If the book comes back, you will not be able to remove the sticker, so you have to destroy the book or replace the jacket.

2. The price is reflected in the price extension of the bar code, and any savvy buyer can decipher the code. Today, your book must have a bar code or it will not flow through the book distribution system.

3. Your book should have an order blank on the last page—facing out. For example, see the last page of this book. We sell more books each week on these order blanks than on any other promotion we do.

So, if you are pricing your book on the order blank and on the back cover in the bar code, why not print the price on the back cover in Arabic numerals, too?

The price should be at the bottom of the back cover on a softcover book and at the top of the left jacket flap of a hardcover book. Do not place the price at the top of the back cover where it may turn off potential buyers before they read the sales copy.

How many books? You must consider both your purpose for writing the book and how many you can expect to sell. Do you want just a few books for family and friends? Will it be a high-priced, mail order book with a small target audience? Or will it be a popular book, with a wide audience, that should sell well in bookstores? How many will be used for review copies, gifts and other freebees? Make a list.

Initial press runs should normally be limited to the number of books one can reasonably estimate will be sold in the first year. Unless you have a substantial number of pre-publication sales (such as to a book club), it is a good idea to limit the first printing to 3,000 books. No matter how diligently you proofread, some errors will not surface until they appear in ink. Also, once you see the book in its final state, you will wish you had done some things differently—especially on a first book. By printing a smaller number, you can use the next few months to catch your errors and make some design changes. Then you will be much happier about the revised second edition.

Set the first press run conservatively. It is better to sell out and have to go back to press than to find yourself with a garage full of unsold books. You will be spending a lot of money on promotion, so it is best to hedge your bets by tying up less money in the book, even though you have to pay a slight premium in printing costs to do so.

But do not be too conservative. All the books will not be *sold*; many will be used for promotion. If you print 1,000 copies and send 500 out to newspapers and magazines for review, there will be only 500 copies left to sell. Reviews are your least expensive and most effective form of promotion, and 500 review copies is a realistic figure (see Chapter Seven). Many publishers figure 10% or more of their print run will be used for review copies and promotion. Except for highly specialized topics, 3,000 makes a good initial print run.

The economics of printing are as follows: the greater the quantity of books, the higher your bill, but the less each book will cost you. The "start-up costs" make the first press run much more expensive than reprints. The major expenses are the start-up costs of composition, layout, camerawork, stripping, press setup, etc. Once the type is set, you only pay for the paper, binding and press time. The more copies printed at one time, the lower the price per copy.

Economy of scale is only true up to a point, since the differences become smaller and smaller as the press runs increase. Each next thousand books becomes cheaper. The price breaks fail to maintain significance after about 9,000 copies. Normally, between 9,000 and 10,000 copies, you save so little that it isn't worth the storage space or the price of borrowing money. Therefore you do not want to print over 9,000 unless you are certain that number will move out within the year.

For example, you might receive printing/binding quotes such as:

No. of copies	500	1,000	3,000	5,000	7,000	9,000	10,000
Total cost	$1,495	1,784	4,485	6,778	8,750	10,530	11,300
Unit cost	$2.99	1.78	1.49	1.36	1.25	1.17	1.13

So it is to your advantage to order as many books as possible in order to get the best unit price. And you want the best price, as long as you are fairly sure you can sell the higher number.

Remember that a printer makes money on printing. Do not let him talk you into more books than you need. There is economy in scale, but there are no savings in paying for books you can't turn into cash. Consider the total printing bill as well.

Print runs are never exact. Printers always run a few extra pages, expecting some to be spoiled. When all the sheets are gathered, there are still some which must be thrown away. Accordingly, it is customary in the trade to have overruns and underruns, and your bill may be adjusted higher or lower, up to 10%. A print run of 3,000 could wind up anywhere between 2,700 and 3,300.

Estimating sales for that first year will be difficult with your initial book, because you don't have other books with which to compare it. You may get an idea from your own previous work experience and may be able to find out what similar books have done. But remember that bigger publish-

Book buyers are less influenced by price differentials than almost any category of customers. —John Huenefeld ers have more clout in the bookstores, as well as other outlets, and already have the connections for promoting and placing their titles; you will not do as well until you learn the ropes. Check with anyone you may know in other publishing companies for their educated estimate, and get a copy of *Financial Feasibility in Book Publishing* by Robert Follet (see the Appendix). It contains guidelines, worksheets and rules of thumb for estimating sales. With proper promotion, any reasonably good nonfiction book, aimed at all but the tiniest markets, should sell 2,500 copies in its first year (plus up to 500 promotional copies). Do some market research. How many associations, magazines and conventions are there in this activity? How many people care about this subject? If you cannot objectively project moving 3,000 copies in the first year, you will have to raise the price to justify printing the book.

Reprints have to be timed just right. If you order a reprint too early, you may tie up more money before the first run is paid for, and many of those books from the last run could be sitting on the shelves in the stores—unsold. It is a good idea to make some telephone calls to find out if the book is actually moving. On the other hand, if you wait too long to reprint, you run the risk of being out of stock and losing the all-important sales momentum the book is enjoying. Reprints usually take three to five weeks. Coordinate with your printer so you can get a fast reprint if necessary. It is much better to be out of books for a few weeks than to have the truck arrive with 5,000 more as bookstores are returning copies.

A "reprint" means there are no changes; a "revision" means you have made updating content corrections. As the publisher, you may decide how many changes are necessary to qualify as a revision. Books may be "revised" or "completely revised." See the copyright page of this book as an example. Always include a new ISBN when you publish a revision. With a new ISBN, the book industry will treat the book as new. Your distributor will put it back in the front of the catalog ("front list").

The book trade is new-product driven. Make a legitimate revision, assign a new ISBN and bar code and keep your book new.

Size of inventory. When your stock is running low, consider printing time (reprints take three to five weeks), trucking time (two to six days), seasonal demand for this title, etc. Then, considering the size of your storage space, amount of money you can invest, need for future revisions, inventory tax dates (if your state has one), etc., print a one-to-two-year supply of books. One great advantage of these nearly annual printings is the ability to make revisions, keeping the text up-to-date.

The demand for some books continues on and on; others have a definite life. The trick is to know when the sales cycle is over. It is nice to run out of stock just before the demand curve ends in a cliff. Watch your sales and do not reorder until the last minute. It is better to be out of books for a couple of weeks than to order too soon.

Discounts must be set down in a definite policy right from the beginning. Discount structures have to be clear to both you and your customers to avoid any misunderstanding.

Ultimate consumers placing individual orders usually pay the full retail price and send cash with their order (CWO). When an order is received without a check, it is best to return it with a copy of your brochure and a short note requesting payment in advance. Circle your prices and terms on the brochure; some people order asking to be billed, because they don't know what the full price will be. Asking for payment in advance will lose a few orders, but it will stop credit losses and cut billing costs. See the order blank at the end of this book, for an example. Avoid COD shipments. They require too much paperwork for a small sale, and the collection charges often upset the customer.

Dealer discounts. The terms publishers extend to booksellers vary so much from firm to firm that the American Booksellers Association publishes a loose-leaf handbook trying to list them all. Discounts are supposed to be based on the theory that there is a saving in bulk shipments. However, bookselling tradition has based the discount rate on the category of the wholesale customer, arguing that certain middlemen need a greater discount because they are providing a service and are passing on part of the discount.

— **Most distributors** take 25% to 30% of the net (what they collect from the stores), which may work out to be around 65% of the list (cover) price. Sixty to 65 percent may sound like a lot, and it is. But most distributors handle only the book trade (wholesalers and bookstores), so you may turn that portion of the business over to them, forget about the stores and go on to the nontraditional markets, which are easier, more lucrative and more fun. You pay the freight to them (FOB destination), but you usually ship directly from your printer. See the distributor discussion in Chapter Eight.

— **Wholesalers** get 50% to 60% off on the theory that they purchase large quantities for resale to retailers and libraries. Often they are regional suppliers providing stores with both one-stop shopping and a short supply line for quick and easy restocking. They allow bookstores up to 40% off depending on the size of the order, but stores are usually allowed to mix titles. In order to maintain large library accounts, they usually extend discounts of 20% to 33%. Wholesalers sometimes pay the shipping (FOB origin) when purchasing from the publisher.

— **Retail bookstores.** Discounts to bookstores start at 40% for single-title orders; this comes as a shock to many new publishers, but one has to consider the high overhead retailers have in the form of rent, taxes, salaries, utilities, insurance, etc. They need at least 40% to stay in business. Incidentally, bookstores enjoy a smaller markup than gift, sporting goods and other stores, which often get 50% or more. The publishing industry has been able to justify the lower discount by making the books returnable if they aren't sold. Fortunately, books are uniform in size, easy to store, simple to ship and unbreakable. Shipping charges are added to the bookstore's bill (FOB origin).

— **College bookstores** get 20% to 25% off on (text) books to be sold to students. The quantity is often large, and any books not sold after the school term begins are returned. There is very little risk to the store, as the store is just acting as an order taker. The "short discount" results in a lower price to the consuming student.

These short discounts are sometimes applied to regular (trade) books, and when this is done, all sales literature should be clearly marked. The book trade will not be too enthusiastic about the poor discount, but they can't complain if they are buying in ones and twos and have been informed of the short discount in advance.

— **Libraries.** Some publishers and wholesalers give libraries a 20% discount, but most libraries do not expect a discount and many orders will arrive with a check made out for the list price. Libraries are only ordering one book so there is no justification for a discount. Most small publishers are charging the libraries full list price and shipping postpaid (at library rate).

The Federal Trade Commission (FTC) requires that the discounts you offer one dealer be offered to all dealers who are purchasing the same quantity. You are not required to extend credit, but if dealers are paying cash and want the same quantity, you must sell at the same discount.

Your distributor will order by the carton, usually one or two thousand books. The wholesaler will order ten to 50 books from the distributor, and the bookstores will take one to three books from the wholesaler. If you select a distributor, you will have few sales to wholesalers or bookstores.

Discount schedules are being used by many publishers in deference to discriminatory tradition. It is based not on the classification of the customer, but on the order quantity. The universal schedule works well for larger publishers, since they have several books and allow titles to be mixed to achieve higher discounts. Smaller publishers will use the universal schedule for bookstores.

The theory of the universal discount schedule is that the wholesaler will earn a better discount by buying in larger quantities. Bookstores and libraries ordering smaller quantities get a "courtesy discount." This encourages the purchasers of small quantities to order from wholesalers with a great title mix, where they can get a better deal and reduce their paperwork with one-stop shopping. Remember that these small quantity special orders from the stores are not getting your books on the shelf for all to see. The book has already been sold and will go straight to the customer.

Outside the book trade. No single plan fits all types of publishers. For example, if you have one book or a single small line of specialized books, cater primarily to a specific class of people, and expect to have several large dealers who purchase hundreds of books at a time, you may wish to consider a simplified discount schedule. The simplified schedule works best for sales to stores other than bookstores.

1-2	no discount
3-199	-40%
200-499	-50%
500 and up	-40%, -25%

Simplified discount schedule

"Less 40%, less 25%" amounts to 55% off. First you deduct 40% and then take 25% off what is left. Wholesalers reselling to retailers make 25% on their investment, which is a good amount.

The simplified schedule gives every dealer the 40% they need, allows you to serve the non-book industry with large orders while not upsetting the book trade with its small orders, and leaves you with just three figures to remember. Whatever discount schedule you choose, make it simple. You will have to use it to compute each order.

Titles may be mixed to achieve higher discounts, except where there is a great difference in price. You wouldn't mix a $1.50 title, normally wholesaled 500 at a time, with a $40 book usually purchased three at a time.

Dealer Bulletin

January 1, 1995

Featuring new and better discounts as well as a greater selection. See brochures for descriptions and list prices.

Discounts

1	book	no discount
2-4	books	20% off
5-9	books	30% off
10-24	books	40% off
25-49	books	42% off
50-74	books	44% off
75-99	books	46% off
100-199	books	48% off
200	or more books	50% off

STOP orders earn a 40% discount. Please add $1.75 per book for shipping. Order using full title and/or ISBN for identification.

Terms. Our terms are net 30 days from date of invoice. A finance charge of 1 1/2% per month will be added to all overdue balances over 60 days.

Credit. Please submit orders on your purchase order form or letterhead. Orders over $50.00 must be prepaid—or send three trade and one bank reference.

Resale Numbers. California dealers must mention their resale number with their order.

Shipping. Books are best shipped via the Post Office's "book rate." We can ship via truck, UPS or Federal Express but do not recommend them for long distances, as the rates are considerably higher. Shipping is FOB Santa Barbara.

Shortages or non-receipt must be reported to us within 30 days of the order date.

Promotional materials. We can supply photographs of all our publications for your catalog work.

Book Trade. Our distributor is Publishers Group West. Our books are also available from major wholesalers such as Baker & Taylor, Ingram, Bookpeople, Pacific Pipeline, the distributors and others. See their microfiche.

Orders may be sent to P.O. Box 8206, Santa Barbara, CA 93118-8206. Telephone orders may be made to (805) 968-7277 9:00 a.m. to 5:00 p.m., Pacific time. Purchase orders may be FAXed to (805) 968-1379 at any time.

Example of discount schedule

Don't confuse "discount" with "markup." A discount of 50% from $2 to $1 is the same as a 100% markup from $1 to $2.

When figuring your discounts, total the order and then subtract the discount. You will come out with a slightly higher figure than if you figure the discount per book and then extend it out. For example, buying 200 $5.95 books at 50% off, there is one dollar difference. $5.95 x 200 - 50% = $595.00, but $5.95 - 50% = $2.97 x 200 = $594.00.

Your discounts and terms should be printed in your dealer bulletins, listed in the ABA *Book Buyer's Handbook* (560 White Plains Road, Tarrytown, NY 10591), etc., where they will be easily found by your dealers.

Once you have published your prices and terms, stick to them. Besides the need to obey the FTC rules, it just is not profitable to deviate from those figures which took you so long to calculate. Some dealers will be asking for a better deal, and some publishers feel that any sale above their cost is a good one. But it is not fair to give one customer a better deal than another. You have to draw the line somewhere. Your valuable time should be used to generate additional net income, not more marginal gross.

Consignments make you into a banker as well as a publisher. Consignment is when the dealer takes delivery on the books, but doesn't pay the publisher until they are sold. Most distributors operate on consignment inventory and pay 90 days after they sell the books to the bookstore or wholesaler. While publishers should avoid selling to small accounts on consignment, there are good arguments for these terms with major distributors. Book manufacture requires large print runs, so part of your inventory might just as well sit in another warehouse as your own.

Shipping charges are usually included in the price charged on individual retail sales. The book may be adver-

---

Before you can sell a person anything you have to make him or her want it more than the money it cost.

tised at "$19.95 ppd" (postpaid). While you have made an allowance for postage in the list (cover) price, the buyer feels he is getting something for nothing. As noted above, most distributors and wholesalers do not pay for shipping, but most libraries and retail customers do.

Book rate postage is spiraling upwards, and both publishers and booksellers are becoming very conscious of the shipping expenses. Similarly, the costs of packing materials and labor are high, and some publishers try to offset some of these with a "handling charge." The term "handling charge" is sure to evoke a nasty response from the customer, no matter how small it may be. If "postage" is not the same as the amount on the package, you will also hear about it. So, if you do plan to tack on a little extra to pay for the invoice, its first class mailing, envelopes and shipping supplies, call the postage and handling charge "shipping."

Some publishers tack a processing charge of 50 cents onto all orders. This is a lot on a single book, but it is only a penny each on a carton of 50. Processing the orders costs the same.

Those dealers who object to any figures higher than the postage on the carton usually just scratch it off the invoice when paying the bill. Invoice altering becomes more frequent after each postal rate hike.

STOP stands for "Single Title Order Plan" and, like SCOP or "Single Copy Order Plan," it consists of a special multi-part order form which arrives with a check. Because the store is paying in advance, they assume a discount of 20% to 40%. The check may be filled in or blank and restricted to a certain maximum amount. Sometimes the order asks that the book be shipped directly to the customer and other times to the store. Part of the purchase order may be used as a shipping label.

> *We are in a consignment business that pretends it is not.*
> — Sol Stein, President of Stein and Day

Contact the American Booksellers Association for an application form for a listing in their ABA *Book Buyer's Handbook*. When you fill it out, indicate that you wish to participate in STOP and list your terms. Many publishers agree to accept STOP orders based on the list price, less a 40% discount, plus $1.75 for shipping.

Terms and credit are different in the book trade. Most wholesalers and bookstores routinely take 60 days to pay, many take 90, and some get around to mailing out checks in six or eight months. This forces the publisher into a frustrating banking situation. There are very few small publishers who can afford to finance the inventories of their dealers.

The customary terms for the book industry are that invoices should be paid within 30 days of an end-of-the-month statement (30 EOM). This is up to 30 days longer than "net 30 day" terms. Some publishers, eyeing other industries, offer "2% ten day" terms, but the dealer usually

A STOP order

pays late and still takes the 2%. Another way to get most of your money faster is to offer 5% for "cash (or check) with order" (CWO). Unfortunately, this offer is usually taken by the financially sound "good pay" store who would pay on time anyway, not by the slow pay store you will have to chase for months. Many of the newer small publishers don't subscribe to the 30 EOM terms or discounts for fast pay; they quote strictly "net 30 days."

"Advance dating" of invoices is sometimes done for seasonal businesses and catalog houses. The invoice is dated a couple of months later. This provides the dealer with the opportunity to get the books into stock before the rush—important where timing is critical and sales will be late.

Ship your invoices separately via first class mail; don't just enclose them in the carton with the books. The longer it takes the invoice to reach the customer, the longer the customer will take to pay it.

Once you have decided on your terms and have published them, stick to them religiously. Any sign of relaxation will be evidence that you don't mean what you say, and some dealers will take advantage of you. You are a publisher, not a banker, and if you were in the loan business you would charge interest.

Credit. It is only practical to extend credit and ship quickly to new accounts. You will receive all sorts of small orders from distant stores, and it is not worth the time and effort to run a credit check on each one. It may cost $50 or more to run a credit check, even if you do it all yourself by telephone, and it will take a lot of time. On one- and two-book orders, credit checks are not worth the effort for the occasional bad pay or bankruptcy.

If a large order out of nowhere seems too good to be true, it probably is. A few people have ordered large quantities of books (200 of a title) from small publishers without ever intending to pay for them. They turn around and sell the books to stores and remainder houses at a great discount.

In 1982, the author suffered a bad accident just prior to the ABA·book fair. He was in the hospital for five weeks and could not work for almost six months. While in the hospital, he received a very large order from someone who pretended to be a big wholesaler in Michigan. The buyer even had the nerve to write across the bottom of the purchase order: "Missed you at the ABA, get well soon." It took several years to put him out of business, and at last report even his bankruptcy trustee couldn't collect from him.

Set a limit of, say, $50, for any dealer order coming in on a letterhead or purchase order. Enclose your brochure, statement of terms and return policy with the invoice. You might also like to slip in a form letter welcoming their account, explaining that you are happy to extend credit and that prompt payment of this invoice will raise their limit to $100. Beyond that, you will require trade and bank references. Those who do not stand your test, or who are awaiting a credit check for a large purchase, may be urged to pay in advance via a "pro forma invoice" (you make out a complete invoice to include shipping charges but you don't ship the books until the invoice is paid). Another clever trick is to ask for 50% of a large invoice in advance—then ship just 50% of the order.

Schools, libraries, state and federal governments are "good pay" but often "slow pay." They have taxing authority, so it is hard to go bankrupt no matter how badly they are managed. Just make sure their request comes on their purchase order. Too often someone in the Park Department will write to you on city letterhead asking for a book, with no mention of money. This may well be an unauthorized order.

Sometimes schools or government agencies will telephone or fax an order and then will follow with a written purchase order. If you are lucky, they will mark the second message: *Confirming order—do not duplicate.* Otherwise, you may wind up shipping twice.

Join a local publishing association and meet some of the people in other book firms. If you question an account, often a call to one of your contemporaries will provide the credit information you seek.

Foreign orders may be treated in the same way as domestic ones. There will be a difference in shipping charges, sometimes higher and sometimes lower. Unless they pay in dollars drawn on a U.S. bank, there may be a check cashing charge. Foreigners have about the same payment history as U.S. customers.

Some publishers place a surcharge on foreign orders, and it might be appropriate to add a small paperwork fee to very large orders requiring customs forms, but since most foreign orders do not require more work than domestic shipments, a surcharge discourages foreign sales and insults foreign customers.

Statements. Wholesalers and bookstores are accustomed to receiving end-of-the-month statements of their accounts; they want a recapitulation of the many small orders they have placed. Statements are not a requirement, but they may speed payment when these customers are waiting for one. You can type up statement forms, but initially it will be far cheaper, easier and faster to photocopy your invoices. Often the copy shops near colleges charge as little as five cents each for photocopies. Check the *Yellow Pages* and make some calls. Once you are computerized, printing statements will be easy.

Photocopy the invoice and stuff the copy into a windowed #10 envelope. This system avoids separate statements, transposition errors, small envelopes, typing and collection stickers. Hand-write your collection message on the copy. The collection messages may include:

1. Is there any reason why this past due bill has not been paid?
2. If you are unable to pay the whole bill, won't you evidence your good faith by sending us a partial payment?
3. We subscribe to Dun and Bradstreet's Commercial Collection service.
4. If payment is not received within ten days, we will be forced to turn this matter over to our attorney for collection.

Enclose brochures on new books with the statements. You might as well fill up the envelope to its full postage limit.

Collections. When the money does not come in on time, you have to exercise your collection process.

When keyboarding invoices, always include the name of the person signing the order. This focuses your claim on a specific individual, where it will have more impact than if you simply send invoices and statements to the company. Now pen a nice personal note to this particular person, on the bottom of the statement.

If the account goes another month without a response, pen a stronger note on the bottom of the statement. Then wait two weeks and make a telephone call. If they don't pay in 90 days, cut them off. You don't need customers like them. In most other industries, 30 days would be the limit; the book industry is much slower.

After this, there are a couple of options. You may arrange with your attorney to send a standard collection letter which will be typed out automatically on a word processor. The charge may be $10 to $15, and the attorney may give you a better price on a quantity of collections. You may also consider a collection agency. Your local firm will have affiliates all over North America, or you might contact a large firm with many offices, such as Dun & Bradstreet. Collection agencies usually take one-third as their collection fee, and they prefer the easy cases. They have little power and usually get their money through a personal visit, which embarrasses the bookseller. They will threaten legal action and will turn the case over to a local attorney if they fail to collect. Generally, the older the debt, the harder it is to collect.

SKO-Brenner-American is a collection agency that specializes in the book trade. They publish a monthly confidential list of delinquent bookstores and wholesalers. They will also handle collections. For information on their services and a subscription to their newsletter, contact SKO-Brenner-American, 196 Merrick Road, Suite 101, Oceanside, NY 11572, Tel: (516) 764-4400.

Collections Plus is a computer program that automates your collection process. For details, Contact Tag Powell, Tel: (813) 530-0110.

The telephone is a powerful collection instrument and a good supplement to dunning notices. Many callers use guide scripts to make sure they get their complete message across quickly.

Remember, it is better to have the books returned unsold than to have the books sold and not get paid.

If a customer has been bouncing large checks on you, put the next one in "for collection." Your bank will send it to the customer's bank with instructions to hold the check until there is enough money in the account to pay it.

To collect a large bill from a foreign customer, try calling the cultural attaché at the nearest embassy or consulate. Often the attaché will relay your message, and this puts pressure on the foreign debtor.

Whatever collection system you select, make it automatic, so that you can be objective and will not allow deadbeats to negotiate delays. Let customers know you mean business. See *Business Letters For Publishers* for some suggested collection letters. See the Appendix.

The accounts receivable operation is one of the most pleasant, because it is always fun to count your money. As the checks arrive to pay for due bills, match them with the invoices. (If only everyone would note the invoice numbers on their checks!) Mark the invoice with a date stamp to indicate when the payment was credited. Put this pink file copy in a record storage box or binder. See the invoice handling discussion in Chapter 10.

Checks will be received made out to the publishing company, the author or the name of the book. Name them all on your check deposit stamp. Pay a little extra for a self-inking stamp; it will save you a lot of time.

Deposits may be made up every week or so. Endorse the checks with a rubber stamp and list them on an adding machine tape. If your bank wants you to list each check individually on the deposit slip, threaten to go to another bank.

The higher your markup, the better you can afford mistakes.

Big corporations do not have to do this, and you won't either if you are assertive. Keep it simple!

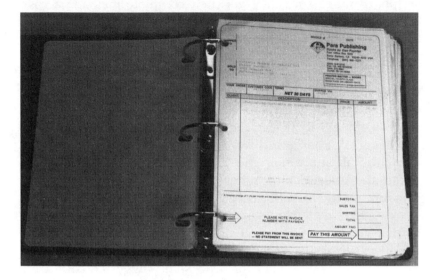

Invoices may be stored in a binder

Returns are one of the biggest controversies in the book business. Distributors, wholesalers and bookstores expect to be able to return all books they do not sell. Bookstores return some 18% of the books they order to the distributor, but the distributor returns just 2% to the publishers and they are shelf-worn. If this still sounds like a lot, then consider that the figure is so high for mass-market paperbacks that the dealers save shipping by stripping the books and sending back only the covers for credit.

The returns system almost amounts to consignment, and the publisher is caught in a bind, because if the booksellers did not have the return privilege, they would be far less likely to carry his books. The publisher wants his books displayed and so has to take the chance of having several of them come back. Therefore, there is little difference between consignment and a no-strings return policy. Returns result in zero profit transactions (ZPT's). The books went out with pa-

Book Return Policy

1. Our books are returnable. If a title isn't moving in your market, we want to get it back before a new edition makes it obsolete. Thank you for giving it a chance on your valuable shelf space. Our return period is normally between 90 days and one year of the publisher's invoice date; however, we will accept the book for return after one year as long as the edition is still in print. To keep our products current, we update our titles every one and a half to two years.

2. Return permission must be requested, so that we may issue detailed packing and shipping instructions.

3. Notice of shortage or non-receipt must be made within 30 days of the shipping/invoice date for domestic shipments; 60 days for foreign.

4. Books damaged in transit are not the responsibility of the publisher. Please make claim to the carrier.

5. Returns must be accompanied by your packing slip listing quantity, title, author, original invoice number and invoice date. Books returned with this information will be credited with 100% of the invoice price, minus shipping. Otherwise, it will be assumed the original discount was 60%. Some books have been returned to us when they should have been directed to our distributor; books should be returned to their source.

6. Routing: Ship books via parcel post (book rate) prepaid or UPS prepaid to Para Publishing, Attn: D. Poynter, 530 Ellwood Ridge, Santa Barbara, CA 93117-9700. Note, this is not the same as our order address.

7. To qualify for a refund, returned books must arrive here in good, resalable condition. If they are not now resalable, please don't bother to return them. If the books are in good condition but you are not willing to package them properly for the return trip, please don't waste your time and postage.

To package the books so that they will survive the trip, we suggest you wrap them in the same way that they were sent to you. There are two important steps in successful book packaging: Keep them clean and immobilize them. Place the stacked books in a plastic bag. This will separate the dirty newsprint and greasy Styrofoam peanuts or discs from the book edges and will prevent grit from creeping between the pages. To keep the books from shifting (which causes scuffing), cut a shipping carton to the right size and stuff it tightly with dunnage.

Continued next page

Since it has been our experience that books shipped loose in oversize "Jiffy bags" always arrive scuffed, it is now our policy to refuse them at the post office so that they will be returned to the bookstore. Do not use Jiffy bags!

8. A credit memo will be issued toward future purchases.

9. Industry tells us that it now costs more than eight dollars to write a letter. Correspondence, packaging and postage cost us all a great deal in money and time (and time is money). Years ago when postage was cheap, it made sense to return slow-moving books. Today, however, many bookstores are finding it is more cost effective to mark down the books and move them out.

Thank you for contacting Para Publishing.

Sample return policy statement

perwork and came back with paperwork; everyone was busy, but nothing was sold.

From time to time, people in the book industry suggest changes to the system of returns. One recommendation which is often heard is to eliminate the returns and to pass the savings on to the bookstore in the form of higher discounts. Because we operate in a free-market economy with a lot of competition, none of these suggestions have ever caught on.

Make up a return policy and send it to anyone who requests it. Baker & Taylor and some of the other wholesalers will probably ask for your return policy when they first open an account with you. Also send the policy when a bookstore or wholesaler requests permission to return some books.

Most publishers will allow returns between 90 days and 12 months of the invoice date. They specify 90 days because they want to make sure the books were given a fair trial on the shelves, but 12 months because they do not want them sitting around too long; the title may go into a new printing.

Most publishers require the bookseller to request permission and specific shipping instructions first, but few stores do. They just ship the books back.

The paperwork with the return should identify the original invoice number under which the books were purchased. You want to credit the bookseller with the correct amount, the amount they paid. You also want to make sure the books came directly from you. If the books were purchased from a wholesaler, they should be returned to the wholesaler.

Books must arrive back at the publisher in good, unblemished, resalable condition, so that they may be returned to stock. This is the biggest failing of the bookstores. They almost never pack the books properly. They just throw them in a carton, often without cushioning material, and send them back. During the long trip, the books chafe against each other and the carton and consequently arrive in a scuffed, battered condition.

Large publishing firms usually do not send refunds on returns. They issue credits, because they are dealing with the customer on a continuing basis. Small publishers, with few other titles to offer, should send a refund check.

Make effective use of your most valuable asset, your time.

The worst thing that can happen to a new publisher is to have a phenomenally successful first book. They think they know the secret and that publishing is easy.
— Tom Drewes, Quality Books

Chapter Seven

Promoting Your Book

Making the Public Aware of Your Book Without Spending for Advertising

If you intend to be a successful author, you will measure your success with money. To make a profit, you will depend on good promotion and marketing. This chapter covers promotion: those methods which require some time and effort but no big advertising dollars. Of course, there will be a certain amount of overlap.

Your most important reference book will be *Literary Market Place*. While you may use the copy in your local library, this reference will be used so often, you should buy one for use at your desk.

> *Being an author is 5% writing and 95% promotion.*
> — Russ Marano, *Hi-Tek Newsletter*

The secrets to book sales are, first, to produce a good product and, second, to let people know about it. Many small publishers receive very little publicity for their books. This lack of attention is not because of any great conspiracy between the big (New York) publishers and the media; it is simply because the neophytes do not ask for coverage. Many small publishers are good at publishing but haven't any experience in marketing. They seem to have little interest in their books beyond the editorial work and production; they do not want to sell, they just want to create. Some beginning publishers seem to feel the marketing end of publishing is "too commercial," and this becomes their excuse for neglecting the most important part of any business: informing the buying public of your wares. For, obviously, if you cannot sell your product, you will not be able to afford to produce more editorial material.

Cost to advertise. Selling books through space advertising is expensive, because books are a *low ticket* (low selling price) item. If you were selling airplanes, one sale would pay for a lot of ad space, and if you were selling less expensive candy, you would sell to so many people that the ads might pay. It is tougher to break even when advertising a low priced product to a small and scattered group of people. For example, a one-half page ad in a national book-oriented magazine might run you $1,850.00. Using round numbers and assuming you printed the book for $2 and are selling it for $20, you would have to sell 102 books at retail, or 308 books at wholesale, just to break even on the ad. Experience tells us you will be lucky to get five orders.

Do not spend money on advertising when you can get publicity free. Put your time and money into less expensive review copies and news releases. Use the free publicity to find which magazines are right for your book, then spend your advertising money there. Always test before you spend

---

Do not spend a nickel on paid advertising until you have exhausted all the free publicity available.

money. Too many publishers start with large ads and blow their promotion money in the wrong places.

Publicity vs. advertising. The major differences between *publicity* and *advertising* are cost and control. Publicity is free, while advertising is not. On the other hand, you may control your advertising, while your publicity may be rewritten by the editor or not run at all.

Book promotion is less expensive and more successful when you use book reviews, news releases and, if appropriate to your book, a limited amount of highly targeted direct mail advertising. Book reviews are editorial copy which is far less expensive and far more credible than space advertising. For most nonfiction books, there are over 500 appropriate magazines and newspapers columns that should receive review packages. Then you should follow up with news releases every month to the very same magazines and newspapers. Let these opinion-molding editors know what you are doing and why your book has the information their readers need.

Book promotion takes time. Writing the book is the easy part—the tip of the iceberg. The real work begins when you switch hats to expend time and money on promoting the book.

Book reviews take three months to three years to appear, because magazines and even daily newspapers have long lead times. Do not get discouraged. The easiest mistake is to send out books for review, news releases on your book or a direct mail offer and then to sit back and wait for the results. The secret of savvy book promotion is to keep up the pressure: Keep sending out the packets and keep making the telephone calls.

Editorial copy vs. advertising copy. On the average, people spend seven minutes with their magazines. Obvi-

---

Just as a parent's responsibilities do not end with giving birth, an author's do not end with publication. The child must be raised and the book must be marketed.

ously, they see very few of the ads. Of those ads they see, they read very few. Of those ads they read, they believe very few. Of those ads they believe, they act on very few. People are skeptical of advertisements. On the other hand, readers believe editorial copy. Now ask yourself: how much advertising space can you buy for $1,500? Not much—and it won't sell many books, anyway. For the same amount, you may send out 500 review copies that will result in editorial copy that people will believe. The public is usually more receptive to publicity because editorial copy is viewed as news. Advertising is perceived as self-serving. An industry rule of thumb is that editorial coverage is seven times as valuable as paid coverage.

Competition for free space is a tough proposition. Hundreds of new books are published for every day the bookstores are open; the crowd is thicker in the fall than the spring. You have to compete for attention in a crowded field and against much larger, more knowledgeable firms. But you will be surprised at how successful you can be when you jump into the fray, exploiting the media through news releases, review copies, radio and TV appearances, feature stories, lectures, etc.

Large publishers are lucky if 40% of their titles make money, and they have departments of experts to launch their promotion. They also have built up thousands of key contacts during their many years in the business. You have only one book, your first, and therefore, you have only one chance to make it. But look at the brighter side. The big firms often work through routine and without imagination. Your overhead is much lower, and you are cutting out the middlemen by publishing yourself. You will do a more effective job of promotion because you have a greater interest

---

Many, many times, I have said, "This is too hard. I am getting out of this business," but then something good will happen and my enthusiasm is replenished.
— Patricia Gallagher

in the book than a publisher who is looking after several titles at one time. There is a lot of room for the very small independent publisher with imagination, initiative and a well-defined target market.

By doing the promotion yourself, you are avoiding the most common problem in author-publisher relationships: differing views on the amount of effort which should be invested in each area of promotion and advertising. The author cannot be objective about his product and is convinced that the book would sell better if only the publisher would spend money to promote it. The publisher, on the other hand, needs more sales to convince him it is worth investing more dollars in advertising.

Analyze the market by determining who might purchase your book, and then figure out the best way to reach them. Your buyer must be *identifiable* and *locatable*. Ask yourself what stores they frequent, what magazines they read, what associations they join and what conventions/events they attend. Before long, you will be able to ask what channels they watch.

If your book is on auto repair for the car owner, one prospect is the car enthusiast. What does he read? You will want to send news releases, review copies, ads and maybe even articles to auto magazines. Since there aren't too many little old ladies who are going to purchase such a book, you won't send review copies to women's magazines. Where do car enthusiasts congregate? Auto supply stores, car rallies, auto shows? If this repair manual covers a single type of car, you may be able to find a highly targeted mailing list of male owners of that type of car. The trick is to think about who the buyer might be and then think about where this type of person can be found. Rarely is the answer: bookstores or libraries.

> *Analyze carefully the type of person who is a prospective purchaser of your book. This is perhaps the single most important thing to consider.*

As you read through the next few chapters, think about your book and its market. Make a list of, or underline, those ideas mentioned that best fit your book. Then go back and work out a promotional schedule, by the week, for several months. Set a schedule so you won't lose sight of it later when you are busy keyboarding orders and stuffing boxes.

A common complaint by those who use a Hi-Liter felt tip marker to indicate the important parts of this book is that their copy of *The Self-Publishing Manual* winds up completely yellow.

If you are approaching bookstores, college bookstores, public libraries or school libraries, you will want to determine their seasonal buying patterns. If you are pursuing direct mail sales, you will want to set up a system of mailings and emphasize the program in certain seasons. The keys to your promotion are market targeting and timing. More on all these later.

Binder organization. Organize your thoughts and record your work by setting up a binder for your book. Use a 2" or 3" three-ring binder with dividers for five sections. The *slant-ring* binders with inside pockets are best. Now set up each section, as follows:

— *Section one* is where you record your promotional plan. Type up your initial plan, and check off the items when completed. Whenever you have a new idea, turn to the second page of section one and make a note. Use the balance of this section to store every news release you write, every mailing you make and every brochure you design. Date each promotional piece and record the results.

> *Our book marketing philosophy. We firmly believe the best way to sell most nonfiction books is with book reviews, news releases and a limited amount of highly targeted direct mail. Then once you have established your book in the U.S., it is time to explore the foreign markets. Book reviews and news releases result in free publicity, while direct mail delivers your sales message directly to potential customers.*

Set up a red promotion binder for each book

— *Section two* is for all your costing information. Store copies of all the printing, artists', trucking, etc., bills as well as all the printing quotations. With this information all in one place, even after six printings you will know exactly how many books have been printed and what each print run cost.

— *Section three* is where you store the reviews, testimonials and other publicity you have generated. All the good things which have been said about your book are kept in one place, so that when you want to make a list of testimonials, they will be easy to find.

— *Section four* is for any important correspondence. Here you will store some of the more interesting letters which do not fit in the other sections.

— *Section five* is the revision section. As you come across new material or think of something that should be included in the next edition, make a note and store it here. Also take one copy of the book, mark it "Correction Copy," and keep it near your desk. Cut off a corner of the front cover, so that it won't walk out of your office or find its way back into stock. As you find small errors or want to make changes, mark this book. Then when it comes time to return to press, all your revision information will be in the correction copy and the fifth section of your binder.

You will appreciate the promotion binders even more after you publish several books. All your costing, promotion, review and revision information will be easy to find.

Rate of sale. You can expect your sales to take on an airfoil shape if your promotion is well organized. For most books, sales will climb rapidly, level out, taper off and become steady. Thereafter you will notice bumps in response to seasonal changes or when your advertising or promotional work is successful. The big initial jump is due to your pre-publication publicity.

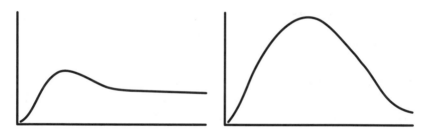

Your sales chart   Typical big firm's sales chart

The big New York publishers market books in the same way Hollywood sells a motion picture. They throw it out on the market to see if anyone likes it. If it gets a response, they dump in a lot of promotional money. Then they push it for a couple of months. When the interest cools, they bring out another product and start all over. As a small publisher, it makes more sense to market your book like breakfast food or soap. Develop your product, pour on the promotion, carve a niche in the market and then continue to sell at the same level for years. This can be done with a nonfiction book which is revised at each printing.

"Best-sellers" are only a name, a myth. This is not like a gold record in the music industry or another service to the trade, run by Bowker. National best-seller lists (there are several, and they do not often agree) are assembled from certain bookstore and other sales reports. Even if you move a million books via mail order distribution, you won't make a best-seller list. On the other hand, you may calculate that your book is the best-selling book in its field, and there is no reason you can't mention this in your advertising. For example, *Parachuting Manual with Log* is the best-selling skydiving book of all time.

Promotion is up to you. Whether you self-publish or go with a large publisher, *the author* must do the promotion. (Large New York) publishers do not promote books. One of the major problems in traditional publishing is that the author assumes the publisher will take care of all the promotion. Publishers do not do much promoting, and by the time the author figures this out, the book is "not new," making any promotional efforts too late. The media does not pay attention to old books. Many publishers will welcome active promotional participation from their authors. They want to sell the book as much as you do. The author can start by searching for mailing lists, sending for ad rate cards and drafting news releases (more on these later). There is a lot to learn from this chapter even if you aren't self-publishing.

Bookstores make your book available, but they do not promote it. These outlets provide availability, but you must encourage people to go into the stores. If your book is a hot seller, the bookstores will want to carry it. If no one asks for it, the stores will not touch it. You must create the demand.

Key contacts are those people who can help you move the greatest volume of books with the least expenditure of time and money. These contacts must be developed if you

---

The main difference between marketing a book and marketing soap is that a book is a one-shot deal . . . a book usually has only 90 days to make it or it's dead.
— Carole Dolph, Promotional Director,
   Doubleday & Company

are going to promote your book properly. The only difference between you and a professional book publicist is that the professional already has the media contacts. There are many wholesalers, TV people and subsidiary rights buyers who are just waiting to "discover" you and your book. While most are very busy, they want you; that is what their job is all about. You will meet a great number of nice, helpful people, but only a few "key" contacts will do you a great amount of good. What you have to do is to locate and then carefully cultivate them. Some of the people will be listed in *Literary Market Place* and other directories available at your library. For others, you may have to call the company and ask for the name of the "buyer," etc. Tell the company operator who you are and ask who you should properly correspond with. Write or call this contact and field your sales pitch; establish a rapport. Maintain credibility, and remember that they are everyone else's key contact, too. Do not expect them to return calls. Send review copies of your book and follow up in a few days with a telephone call asking, "Have you received it?"

Start files on these key contacts and fill the folders with letters and notes of your telephone conversations. Note the personal likes and dislikes of your contacts, so you can bring them up in future conversations. Treat contacts well, and they will be there to help you with your next book, too.

Address codes. Tracing each order you receive back to a specific promotional effort or paid advertisement provides you with important business intelligence. Without this information, you may be unknowingly spending your energy and money in the wrong places. Waste becomes tragedy when you continue blind promotional spending, because you are not certain which projects are paying off by bringing in book orders. Both your time and money are limited; you must spend them in those places which will bring maximum return. The trick is to add a code to your address.

To code your address, just add an extra letter or number to your street address or P.O. box. Code everything! Every brochure, ad, order blank, press release, directory listing, everything. Then, you will receive only a few orders you cannot trace. Some people will be influenced by your promotion and will seek your book through their library or bookstore. But coding will indicate the source of most of your orders.

List your address as *4759 Walker Street, Suite 712*, or in a classified ad where every word costs, *4759-712 Walker*. Many customers figure out the obvious codes and, knowing they aren't important to the address, leave them off. So, if you are advertising in *Popular Science* in August, 1995, don't use *4759 Walker Street, Dept. PS-8-5*. Use a plain number or a *suite* number; they appear important to the address. Never use a *department* number, which is an obvious code. Careful coding is even more important with news releases and those items not going directly to the general public, because the media are conscious of these codes and often won't repeat them. An address code is of no value to you if it doesn't get used.

List all the places to which you are mailing news releases and other promotional material, and give a short code to each. Letters are good for a start, but there aren't enough of them and some can be confused when rendered in script on an envelope. Avoid "I" and "1," "u" and "v," "G" and "6," "Z" and "2," "0" and"O," and "4" and "H".

Many people ask, "But won't the post office object to all this added information?" The answer is no, as long as the essential addressing information is there so they may easily determine where to direct your mail. On the other hand, you may confuse visiting customers who drive down your street looking for a building tall enough for a *Suite 712*.

If you have more than one title (book) or edition (binding) and are advertising or promoting two or more in the same market, make a notation on each envelope as you process orders, indicating which book was ordered. Then total

Show me a publisher who says you can never tell which book is going to make it and I'll show you a publisher who evaluates manuscripts without considering the market.

up the responses at the end of the month and record them by code letter or number on a ledger sheet. Also enter on the sheet when certain advertising and promotion hit, so you can better visualize the reasons for the results. These tallies aren't hard work and can even be done spread out on the floor in front of the TV set. Or add a field to your order-entry program and record the source of the orders as you enter them.

Where some of your orders come from is terribly revealing. How else would you know, for example, that a mention in a *Changing Times* article brought in 140 orders? Or that most foreign bookstores find you in *Books in Print?* With this information, you will be able to assess what works and where you can most effectively spend your time and money to generate more sales. After a few months you will wonder why address coding wasn't obvious to you from the beginning.

Promotional materials take many forms, and many are already at hand. Think of the ways you can use photocopies of your manuscript, folded and gathered pages, overruns on covers, photocopies of the boards, etc.

Consider combining the jacket of your book with a cover letter and an order blank for a mailing. Another successful and popular promotional piece is to make press kit folders with overruns of the cover. Just ask the printer to print a few hundred extra covers. Then fold them, tuck in your promotional materials and mail them out. The result is an inexpensive yet impressive, professional-looking press kit.

Professional book-promotion services are available for those who haven't the time or desire to do their own work. These professionals can be a great help, especially on your first book when you are just learning the ropes. Book publicists write and place news releases, organize autograph parties and place authors on TV.

Publicity companies usually work on a retainer basis or a per-placement basis. The average monthly retainer is between $2,000 and $4,000. For radio and TV placement they might ask for $1,500 for the first city they serve and $500, plus expenses, for each additional city. In each city, you might do four radio and TV shows each day for two days. If you decide to hire a professional publicist, start early. Do not wait until your pub date, but do not go on the shows until your books are in the stores.

More and more authors who are published by large New York publishers are hiring their own PR firms to promote their books.

Large publishers have their own in-house promotion departments, while *Publishers Weekly* estimates there are close to 200 independent book publicists. Some are listed in the Appendix. More may be found in *Literary Market Place* under "Public Relations Services." Also see Para Publishing's Instant Report *Interviews, How Authors Get on Radio and TV*. See the Appendix.

Testimonials and endorsements. Testimonials sell books because many people feel that there is no greater credibility than a recommendation from a satisfied customer. Testimonials and endorsements will be used in two places: on the back cover of the book and in your sales literature.

— Back cover. Endorsements may be gathered from peer reviewers who read and comment on chapters or your complete manuscript. You want their comments as peer reviewers to double-check your work, and you want their praise to quote, since they must be opinion molders. This means you want people known in the book's field or known to the general public. They should be people with recognizable names or recognizable titles.

Please do not ask Dan Poynter to endorse your book unless it is on publishing or skydiving. His endorsement on other subjects would not be appropriate or valuable.

— Sales literature. You will want to add testimonials and excerpts from your reviews to all your brochures, as well as to your "review and testimonial" sheet. The rev/test

> *Hiring a publicist isn't a vanity; it's a realistic commercial decision.* — Paul Cowan, author of *Mixed Blessings*

sheet is an important piece of your publicity package, in that it indicates that other people like your book. This sheet should be sent to later reviewers, prospective dealers and anyone else you are trying to convince the book is a winner.

You may need endorsements on a particular point, or you may need a variety of endorsements. You do not want all the endorsements to say the same thing, or to be very general, such as *it is a great book*. After someone has reviewed your manuscript, approach them again. Write out an endorsement making a particular point (relating your book to *their* audience), and ask the peer reviewer to look it over and edit it. Say that you need a quote in this area. Editing is much easier than creating, and most people will accept the prompting quickly.

The best way to collect testimonials is to ask for them. It is easier than you think, because people like to see their name in print. As long as your book is good, experts in the field will jump at the chance to be mentioned. If they sell products or consulting, the exposure is valuable to them. Whether due to vanity or possible financial gain, recognizable people want to have their names in print. Do not pay for endorsements; quotes cannot be considered valid if payments are involved.

Shoot high; solicit testimonials from the most important and most recognizable people in your industry or activity.

Unsolicited testimonials will arrive after the book is published. They should be answered and filed for future use.

Your publication date is a place in the future, well after your books are off the press, when your promotion hits and your books are available in the stores. The publication date is a means of focusing attention. The idea is to have the product accessible when public attention peaks in response to your promotion. You want to time book reviews, TV appearances, autograph parties, etc., to hit after bookstore deliveries.

> *Books do not sell themselves. People sell books.*

The publication date has nothing to do with the date your book is published—the day it comes off the press and you have finished books in hand. It is the date you list on the ABI (Advance Book Information) form, but it is not the *day of publication* you list on the copyright form. The publication date is a *fiction* for the benefit of a few big, important pre-publication review magazines such as *Publishers Weekly*. There is nothing to stop you from selling or shipping books. Sometimes entire print runs are sold out prior to the publication date.

After your publication date has passed, remove mention of it from your review slip, news release, etc. There is no need to remind the media that your book is no longer new. Let them focus on the issue and the quality of the book.

The big, important pre-publication reviewers need 12 to 16 weeks lead time, so you will have to pick a publication date at least four months after the books are scheduled to roll off the press. *Publishers Weekly* and the other *wholesale trade* review magazines need this time to evaluate your book, assign it to a reviewer, write the review and get it into print for the benefit of the stores. Monthly and bimonthly magazines such as *The Kirkus Reviews* need even more lead time. The stores, in turn, need time to order the book and receive it into stock so it will be available to the public on or before your publication date. When planning your publication date, remember that book rate shipping can take three weeks from coast to coast.

Newspapers have shorter lead times than magazines. Since they are dailies or weeklies, they require books just a few weeks prior to the publication date.

Production is always subject to delay, so it is recommended that for your first book, and until you learn the problems exacted by the printing trade, you wait until the book is off the press before you set your publication date.

> *There is no way anything you send to PW can be too early.*
> — John Baker, Editor-in-Chief, *Publishers Weekly*

If you have achieved sufficient pre-publication momentum, you should make a significant amount of sales before the printing bill arrives. It is a matter of planning, scheduling, timing and work. The big publishers expend 90% of their promotional effort by the publication date. You, of course, will keep up the pressure.

The best publication dates are probably in the first quarter of the year. Most of the big publishers aim for October and November to take advantage of the Christmas gift-buying season. Avoiding the last quarter of the year will decrease your competition for publicity. But get your book to market; never hold it back for a better release date. Sell fresh information.

Some publishers will tie their publication date to a significant date in order to hitch on to publicity naturally occurring on that date. For example, if you have a book on Spike Jones, you might want to schedule your publication date for his birthday. If your book is on an aspect of World War II, you might tie in to D-Day. People will be thinking about the war on this date, so your book will benefit from the memorial publicity. If you know your book and its subject area well, finding a date to link to should be easy. If you need help, check *Chase's Annual Events* and Beam's *Directory of International Tourist Events*.

It is always smart to take advantage of a prime selling season. A book on a summer sport should come out in early spring, when people are making plans for the summer, but not in summer when they are outside and not reading. A book on skiing should come out in the fall.

The ship date is the month your book arrives from the printer and will be available to your distributor and dealers. It is three to four months prior to the pub date.

Book reviews sell books. They are the least expensive and most effective promotion you can possibly do for your book. Considering the cost of producing the book, promotional materials, mailing package and postage, each promotional package usually costs less than $3 as it goes out the door. That means you can send review copies to over 300 appropriate magazines for less than $900. If you are writing on a subject of interest to business people, your book should be of interest to over 1,200 business-oriented magazines, newsletters and newspaper columns in the U.S. Unfortunately, most large New York publishers are very cheap with review copies—sending out less than 50. Reviews are not difficult to get, while they cost you very little in time and money.

There are two major types of book review media: *pre-publication date* or *wholesale reviews* and *post-publication date* or *retail reviews*. They cater to separate markets, and the approach to each is different. In addition, there are early reviews and continuing reviews. Book review order and breakdown look like this:

1. Pre-publication date reviews aimed at the wholesale market.
2. Early reviews, copyright and directory listings.
3. Post-publication date reviews aimed at the retail market. These include:
   a. The sure bets; those that *will probably* review the book.
   b. The rest; those that *might possibly* review the book.
4. Continuing review program.

— **Pre-publication reviews** are directed toward the industry. Certain magazines will review your book prior to publication so that the bookstores and libraries will have the opportunity to stock it before patrons start asking for it. Since over 100 new titles are published for each day the stores are open, there is no way a store can stock every book. In fact, booksellers can't even spend the time to evaluate them all. Consequently, many book dealers and librarians depend on the concise summaries in industry review magazines when making their purchasing choices. Pre-publication reviews are directed at the trade and should not be confused with the regular book reviews aimed at the ultimate consumer/reader. Good reviews in the pre-publication review magazines will bring you more good reviews in other publications later.

Galleys may be the same as the laser output you sent to your printer, but you stand a much better chance of review if the pages are perfect-bound with a plain cover. Pre-publication reviewers are used to receiving bound galleys in a book-sized format. If you send a *finished* book to a pre-publication reviewer, it will not be reviewed, because it is obviously not "pre-publication." For instructions on preparing galleys or *Cranes*, see the Special Report titled *Book Reviews*. See the Appendix.

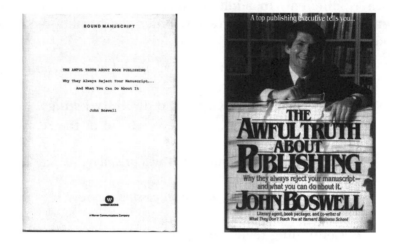

Bound galley and finished book

Three to four months prior to your publication date, send bound galleys with a cover letter and a news release to the following pre-publication reviewers:

1. *Publishers Weekly*, Forecasts, 249 West 17th Street, New York, NY 10011, Tel: (212) 463-6758; Fax: (212) 463-6631. *PW* is directed at the book trade (bookstores, libraries and publishers). A good re-

If your book fails to sell, you don't know your market.

view here will result in many bookstore orders; most will come through wholesalers. *Publishers Weekly* gives priority to books with broad general appeal. They review new books only, no reprints, reissues or new editions. Send galleys between 12 and 16 weeks of your publication date. Circulation 38,000. Contact PW for their *Guidelines for Submission,* and see the submission information on the first page of the Forecasts section in each issue.

2. *Library Journal,* Book Review Editor, 249 West 17th Street, New York, NY 10011, Tel: (212) 463-6819; Fax: (212) 463-6734. *LJ* is a magazine directed to general public librarians. They review 4,500 books each year, of the 30,000 received, specifically to assess their value to the library market. For many nonfiction books, a good review in *Library Journal* will sell over 1,000 copies. A rave review on a high demand topic may move 5,000. Most of these library orders will come through a library wholesaler, and some 80% of these through Baker & Taylor. Therefore, it is important to let the wholesalers know about your book, too. LJ will review from galleys or the finished book. Circulation: 28,000.

3. *Kirkus Reviews,* Library Advance Information Service, 200 Park Avenue South, New York, NY 10003, Tel: (212) 777-4554; Fax: (212) 979-1352. *Kirkus Reviews* is a book review magazine directed toward libraries and bookstores. They review most any fiction and nonfiction except poetry, mass-market paperbacks and children's books for toddlers. *Kirkus* likes to see galleys three to four

---

Book reviewing is one of the few activities in the world that could be said to depend largely on love.
— Jack Beatty, Literary Editor, *New Republic*

months prior to publication of the book. Circulation is about 5,400.

4. ALA *Booklist*, Up Front, Advance Reviews, 50 East Huron Street, Chicago, IL 60611, Tel: (312) 944-6780; Fax: (312) 337-6787. *Booklist* reviews books for small and medium-sized public libraries. They review fiction, nonfiction, reference, young adult and children's books. This does not include textbooks, workbooks, pamphlets or coloring materials. Send galleys or finished books. Circulation is 31,500.

5. *The New York Times Book Review*, 229 West 43rd Street, New York, NY 10036, Tel: (212) 556-1234; Fax: (212) 556-7088. *The New York Times* is one of the most prestigious of review publications. *Times* reviews are also syndicated, so a review there may appear in papers throughout the country. The *Times* does not review very technical, specialized or juvenile books. Send galleys and then send books when printed. Circulation is 1,600,000.

6. *The Los Angeles Times Magazine*, Linden Gross, Times Mirror Square, Los Angeles, CA 90053, Tel: (213) 237-7811; Tel: (213) 237-5000; Fax: (213) 237-4712. *Times* editors look for books which are of general interest to their newspaper readers. Circulation: 1,100,000 daily, 1,300,000 Sunday.

7. Quality Books, Inc., New Title Acquisitions, 1003 W. Pines Road, Oregon, IL 61061, Tel: (815) 732-4450; Fax: (815) 732-4499. Quality is a distributor of small press titles to libraries. They want to know about your book early.

The primary book review medium in the United States for popular trade books is The New York Times.
— Nat Bodian

8. **Major book clubs.** Send bound galleys to the major clubs, such as Book-Of-The-Month and Literary Guild and those specializing in the book's field. See *Literary Market Place* for a list of book clubs.

9. **Presentation copies to opinion molders.** The best way to get sales moving is to get the book talked about by the right people. These may amount to just a very few people to hundreds. Sometimes the publisher uses these special bound galleys to get the public talking about the book. Many people feel receiving an advance bound galley is much more impressive than receiving the actual book. Some opinion molders should get bound galleys, while others should receive the finished product.

— **Early reviews, copyright and listings.** In anticipation of your new book coming off the press, address shipping bags to those places listed below and stuff them, as appropriate, with: cover letter, review slips, photocopied Advance Book Information form, and a 4" x 6" or larger black-and-white photograph of the book's cover. Stuff in brochures, copies of early reviews and other materials to convince reviewers the book has been accepted by others. Do not skimp here. Then when the truck arrives from the printer, stuff the books into the bags and ship them off.

Note what is said about each of the addressees below, as some may not be appropriate to your book. If yours is an adult scientific text, do not bother to send it to the *Horn Book Magazine*, which reviews children's books.

"F&G's" are the folded and gathered signatures of the printed book ready for binding. F&G's used to be sent to the publisher for approval prior to binding the print run. Bound galleys are F&G's with a generic perfect-bound cover.

1. One copy to *Publishers Weekly*, Attn: Weekly Record, 249 West 17th Street, New York, NY 10011, Tel: (212) 463-6758; Fax: (212) 463-6631. You should have sent bound galleys to *PW* some months earlier. This is a confirmation copy to show the book has been published.

2. One copy to *Library Journal*, Barbara Hoffert, 249 West 17th Street, New York, NY 10011, Tel: (212) 463-6819; Fax: (212) 463-6734. Again, you should have sent bound galleys some months earlier. This is a confirmation copy to show the book has been published.

3. Two copies to *School Library Journal*, Attn: Trevelyn Jones, 247 West 17th Street, New York, NY 10011, Tel: (212) 463-6759, Fax: (212) 463-6734. *SLJ* prints 2,500 reviews annually by school and public librarians of new books for children and young adults. They will consider for review any book appropriate to school library use. This monthly (except June and July) has a circulation of 43,000.

4. One copy to *Choice*, Attn: Patricia Sabosik, 100 Riverview Center, Middletown, CT 06457, Tel: (203) 347-6933; Fax: (203) 346-8586. *Choice* is a publication of the Association of College and Research Libraries, a division of the American Library Association. *Choice* reviews 6,600 books annually for the $300 million academic library market: high school, college and special libraries. Monthly except August. Circulation: 4,800.

5. Two copies to ALA *Booklist*, American Library Association, 50 East Huron Street, Chicago, IL 60611, Tel: (312) 944-6780, (800) 545-2433; Fax: (312) 337-6787. You should have sent bound galleys to *Booklist* some months earlier.

6. One copy to *Kirkus Reviews*, 200 Park Avenue South, New York, NY 10003, Tel: (212) 777-4554; Fax: (212) 979-1352. You should have sent bound galleys to *Kirkus* some months earlier.

7. One copy to the *Horn Book Magazine*, Attn: Anita Silvey, Park Square Building, 11 Beacon Street, Suite 1000, Boston, MA 02108, Tel: (617) 227-1555, (800) 325-1170; Fax: (617) 523-0299. *Horn* reviews about 420 books each year for children and young adults. It is published bimonthly and has a circulation of 24,000.

8. One copy to *Hungry Mind Book Review*, Bart Schneider, 1648 Grand Avenue, St. Paul, MN 55105, Tel: (612) 699-0587; Fax: (612) 699-0978.

9. One copy to *KLIATT Young Adult Paperback Book Guide*, Paula Rohrlick, 33 Bay State Road, Wellesley, MA 02181, Tel: (617) 237-7577. *KLI-ATT* annually reviews some 1,600 softcover books for young adults. The magazine is bimonthly and has a circulation of 2,300.

10. One copy to *Small Press Magazine*, The Jenkins Group, 121 East Front Street, #4A, Traverse City, MI 49684. Tel: (616) 933-0445; Fax: (616) 933-0448. Bimonthly, *Small Press* reviews 75-100 titles every issue. Circulation: 7,000.

11. One copy to *Small Press Review*, Attn: Len Fulton, P.O. Box 100-P, Paradise, CA 95967, Tel: (916) 877-6110, (800) 477-6110; Fax: (916) 877-0222. This monthly publication has a circulation of 3,500 and specializes in fiction and poetry.

12. One copy to the *Small Press Book Review*, Attn: Henry Berry, P.O. Box 176, Southport, CT 06490, Tel: (203) 268-4878. Books are selected for review not only for merit in their respective fields but for their standard of writing, editing, design

and production. Bimonthly with a circulation of 2,000.

13. One copy to *Belle Lettres*, Janet Mullaney, 11151 Captain's Walk Ct., North Potomac, MD 20878, Tel: (301) 294-0278; Fax (301) 294-0023. This quarterly, with a circulation of 5,000, reviews books by women.

14. One copy to the *New York Review of Books*, Attn: Barbara Epstein, 250 West 57th Street, New York, NY 10107-0001, Tel: (212) 757-8070; Fax: (212) 333-5374. This biweekly (except January, July, August and September when it is monthly) magazine publishes reviews, prints excerpts and buys serial rights. They review 400 books each year, and the circulation is 130,000.

15. One copy to Baker & Taylor, Eleanor Fanicase, Publishers Services, P.O. Box 6920, Bridgewater, NJ 08807-0920, Tel: (908) 218-3803, (908) 218-0400; Fax: (908) 722-7420. Enclose your brochure and a photocopy of the Advanced Book Information (ABI) form.

16. One copy to *Rave Reviews,* Marc Cerasini, 163 Joralemon Street, Brooklyn Heights, NY 11201, Tel: (718) 237-1097. *Rave Reviews* is a bimonthly aimed at consumers and focuses on nonfiction best sellers and all genres of fiction except westerns. Over 100 reviews are printed in each edition.

17. One copy to the *San Francisco Review of Books,* Donald Paul, 2909 McClure Street, Oakland, CA 94609. This quarterly specializes in books published in the West and reviews 120 books per year. Circulation is 7,500.

18. One copy to *The New York Times*, Attn: Daily Book Review Section, 229 West 43rd Street, New York,

NY 10036, Tel: (212) 556-1234; Fax: (212) 556-7088.

19. One copy to *The New York Times* Magazine, 229 West 43rd Street, New York, NY 10036, Tel: (212) 556-1234; Fax: (212) 556-7088.

20. One copy to *Voice Literary Supplement, The Village Voice*, Ms. M. Mark, 36 Cooper Square, New York, NY 10003, Tel: (212) 475-3300; Fax: (212) 475-8846. They review 500 books each year in ten issues. Circulation is 180,000.

21. One copy to *The Washington Post*, Nina King, Book World, 1150 15th Street NW, Washington, DC 20071, Tel: (202) 334-7882, (202) 334-6000, (202) 334-4260; Fax: (202) 334-5669. Circulation: 780,000 daily, 1,100,000 Sunday. The *Post* reviews about 2,000 general fiction and nonfiction books each year. A favorable review in *The New York Times* or the *Washington Post* tends to stimulate good reviews in the book sections of smaller newspapers.

22. One copy to Ingram Book Company, GreenLight Program, P.O. Box 3006, La Vergne, TN 37086. The book must not be marked or identified as a promotional copy. Enclose your brochure and discount schedule. (A higher discount on single orders will allow them to give stores a discount, which will increase sales.)

23. One copy to *The San Francisco Chronicle*, Attn: Patricia Holt, Book Editor, 901 Mission Street, San Francisco, CA 94103, Tel: (415) 777-1111, (415) 777-7042; Fax: (415) 957-8737. Holt covers about ten of the 100 books she receives each week. Like most newspaper editors, she looks for books of interest to her local readers. Circulation: 570,000 daily, 715,000 Sunday.

24. One copy to *USA Today*, Robert Wilson, Book Editor, 1000 Wilson Blvd., Arlington, VA 22229, Tel: (703) 276-3400, (202) 872-8329, (800) 872-8632, (800) 368-3024; Fax: (703) 247-3196. This daily national newspaper prints reviews every Friday and other times under special subject areas such as sports, money, lifestyle, or art and entertainment. Circulation: 1.9 million.

25. One copy to *New York Newsday*, Jack Schwartz, Two Park Avenue, New York, NY 10016, Tel: (212) 725-3600; Fax: (212) 696-0487. *Newsday* reviews general-interest books such as fiction, history, politics, biographies and poetry. They do not review how-to books. Send books to the appropriate departmental editor. Circulation: 800,000 daily, 950,000 Sunday.

26. One copy to Gale Research Co., Attn: *Contemporary Authors*, 835 Penobscot Building, Detroit, MI 48226-4094, Tel: (313) 961-2242, (800) 877-GALE; Fax: (313) 961-6083. *Contemporary Authors* will not list you in their directory if they think your books are self-published.

27. One copy to H.W. Wilson Company, Attn: Nancy Wong, *Cumulative Book Index*, 950 University Avenue, Bronx, NY 10452, Tel: (718) 588-8400, (800) 367-6770; Fax: (718) 538-2716. Books must have at least 100 pages and a print run of at least 500 copies. For a description of services offered by the H.W. Wilson Company, see Chapter Five of *The Self-Publishing Manual*.

28. One copy to the Baker & Taylor Company, Academic Library Services Selection Department, P.O. Box 6920, Bridgewater, NJ 08807-0920, Tel: (908) 218-0400, Fax: (908) 722-7420 for their Current Books for Academic Libraries plan. Enclose a photocopy of the Advance Book Information (ABI) form.

29. One copy to Dan Poynter, P.O. Box 8206, Santa Barbara, CA 93118-8206, autographed. Yes, we receive around 20 books each week. That is why *The Self-Publishing Manual* has been called "the book that has launched a thousand books" (actually many more). All books are acknowledged.

30. One copy to The Library of Congress, Exchange and Gift Division, Gift Section, Washington, DC 20540.

31. Two copies to Register of Copyrights, Library of Congress, Washington, DC 20559, for copyright registration, along with your check for $20 and copyright form TX. See Chapter Five.

32. One copy for Library of Congress cataloging, CIP Office, Library of Congress, Washington, DC 20559, if you are in the CIP program. Once you have published three books, you are eligible to participate in the CIP program and receive library cataloging data for printing on your copyright page. See *Publishing Forms* and Chapter Five of *The Self-Publishing Manual*. The Cataloging in Publication Office supplies postpaid mailing labels once you have been admitted to the CIP program.

33. One copy to LC Acquisitions and Processing, along with your brochure and dealer discount schedule, Library of Congress, Attn: Jane Collins, Acquisitions and Processing Division, Crystal Mall Annex, Washington, DC 20540.

34. Send one copy to each of the 8 to 10 major wholesalers. See Chapter Eight and the Appendix.

35. Send one copy to each of the 6 to 10 most important opinion molders in your field. If these people talk up your book, you will be off to a good start. Autograph the books.

36. One copy to *New Pages*, Casey Hill, P.O. Box 438, Grand Blanc, MI 48439, Tel: (313) 743-8055; Fax: (313) 743-2730. This quarterly reviews 300 books per year. Circulation is 5,000.

37. One copy to *Pacific Publisher Review*, Tony D'Arpino, 1164 Bishop Street, #124, Honolulu, HI 96813, Tel: (808) 488-6402. This quarterly has a circulation of 3,000.

38. One copy to the *Los Angeles Times Book Review*, Jack Miles, Times Mirror Square, Los Angeles, CA 90053, Tel: (213) 237-5000; Fax: (213) 237-4712.

39. One copy to *John Barkham Reviews*, John Barkham, 27 East 65th Street, New York, NY 10027, Tel: (212) 879-9705. They review 600 adult and 200 juvenile books annually for 35 newspapers in the U.S.

40. One copy to Feature News Service, Cozen P. Bantling, 2330 South Brentwood Blvd., St. Louis, MO 63144-2096, Tel: (314) 961-9828; Fax: (314) 961-9828. Reviews books for 87 weekly papers.

41. One copy to Pacific Coast Press Bureau, Randy Reid, 15581 Product Lane, #C-4, Huntington Beach, CA 92649. Sends reviews to 260 newspapers, magazines and radio shows.

42. One copy to *Rainbo Electronic Reviews*, Maggie Ramirez, 8 Duran Court, Pacifica, CA 94044, Tel: (415) 359-0221. Reviews 300 books annually and publishes them on GEnie on-line service.

43. One copy to *American Book Review*, Donald Laing, Publications Center, Box 494, University of Colorado, Boulder, CO 80309, Tel: (303) 492-8947. This bimonthly, with a circulation of 15,000, reviews 240 books each year.

44. One copy to *Bookwatch*, Diane C. Donovan, 12424 Mill St., Petaluma, CA 94952-9728, Tel: (415)

587-7009. This monthly, with a circulation of 50,000, reviews 800 books each year.

45. One copy to Coast Book Review Service, Don Cannon, P.O. Box 4174, Fullerton, CA 92634, Tel: (714) 990-0432. Reviews are sent to 125 daily and weekly newspapers.

46. One copy to Patrician Productions, Victor Kassery, 145 West 58th Street, New York, NY 10019, Tel: (212) 265-5612. Some 500 books are reviewed annually for radio and TV.

47. One copy to *Reference and Research Book News*, Jane Erskine, 5600 NE Hassalo Street, Portland, OR 97213, Tel: (503) 281-9230; Fax: (503) 284-8859. This bimonthly, with a circulation of 1,700, reviews some 600 books per issue.

48. One copy to *Reference Book Review*, Cameron Northouse, P.O. Box 190954, Dallas, TX 75219, Tel: (214) 690-5882. This semiannual has a circulation of 1,000 and reviews some 200 books per year.

49. One copy to *Chicago Tribune Books*, Larry Kart, 435 North Michigan Avenue, #400, Chicago, IL 60611-4022, Tel: (312) 222-3232.

These early review copies must be sent out as soon as the truck arrives from the printer. Reviewers like *new* books, and books are dated, so it is easy to tell when they are not new. Equally important, most of your initial sales will come from these reviews, so if you do not get moving with your review copy program, that inventory will not move out. Meanwhile, the dated books are getting older every day.

— *Reviews to the ultimate consumer.* Now that the pre-publication and early review packages are out, it is time to get to the *retail* reviewers. These are the rest of the book review magazines, the rest of the newspapers with book review columns, free-lance book reviewers, radio and TV stations with talk shows and book programs and, last but not least, periodicals which cater to the book's field.

It would be very expensive and terribly inefficient to send review copies to every reviewer, and yet a lot of publishers do this. Many of the larger publishers automate their review book process. The result of taking the human touch out of the loop is that some reviewers get more than one package, while others receive the types of books they do not review. Reviewers who request a specific title are often ignored by big publishers, because the promotion people are currently concentrating on a new line of books. Smaller publishers tend to be smart enough to send out a requested title, knowing there is a very good chance of its being reviewed.

Since book reviews are very effective, while review copies are very inexpensive, it makes sense to spend more time and effort on reviews than on most other forms of promotion or paid advertising. For most books, it is not unusual to send out 300 to 500 review copies. This may seem like a lot, as many publishers circulate less than 50, but it is a sound investment. First, the complete review package will probably cost you on the order of $3 for the book, promotional material, shipping bag and postage. Several inches of space in magazines, major and minor, are extremely valuable. And this is editorial copy, far more credible than advertising puffery. For example, 94% of the librarians rely on reviews they read in *Library Journal*, while only 35% believe the ads.

If only 30% of the magazines review your book, you are way ahead on your investment. Considering that reviews return so much on their investment, it is wise to follow these two simple rules: 1. Do not be stingy with review copies, but do not waste your money, either; 2. When in doubt, ship it out.

There are different kinds of reviews. A *summary* review relates the contents of the work without issuing an opinion on its value. These reviews help potential readers select books for their particular needs. An *evaluative* review decides whether the author has covered the topic and compares the book with similar works. It usually ends with a favorable or unfavorable recommendation.

Your book is a product of yourself. You poured your time, heart and soul into it. But just because you were interested enough to take the time to write it doesn't mean a reviewer will be interested enough to take the time to read it all. A book critic will read your book, but a book reviewer will probably only check the front matter. Some reviewers write up 10 to 15 books a week. Most of the reviewer's work will come from your news release and other enclosures. Make them good.

It helps to understand the lot of the editor and/or reviewer. Whether they are full-time or free-lance, they have one thing in common: They are very busy. Neither time nor room are available to review all the books that come in, and there just aren't enough book review columns to go around. Even the prestigious and prolific Sunday supplement of *The New York Times* can only cover about 10% of the books received. All books are not assigned; most reviewers select the ones they want to review. You can't change the situation, so you might as well understand and take advantage of it.

A few years ago, this author was dropping off a load of books at the loading dock around back of the post office in Santa Barbara. He saw a young man (not in a postal uniform) with a cart full of packages over near the dumpster, and his curiosity mounted. As he watched, the man ripped open the cartons, took out what appeared to be books and placed them in a large carton. Then he threw the wrappers in the trash. Unable to stand it any longer, he approached the man and asked if these were *lost-in-the-mail* books. Turns out the packages were for Los Angeles book critic Robert Kirsch. This gigantic load of books was being received at his home address (imagine what showed up at work), and he not only didn't have time to pick up the books himself, he didn't have room for the wrappers. There is a second lesson here, too: Much of the material you ship with review copies is likely to become separated from the books.

Ruth Coughlin of *The Detroit News* says, "I arrive at my office each Monday morning to find 200 books in unopened mailing envelopes stacked outside my door." Alice Digilio of *The Washington Post* says, "We have somebody here 20 hours a week whose only job is to tear open book packages."

If your book has special-area appeal, you can greatly increase your chances for review by submitting your book to the special publications reaching that particular group. For example, if your book is on hang gliding, you would send review copies to *Hang Gliding* magazine and *Glider Rider*. Then you would consider every aviation, outdoor, sport, recreation, do-it-yourself, teen, men's, etc., magazines you could find. There are some 60,000 magazines being printed in the U.S. today (and a lot more foreign). There must be some reaching the groups you want.

Be prepared for delays with the smaller associations' publications. They want to review your book, but they have certain staff and budget limitations. Usually they rely on outside free help for book reviews. Typically, the editor will only scan a book before sending it off to an appropriate expert requesting him or her to review it. Often, the reviewer is very busy, too.

Selecting periodicals. For lists of appropriate media, visit the reference desk of a large public library and ask to see the periodical directories; there are at least two for magazines, two for newsletters and several for newspaper columns. (Stop by the bank first for a roll of dimes for the copy machine.) Copy just the pages you need and bring them home to enter the addresses of the periodicals into your computer; you will use these addresses over and over again. Some of the periodicals you will consult are:

1. *Standard Periodical Directory* (thousands of magazines)
2. *Ulrich's International Periodical Directory* (many U.S. and foreign periodicals)
3. Hudson's *Newsletters Directory*
4. Gale's *Newsletters in Print*
5. *Literary Market Place* (with many good lists such as book review syndicates, book review periodicals, book columnists, cable networks, radio and TV stations with book programs, book clubs, news services and newspapers with book sections)
6. *Bacon's Publicity Checker*

7. Gebbie's *All-in-One Directory*

8. *Editor and Publisher's International Yearbook* (the key radio and TV personnel)

9. *Working Press of the Nation* (lists media people at newspapers, magazines, radio, television, syndicated columnists, etc.)

10. *Directory of Literary Magazines* by the Council of Literary Magazines & Presses, 154 Christopher Street, #3-C, New York, NY 10014

11. *Writer's Market* (directed at writers in search of magazine publishers)

12. *Encyclopedia of Associations* directory (lists 18,000 special-interest trade and professional organizations)

13. *National Trade and Professional Associations* (6,000 associations, unions and societies)

14. *The Pocket Guide* (lists major trade, business and general interest magazines and newspapers. 33 pages. Free from Media Distribution Service (MDS), 307 West 36th Street, New York, NY 10018)

Address review books to a *person* or your book may get ripped off by someone else on the staff. When this happens, you not only waste a book, you lose out on a review. Also address review books to the *position*, not just the name, of the editor or reporter. If your recipient is on vacation, your mailing might be pigeonholed for weeks—and no longer considered news once rediscovered upon his or her return. If you cannot find the editor's name in one of the above-listed references, call and ask, or address the package to *The Review Editor*.

Depending on your subject, you may find 400 to 500 potential reviewers for your book. Don't be surprised if you come up with 600. On the other hand, if the topic is very specialized, the print run is short, and the cover price is high, you may find there are only a few dozen interested and qualified potential reviewers. The best rule is to contact everyone who might possibly review the book. Divide the periodicals into two groups:

1. The good bets: those that *will probably* review the book; and

2. The rest: those that *might possibly* review the book.

Some magazines will be perfect matches for your subject, and some will have such a large circulation that they cannot be ignored. Send books to the group of good bets, but send only the literature and a reply postcard to most of the rest. When the cards come back, send out the books and the literature. You are fishing at this point; you won't hook a fish with every cast, but you have narrowed your odds with the postcards.

Para Publishing

P.O. Box 8206, Santa Barbara, CA 93118-8206 USA
Telephone: (805) 968-7277   Fax: (805) 968-1379

Dear Book Reviewer:

Are any of your readers frustrated authors? How would you like to help them, by revealing the secrets of breaking into print?

The Self-Publishing Manual has just been published in an all-new, expanded fifth edition. Known as the book that has launched a thousand books, it brings publishing within the reach of nearly everyone.

Help all your readers, who have a book inside them, by **returning the enclosed post card** today. You might encourage a future Zane Grey, Mary Baker Eddy, Whitman, Poe, Thoreau, Shaw, Paine, Kipling, Sandburg or Twain (all self-published.)

Sincerely,

PARA PUBLISHING

Daniel F. Poynter
Publisher

DFP/ms

Cover letter and request postcard

REVIEW BOOK REQUEST

I would like to receive a review/examination copy of:

Book title: _____

PLEASE SEND THE BOOK(S) TO:

Name of publication or broadcast station: _____
Name of reviewer: _____
Full job title: _____
Mailing Address: _____
_____ Zip: _____
Circulation: _____ Frequency: _____ Av. No. of Pages: _____
Brief description of publication: _____

Audience profile: _____
Comments (optional): _____

Go through the directories and make up lists of newspapers, weekly magazines, review journals and specialized periodicals. Many smaller newspapers do not have reviewers on their staffs; they use syndicated columns. Be sure to send review copies to all syndicated reviewers.

If you do not have time to go through the above-mentioned educational exercise of compiling your own lists, some may be rented—ready to go. Paralists (P.O. Box 8206, Santa Barbara, CA 93118-8206) maintains several up-to-date lists. Write for current list counts and prices.

Reviewer addresses should be entered into the computer so they can be reproduced for use again. A simple mailing list program will do the job, but a data base program such as dBASE IV will allow much more flexibility. Add a code to each record in the address file to indicate what type of review publication it is (e.g., aviation magazines, parachuting magazines, ballooning magazines, in-flight magazines, soaring magazines, etc.). The narrower your classifications, the more valuable your lists.

Most label programs will allow you to print one-across pressure-sensitive labels or four-across Cheshire labels. The pressure-sensitive labels are handy for smaller in-house mailings, while you will want to use the plain-paper Cheshire for the larger mailing-house mailings.

The review package sent to reviewers should include a book, brochure, review slip, sample review/news release, reprints of other reviews, cover letter, reply card and a photograph of the book. Here are the details:

1. **Book.** Do not send a damaged book or *selected second* as some publishers do. You want to put your best foot forward, hoping to get the attention of the reviewer. Pack the book as you normally do so that it will arrive in good condition.

Some reviewers still assume that in real publishing the hardcover edition comes out several months prior to the softcover. If they receive a paperback, they assume the title is old. Today, with the increasing dominance of the *quality* or *trade paperback,* this barrier is beginning to be breached, and many books are being selected for review on their own merits, rather than be sorted by their wrapper. If you are publishing in softcover only, make sure the point is clear in your review package.

2. Brochure. Use the brochure you have drafted for the retail buyer, and make sure it looks professional. There is no need to print a special brochure for the reviewer.

Para Publishing presents for review

Title: *The Self-Publishing Manual*
Author: Dan Poynter
Edition: Eighth, completely revised
Number in print: 95,000
CIP/LC: 94-33200
ISBN: 1-56860-003-8
Pages: 464, 5.5 x 8.5
Price: $19.95
Season: Spring
Publication date: March 1995
Rights:
        Book clubs: Independent Book Club
                Small Press Book Club
                Writer's Digest Book Club
        Condensations: *Publishing Trade*
                Income Opportunities

The book has a new cover, price, ISBN and bar code; more than 50% of the text is new.
As an eighth revised edition, it has the unusual distinction of being **a new book—with a track record.**

A copy of your review to the address below would be appreciated.

Para Publishing
Reviewer Relations Department
P.O. Box 8206-890
Santa Barbara, CA 93118-8206
Tel: (805) 968-7277
Fax: (805) 968-1379

Book review slip

3. Review slip. Many books are sent with book review slips listing vital information, while a lot of other books also have the title, publication date and price rubber-stamped on the inside of the front cover. Most publishers slip the loose sheets into the book. Pasting the book review slip inside the cover will make sure it arrives *with* the book. Some reviewers want the information stamped on for identification in case they lose the book review slip. Review slips may also be made by computer-generating the information on mailing labels and pasting them on the inside front cover or flyleaf of each book.

Book review for *Choices: A Teen Woman's Journal for Self-awareness and Personal Planning*
by Mindy Bingham, Judy Edmondson and Sandy Stryker.

For Immediate Release:

"As a little girl, did you ever wonder what became of Snow White, Cinderella, and Sleeping Beauty after they married their princes and retired to their respective castles?"

And so begins a revolutionary new book, *Choices: A Teen Woman's Journal for Self-awareness and Personal Planning* by Mindy Bingham, Judy Edmondson and Sandy Stryker (Advocacy Press). This refreshing book is a welcome change from the traditional offerings for teenage girls. While the publishing industry continues to produce more and more romance novels for adolescent girls that reinforce the "they-lived-happily-ever-after" Cinderella syndrome, *Choices* gives the message, at a critical time, that the teenage girl has to take charge of her life—that she can't just drift and hope for some Prince Charming who will take all her burdens away.

Example of a sample review

4. Sample review in the form of a news release. Many reviewers use releases verbatim. In fact, it won't hurt to write up two samples, a short one and a long one. See next page.

5. Other reviews. Reviewers are cautious people. They are more apt to review your book if it has been treated favorably in pre-publication reviews by big-name reviewers. One way to convince them your book is worthy of their attention is to include copies of these early reviews. Cut out each review, paste it on a piece of plain paper, and cut out the masthead or title of the magazine and paste it in for source and date identification. Underline the best parts of the review to draw attention to them. Make photocopies for your review kit.

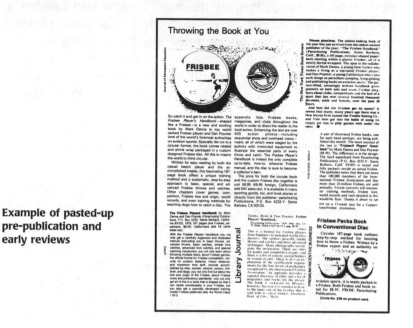

Example of pasted-up pre-publication and early reviews

Take advantage of a good review. Besides being very good for the ego, it can be used to further stimulate your promotion program. You want your wholesalers to know you are promoting the book, so send them a copy. If a review appears in a local newspaper, send copies to the local bookstores. Keep these pasted-up reviews on file and send them out with future review copies, letters to foreign-rights buyers or for use any time you need more promotional material.

6. Cover letter. The cover letter should be short and to the point. If you plead for a review, you will sound as though you need something from them. Make your letter sound as though you are helping the reviewer find something his or her readers will be interested in. Stress benefits to the recipient, not to you.

Mention that you are enclosing a review copy. Suggest an interesting or unique (perhaps local) angle. Introduce the book and its contents. Tell why the book is important to today's reader, and ask for a review.

Some public relations people like to get very personal in review copy mailings. They jot a little personal note to the reviewer, hoping to snow them into thinking they have met before, or that the reviewer may have made some long-forgotten promise at a cocktail party.

7. Reply card. Some publishers like to include a self-addressed reply postcard so reviewers may indicate the response they plan. The reply card is optional. The return rate is not high: Some cards take a long time, and others are not returned at all. Many reviewers just don't know when the review will appear.

It is not necessary to use business reply indicia or a stamp on the postcard. Reviewers in significant periodicals do not buy their own stamps. They throw outgoing mail in the out basket for the mail room.

PLEASE ACKNOWLEDGE

We have received the complimentary review book or galleys you sent of

Book title: _____

☐ We expect to review this book on (date): _____
☐ Please send a photograph of the book
☐ Please send a photograph of the author
☐ We did not find this book suitable for our review.

Name of reviewer: _____
Full job title: _____
Name of publication or broadcast station: _____
Mailing address: _____
_____ Zip: _____
Comments (optional): _____
_____

Review book acknowledgment postcard

8. Photograph. Artwork will get you a lot more space and make the review more attractive—resulting in a higher degree of readership. Enclose a photograph of the book and, if the book is well-illustrated, samples of the interior artwork. Send photos of the book whenever you feel they might be used, and always offer the photos at the end of your news release. A clearly typed, taped-on identifying caption should hang below the photograph. When placing the order for prints, specify that they are *for reproduction*, glossies, and 4" x 6" (or larger) in size. Unless you have a readily recognizable face, send a photograph of the book, not of yourself. Remember what you are selling.

Rubber stamps. Use a rubber stamp to mark review copies *Professional Review Copy, Not For Sale*. Rubber-stamp the *edges* of the pages (side of the book) so that the marking is visible without lifting the cover. It is embarrassing when a marked review copy finds its way back into your for-sale stock. Reviewers often suggest the price, publication date and other important information be rubber-stamped inside the front cover in case the review slip is lost.

Review book rubber stamp

The rubber stamp or pasted slip will not stop the sale of a review book, but it will insure the book will not be returned to you by a bookstore for credit.

In mid-1979, the newspaper and book industries were scandalized when ten newspaper book reviewers were accused of selling review books to the Strand bookstore in New York. Apparently, several bookstores send form letters to reviewers soliciting books. Typically, the stores buy the books at 25% of list price and resell them at 50% of list. One reviewer estimated he received 30,000 review copies in seven years. Many periodicals have a policy of donating review copies philanthropically: to hospitals, charitable bookfairs, foreign libraries, etc.

Certainly the ability to sell review copies may promote the requesting of more books with no intention of considering them for review. There is nothing wrong with a reviewer requesting a book if he or she plans to review it. But it is wrong if they plan to sell the book without first considering it for review.

Review/Testimonial sheet. The "rev/test" sheet lists excerpts from reviews and testimonials along with pertinent printing and rights information.

Read what others are saying about

Parachuting, The Skydiver's Handbook

● *This is only up-to-date basic sport parachuting handbook and it is highly recommended.*--The Next Whole Earth Catalog.

● *For a lesson or just some vicarious thrills, read* Parachuting, The Skydiver's Handbook.--New York Post.

● *A valuable collection of information and a good first look at the sport.*--Library Journal.

● *Dan's strength as a writer lies in his technical descriptions of equipment; these are faultless.*--British Sport Parachutist magazine.

● *This handy volume falls into the "Everything you need to know about..." category and is required reading for everyone who wants to jump out of and aeroplane.*--Flight International.

● *All aspects are covered in a clear and authoritative fashion.*--Air International.

● *Poynter's latest fills the bill of educating while entertaining. He says it well.*--Parachutist magazine.

● *Chapters cover an overview of the sport, detailed discussion of each facet of the first jump, the history of parachuting, and an in-depth study of parachuting emergencies. Other sections discuss specialized jumping and equipment. Appendix contains a glossary and a list of drop zones, books, magazines and films.*--Sporting Goods Business.

● *Well-written, this volume is profusely illustrated with photos and drawings. A useful addition to the public library collection.*--Choice.

● *Dan Poynter has done it again.*--Spotter NewsMagazine.

o - o

● After five revised editions, over 45,000 copies are in print.

● **Selected** by the U.S. Parachute Association, the Canadian Sport Parachuting Association, and other national organizations for sale to their members.

● **Serialized** in *Parachutist* (USA), *Free Fall Kiwi* (New Zealand), *Fritt Fall* (Norway), and *CanPara* (Canada).

● **Mentioned** in *Joint effort, Aviation/Space, SAFE Journal, Flyv* (Denmark), *Soldier of Fortune, Thrill Sports Catalog,* Alaska Flying, Skydiver Magazin (West Germany) and many more.

● **Selected** for transcription for the blind by the Milwaukee Public Library and the Florida Department of Education.

● **Translated** and published in Spanish by Editorial Paraninfo of Madrid.

Parachuting, The Skydiver's Handbook by Dan Poynter. All new, completely revised, fifth edition. 5.5 x 8.5, 400 pages, 260 illustrations. ISBN 0-915516-65-9, LC 88-32405. $19.95. Publication: Spring 1989.

fmi: Para Publishing, P.O. Box 4232, Santa Barbara, CA 93140-4232. (805) 968-7277

Review/Testimonial sheet

Unsolicited testimonials. There is no better promotion than a recommendation from a satisfied customer.

Save all those unsolicited testimonials and nice letters; bank them for future use. When you have ten to twenty of them, photocopy them, cut them apart and arrange their best, most quotable parts in a logical order. Put duplicate praise aside and try to arrange the testimonials so that they flow, tell a story and follow one another. Then either get permission to use their signatures, or paste the testimonials to a sheet of blank paper, omitting the names and addresses of the writers. Start the page off with "What readers are saying about *(name of the book)."* Since all the typewriter and handwriting styles are different, the page will have good credibility.

Approaching other periodicals. Now that you have mailed books to the *good bets*, those periodicals that match your subject and are very likely to review the book, it is time to approach others. Your second list may total 1,000 or more.

Send a cover letter, brochure, news release and a reply card. The reviewers will request a review copy if the book looks as though it might interest their readers. Some will print your release without asking for a book.

A mailing to 1,000 reviewers may bring a response from 200 or so. The mailing and the resulting book shipment will be far less expensive than sending books to the original list of 1,000.

— **Continuing review program.** Your review copy program will not end at the publication date. Requests will come in as other reviewers hear of your book, and you should be on the lookout for new reviewers. For example, keep an eye on the Media section in *Publishers Weekly*.

There were 1,733 daily newspapers in the U.S. at last count; 458 are morning and 1,275 are evening; 783 newspapers publish on Sunday. Only three papers have Sunday book review sections: *The New York Times, The Washington Post* and *The Los Angeles Times*. They were discussed earlier under pre-publication reviews. There are approximately 7,700 weekly newspapers. Then, there are magazines. There are a lot of possibilities.

Three to four months after your initial review copy mailing, hit those sent the cover letter, news release and reply card again. Send them the same package (deleting any reference to the publication date), but this time handwrite across the top of the release: *This book is available for review.* A lot of reviewers will have missed your first mailing, or they may decide to look at your book because they have read of it elsewhere. You will be amazed at the response. A year later, re-slant your release and try this again.

Here are some response numbers: In 1983, 19 publishers joined in a *Books for Review* program. A very attractive brochure offering 29 books was sent to 1,800 reviewers. The participation cost was $46 per book, or about 2.5 cents per contact. Approximately 8% of the reviewers responded by requesting some 700 books. Over 50 requests were received for some of the more popular titles. The publishers were able to approach reviewers inexpensively, while not wasting books or material on reviewers who were not interested. The *Books for Review* program is a good example of how publishers can band together to exploit free publicity while keeping their promotion costs down. *Books For Review* was turned over to the Publishers Marketing Association and is currently being mailed to 3,900 daily and weekly metropolitan newspapers.

Be on the lookout for review possibilities outside the book pages of magazines and newspapers. Depending upon your subject, contact cookbook editors, lifestyle editors, sports page editors, etc. Watch for special sections.

Unsolicited requests. From time to time, you will receive unsolicited requests for review copies. You may wish to look up the periodical for its frequency, circulation and audience match, as well as whether this person is really on the staff or a bona fide stringer. Is the request on credible media letterhead? However, since the review package costs you so little, the better procedure is probably just to respond cordially. Certainly the free publicity a review can provide is worth many times the cost of the book. When in doubt, ship it out.

Press clipping services have people who regularly read all major publications and clip out mentions of their clients. You may subscribe to one of these services (see listings in

Literary Market Place), but it probably is not worth the expense. The clipping services cannot read every periodical; they often send clippings which mention your key word but not you, and you do not need all these clips anyway. Many smaller periodicals will send you copies of their magazine containing the review. Some people enclose a clipping with their order. There will be very few reviews you do not hear about.

Advertising. Never suggest to an editor that you might be willing to advertise in the magazine, as a way of gaining a review. Most editors do not sell advertising—that is the job of the advertising department. Petty bribery will repel most review editors, who view themselves as independent. On the other hand, when the ad sales representative calls it is OK to say that you are *waiting for the review to test the match between your book and the magazine's audience.*

Once you receive a card notifying you a review will appear in a given publication, you may like to advertise in it, too. Some publishers feel this double impact is worth their while, though others do not. Many like to see how the review pulls before investing in an ad. They let the review test the medium, and then they quote the review in the ad. The major advantage of the ad is that it is more likely to have specific ordering information. Since it isn't likely your book will be reviewed twice in the same publication, advertising is the only way to continue contacting the readers.

Bad reviews. Some of your reviews may be negative, and one reason (but not the only reason) is that some reviewers are negative. Some of these critics are frustrated writers who try to bring all other published authors down to their level. They take cheap shots or use the book as a springboard for lofting their own views.

Reviewers tend to be very cautious people. Even a very favorable review will probably contain one negative sentence or paragraph. This is a cover to save the reputation of the reviewer in case the book turns out to be a loser.

In smaller publications aimed at a select target audience, the author will probably know every qualified reviewer.

Skydiving books have to be reviewed by experienced parachutists. In this case, the author may ask a colleague to review the book.

Some reviewers write negative reviews on purpose. In an effort to find a qualified reviewer, the editor will look for someone with a background in a book's subject. Books are sometimes unknowingly assigned to a reviewer who has an ax to grind with the author.

Don't worry about a negative review. Any review is better than no review, because people tend to remember the subject more than the details of the critique. Even a bad review will arouse reader curiosity. Libraries must cover every subject, and acquisition librarians are always searching for something new.

When you quote the negative review, just use the good parts. If there are no good parts, just say "as reviewed in *The Washington Post*" or "find out why *Consumer Reports* hated this book." Do not edit out the bad words so that the review appears to be favorable. According to Brigitte Weeks, editor of *The Washington Post Book World:* "Ellipses are often the enemy of truth." It is flagrant misrepresentation to edit out less-desirable phrases if they change the meaning and intention of the review. Reviewers and editors are writers, too, and most have excellent memories. If you misquote them,

---

There is nothing like a good negative review to sell a book.
— Hugh R. Barbour, bookseller

Many book reviews are mean-spirited. Even if a reviewer likes a book, he or she must find fault and write snide and/or patronizing little asides about the author's character or motives that demonstrate the reviewer's intellectual and moral superiority.
— Author Andrew Greeley in *Publishers Weekly*

they will probably catch you and will certainly remember you when next you send a book for review.

Learn from negative reviews. Perhaps your promotional approach is misleading. Think about changing your news release. Help the reviewers to understand the book. Try to direct their thinking. The same goes for good reviews. Focus on the praise—the parts of the book reviewers like. Emphasize these parts in your news release.

Why reviewers review books. Many reviewers will spend some ten hours reading a book, a couple of days thinking about it, and perhaps six hours writing up the review. Some reviewers are paid a small amount and many do not get paid at all. They get the book and the satisfaction of being on the inside of publishing and/or their area of specialty, expertise or profession. To add insult to injury, the Internal Revenue Service has attempted to tax some reviewers for the value of the books they have received.

Local newspapers, magazines, radio and television almost *have* to cover you, because you and your book are local news. Get out the *Yellow Pages* and make up a list of local media. You will probably find more than you first thought. Send a review package to each periodical, addressed to a particular features editor. They may not have a book review section, but you would rather have a half-page feature on yourself and your book anyway. Follow up in a few days with a telephone call to the most important ones. Next, do the same for local radio and television stations.

If you know a free-lance or staff reviewer personally, send him or her a review copy. Use every possible *in* you might have. Hit all your hometowns, where you live now, where you grew up, where you went to school, all of them.

Someone once remarked that we have the power of life and death over a book. Life perhaps, but not death. We could devote our entire section to loathing the latest Sidney Sheldon, and it would make no difference.
— Stefan Kanfer of *Time* magazine

You may get not only a nice review, but a special feature story as well.

Follow-up calls increase your chances for a review. Don't be a pest, but it is acceptable to call to see *if a book has been received*. You may find your package has not been received or that your book or news release should have gone to another editor.

Acknowledge all reviews with a personal note; praise and thank the reviewer. They will remember you when you send your next book. The easiest way is to photocopy the review and write a short message on it. A small amount of time spent on letters here is an investment in the future. Annotate your computerized list of reviewers to indicate that this reviewer has performed for you.

How to ship. Review copies may be sent to most reviewers via the Postal Service's book rate. If the author lives near any of the reviewers on the list, hand delivery never hurts.

When the *Frisbee Player's Handbook* rolled off the press, Santa Barbara co-author Dan Poynter made up a list of reviewers in ZIP code order. New York co-author Mark Danna made the systematic rounds of reviewers in Manhattan and *threw the book at them*. The unique circular book was brought to their attention, made an impression and was very well reviewed.

If the reviewer requested the book on one of your reply cards or on letterhead, make a photocopy of the card and place it on top of the book. Everyone recognizes and takes an interest in their own handwriting. Seeing their own writing will remind the reviewer the book was requested.

Credit the reviewer. Reviewers like credit for their work, so mention their name as well as that of the publication. For example, end the quote with: "Kevin Gibson, *Parachutist Magazine.*" In fact, if the reviewer really likes the book, he or she will try to provide a few quotable lines, hoping for a mention.

Permission to quote. Reviews are written to be quoted. You do not have to contact the reviewer or periodical for permission. However, in the last few years, a few isolated review publications have begun requesting payment for reprinting their reviews. This is a new development.

Put a lot of effort into reviews. Far less expensive than display advertising, they are the best promotional investment you can make. For more details on setting up your review program, see the Special Report titled *Book Reviews*. See the Appendix.

News releases. Most small publishers receive very little free publicity for their books. This lack of attention is not because of any great conspiracy between the big (New York) publishers and the media; it is simply because the neophytes do not know how to ask for free coverage. News releases are used to announce products, promotions, and events. They accompany galleys and review copies of books and are included in press kits for radio and television stations. Sometimes a release accompanies other promotional or informational material, and sometimes a release is mailed alone.

> *News release* is the modern term for *press release*. Your message will be sent to all forms of media such as radio, television and other opinion molders, not just the print media.

The media are in the news gathering/publishing business; they want to hear from you. Publicity is not expensive advertising; it involves the use of inexpensive news releases. News items receive a much higher degree of readership than advertising, and greater readership leads to more response (sales). News releases generate publicity and invite book reviews. Releases may be used to announce publication of your new book to newspapers, magazines, libraries, radio and TV. In fact, they should be sent to anyone who will listen.

Many of the articles and news items you read were written by the people mentioned in them. Editors may use only one news release in ten, but news releases make up 20% to 25% of the editorial space in many newspapers and magazines. Some of the smaller, more highly targeted publications use an even higher percentage.

Editors would use more outside material if the news releases they received were more interesting. Your challenge is to draft copy that is irresistible to the editor—to come up with interesting information the editor will want to pass on to his or her readers. You want the editor to open your monthly mailings first, while thinking: "I wonder what good material John is sending me today?"

Remember, you are providing a service to editors. As an author-publisher, you are an expert in your field and an information source. You are providing important, timely and interesting information to the editor and his or her readers.

On your first book, while you are still learning about the printing trade and your own schedules are apt to slip, it is probably best to send out your first news release when the manuscript is actually delivered to the printer. When you are working on your next book, you may start sending out the releases earlier. These early releases should contain a more generalized publication date, such as "March, 1996." Later it may be moved, or the specific day may be added. Do not send early releases to newspapers. Publicity is wasted when mailed before your books are in the stores.

Some authors do not like to reveal their project too early, and hold off on their releases. They are afraid someone might pick up on their good idea. But other writers purposely get their releases out very early in the hope of scaring off the competition. Whichever approach you take, someone will call to say, "Don't write it, my book is at the printer now!" "At the printer" usually means they may sit down at their keyboard soon.

The four steps to placing your news releases are:

1. Develop an interesting angle that shows how your book will benefit the reader. You need a hook, an issue.

While publicity misused can be nothing but an ego trip for the author, well used it can be a powerful sales tool. — Al Lind

2. Locate and cultivate the appropriate media contacts.

3. Deliver the information in the proper form.

4. Be persistent and follow up.

News release layout. Give the editors what they want and need; deliver the information in such a way that it is useful and newsworthy. The less rewriting your release requires, the more chance that it will be used. You will draft some releases specifically for distribution to a single publication. Study the publication, imitate the writing style and follow the same article layout. The secrets are to know what the editor considers good news value and to know how to write in good press style.

Word processing programs make news release tailoring easy. Most of your release will remain the same, but you will tailor the headline and lead paragraph to the target audience. For a book on publishing, we would have different pitches for magazines sent to publishers, writers or printers. Just change the headline and lead paragraph and let the machine copy the rest of the previous release.

— Format. The format of the release is standardized. The easiest way to design it is simply to type "NEWS RELEASE" on your own letterhead stationery. The release will look fancier if you have special forms typeset. By using your own stationery, you automatically have the important information, such as company name and address, at the top. Then just type in the release date (*For Use the Week of September 17th*) or (*For Immediate Release*).

Place a contact name with telephone number in the upper right-hand corner. If your name is Greg Godek, the book

---

Releases should, like all writing, be accurate, consistent, clear, concise, persuasive, interesting, and above all, correct in spelling, punctuation, and grammar. (I didn't say this would be easy!) — Rose Adkins, past assistant editor of *Writer's Digest* magazine

(Letterhead)

NEWS RELEASE

For Immediate Release. . .

Contact: Joyce Ready (805) 968-7277

Headline
Type a descriptive, clever and catchy headline in capital letters and center it. Lure the editor to read more. Then space down four lines and get into the body of the release.

Issue or problem
The lead paragraph is designed to invite the largest number of people to read the article. It must have broad appeal; make it interesting. The release should be *issue oriented*; write about the *problem*, not the book. The release should begin by stating the problem and telling why this is an important subject. Make it provocative.

Development
Spend a second paragraph developing the message. Put the most interesting information first to keep the reader reading. Recite the most important items in descending order so that if some are cut from the end, the most important will remain. Provide interesting facts and statistics.

How the book solves the problem
Now move from a *what* orientation to the *how* orientation. It is not necessary to dwell on the book. Anyone who finishes the article will be interested in the book. Then describe the contents of the book; mention it as a resource. Continue with some background on the topic and show why your book is unique, useful and timely. Recite benefits to the reader.

Author
Spend a paragraph on the author and tell why the author is an expert on the subject.

Ordering information
Give the price and mention that the book is available from the publisher as well as the stores. List your address so the reader will know where to send the money. Code your address.

End the release with the newspaper termination sign: *-30-*.

News release outline

One reason the demand for books is constant is that the book-buying public is not static. It is constantly changing. New readers are entering the bookshops all the time, while old readers are going to that big library in the sky. — Max Alth

Para Publishing

P.O. Box 8206, Santa Barbara, CA 93118-8206 USA
Telephone: (805) 968-7277   Fax: (805) 968-1379

For immediate release . . .

Contact Monique Tihanyi (805) 968-7277

Skydiving = A New Way to Fly

Skydiving! Not just falling out of an aircraft in a rapid vertical tumble for thousands of feet, but exhilarating horizontal flying; the closest we humans have ever come to unencumbered bird-like flight.

Skydivers can deflect the air to fly horizontally. In fact, they can achieve an angle of 35 degrees or more from the vertical, or approaching 1:1. This means that on a sixty second skydive from 12,500' providing 10,000' of freefall, a jumper can cover 7,000' of ground, or 1.35 miles.

Skydiving also takes place at controlled vertical speeds between 110 and 190 mph. This is why the *Guinness Book of World Records* awards skydiving the record for the world's fastest non-mechanical sport. Freefalling jumpers spread their flying surfaces (arms and legs) to fly prone like Superman or sweep them back to stand on their heads. Since their weight remains constant but their drag area can be changed, skydivers can go up and down--relative to each other. They pile out of aircraft one-after-the-other and then swoop down to make a formation on the same level.

Today's parachutes are exciting too. Gone are the traditional round canopies which were purely drag devices. The new airfoil-shaped, ram-air inflated wings provide lift and are flown like a glider. They have a 20 mph airspeed, a ten foot per second sink rate and can be flared for tip-toe landings. Whether you want to try another aviation activity or learn more about parachutes, where can you find more information?

News release example (first page)

I never said starting your own publishing company would be easy. I only said it would be worth it.

is authored by Greg Godek and the book is published by Greg Godek Publishing, make your company look a little larger by selecting another (*pen or PR*) name for the contact person.

— **Layout.** Double-space on 8.5" x 11" paper. Some publicists use legal-size paper, which has the advantage of sticking out of a pile of papers—the release is more easily noticed. Begin a third of the page from the top and leave one-inch margins on the sides and bottom. The release may be any length, but one page is usually best. If the release runs more than one page, identify the story with a header in the upper left-hand corner of the second page. Or excerpt a portion and place it in a separate background release or author biography. One way to condense a release to a single page is to use the word processor's ability to change from double space to 1.8- or even 1.5-line spacing. Do not use a staple to bind pages together; use a paper clip. Never type on the back of the sheet.

An alternative format is to set the type one column wide on slick stock so that your piece is camera-ready. This format is useful to smaller publications since they may strip-in your piece without resetting the type. The difficulty is that you must submit several formats, as magazine and newspaper columns are not of uniform width.

More and more news releases are being submitted on disk today. Editors are more likely to use a news release they do not have to retype.

— **Style.** Observe basic journalistic style: Keep your sentences to 23 words or less; *3 p.m.*, not *4:00 P.M.*; commas and periods inside closed quotation marks; no capital letters for anything in the text but initials, first letters of proper names and first words of sentences (exception: TV, not tv); no extra space between paragraphs (double-space, same as the rest of the text); the first mention of the author should include first name, middle initial and last name (subsequent mentions should include last name only). Magazines like book titles in italics, while newspapers place quotation marks around them.

Use the fewest number of words to communicate any thought. Circle all repeated words in a paragraph and select alternates. Cut unnecessary words. Never use a less common word when a familiar one will convey your meaning. Use simple sentences; complex sentences can be hard to read. Do not make judgments. If you say the *book is the most important contribution to literature since the Bible,* the editor will cut it out or trash your release. On the other hand, it does not hurt to quote someone else who says something nice about your book. Proofread and re-proofread!

Take your time and compose a good release. Not all news gatherers do their own work all the time, so your release may appear verbatim in print. It may even be reprinted word for word as a book review.

A release which starts out, "Festival Publications is happy to announce . . . " is self-serving. There is a much better chance your release will be used if the headline begins, "Breakthrough found in . . . ." The release is being written for the readers of the periodical; it isn't an announcement for your company picnic. When drafting a news release for a specific section, such as *Publishers Weekly's* "Back to Press" column, write it in the same format, no more and no less. Do not make the editors rewrite the release; they may "round-file" it instead.

If possible, include a photograph. One from the book illustrating the point you are making in the release is best. Remember, you want the release to push your issue; the book is secondary—almost subliminal.

Print out the releases and ship them off with a photo of the book, and enclose a reviewer response card (below).

Send the releases to all appropriate magazines, book clubs (see Chapter Eight), subsidiary rights contacts (Chapter Eight), wholesalers, libraries, sales representatives, hometown papers, etc. Don't forget alumni, fraternal, trade or church publications with which you may have a connection. Spread them around. Follow up with a telephone call to the most important periodicals. Think of this news release as your brochure before you make up a brochure.

News releases to local periodicals may be hand-delivered. Personal delivery not only receives more attention, meeting editors will be a great education for you.

Use news releases liberally. Every time you go back to press, issue a release to herald it. Magazines such as the prestigious *Publishers Weekly* will give you a few lines if you just let them know. Releases should also be issued to announce speaking engagements, TV appearances, autograph parties and any other newsworthy event. If business slows down, think up a newsworthy event and write a release on it.

PLEASE ACKNOWLEDGE

We have received your News Release about (book title): _____

We will take the following action:

☐ Your book will be featured on (date): _____

☐ Your book will be featured in the near future

☐ Please send a photograph of the book

☐ Please send a photograph of the author

☐ Please send a complimentary copy of the book

Name: _____

Full job title: _____

Name of publication or broadcast station: _____

Mailing address: _____

_____ Zip: _____

Comments optional): _____

Release Response Reply Card

An enclosed Release Response Reply Card will provide instant feedback. The cards will tell you if you are writing good releases and if you are sending them to the right people. You won't have to wait months wondering if the articles

---

Never talk about what you are going to do until after you have written it. — Mario Puzo

will appear. You will be ready to collect clippings, and the responses will provide leads for possible book reviews.

Always respond to *PW's* requests for information for their spring and fall announcements issues. Once you register for an ISBN, you will be on Bowker's mailing list and should receive these requests automatically. If you are going on tour, send a short release, listing the places and dates, to PW's "Author Publicity" column. Also be on the lookout for special editions of *Publishers Weekly* and other magazines. Some of the special editions are on cookbooks, travel books, sports books, etc. Listings are usually free.

Remember that media people work in a pressure-cooker world. Be polite; they won't expect it. You will get a lot of mileage out of one kind word.

For more information on news releases and paint-by-the-number instructions for drafting and using them, see the Special Report *News Releases and Book Publicity*. See the Appendix.

Press kits. Some publishers like to get fancy and issue a "press kit." While it isn't necessary to send a kit with a review book, there are other events where you may like to hand a kit to a reporter. The press kit is a pocket folder containing news releases, early reviews, letters of endorsement, an author biography, a cover letter, touring dates, testimonials, photographs, a business card, etc. The folder may be from a stationery store or, if the book measures 8.5" x 11", may be made from book cover overruns.

Use cover overruns for book promotion. Print your promotion copy on the other side and mail them out. If your book is 8.5" x 11", fold and trim the extras into file folders and hand them out at appropriate conventions. Delegates will carry your folder around, using it to collect other papers, for days. If you have a hardcover book, get extra jackets—not just for promotion but for replacements. Jackets become shelf-worn quickly in the stores. A new jacket will make the book look crisp again. Always ask your printer for the overruns and order a few hundred extra—"run-on printing" is very inexpensive.

Notify your friends of your new book by mailing them a news release and an order blank. Send these mailings to friends, relatives and influential people in the field covered by the book. They are prime prospects and will help to promote your book by just talking about it. For those mentioned in the book, send a flier with a rubber-stamped message, "You are mentioned in this book." A very high percentage will respond.

Influential people in the field should receive a complimentary copy; you want these opinion molders on your side.

Radio and television talk shows. Every day, more than 10,200 guests appear on some 4,250 local interview and talk shows across the U.S. The shows run on a total of 988 TV stations. And, 94% of the guests do not have recognizable names.

Authors are interesting people. Most people think that authors are experts and celebrities. Radio and television talk shows need interesting guests to attract listeners and viewers.

Your book will get you on; then you must have something interesting to say which is unique, controversial or fascinating.

Most of the guests booked by the shows are authors, so your book is your entrée to the airwaves.

Do talk shows sell books? Sometimes, oftentimes, but not all the time. We hear when a show works, but we usually do not hear the rest of the stories. If you enjoy talk shows, do them; if you do not like talk shows, do not feel obligated to go on the air.

Pay. Never pay a station for an interview. If a radio station is charging you, it must be because they don't have advertisers or listeners. Conversely, stations do not pay you for an interview. They are giving you exposure.

Start with telephone interviews on radio. They are fast, easy, inexpensive and you do not have to get dressed up or travel. Start with local radio shows and work your way up. Then graduate to local television shows and work your way up. Do not try to start out with Donahue or Oprah or Sally.

You have only one shot at the top shows, and if you blow one, you will not only not be invited back, you won't be invited to any of the others. They monitor each other.

How to get on. There are several ways to get on the shows. You can do it yourself, get yourself listed in the publications the producers read, or hire a public relations agency to contact the producers for you. For a complete explanation and the very latest in contact names and addresses, see Para Publishing's Instant Report *Interviews, How Authors Get on Radio and TV*. You may also take out a listing in the *Radio-TV Interview Report*. For an application, contact Bradley Communications, Bill Harrison, 135 East Plumstead Avenue, #125, Lansdowne, PA 19050-8206, Tel: (215) 259-1070, (800) 989-1400. Also see *On the Air* by Al Parinello. See the Appendix.

— **Television.** The big television shows are best, of course, as they reach more people. "Today," "Tonight," "Phil Donahue Show" and "60 Minutes" are the most influential in book selling. The best plug for a book is when Oprah Winfrey or Phil Donahue takes a personal interest. According to *TV Guide*, an appearance on *Today* can sell 3,000 copies of a book, while a few minutes on *Donahue* have moved 50,000.

Do not overlook the smaller and local shows. They are much easier to get on, and you may use them to work your way up. Many stations have special shows for interviewing authors, and most have at least one talk show. The local station will want you on its community affairs program. Depending on your subject, the station may even produce a short clip for their news broadcast. Once you have appeared on one local station, don't give up on the others. Use another interesting angle.

To get on a show, find out who the producer is. Locally, you may simply call the station and ask the switchboard op-

---

Many people love to go on radio and television. In fact, I think some people write books just to get on the air.

erator. For other stations, call the station or consult the directories in your library.

When on a television tour, try to book print media, too. Make the most of your time by granting interviews to the newspapers and magazines in the same city. Also try to schedule author signings at bookstores. The fact that you are appearing on radio or TV will tell them you are important.

Once you appear on TV, you may want a *clipping* of the show. Some services tape everything on the air and will sell you a copy. Contact Radio TV Reports, Tel: (212) 309-1400, and Video Monitoring Services of America, Tel: (213) 380-5011.

— **Radio.** There are 700 U.S. and Canadian radio talk shows that will interview you by telephone. With telephone interviews, you do not have to leave home. The scheduling can be tighter—very efficient. Radio stations like telephone interviews because they make even very busy celebrity authors available at very low cost.

Example of
a media
brochure

One way to let the talk shows know you are available is by sending them a *media flier*. The media flier stresses an interesting *issue* and offers you as an expert to explain the subject. The back of the flier may describe the book. The book is not the main subject; it is simply giving credibility to the expert.

The show's producer will call you to set up an appointment and then will call you at the appointed time. (Always clarify whether they will be calling at 7 a.m. your time or their time.)

Respond by sending a copy of the book, your news release, and photocopies of any reviews you have received. If you send a list of questions, most hosts will use it.

When you go on the air, be prepared. Do not use a telephone with *call waiting*. The clicking is annoying. Since several months have passed since you wrote the book, reread it. Practice public speaking. Think over the best answers to the questions most likely to be asked. Rehearse the stock answers and use high-impact words: sound bites. Go over the main points you want to make, and slip them in no matter what the questions. The talk show host may frustrate you by bouncing from subject to subject, so don't be caught with nothing to say. Push the subject, not your book. Do not mention the book at every opportunity—it turns off listeners and wears out your welcome.

On the big morning shows, you will be lucky to have 60 seconds on the air. Later in the day you may have four to eight minutes. Evening shows may run an hour.

A few years ago, this author was listening to a local radio station while running errands. He heard a disc jockey talking about making his first parachute jump. Since the author had written several books on skydiving, he called the disc jockey, who spoke to him between record breaks. An invitation was extended, and the author dropped by the radio station for an impromptu interview which lasted all afternoon.

Media people are busy and are under a lot of deadline pressure. While your book is the most important thing that has happened to you lately, it is just another news item to them. They are not easily impressed; they deal with news-making personalities all the time. Be polite; they won't expect it. Everyone around them is tough and short. A kind word from you will go a long way. A thank-you note afterwards will leave a nice memory, and you will receive great treatment for your second book.

The biggest problem all authors have with interviews is when their books are not in all the stores. Listeners may make one attempt to buy the book and then forget about it. One way to handle this potential disaster is to tell the host you will send a free *information kit* to any listener who will drop you a card. Talk show hosts love to give things to their audience, and most will repeat your message and address again and again. Now the responses will come directly to you, so that you may add these hot prospects to your mailing list and send them a brochure and other information on the subject.

Author's tours are the way you promote your book out of town, and they are very hard work. There was a time when all the author did was to deliver his manuscript to the publisher and then go home to await his royalty checks. However, with the advent of TV and more hype in the book business, the major effort for the writer now is in criss-crossing the country, selling the book. According to *The Wall Street Journal*, "For the publisher it is publicity at low cost. For the author it is an endurance test." It's a tough, grueling experience and it isn't inexpensive, but there is no cheaper way of reaching so many of the book-buying public.

Author tours mean going on as many radio and TV shows as possible and visiting bookstores between shows. It is terribly discouraging to find that most of the stores do not have your book in stock. Some self-publishers fill their van with books, so they can make store deliveries before going on the air.

When you know you are going to be on a show, try making a postcard mailing to all the bookstores in the broadcast area. Let them know who your distributor or wholesalers are so they can order easily in anticipation of your appearance.

Advertise your itinerary in ABA's *Bookselling This Week* several weeks before you are scheduled to leave. The American Booksellers Association publishes this newsletter for the bookstores. They will order your book and anticipate your visit to their area.

For more information on author tours, read Peggy Glenn's book; *Publicity for Books and Authors*. See the Appendix.

TV giveaway programs will provide you with great exposure, and all you have to do is donate a book. These programs are presented to raise funds for charitable organizations. Be on the lookout for them.

News conferences are often staged by big firms by hosting a lavish party for the press. But there is nothing wrong with a small gathering. If you have something provocative to say on a timely subject, if it would normally be mentioned as a news item, you may be able to draw out the media. You do not have to rent a hotel suite. News conferences may be called in a friend's home or in a public meeting place. Press people just want the information as quickly as possible. Be prepared with press kits.

Featured articles on yourself are another way to gain publicity. Local papers, company magazines, alumni publications, etc., are always looking for interesting news about their people. Let them do a story on you and they will mention your greatest accomplishment—your book. You are now an expert, an interesting person, just because you are a published author.

You are news to every publication with which you are connected, from a national association to a local newspaper.

When promoting your book, speak proudly about it. You worked hard on it and should be proud. False modesty will get you nowhere. — Mark Danna

Take advantage of them. Remember, book reviews sell books, but featured stories sell more books.

Book promotion through magazine articles is another way to gain publicity for your book while furthering your writing career. It is easy to spin off articles from the chapters of your book. You can sell the articles, build your reputation and help to sell the book, too.

First of all, you will be pleased to find that you have less difficulty selling articles to magazines now that you are a published author. You are an expert, and magazines want authoritative articles. Of course, you will want to end the article with: "Editor's note: Jan Nathan is the author of . . . which is available from . . .," and type the notice in just as you want it to appear; do not leave this up to the editor. Those who read the article will be interested in the subject or they wouldn't be reading about it. Many will want to know more and will seek your book. So, while you are making sales on books, you might as well get paid for the article.

Most national magazines do not pay a great deal for articles—usually just a couple of hundred dollars. However, the exposure is more important to you than the money. You even might like to consider that if you offer the article free, you have a better chance of its seeing print. Write to the editor, enclosing a few applicable pages from your book, and offer to write an article with the magazine's editorial slant. Offer to send an outline, or include it with this first mailing. It is easy to extract a section, add an introduction and a conclusion and edit it slightly.

Speaking engagements are another way to publicize your book. As an expert on your subject, you are in demand by service organizations, adult education programs, church groups, PTA's, the Chamber of Commerce and others. Many of these groups feature a guest speaker at every meeting. Sometimes they rotate the responsibility among the membership to find a speaker. Your call to them may actually get someone off the hook.

The possibilities will become obvious once you begin to think of your topic from the marketing standpoint. If yours is a carpentry how-to book, a hardware store or lumberyard might like to build a seminar around you. Your presentation might turn into an annual affair. Think of the nurseries which hold pruning classes every spring. You will make good contacts and develop new ideas; it is stimulating.

When you make your speaking appearance, always mention your book. Have one on display, and make several copies available for sale and autographs in the back of the room. Authors often make more on book sales in the back of the room than they do on the speech. Prepare a short, powerful speech on one small, very interesting, related item, and leave plenty of time for questions and answers. Always write out your introduction, so the host won't stumble around trying to explain who you are.

Speaking engagements will do three things for you; they promote your book, you may receive a fee for speaking and they add to your professional portfolio. Now, in addition to being an author and a publisher, you are a presenter, too. You must be an expert!

Seminars are speaking engagements you organize yourself. You set up the daylong program and collect the admissions. A General Motors study found approximately 40,000 seminars are given in North America each year and generate revenues of $100 to $160 million.

Use your book as a text for the seminar and include it in the admission fee. Display related books in the back of the room and sell tapes of your lecture. If you have an idea, you can get $20 for the book, $80 for the tape, $200/hour for private consultation and $300 or more for the seminar. For information on setting up seminars, write: Communications Unlimited, Gordon Burgett, P.O. Box 6405-B, Santa Maria, CA 93456.

Autograph parties are a good ego trip when successful and can help to make your other advertising more effective. Normally these events are scheduled by the publisher for the benefit of the author. However, unless the author is well known, the autograph party rarely pays. The best scheduling is to tie in with a radio or TV appearance and some local advertising.

Contact a local bookstore and ask if you may set up a table, erect a sign and provide some refreshments. The bookstore may be reluctant to sponsor such an event unless you are willing to underwrite some of the cost. The expense won't be small because, in addition to the refreshments and sign, you will have to consider a good deal of advertising via mail and space ads. But the store may pay half. Even if they fail to sell a lot of your books, this "event" you are staging will bring new customers into their shop. Once introduced to the bookstore, they are more likely to return in the future.

The store will provide the place, but you must get the people in. Do not rely on the regular customers to buy your book. Mail announcements of your appearance to every friend, relative, acquaintance and prospect in the area. Make the event sound big and important. Make everyone in town think that everyone else is going, that if they don't go they will be the only one not there.

Once you know a local paper is going to review your book or do a feature article on you, visit the bookstores. Suggest they might like to place an ad in the same edition to draw readers into their store. Offer to stage an autograph party—another fine tie-in.

Don't overlook fund-raising event autograph parties. Here, you would do the selling and would donate part to the club or organization.

When traveling, drop in on bookstores, and when you find your books on display, offer to autograph them. An autograph makes the book more valuable, and this will provide an opportunity for the staff to become familiar with you and your book. Sometimes you will wind up doing an impromptu presentation.

Book awards. There is probably no greater satisfaction to a writer than having her book selected for an award. Some book awards are big and well known, and some are small. There are those that are general while others are quite specialized, but all are awards, and just being nominated for one looks good in your advertising.

Awards may be mentioned in advertising, and announcement stickers may be applied to the books. These stickers are a bit of extra work, but they get attention. If the organization making the award does not sell the stickers, have them made at a quick-print shop. In later printings, the "sticker" may be printed on.

According to *Publishers Weekly*, the big publishers say that awards do not sell books. By the time the award is received, the book has been pulled from the stores and the publishers are promoting newer books. So what is the effect of an award? "It makes the author cost more when contracting for their next book," said one (large New York) publisher. Fortunately, smaller publishers benefit from awards, because they keep their books alive longer.

Book awards, contests and grants are listed in *Literary Market Place* and *Writer's Market,* available at your library, and in a pamphlet titled *Grants and Awards Available To American Writers,* published by P.E.N. American Center. See the Appendix.

Related book lists can be used to plug your other books. Each of your books should carry a list of all your books, and these lists should be updated at each reprinting. The list may appear on the rear jacket flap or in the appendix of the book. This is a way to get your sales message to potential buyers in the same field at little cost.

Be prepared to move when your book takes off. Have your promotional plan organized so you will be able to gain maximum mileage from your publicity. Capitalize on each piece of publicity. Have your releases, ads and letters drafted.

Take advantage of every possible market. Pursue the most lucrative, but don't overlook the marginal ones. It costs very little to serve more markets, once you have done the initial organization.

Chapter Eight

Who Will Buy Your Book?

Distribution Channels

Your marketing effort is vital to the success of your book. Yours may be the greatest tome ever written, but if your sales message fails to reach its intended customer, your book won't sell. People just will not line up automatically to purchase your book. You have already expended a great deal of effort in writing and publishing your book, but it is the energy you expend now that will make your earlier effort pay off.

Unfortunately, many creative people recoil at the thought of selling their own product. But they must promote their book. It makes no difference whether they went with a large

> *The writing of a best seller represents only a fraction of the total effort required to create one.* — Ted Nicholas

New York publisher or elected to do their own publishing. If the book is to sell, the author must do the promoting.

The role of marketing is to return maximum sales on minimum promotional investment, "to get the most bang for your buck." You want to invest your money where you will get the best return. This means placing promotion and advertising where you receive the best response per dollar and hour invested.

An often heard rule of thumb for response percentages— for example, the number of orders received from a mailing— is 2%, and there are many entertaining stories of much better returns. What really counts is the return in sales on the promotional investment. A cheap ad becomes expensive if it fails to bring in any sales. To determine your results, you must total your alternatives before you sign up. The woods are full of ad salespeople, and their primary mission, like yours, is staying in business. They will promise you anything to get into your promotion budget.

Consider the amount of work which will go into the promotion. Total up your office expenses ("licking and sticking") and the direct costs such as stamps and envelopes, and balance these against the selling price (if to wholesalers, you will get less per book) and the expected response. Total these up and make the decision, but try to be objective. Run small tests before rolling out into a large investment. Code your address in all marketing efforts as described in Chapter Seven, so you can trace the source of each order.

Who is buying books? A 1990-1991 survey of 16,000 U.S. households by the Association of American Publishers and the Book Industry Study Group revealed some interesting figures:

Some 60% of the households did not buy a single book in the previous year. Of the 40% that did, 99% of them classified themselves as "white." Popular fiction accounted for

> *Selection is directly related to sales.* — Jon Glazer, Little Professor Book Centers

two-thirds of the sales. People 65 and older made 16% of the purchases, the largest group. Popular fiction increases in popularity with the age of the reader.

Higher-income groups ($50,000 and up) buy higher-priced books: 21% of the unit sales but 41% of the dollar sales. Lower-income groups ($30,000 and under) accounted for half the unit sales but only one-quarter of the dollar sales. Single households made 34% of the book purchases. Professional and white-collar workers made 50% of all book purchases. Residents of cities with populations of 1.0 to 2.5 million were disproportionately heavy book buyers.

Buyers under 35 and aged 55 to 64 buy more hardcovers, while those between 45 and 55 and those over 65 were heavy buyers of mass market paperbacks. 91% of all mass market paperback sales were popular fiction. Of these, 46% were in the romance genre. Eighty-six percent of all books were purchased for the buyer but 26% of the hardcovers were purchased as gifts.

The average home in the U.S. has 154 books in it. The range is from 74 books in homes where the residents have less than a high school diploma to 249 in homes of college graduates. Only 16% of the homes have fewer than 20 books. But, Jerry Jenkins says 57% of the books purchased are never read.

Where are they buying books? According to studies by the American Booksellers Association and the Association of American Publishers of 1993 book sales, 915 million books were sold for a total of $18 billion. 55.6% were sold through bookstores, 18.6% through the mail, 17.3% through supermarket, drug and discount stores and 8.4% "other."

Of the books sold through bookstores, 47.3% were sold through independents (down 3.9%), 44.1% through chains, including superstores (up 4.3%) and 8.6% through used book shops. Warehouse clubs, such as the Price Club, moved 46 million books (up 82%).

Independent bookstores sold 28% of the books, the chains 20%, book clubs 16% and food/drug/discount stores

19%. Over 77 million books were sold through department stores, card/gift stores and hobby/craft stores (up 27.4%.)

18.6% of the books are sold through the mail (mail order and book clubs); in fact, books account for 6% of all purchases made by mail.

No figures were available for book sales outside of the book trade. It is suspected that a very large, unreported number are sold through specialty shops (e.g., parachute books in parachute stores), catalogs, as premiums, etc. These nontraditional sales are usually easier to make, very large and much more lucrative.

The chain superstores are growing, the chain mall stores (with smaller selections) are shrinking, the independents are being killed off by the chains, more and more specialty stores are carrying books and mail order is growing.

Audience specialization is concentrating your promotional efforts on those most likely to buy. Before you wrote your book, you analyzed your potential audience, and then you slanted your text toward them. In producing your book, you considered how it might be marketed and made your product attractive in this medium. Perhaps you put extra effort into the cover. The selection of your marketing channels is very important. For example, the chains seem to concentrate on fast-moving books. If your book does not have a wide audience, you do not want to be in the chains. The unsold books will only come back. Even if you get your book into a nonbook market where there aren't any returns, you want the books to sell, not to sit on the shelves forever. So consider who patronizes each of the various outlets, and be objective in considering whether they are your audience.

In analyzing the market, you will consider your principal marketing concerns, your customers (individuals, schools, libraries, international markets, subsidiary rights, industry, government, etc.) and your distribution channels (mass-market outlets, distributors, wholesalers, bookstores and book clubs). Your marketing tools are book reviews, news releases, direct mail advertising, sales representation, etc.

With a specialized nonfiction book, you can avoid the expensive, traditional big publisher methods of marketing to everyone and concentrate on the more profitable areas. Work smarter, not harder. Define your core audience, and then get to work. Select your special audience and find a way to reach them. You will find your target group is served by magazines, stores, catalogs, broadcast interviewers, specialized book clubs, columnists, associations, conventions and others. For example, if your book is on skydiving, you know you can reach your customers through the U.S. Parachute Association, the Para-Gear catalog, *Parachutist* magazine and at the national championships. Who is your customer? What is his profile? Where can you find him? Where does he congregate with others like him? What magazines does he read? What clubs does he join? Where is he?

You do not have to attack the whole group; you can go after just the cream off the top. Mail to the libraries with the biggest budgets; visit the buyers of the larger chain stores and select the wealthiest of the direct mail purchasers. Ads and mailing lists can be purchased selectively by region and other criteria; you do not have to buy the whole country.

Hedge your bets by balancing your markets. Put most of your energy into selling your target group. Sell to the rest, too, but don't spend a lot of time courting them. Invest your time and money wisely.

Repetitive audience contact is your mission once you have identified your marketing area. A repeated promotion in direct mail advertising, space ads, etc., will normally bring the same response as it did the first time. Naturally, the returns will drop off if done too often, but many agree that six weeks is sufficient spacing. And there is some value to repetitive exposure; after a while, people begin to recognize and become comfortable with you. It is wise to change your message occasionally, as some in your audience will

---

There is no secret formula. It is simply a good item for which there is a need, at the right price, offered to the right market.

pass over it, having seen it before. But don't change for the sake of change. Repeat what works; go with a winner.

It helps to have more than one product, because each customer who buys is a prime target for similar books on the same subject. People who buy how-to books on a specialized subject collect them all. Slowly build your clientele and your product line.

Multiple markets will cost more in time and money but will stabilize your financial position by smoothing out the peaks and valleys. It is wise not to have all your eggs in one basket. With a how-to nonfiction book, you may concentrate on wholesalers, catalogs, and direct mail. Some of your effort will depend on you. If you like personal contact, you might do more talk shows and visit more bookstores. If you like your privacy, you might use the mail. Book promotion should be fun, so do what you enjoy most.

Seasons will affect your sales, and you should plan your major marketing efforts around them. The big publishers bring out most of their new titles in the fall, targeting them at Christmas. Their second major season is in the spring. June graduates are a good market. Business books move best in the late spring and late fall, not during the summer. Outdoor books do best in late winter when people are confined indoors and thinking about the activities of the coming summer. Travel books will do well a few months before the applicable travel season.

Most publishers find December and late August to be slow. Business picks up after the first of the year and after Labor Day.

The public, or ultimate consumer, may be approached directly. Books have been sold door-to-door, hawked on street corners, at street fairs and flea markets. The advantage of selling directly is the elimination of the middlemen; you

> *The fact is, do-it-yourself books have never been more popular than they are now, and their popularity is growing steadily.*
> — Arnold F. Logan, Petersen Publishing Company

keep the entire list price for yourself. But approaching the ultimate consumer requires greater effort, and the books are sold one at a time. It is far more efficient to use distributors and wholesalers.

The other method of reaching the public is by mail. Direct mail advertising is less personal but more private; it appeals to many authors. Pre-publication offers to the consumer usually pull very well. Direct mail advertising and mail order distribution are discussed in detail in the next two chapters.

Microfiche card

Microfiche systems. Some of the larger wholesalers, such as Ingram and Baker & Taylor, have microfiche systems. They ship these 4" x 6" film negative "fiche" inventory lists to the stores every week. Now when a customer asks for a book not on the shelf, the bookstore can look it up, verify that it is available, make a toll-free call and have it delivered by UPS in a couple of days. The customer may pay for the book then and return to pick it up, or have the book delivered to his or her home. Bookstores like making sales when they do not have to inventory books. Even the chain stores use the system because it is sure and fast.

While you cannot place your book in every bookstore, you can make it available through every store with these microfiche systems. A listing in *Books in Print* is not enough, since stores do not want to spend the time and bookwork to order directly from publishers. Your book must be available from one of their large, established suppliers. You must have your books with Ingram and Baker & Taylor and your book must be listed in their microfiche. Visit a bookstore and ask to use the microfiche reader—see for yourself.

Books must show some activity to be included on the wholesaler's microfiche. Your distributor should get you into Ingram and Baker & Taylor. Then you must get customers into the store to pull some books through to earn your way onto the microfiche.

Books in Print is distributed annually in print form and monthly on CD-ROM disc. Some of the microfiche systems are being switched to CDs, too.

Times have changed. We used to recommend that non-fiction book publishers serve the book trade (mostly bookstores) through wholesalers. We went on to suggest you place your books with as many wholesalers as possible so as not to place all your eggs in one basket. Times have changed.

Distributors, led by Publishers Group West, have carved out a large niche in the distribution of books. Bookstores would rather order from distributors and wholesalers for several reasons. Historically, publishers have been slow to fill orders. Stores would rather write 15 cheques at the end of the month, not 15,000. Stores prefer to deal with suppliers they know, those with whom they have established accounts. Bar codes make instant inventory control and just-in-time delivery possible. One wholesaler, Ingram, has a warehouse within one-day UPS delivery of 95% of the bookstores in the country. Store buyers know they can pick up a telephone, use an 800 number, consolidate an order, and have delivery in two days.

Bookstores will order from a wholesaler before they will consider a distributor or a publisher since the selection of titles is greater.

Wholesalers are *warehouses* for bookstores. With quick service from wholesalers, stores can carry more titles on their shelves because they need less depth.

Today, we recommend publishers select a single distributor on an exclusive basis (to the "book trade"). Let that distributor handle the bookstores, so you can concentrate on other stores, mail order and other markets.

How much and why? Most distributors take 25% to 30% of the net (what they collect from the stores—which varies according to how many books the store orders), which may work out to be around 65% of the list (cover) price. Basic services to publishers include warehousing, cataloging, sales representation (to the independent bookstores and chains), shipping, billing, collections, marketing and editorial consultation. Many distributors provide other services at additional cost. Some of those services are filling individual (retail) orders, co-op advertising in book trade publications, postcard mailings to bookstores in areas where you are appearing on radio or TV, etc.

Sixty-five percent may sound like a lot and it is. But, most distributors handle only the book trade (wholesalers and book stores). So, you may turn that portion of the business over to them, forget about the stores and go on to the nontraditional markets which are easier, more lucrative and more fun. Your distributor will send you a nice cheque each month and will move a lot of books into the stores. Now, when you go back to press, you will print more books and achieve a lower per-unit cost. So while you are sharing around 65% with your distributor, they are providing many services and are helping you to move more books and to get them cheaper.

More and more of the chains and larger independent stores are requiring electronic ordering systems (EDI). Few publishers can afford them, so here is another reason to use a distributor.

The distribution industry—definitions. Here are some general definitions of those "middlemen" between the publisher and the bookstore, to help you understand the book-supply pipeline. Several of the companies are evolving and growing. Some started off in one category and changed.

Distributors act as the fulfillment department for their publishers. More publisher-driven; their mission is to create orders from stores. They carry each publisher's entire line of books. Most have a catalog and sales reps who visit the stores. They try to create demand. They also supply wholesalers. Your distributors will launch your books each season in a catalog. Typically, distributors pay 90 days after they ship the books.

Your distributor's will serve the wholesalers (especially Ingram and Baker & Taylor), send their sales reps to the independent book stores and will sell your books into the chains.

Wholesalers are more demand-driven or bookstore-driven; they respond to orders and they do it quickly. They carry just those books that are in demand and fill orders when received. Most do not have reps, some do not even stock the books and they do little, if any, selling. They carry books from most publishers because their main service is delivering books quickly.

Jobbers generally buy books from wholesalers and carry a predominance of mass-market paperbacks. You probably will not deal with many jobbers.

Independent Distributors (IDs) carry magazines and mass-market paperbacks and serve drugstores, supermarkets and airport outlets. IDs are magazine distributors who carry paperbacks and treat them the same as magazines: the books go on the rack for one month and then only the covers from

---

A distributor is a surrogate sales department for a group of independent publishers. — Julie Bennett

unsold books are returned for credit. You probably will not deal with many IDs.

Library wholesalers are companies that find books for libraries. Larger ones stock some books, but most order from publishers only when filling a library order. They will be discussed in more detail in the next section on libraries.

Chain stores are stores that are related to each other and usually have a single central buying office.

How the industry is organized. Here is the layout for the book industry's distribution service to bookstores. Later in this chapter, we will discuss the individual firms and tell what subjects they specialize in. Some of the major players are listed here, but there are many more. See *Literary Market Place*.

National Distributors (or master distributors)

Associated Publishers Group

Atrium Publishers Group

BookWorld Services

Children's Small Press Collection

Consortium

Hispanic Books Distributors

InBook (Inland)

Independent Publishers Group

Independent Publishers Marketing

International Book Distributors

Lifetime Books

Login Publishers Consortium

National Book Network

Publishers Distribution Service

Publishers Group West

Raincoast Book Distribution

Samuel French Trade

SCB Distributors

Seven Hills Distributors

Small Press Distribution (SPD)

Spring Arbor Distributors

Talman Company

American Software & Hardware Distributors

Art Book Distributors

Book Tech Distributing

Cromland

(Major publishers, such as Harper-Collins, St. Martins, Random House and others, distribute books for some smaller publishers.)

National Wholesalers

(with multiple regional warehouses)

Baker & Taylor

Ingram Book Company

Golden-Lee

Specialty Wholesalers

Advanced Marketing Services (warehouse clubs)

Devorss & Co. (metaphysical)

Moving Books

NASCORP (college bookstores)

New Leaf (new age)

Nutri-Books (health and fitness)

Regional Wholesalers

(Many of these are loosely linked in the American Wholesale Booksellers Association.)

Book Dynamics

BookLink

Bookazine

Bookmen

Bookpeople

Bookslinger

Booksource

Cannon Book Distribution, Ltd.
Inland Book Co. (InBook).
Koen Book
L-S Distributors
Merle Distributing
New England Mobile Book Fair
Pacific Pipeline
Publishers Distribution Center
The distributors
Richardson's Books
Southern Book Service
Sunbelt Publications
Gazelle BookServices
Airlift Books

Library Wholesalers
(Listed in the next section on libraries)

National Chains
Barnes & Noble/ B. Dalton Bookseller
Waldenbooks/Borders (Kmart)
Crown Books
Book-A-Million
Encore Books

Regional Chains
Kroch's
Lauriat's
Stacy's
Tower Books
Classic Bookshops
Coles Book Stores

Wholesaler vs. Distributor. Wholesaler and distributor
are often used interchangeably; they are the "middlemen"

between the publisher and the bookstore. Technically, wholesalers stock books for many, many publishers on a non-exclusive basis. They do not push books with sales reps, and most place orders with publishers only when they receive an order from a bookstore or library. Distributors act like an arm of the publisher. They represent a few publishers on an exclusive basis, warehouse the stock, and send sales reps to the stores. The problem is that many of the wholesalers and distributors have reformulated their businesses so they have moved out of their original mold. Many do not even know which one they are.

Remember that distributors replace part of your shipping department but not your marketing department. You must always do the marketing yourself.

More than 30% of the bookstores buy from wholesalers regularly and most depend on wholesalers for some of their stock. These wholesalers ask for a 50% to 60% discount from you and sell to their customers at 20% to 40% off depending upon quantity (titles may be mixed). Even the big chains make use of wholesalers when they run out and are desperate for books.

Many wholesalers cater only to libraries. Seventy percent of the libraries buy from wholesalers. These wholesalers provide a valuable service, by combining orders and saving the librarian from thousands of single-title orders.

Which distributor? Now the question is how do you find the right distributor? The secret is to match your book (or line of books) with a distributor that already offers titles of the same type. They will have a relationship with stores that have major sections of that type of book, and they may be serving other appropriate stores outside the book trade. For example, if you have a business book, you might approach Publishers Group West or Publishers Distribution

---

Wholesalers perform a valuable order-consolidation and distribution service but they don't market individual titles.
— Mark Sexton

Service. If you have a traditional religion or new age book, you might contact Atrium. If you have a health and fitness book, you might check with Nutri-Books. If you strike a deal with Nutri-Books, for example, they will get your book into bookstores with significant health and fitness sections and into health food stores. You want a distributor that is already plugged into the right markets for your book.

Selection criteria. Distributors will consider the following when deciding whether or not to accept your book:

1. Is the book manufactured to accepted industry standards in terms of binding, cover design, type style, size and so on?
2. Is the book backed by any advertising or promotion budget or plan which will bring it to the attention of readers, libraries and/or bookstores?
3. Does the publisher have more than one product? They like to open accounts with established, ongoing businesses.
4. Do they feel they can move this title?

Your next move is to call the distributors that appear to best match your book(s). That way, you will not waste their time or yours. Ask if they would like to see your book and request submission forms. For a current list of distributors, noting the categories of books they want (as well as those they do not want), see Para Publishing's Special Report *Book Marketing* or our Instant Report *Locating the Right Distributor*. If you just want addresses and telephone numbers, see *Literary Market Place*.

If a distributor turns down your book, it may be because the book is not right for *their* particular market, the book may be poorly executed or because they fail to see its sales potential in a very brief evaluation. Distributors, like bookstore buyers, have little time to evaluate the dozens of books they receive every day. Try again. Wait a few weeks or months to build up a track record. Then resubmit the book and send along sales figures, reviews, endorsements—anything that will demonstrate that the book is selling and that customers are responding to it. If the book is moving, the distributors will want to get in on the action.

Distributors are often reluctant to open an account with a one-book publisher. Therefore, if you are new or small, you must be persistent. You must convince them this is the first book of many and that this book will move.

If you call a distributor and they do not feel your book is right for their line, ask them for a recommendation. They know the industry and will not consider other (non-competing) distributors as a threat.

Exclusives are necessary in the book trade because books are sold on a returnable basis. Publishers need a single-source representative (distributor) to the stores, so that books may be cycled back and forth, ordered and returned to one place.

Consignment. Most distributors operate on consignment inventory and pay 90 days after they ship the books to the bookstore or wholesaler. This means they have very little invested in their operation. While publishers should avoid selling to small accounts on consignment, there are good arguments for these terms with major distributors. Book manufacture requires large print runs, so part of your inventory might just as well sit in another warehouse as your own.

Remember, however, title (ownership) to the books is still yours. If the books are lost or damaged, if the wholesaler does not have insurance, the loss could be yours.

Sending 20 cartons of books to a distributor requires the same amount of paperwork as sending a single book to a bookstore. Accordingly, distributors are very important to you. In fact, if your dealer price list requires a large number of books for a discount, it will force more stores to order from wholesalers, which may simplify your business.

Baker & Taylor is headquartered in Bridgewater, New Jersey, with nearly autonomous warehouses in Somerville, New Jersey; Reno, Nevada; Momence, Illinois and Commerce, Georgia. The company has an additional 100,000 sq. ft. "consolidation center" in Franklin, New Jersey, which stocks 15,000 titles and acts as a backup for the other regional warehouses.

While the company is education-oriented and much of their effort is directed toward finding books for libraries, the bookstore market is served with a microfiche system listing 100,000 current and 10,000 forthcoming titles. Baker & Taylor is a mirror of library demand. If you receive a good review in *Library Journal,* some 75% of your library orders will come through B&T.

Baker & Taylor stocks more than 120,000 different titles, over 3 million books in all. They have 1.2 million titles on their CD-ROM database. On heavy days, they receive over 90,000 books and ship over 90,000 books. In a recent year, B&T returned 2 million overstock books to publishers. B&T added 3,000 new publishers last year, and they currently solicit new title information from some 14,000 publishers. The company employs over 1,700 people and grosses about $800 million. Its 38 salespeople call on some 105,000 libraries across the U.S., and its representatives attend more than 500 library meetings each year.

Baker & Taylor wants a 55% discount, net 90 day payment terms, FOB destination (free freight) and fully returnable. They also charge a one-time $100 set-up fee for new vendors. In return, B&T will enter the publisher and all books into their database and CD-ROM product. The top-selling 120,000 books are inventoried and are included in the microfiche. To get onto the microfiche, the book must be ordered (by a library or store); to stay on, the book must be ordered repeatedly.

If you do not choose to be in the system, you may allow Baker & Taylor any discount you wish. Since they are usually waiting for your book to complete a large order, they won't quibble over the discount and will even pay a pro forma invoice (in advance). However, being a stock publisher with a listing on the microfiche makes your books available to many more stores and buyers, which is easily worth the 55%.

B&T's first notice of new books often comes from The Library of Congress, so make sure you apply for a Library of Congress number for each title. About half the orders received by B&T come in electronically and reference the ISBN. Make sure your numbers are correct in your brochures and listings. But, they want to hear from you as soon as possible—don't wait for them to find you.

Contact Baker & Taylor in Bridgewater and ask for a copy of their *Information Outline For Publishers*. This multi-page document explains all of the Baker & Taylor programs. Fill out and return their *Vendor Profile Questionnaire* and their *New Book Information Form*. Ask for a copy of their media kit, which outlines their marketing programs. Work with the Publisher Contact Section in Bridgewater, but also contact the facilities in Somerville, Commerce, Momence and Reno for a stocking order.

Baker & Taylor
Publisher Contact Section
P.O. Box 6920
Bridgewater, NJ 08807-0400
Tel: (908) 218-3803
Tel: (908) 218-0400
Fax: (908) 218-3980

Send a review copy of the book to Publisher Services in Bridgewater before publication date. Review copies are evaluated and processed for the Academic Approval Program and cataloging card sets for libraries. Selections for the Approval Program are not confirmed but will result in an order for up to 100 copies as well as automatic inclusion in their monthly journal *Directions*.

Ingram Book Company is the largest wholesaler to independent (non-chain) bookstores; it has been growing very rapidly. Headquartered in Nashville, Tennessee, Ingram has regional warehouses in Walnut, California; LaVergne, Tennessee; Fort Wayne, Indiana; Avon, Connecticut; Roseburg, Oregon and Petersburg, Virginia. With this spread of warehouses, Ingram can provide next day delivery to over 95%

of its (bookstore and library) customers. Ingram stocks fewer titles (some 100,000 in each warehouse) than Baker & Taylor but stocks the books in greater depth. Ingram serves 18,000 bookstores and libraries. Ingram does not promote books, they make them *available* to retailers.

Ingram sells over $2 billion in books each year from some 2,000 publishers and distributors.

Normally, Ingram wants to buy your books from a distributor they already deal with. Your distributor will present your book(s) to Ingram. Then you may work with your distributor to take part in some of Ingram's promotional programs. A few smaller and newer publishers with a line of books have been successful at approaching Ingram directly.

Ingram is very business-oriented. You must convince them there will be demand for your books. Their decision to buy or not to buy your book will be based on your promotional plans as much as the quality of the book itself. Most of the buying for the regional warehouses is controlled from Nashville. There are several buyers, each responsible for a particular area. Try to get to the computer book buyer, the trade nonfiction buyer, etc. Call Ingram for the name of the current category buyer. Ingram wants a 50% discount and pays the freight, though some new publishers have been unable to negotiate a deal better than 55%, FOB destination.

Ingram mails its microfiche listings to over 9,000 bookstores each week. Getting on the fiche is a respected accomplishment, but staying on it through reorders is more difficult and a more accurate measure of your book's success.

Ingram runs special promotions. For a price, your book can be featured in a circular mailed with the monthly statements or microfiche mailings (cost was about $1,150 in 1992), or the book can be mentioned by the order operators ($1,100 to $1,500 in 1992). This statement-stuffing works very well for books that have been out for a while as it reminds the bookseller to reorder.

Bookfax is a promotional program where publishers can place up to 50 pages of sales information in Ingram's fax-on-demand system. Customers can call for more information on specific titles. Cost is $950 for six months.

GreenLight Program. Ingram will special order titles they do not carry. They expect a 50% discount and free freight. Ingram promotes GreenLight as a faster alternative to STOP programs. So that Ingram will know your book exists, send a brochure to the GreenLight Program in LaVergne.

Your distributor will present your book, but you may also make a presentation and let your distributor fill the orders. Send a copy of the book, with a brochure and any other promotional materials, to:

Ingram Book Company
Wanda Smith, Publisher Relations
One Ingram Blvd.
LaVergne, TN 37086-1986
Tel: (615) 793-5000, Ext. 7563
Tel: (800) 251-5900

Chain bookstores. The chains are important to publishers because the top five chains control one-third of the bookstore market, for $3.2 billion in sales. So, five buyers control one-third of the books sold. They are easy to reach and sell since they have single central buying offices.

According to *Publishers Weekly*, Barnes & Noble is the largest hardcover retailer in the U.S. and they have the lowest unsold book return rate in the industry. Their operations are computerized, so they know what is selling and can plan reorders.

Many of the chain stores have their cash registers tied into the central computer to monitor sales. They purchase by category and demographics, matching books to the store's clientele. Often the computer will throw a large number of books out to a store as a test only to be sent back if unsold after a period of time. This instant access to sales information enables the headquarters to stay on top of fast-breaking books. They can reorder sooner to maintain inventory levels.

Chains are easy to reach. Since each has a single buying office, one sale places books in many stores. Visiting one chain buyer is more efficient than sending sales reps to thousands of individual stores.

Chain buying is centralized, but most local outlets are authorized to make small purchases, and they are especially receptive to regional books and local authors. Walden does not permit local managers to make purchases, but headquarters does listen to them when they request a local publisher's book. Most chains expect a 40% discount, FOB origin, and many pay in 60 to 90 days.

The larger chains have stopped buying directly from smaller and newer publishers. However, you can still reach them through your distributor. So, approach the chains in two steps:

A. Find a distributor, and then

B. Let your distributor pitch the chain on the book.

Or, reverse the process by using the PMA chain service. PMA has a chain program with Walden, Barnes & Noble and Independent Publishers Group. PMA members may submit books to a member-committee. Books are screened for bar codes, suitability for general-interest bookstores, etc. Then the books are displayed for a visit by the chain buyers. IPG has agreed to carry all books selected. This is a great service for the chains, as they get access to preselected, prescreened (otherwise unseen) books. It is also a great program for the smaller and newer publisher, as it provides access to the chains. Contact PMA for details on the program. See the Appendix.

> *What really interests us are print runs and promotions. We want to know what is the publisher going to print? What is it going to put behind the book? Is the author good on talk shows? And is there going to be a tour?* — Harry Hoffman, former CEO, Waldenbooks

National chains

Barnes & Noble is a national chain affiliated with B. Dalton, Bookstop, Doubleday and Scribners stores. Some 203 of their stores are superstores. They did $1.3 billion in business in 1993. Barnes and Noble tries to tailor the books in each store to its local community. Barnes & Noble buys by format and publisher rather than by subject category. This approach fosters and permits the establishment of a publisher or distributor-buyer relationship.

Barnes & Noble Booksellers
Buyer (Specify hardcover, trade paper or
mass market or call for the current name.)
105 Fifth Avenue
New York, NY 10011
Tel: (212) 206-8800, Ext. 360

Borders-Waldenbooks-Bretano's (Kmart). Walden has 1,045 stores and is closing some of the mall stores that are not performing. Walden purchases books from some 7,500 publishers, but they prefer to deal with (many fewer) distributors. Sales are $1.1 billion.

Walden watches social trends and tries to match the stock to the community. About 150 Walden stores are carrying Spanish-language books, and some 300 have Black-American books. Walden buys by category.

Waldenbooks
Buyer (Specify: call for the current name.)
201 High Ridge Road
Stamford, CT 06904-3417
Tel: (203) 352-2000, (203) 352-2018
Tel: (203) 356-7626

Crown Books. Crown has numerous discount stores in major cities.

Crown Books
John Sutton
3300 75th Avenue
Landover, MD 20785
Tel: (301) 731-1200

Books-A-Million has 109 stores, 26 of which are super-stores. Many are combination book and greeting card stores operating under the Bookland name.

Little Professor Book Centers has 10 stores and is expanding its superstore division. They do about $70 million a year.

Little Professor Book Centers
John Glazer
130 South First Street, #300
Ann Arbor, MI 48104-1304
Tel: (313) 994-1212
Tel: (800) 521-6232

W.H. Smith Ltd. (and Waterstone's) is expanding into airport shops in the U.S.

Waterstone's
Buying Manager
113 Merton Street
Toronto, ON M4S 1A8
Canada
Tel: (416) 485-6660

Bookstores, individual but not necessarily independent, are a diverse group of retailers. They include the downtown bookstore, the college store, the religious bookstore and others. There are over 15,000 stores that carry books. They come in all sizes: some sell books exclusively while others carry books as a sideline, some stores are general and some are specialized, and some are attached to museums or libraries.

— **Bookstore patron profiles** consist of the book addict and the occasional buyer. Recreational readers are used to plunking down $19.95 for hardcover fiction. Fifty percent of the customers in a bookstore are looking for a particular book. These particular-book seekers are more likely to be younger and female. Forty-seven percent are looking for a nonfiction title, 27% for a particular book of fiction and 28% want textbooks. While 20% do not find the book they are looking for, 54% buy one or more books before they leave. Then there are those people who never visit a bookstore.

Modern booksellers are faced with trying to attract and sell to all these people. To do so, they have to locate in high-rent, heavy-traffic areas. Stores report an inventory turnover of two to five times a year, with an average of 3.3 times. If a book hasn't moved in six months on the shelf, it is usually returned. The newer and smaller publisher is trapped between the Scylla of wide exposure and the Charybdis of massive returns.

Many small publishers tolerate, but don't pursue, small individual bookstores. The major problems with stores are that they order just a few books at a time, complain about the 40% discount, seldom pay in 30 days and often return the books for a refund—damaged. You wind up processing a lot of paperwork for many small orders and returns, while making very few sales. The best approach is to let the distributors and wholesalers handle the stores. Once the wholesalers make your book available to the stores, you may spend your energy creating a demand.

Try visiting local bookstores; it will be a good education. Tell them you are a local author and, therefore, local people will be interested in your book. Mention any local publicity such as talk shows which are planned. Stores want to know if the book will be promoted. Reviews and author appearances are more important than advertising. If the book is

> *If selling books through bookstores was good business, the stores might be paying their bills.*

professionally produced, a sale should not be difficult. Be ready with the stock phrase: "I can offer you the books at a full 40% discount, without delivery charges, and they are fully returnable, of course." The whole pitch will probably run five to ten minutes.

If you still can't persuade the buyer, you might like to try "consignment." Here the store pays for the books only after they are sold, that is, when they need more of them. Keep the initial order small. It won't help to overload the store only to get the shelf-worn books back in a few months. It is better to keep the inventory turning over.

— **College, school and textbook stores** also respond best to face-to-face sales calls. There are some 2,800 college stores serving 2,200 U.S. colleges and universities with over 11 million students. These stores are on their own schedule, depending upon whether they are on the semester, quarter or early semester system. Don't put too much energy into college stores. Students don't spend money on much more than assigned texts, recorded music and beer. Large textbook orders go to the publisher. About one-third of school store orders are through wholesalers, so wholesalers may be a better way to reach this market.

— **To get your message to bookstores**, use co-op mailings, targeted mailings and trade magazines, but let the wholesalers do the fulfillment. The Publishers Marketing Association makes co-op mailings to the 4,500 members of the American Booksellers Association (independent bookstores). Your message can be included for just $180, and you do not have to do all the licking and sticking. PMA's address is in the Appendix.

Targeted mailings may be made to bookstores with special-interest sections. Ask to see the bookstore directories at the Reference Desk of your public library.

Libraries come in several types: public, private, special, school, government, etc. There are almost 15,000 public libraries (9,050 public library systems, some with branches). Three thousand more can be found in colleges, 15,000 are special (including 1,700 law), 20,000 libraries are in high schools, 50,000 in elementary schools, 1,000 are governmental, and over 1,000 formal libraries exist in larger churches.

Even though orders are for smaller quantities, libraries offer greater potential to the small publisher than bookstores. The size of the market is hard to verify, however. Over 90% of the libraries that respond to your mailings or a review in Library Journal will order from a library wholesaler, and 75% of those orders go to Baker & Taylor. Rather than place thousands of orders with individual publishers for single titles, libraries save time by sending all orders to a wholesaler. They are extended a 20% to 33% discount by the wholesaler, so they are receiving both price and service.

Their problem is money. The cost of ordering and processing a new title can cost as much as the book itself. Many libraries are spreading their already tight budgets even thinner now by adding audiovisual and other non-print items. In 1991, 64% of their budget went for personnel; 15.4% was spent on books and other media.

— **Market size.** Libraries spend around $3 billion each year for books, buying some 14% of the books published. Public libraries buy 23%, el-hi school libraries 33%, college libraries 27% and special (e.g., law, medical) libraries 17%. Many of their purchases are for books with press runs under 5,000, which would not get published without their support.

Public libraries spend $700 million on books and audiovisual materials. Sixty-one percent serve populations under 10,000, and 43% spend less than $50,000 a year for all expenses, including purchases.

Most of the libraries with purchasing budgets over $2.5 million are members of the Association of Research Libraries. Five percent of the university libraries have $1 million to $2.5 million to spend on books, 40% have $300,000 or more and 40% have $100,000 or more. Most community and other two-year colleges have only $20,000 to $100,000.

> *Many librarians view the publisher as being the money-grubber between the author and the reader.*

However, university libraries spend 40% to 80% of their budgets on books, with most of the rest going for periodicals.

If libraries bought one copy of every book published in the United States, they would each need a budget of over $2 million per year. Yet less than 2,600 public libraries have an annual book budget of $25,000 or more, and most have much less. They have to be selective in their purchases. Contact only those libraries that can afford to buy your book. Do not waste your energy and money pursuing the rest.

Libraries do not buy fill-in type books—librarians do not want people writing in their books. If your book has to be filled in, you must accept that libraries will not buy it. Some fill-ins can be changed to "lists." Or you might print "SPECIMEN" across the page to encourage photocopying of the page.

As could be expected, children's books and fiction aren't of any great interest to college libraries. Send your brochures to the right type of libraries.

Many libraries buy more for topic than quality. They have to justify their budgets to the community (if public) and try to get something for everyone. It is said that better judgment is shown in the purchasing of children's books and fiction. One librarian recently explained: "When material is scarce on a topic and interest is high, we will often buy any reasonably priced new book through an ad in *Library Journal* or even a flier. However, we usually don't buy if the book receives a bad review."

— **Do library orders kill sales?** Some book publishers question the wisdom of selling to libraries, on the theory that this one sale will kill several others when many people read the book free. They note that many magazines charge libraries a higher price for a subscription on the theory that more people will read the periodical.

Other book publishers feel the libraries are showcasing their book—and are paying to do it. At least four orders for *The Self-Publishing Manual* are received each week with a letter starting, "The library will not let me check the book out again so I guess I'll have to buy my own copy."

Library loans may hurt sales of fiction, which is only read once, but not reference books, which are used over and over. Mailing a free copy of a new book to major libraries might even be a good promotional investment.

— **Approval plans.** Some wholesalers serve their library accounts automatically by sending collections of books in specific categories *on approval*, allowing the library to return the unwanted titles. Because the wholesaler has *prescreened* the books and matched them to the library's special collections, few are returned. Academic and special libraries may buy 30% of their books this way, while public libraries buy some 10% of their books through approval plans. Obviously, it is to your great advantage to have your book included in these computer-matched offerings, especially in the Baker & Taylor system.

— **Ordering cycles.** Libraries tend to do most of their ordering around the beginning/end of their fiscal year (usually December 31 or June 30), when they try to use up their old budget or break into a new one. This is when they may show slightly less buying discrimination. Your book might be selected at this time even if it is an afterthought, not a first choice. At the three-quarter point in their fiscal year, libraries are often out of book purchasing funds. School libraries usually use the slow summer months to work on ordering.

— **Acquisition librarians.** Some libraries have acquisition librarians, while in others book selection is done by committee. Because more than one person is often involved in acquisitions in the larger libraries, it is wise to send more than one copy of each piece of literature.

Do not send your promotional material to the *head librarian* or *acquisition librarian*. In large libraries, it is best to direct mailings to the subject area supervisor who makes the actual buying decisions. These supervisors are in charge of areas such as: *children's books, adult fiction, reference,* etc. Ask about these categories at your local library.

Since libraries want to order from wholesalers, you must let them know which wholesalers carry your book. Make ordering easy. Librarians want all the numbers: ISBN, LC number, Dewey classification, copyright date, number of pages, etc.

It helps if you build consumer demand, as most libraries respond when a title is requested by a library patron. For example, school libraries are responsive to the wishes of their faculties. Mailings to teachers often result in school library orders.

— **Books wear out**; they can be lent out only so many times; a softcover book is good for about 18 cycles. The lifespan of most books is one-and-a-half to two years. Unless a worn-out title has seen a lot of recent use, it usually isn't reordered. On the other hand, if the book has been very popular, the library may order several copies. Books are also stolen—Despite the electronic security systems, some 20% of the collection is lost each year. So many books are kept past the due date that librarians do not have time to look up their price. Many libraries have a flat fee, say $10, for any overdue or lost book.

In 1979, when *The Self-Publishing Manual* was first presented to a librarian in Santa Barbara, she said, "We will have to order several of these. This is the type of book our patrons keep." During the next few years, the library went through more than 30 copies, and this is despite the fact the book is available for sale in several bookstores, instant print shops and office supply stores around town.

Do libraries want hardcover or softcover books? Neither: more and more, they want electronic books, because they do not have shelf space for books. Fiction is still being stocked in print form, but reference materials are on CD-ROM disc. Now when people want to take research material home from a library, they do not photocopy or print out a hard copy, they download onto a floppy. The world of electronic books is not coming; it is here!

— **Dealing direct**. Some publishers have elected to deal directly with libraries instead of using wholesalers. Most of these publishers specialize in higher-priced reference books for which libraries are their largest market. They make regular mailings to libraries, count on getting full price and like to stay close to their market. But most libraries prefer to use wholesalers.

While librarians don't throw out as much mail as bookstores do, they are likely to purchase only one book per branch. It is hard to justify a mailing when more often than not, the library will order it through a library wholesaler to whom you give 40% to 60%.

The librarians say they buy to cover a subject; they will buy a higher-priced book if it meets the need and is the only one available. Libraries do not expect a discount unless they order several copies. Some publishers follow a universal discount schedule, giving 10% for an order of five, 20% for 20, etc. Some big-city public libraries will take advantage of quantity deals because they are buying for several branches.

— **Your local library** should buy your book just because you are part of the community. Some even have a special private room for books by indigenous writers. If so, it may be appropriate for you to donate a copy to this reference section. If you do make such a donation, be sure the local paper is notified with a news release, so you can get some promotional mileage out of your largess.

> Dan Poynter donated a couple of his new books to the local public library when he lived in Quincy, Massachusetts. The books were placed in a special room reserved for local books. This was quite an unexpected honor in the hometown of two U.S. presidents.

Marketing plan for libraries. The best way to handle the library market is to strike a deal with Quality Books, become a stock publisher with Baker & Taylor, let all the library wholesalers know where to find you by sending them a brochure, join the PMA library mailing, make your own mailings to libraries with special collections, and prepare a great review package for *Library Journal*. Here are the details:

— **Quality Books** uses sales reps to sell books to libraries. They have some 6,000 active library accounts. Quality needs 100 new titles each month and actively seeks new books. They sell to libraries at list price or at a 20% discount.

Quality wants 55% off, consignment, returnable and 90 days to pay. If you will agree to a 60% discount, they will pay in 60 days. Fifty-five percent may sound like a lot, but Quality buys by the carton and pays on time. Returns to publishers average 2% to 3%, and Quality pays the return shipping.

Write to Quality for a *New Book Information* form and a sample *Distribution to Libraries Agreement*: Quality Books, Inc., 1003 W. Pines Road, Oregon, IL 61061, Tel: (708) 295-2010.

> Quality rejected *Parachuting, The Skydiver's Handbook*, when it was initially published. The selection committee just didn't believe the library market was large enough for such a specialized sport. Quality was handling a number of the author's other books and gave the handbook another look soon after company president Tom Drewes took up skydiving in 1983. Everyone has been pleasantly surprised—Quality has moved several hundred copies.

The Quality Books Selection Committee looks for the following when evaluating a book for library use:

1. Adult nonfiction.

2. New—copyright in current year. The book must not have been exposed to the library market previously. Publisher's primary market must be outside the library market. Book must be submitted to Quality books prior to official publication date.

3. Book is well organized.

   a. Good title and subtitle. Must be informative, not cute. Must clearly and instantly convey the book's purpose. Title must be the same on cover, spine and title page.

   b. Includes table of contents and index.

   c. Book is clearly different from others in its field. Librarians like to fill information gaps.

   d. Information is readily accessible—the book is *user-friendly*.

4. No fill-in books. The book must be usable by several customers.

5. Cataloging-in-Publication data to help in cataloging the book.

6. ISBN to aid identification of the book.

7. Binding. More and more of the books purchased by libraries today are softcover. The less-expensive edition allows librarians to order more books from the same budget. However, the perfect binding must be durable. The book must have a spine to display the title (no spiral binding) and must be shaped to fit a library shelf, not long, low or round.

8. A topical subject. Book must be the type customers want to borrow from the library.

9. Sales aids. The publisher should supply extra covers for the reps to show to the libraries.

The selection committee turns down 700 to 800 titles each month. Some books do not meet the selection criteria above, but most rejected submissions are older books from larger publishers. Think about these criteria when writing/designing your next book.

The secret to having your book accepted by Quality Books is to notify them of the new title early. Quality has to get the jump on the regular wholesalers if they are to be effective in moving books for you. The time to send in the *New Book Information Form* is before you go to press. Then books may be shipped directly to Quality from the printer. It is a great feeling to go to press knowing that 400 books are already sold.

— **Baker & Taylor.** Become a *stock publisher*. Library sales account for 68% of B&T's business. Contact should have been made as you worked through the previous bookstore section.

— **Notify other library wholesalers with a mailing.** The smaller library wholesalers are Coutts Library Service, Midwest, Ballen, BroDart, et al.

— **Book reviews** in library review magazines. Since a good review in *Library Journal* or *ALA Booklist* will move around 1,200 copies of most books, book reviews are worth some extra effort.

Book reviews are librarians' overwhelmingly most popular tool for making selection decisions. Acquisition librarians just do not have the time to read and evaluate all the new books. Librarians rely mostly on *Publishers Weekly, Library Journal, ALA Booklist, Kirkus Reviews, Choice* and *The New York Times Book Review*. Ninety-four percent of the librarians rely on reviews in *Library Journal*, while 91% read the reviews in *ALA Booklist*. Only 44% believe thc ads in *LJ*, and only 35% have confidence in the ads in *Booklist*. The figures for *Publishers Weekly* are 75% and 53%. See the addresses for the magazines in the Appendix. Also see the *Book Review, Selection & Reference* section of *Literary Market Place*.

Follow up on review packet mailings to the above-mentioned library review magazines with a telephone call. Never ask if they plan to *review* the book but rather if they have *received* the book. If not, or they can't find it, get a name and send another book.

— **PMA co-op mailings to libraries.** Four times each year, The Publishers Marketing Association mails a flat envelope containing individual book fliers to 2,500 public libraries across the U.S. which have a purchasing budget of $25,000 or more. These are just public libraries, and then only those that can afford to buy. Cost for participation is $125 plus your flat (unfolded) flier on one or more books. PMA also makes co-op mailings to K-12 libraries and university libraries. Contact PMA; the address is in the Appendix.

Consider the type of library most likely to buy your book: Maybe you just want school, medical, or law libraries, or maybe you have a regional book and just want public libraries in New England. Then make a mailing either alone or in cooperation with other publishers.

— **Mailings to special libraries and libraries with special collections.** Look for special libraries or regular libraries with special collections. If yours is an aviation book, send brochures to libraries with an aviation section. Do not go to the expense of mailing to all libraries when you can isolate those that have a particular interest in your topic. Gale Research rents lists of libraries with **special collections**. Gale Research Company, 835 Penobscot Building, Detroit, MI 48226-4094, Tel: (313) 961-2242, (800) 877-GALE; Fax: (313) 961-6083.

For a list of **special libraries**, contact the Special Library Association, 1700 Eighteenth Street, NW, Washington, DC 20009-2508, Tel: (202) 234-4700; Fax: (202) 265-9317.

Many individual library associations will rent their mailing lists. For example, The American Association of Law Libraries can supply a list of 2,300 law libraries on labels. For more information on contacting special libraries, send for *Marketing to Libraries Through Library Associations*, from the American Library Association, 50 East Huron Street, Chicago, IL 60611, Tel: (312) 944-6780; Fax: (312) 944-8741.

When you plan to make a mailing to specialized libraries, invite other publishers to join you. Co-op promotions can save a lot of money and help justify otherwise marginal mailings. Contacting other publishers is easy. Just send a notice of your proposed mailing for listing in the Publishers Marketing Association *Newsletter*.

— **Library review magazines**. *Library Journal, ALA Booklist* and other trade magazines run special editions and special sections throughout the year. Areas covered are travel books, children's books, metaphysical books, cookbooks, religious books, etc. Listings are usually free. Advertising and listings should be planned for these special editions where attention is being drawn to a particular subject.

Write to each magazine for ad rates and announcements of special editions. The addresses are in the Appendix.

The school market spends over a billion dollars each year for textbooks, and while most of these books are developed especially for certain courses, many are regular books developed for other markets but adopted as supplementary educational aids. While educators want the very latest information, most are leery of being experimental. Teachers need to be assured that the book is up-to-date and has been accepted by experts elsewhere. Educators are the most price-conscious of all the book markets, even though they aren't spending their own money. Textbook publishers respond by keeping their prices lower than normal and extending only a 20% (short) discount to the school bookstores.

— **Elementary and secondary schools.** In the U.S. there are some 64,000 public elementary, 24,000 public high and 1,800 combined schools in 18,000 school districts. Additionally, there are some 14,000 private elementary and 4,000 private high schools. Together they employ 2.3 million teachers.

In 22 states, schools purchase texts under a state adoption system, where titles are approved by a board for a five-year period. State adoption is a hunting license and allows the salespeople to try to sell the book to the schools. Even where there is no state adoption system, planning seems to follow a five-year cycle. In some areas, publishers have to ship to central depositories, where the schools draw on books as needed. This usually means a consignment inventory, and the publishers aren't paid for the books until requisitioned by the schools. The school market is tough and very competitive.

To reach the home school market, see *Selling to the Other Educational Markets* by Jane Williams, Bluestocking Press, Tel: (916) 621-1123.

— **Colleges and universities.** Colleges are changing. There are more students over 25; more women are going back to school; and more people are turning to continuing-education courses in their specialty.

There are three types of college bookstores. Some are owned by the institution, some are private and some are college stores with a private lessee. Those connected with the institution may take advantage of "library rate" postage schedules.

Textbook publishers concentrate on wooing the instructors who must select books for their courses in more than 3,000 schools. This decision is easy for some professors, as they pen their own. Normally the purchasing is done by the local bookstore, and the instructor notifies them of his or her choice by April for the fall term. Of course, there are problems. The choice is made late and the estimate of the number to be needed is frequently wrong. Then some students avoid buying the text by sharing or making repeated visits to the school library. The result is a store return rate on textbooks of more than 20%.

Teachers expect to get free examination copies of books, and while some treat this privilege with respect, others just collect books or sell them to the bookstore. The bookstore, in turn, sells the book to a student or returns it to the publisher for a refund. The bookstores even supply the educators with blank "Desk Copy Request Forms" designed to be sent to the publisher for freebees. Often the younger instructors are trying to build up their libraries. The older professors, who have more say in book selection, do much less collecting. Some publishers like to request more information about the size of the course, the requester's academic position, etc. Sol Marshall of Creative Books answers desk copy requests with a form letter offering the book at a greatly reduced price. This way he at least covers his costs.

> During the last 20 years, this publisher has sent out scores of requested "desk copies" and so far only two have resulted in large school bookstore orders.

To attack the college market, analyze your book's subject and determine which course might find it useful. The educators are easy to find, and direct mail advertising is the most effective method of reaching them. In fact, some publishers find the lists so specialized that they use them to send free, unsolicited examination copies.

Mailing list information can be found in your library. See *Direct Marketing List Source, An Advertiser's Guide to Scholarly Periodicals* and *Direct Marketing* magazine. Check the *Yellow Pages* for local list brokers, and see the listing of mailing list sources in the Appendix.

Another way to reach the educational market is through book exhibits at academic bookfairs and conventions. With only a title or two, you may like to share a booth with someone else, or turn your book over to a firm which will represent you for a small fee. See the paragraph on bookfairs, later in this chapter.

College buying patterns are affected by school schedules, depending on whether they are on the semester, quarter or early semester system. The best months to make mailings to colleges are February, April, July and October. Once you make contact with an instructor, add him or her to your mailing list; they are valuable. Once a professor has adopted one of your books, some say he or she is twice as likely to do it again.

Pre-publication sales will bring in some money early and help you pay the printing bill. But it isn't wise to start too soon on the pre-publication publicity for your first book. The first time around is a learning experience, and there will be countless delays. You do not want to find yourself spending all your time answering the question: "Where is the book?" With the first book, hold your announcement until it is on the press. The next time, adjust and start earlier.

> Once you learn the promotion ropes, you should be able to sell enough books through pre-publication sales, to both wholesale and retail customers, to pay the print bill.

Write up a news release, send in your ads and make a mailing. Offer an early wholesale deal ("to be shipped direct from the printer") to associations and specialty dealers. It is nice to have a pile of orders on the desk when the book comes off the press. But timing is important; these orders must not pour in too early or too late.

If your book is specialized and you are able to find an appropriate mailing list, you should consider a pre-publication retail offer. Tell the potential buyer the book is being printed, and if they want one hot off the press, to send their money now; that you will be shipping on a first-come, first-served basis. Include an early order deal such as "postage free if you order from this ad." This mailing should also be sent to all your friends and acquaintances; many will respond and be pleased that you thought of them. If a prospect is mentioned in the text or the acknowledgments, he is sure to buy one.

Never discount a brand-new book. Many new publishers feel they have to offer a deal. Discounting a new book makes you appear to be in a distress situation. You are in a very strong position. You have a new book. You need every penny of profit; do not give it away.

Specialty (nonbook) outlets offer many nonfiction publishers their largest market. For example, a book on mountain climbing will sell better in backpacking shops than bookstores, and the size of the store's purchases will be larger. Sales to stores other than bookstores are often called *nontraditional sales* or *special sales.*

Warner Publishing cracked a new market in 1978 when Karen Lustgarten's *Disco Dancing* was sold in record stores.

At Para Publishing, we tolerate but do not pursue bookstores. The only relationship between nonfiction books is their packaging; the subject matter of each book is unique. Nonfiction should be sold where customers for it can be found. Boating books should be placed in nautical shops, tourist books in tourist shops and football books in sporting goods stores. Sell your books where the highest concentration of potential customers can be found. Most of your prospects probably never go into a bookstore. So, make your books available through bookstores, but do not confine your sales efforts to these shops.

— Stores. Many specialty shops will want a 40%, 50% or more discount, but they usually buy outright. There are no returns.

In these specialty shops, it is very important to establish, cultivate and maintain as close a personal relationship as possible with the management. It is of the utmost importance that they like you and your book so they will promote it at every opportunity. Selling them the first time often requires a personal visit to prove the sales potential of the book. When making a direct mail promotion to these firms,

Bookstores are lousy places to sell books.

remember their peak selling seasons and the required lead time.

One innovative book marketer is Bruce Lansky of Meadowbrook Press. He is good because he markets books the way he used to market candy. His (then) wife Vicki wrote a book on nutrition for babies called *Feed Me, I'm Yours*, and the Lanskys decided to publish it themselves. First Bruce tried a local children's clothing store. They bought, so he approached a wholesaler of infant items but was turned down flat. He had to offer consignment and counter racks to let the wholesaler prove to himself the books would move. The wholesaler called three days later and ordered 12 dozen more—they were in business. Next Lansky created a mailing stuffer for the wholesaler to put in with the statements sent to his 1,000 accounts. Sales soared. Lansky's secrets are:

1. Play dumb. Visit the account and learn all about terms, key accounts and trade reps in that field.

2. Don't act like a publisher; act like you are in the same business. Bruce was in *infant accessories* that day.

3. Use success to breed more success. Do your research, run small tests and learn the industry. Subscribe to their magazines, join their associations, exhibit at their trade shows. Make a mailing to distributors and retailers and follow up with calls.

Other nonbook retail channels include gift shops, hardware stores, garden shops, sporting goods stores, etc. Many are establishing book corners for an additional profit center, as well as to lend prestige to their line.

Run a test in a few local shops. Develop your approach (posters, counter displays, price, etc.) before rolling out in a wider promotion. Just as there are wholesalers serving the bookstores, there are those who cater to the nonbook outlets. Check these stores and look for books. Find out who distributes them to the store.

> *The smallest houses were relatively more successful in using non-book retail outlets than the largest houses were.*
> — Judith Appelbaum in *Publishers Weekly*

If books are not being carried, you will have to reach the stores through direct mail, advertising in their magazines or sales reps of other lines. Search for lists of that type of store. Ask the local store manager for names of hot sales reps and rep groups who handle other lines of products. Sales reps will want 10% to 15% of the *net billed amount* (a commission on the books after discount, not the shipping charges).

If the specialty shop is a franchise, make a pitch to the headquarters. Many franchisers do not control the buying of their franchisees, and even if they do, the sale will not be easy. However, the hope of making one large sale to the whole chain is worth some of your sales time.

> A few years ago, the author was in a local instant print shop when the owner began asking about *The Self-Publishing Manual*. Forty percent off sounded good, and the printer wanted to put some books on the counter. The author doubted the books would sell, but brought in eight copies in a (cut-down carton) counter display to humor the printer. Three days later, the printer called for more. Apparently, the type of people who frequent copy shops are the type who work with the written word—a good market after all. This lesson resulted in an expansion into other instant print shops and a book on how to paste up. Some outlets for books may not be obvious at first.

If you receive an inquiry from a market you never thought would be interested in your book, draft a letter to similar stores or groups saying, "This store or group ordered the book and we thought you might be interested, too." The mailing may be just 100 pieces—no great investment—and there is a good chance of a payoff.

If the Appendix of the book has a source directory, make a mailing to each firm saying, "you are mentioned in the book; thought you would like to know, and we think you might like to offer this book to your customers." Build up a strong, reliable dealer network.

— **Selling to the U.S. Government.** There are 2,300 libraries in the federal government library system and 80 agencies which purchase books, according to *Publishers Weekly*. Most of the libraries come under the Defense Department. The Office of the Director of the Army Library Program procures hardbound books for Army libraries around the world and paperbacks for distribution in the field. Of approximately 60 clothbound titles chosen monthly, some 60% are nonfiction. About 100 paperbound titles are procured each month and distributed in 900 kits; selections are highly recreational. Centralized purchases are made under annual contracts with wholesalers. Navy libraries spend over $3 million each year. The U.S. Information Service runs 129 libraries in 110 countries, with 6,000 to 25,000 volumes each, and devotes about $2 million each year to procurement. They like to see brochures and review copies. The Veterans Administration operates 392 libraries, with a budget of more than $2 million.

The secret in selling to the military is to approach the "specifier." For example, the author's *The Parachute Manual* is of interest to parachute riggers, both civilian and military. A mailing made to all military parachute lofts generated private sales and the brochure was passed on to procurement offices, so that the book could be ordered for the library or the loft. Brochures sent to the ultimate user often get a much better response than those sent to procurement offices.

— **Premiums** are products which are given away or sold at a discount to promote business. Premiums may be given away by a store or other business to encourage people to come in. According to *Potentials in Marketing* magazine, 16.8% of the companies using premiums, use books. The premium market is estimated to amount to $11.5 billion annually, and about 1/2 billion is spent on books. Books make especially good premiums, as they may be customized by printing a special cover and they are held in higher esteem than some other premium trinkets.

If your book covers a regional topic, try local businesses. Small quantities of books may be rubber-stamped with *Compliments of Valley National Bank*, as an example. If you cover a subject with wider appeal, such as a book on beer can collecting, contact the beer, aluminum, steel, can and packaging companies. Such a book would make an ideal corporate gift or might be worked into a promotion. A travel book might be sold to a motel chain.

Judy Dugan was working in a graphic arts shop when the first edition of *The Self-Publishing Manual* was being typeset. As she pasted up the pages, she read the book and became increasingly interested. She had been toying with a local history-geography manuscript for years, and began asking the author all sorts of questions about the possibilities for her book. One problem she had was a lack of money to invest.

The author noticed that Valley National Bank was moving into a building in downtown Santa Barbara. He explained that they were a prime candidate for a regional book, as it would tie the out-of-town bank to the local community. A premium could be used to lure potential patrons into the bank.

In two short visits, she walked out with a purchase order for 5,000 copies in softcover and 1,000 copies in hardcover. She was paid one-half on signing and one-half on delivery, at full list price. She had 30 days to deliver but had not finished the book yet. Fortunately, Judy was a graphic artist, and there was a printer right next door. *Santa Barbara Highlights and History* was delivered on time. The money allowed her to print 11,000 books so she could serve the local tourist market with her 5,000.

The bank's copies had special back cover printing: *Compliments of . . .,* and the bank advertised in newspapers, on radio and television. They invited people to come into the bank for a free autographed copy of the book. They set up a table and a sign, and Judy spent the week greeting people and signing her name. Judy's book became a valuable traffic-builder for the bank.

Premium orders are large, usually 1,000 or more books, and the customer may ask for 60% off. Such a discount can be justified for a large order which eliminates the problems of financing, storage and individual shipping. A typical premium discount schedule might look like this:

Number of copies	Discounts
25-99	20%
100-299	40%
300-499	45%
500-999	50%
1,000-14,999	60%
15,000 up	Cost of printing plus 10% of list price

Discount schedule for premiums

If you can strike some premium deals before going to (or back to) press, you may increase your press run and achieve a smaller per-unit cost. Early sales are also a great help in paying the first printing bill. Be prepared to do a lot of legwork. Premium sales are tough and time-consuming, but the payoff is big.

— **Fund raisers.** Nonprofit organizations are always running sales to raise money for their cause. These flea markets, bake sales and auctions, promoted by church and civic groups, can provide you with an opportunity to move some books. Try approaching some local organizations first, to get a feel for the way they operate. If you are successful, consider a mailing list to similar groups. Don't forget to tell them of your past good track record for sales and assure them that the unsold books may be returned. Local clubs and local chapters of national organizations raise funds, too. If your book is appropriate, you might strike a deal. A gar-

> *Unless the group is the National Association of Cookie Products, a book makes a better fund-raiser than a bake sale.*

dening book might be sold by a gardening club, for example. By making the nonprofit organization a dealer, they raise money for their group and you gain access to a new audience.

To find organizations, consult *National Trade & Professional Associations of the U.S. and Canada* and Gale's *Encyclopedia of Associations,* available at your library. Write to these organizations, enclosing your brochure, news release, etc. Tell them why your book would be valuable to them, but hold off on the price until you get a bite. The price will depend on the number they want, and the number could be in the thousands.

Subsidiary rights. Essentially, subsidiary rights give someone else permission to reproduce (repackage) your material. They include book clubs, mass-market paperbacks, film rights, translations, etc. The two major classes of subsidiary rights are *print* rights and rights to *non-print adaptations.*

Subsidiary rights are so important to the big publishers that the rights are often auctioned off before the original book is printed. However, most publishers report that less than 2% of their income is derived from subsidiary rights sales. A condensation or small book club sale usually brings more fame than fortune. Such a sale is also a great morale booster for both the author and the publisher, not only for the money but because someone else obviously likes the book.

The main reason publishers can sell the subsidiary rights for so little is that they are not paying production costs to their printers or, more important, royalties to their authors. Most author-publisher contracts call for a 50/50 split of subsidiary rights *revenues.* Some contracts give 90% of revenues to the author on any non-print (e.g., film) subsidiary rights. The publisher gets 10% as an *agent.*

A publisher's attitude toward a manuscript ought to be similar to a coal mine operator's attitude toward coal: get every last bit of value out of it.
— Sol Stein, President of Stein and Day

Some subsidiary rights require only a continuation of the same printing (book club rights), but don't let your customer get away with just paying for the additional press time. They should pay for all your set-up and overhead costs. If you aren't familiar with negotiating rights, get a literary agent or an attorney who understands the publishing business, when a book club or other subsidiary rights buyer becomes serious. The agent will get 10% to 15% of whatever he or she brings in, while the lawyer will work for a percentage or a straight fee for checking the contract. Agents are listed in *Literary Market Place*. For a list of book attorneys, see Para Publishing's free Fax-On-Demand Document 113. See the Appendix.

— **Mass-market reprint rights** are for those pocket-sized books selling from $1 to $5 in the supermarkets. This is the one market where it is easier to sell fiction than non-fiction. Mass-market publishers like seven-year contracts with renewal options and initial print runs of 30,000 to 50,000 copies. Mass-market publishers offer 4% to 7.5% in royalties; the cover price is low and the scale does not slide up until sales reach 150,000 copies. Advances are usually just a few thousand dollars. Unless you have a *very* popular book, the mass-market firms won't be interested.

The secret is to match your book with a publisher that has experience with that type of material. Look over other books, and search for publishers who have produced the same subject matter. Not every editor in every house is interested in everything. Mass-market publishers may be contacted after your book has been out for a year or so.

— **Periodical rights.** Serializations and excerpts by magazines and newspapers may be *first serial rights*, if before publication, or *second serial rights*, if afterward. Both generate a lot of good publicity. Big publications pay more than small ones, and first rights are more valuable than second. The subject matter has to be of great interest to the publication's readers.

Serializations help generate sales for the original book. Always request that the periodical print ordering information for your book. Place exact wording in your contract or letter as well as on the material submitted, such as:

"Reprinted with permission from *The Self-Publishing Manual* by Dan Poynter, copyright © 1995. Available from Para Publishing, P.O. Box 2206-802, Santa Barbara, CA 93118-2206, for $21.95 postpaid."

Such a notice will generate a lot of individual mail order sales. Anyone who reads the whole article will be a prime candidate.

Magazines will probably contact you regarding serializations after receiving a review copy of the book. However, you should make the offer to *appropriate* magazines prior to going to press. Send a Crane-type galley to those magazines with good readership-to-book match. For specific details on Cranes and galleys, see the Special Report titled *Book Reviews*. See the Appendix.

— **Condensation rights.** Book condensations in magazines do not normally pay a lot, but the publicity they provide will sell more books. Make sure the magazine is a quality product, one you will be proud to be associated with. Check their past condensation work, and call the publishers of the subject books. Ask if they are happy with the way they were treated and with the quality of the condensation, and compare the price they were paid with the one you have been offered.

The magazine normally farms out the rewrite, and the work should be a condensation, not a reprint of the two meaty chapters. You can expect them to offer a couple of hundred dollars, up to several thousand, depending upon the publication. Expect an offer of $600. Remember, they have to rewrite the text and that costs money. Sell the condensation rights on a non-exclusive basis; the magazine will be first in print but you want to retain the right to sell again to other publications. Always obtain *text approval*. They could completely miss your point in making the condensation.

> *Without subsidiary rights, publishers would operate in the hole.* — John Dessauer

Read the draft over carefully, and make corrections; your name is on the piece, and the condensation will be a major sales tool for your book. You want it to be right. Make sure the condensation includes information where the original book may be purchased, complete with price and address. See the example in *Periodical Rights*, above.

Magazines will probably contact you regarding condensations after receiving a review copy of the book. However, you should make the offer to appropriate magazines prior to going to press. Approach just a few magazines with a good book-to-readership match.

— **Anthology rights.** An anthology is a collection of writing selections from one or more authors, usually on the same theme. Editors of anthologies may offer you a flat fee or a percentage of a normal royalty. If ten authors are each contributing a chapter, each might be offered 1% of the list price or 1/10 of a 10% royalty.

You might decide to spin off a piece of your book into your own anthology by contacting authors in the same field for submissions.

— **Book club rights.** Book clubs offer you some money and a great deal of prestige. Since they were established in the mid-twenties, the Book-of-the-Month-Club (BOMC) and the Literary Guild (each with over a million members) have been helping their members by selecting the best books of the thousands available, at lower than normal prices. Now there are more than 200 book clubs, moving over $500 million worth of books each year, most of which cater to highly specialized groups.

The usual book club royalty is 10% of the list price plus production expenses. For example, say it costs you $2 to print the book and the list price is $20. The clubs like to discount to their members, so knock off 20% and you have $16. You will receive $3.60 per book, representing $2 for production and $1.60 as a 10% royalty on the $16 selling price. If the book club invests in the printing, you get just the *royalty* of 10% of the club's selling price. Book club purchases are usually non-returnable.

Larger clubs will make their own printing or join you in your original print run. Smaller clubs will want to buy from your finished stock. Those doing their own printing or joining yours should benefit from a 10% royalty deal. Book clubs buying 500 to 1,000 books from your stock should be treated as a large dealer and be given a discount of around 60%.

The larger clubs usually want an exclusive; they don't want other clubs to carry the book, too, at least not at the same time. Smaller clubs aren't so particular, because their memberships do not overlap.

A book club sale is an important endorsement. If you can make the sale before going to press, the endorsement can be noted on the back cover as well as on all your promotional materials. For example: *Writer's Digest Book Club, Main Selection.*

Do book clubs hurt regular sales? Absolutely not! They help you start off with a large number sold, provide you with a valuable endorsement and draw a lot of attention to the book in their promotions.

Approach book clubs when you have a completed manuscript or galleys to show them. If they don't respond, write them again after publication and enclose photocopies of your reviews. They have to be convinced it is a desirable book, and that is where clippings of reviews can help. Send a letter to every club that might possibly be interested. Check *Literary Market Place* for book clubs and make up a list for a mailing.

— **Performing rights** cover stage, motion pictures, radio and television. Film rights will be somewhat unusual for a nonfiction book, but it does happen.

The usual royalty rate is 15% of the net and this is usually a bad deal. Film companies are notorious for their unusual accounting procedures, which result in a very small net; some have been known to write off everything possible

---

The bottom line makes it abundantly clear; subsidiary rights have become less and less subsidiary. — Nancy Evans

against the film. Always insist on a smaller percentage of the **gross**. The gross figure is much more objective.

Performing rights involve complex contracts and should not be negotiated without special advice. If you receive a firm offer, see a book attorney.

— **Translation rights.** A publisher in another country may wish to buy the translation rights. The foreign publisher will pay you a royalty and take care of everything. Normally you supply the photos and a couple of copies of the book with late changes noted. They translate the text, change the measurements to metric and take care of all the printing, distribution, etc. Royalties may be 5% to 7% for hardcover rights and 5% to 10% for softcover.

Foreign publishers and foreign rights representatives are listed in *International Literary Market Place*.

When negotiating a foreign rights contract, consider the number of copies to be printed, the printing schedule, cover price, royalties for both hardbound and softcover editions, the advance and the government tax, if any. Some countries impose a tax on exported royalties; Japan, for example, charges 10% of the remitted amount.

For complete details on foreign sales, see the Special Report titled *Exports/Foreign Rights, Selling U.S. Books Abroad*. See the Appendix.

— **Merchandising rights.** If the subject of your book suddenly becomes hot, customers will beat a path to your door with offers to put the character or words on tee shirts, decals and coffee mugs.

See *Literary Market Place* for more subsidiary rights possibilities. See *Publishing Contracts on Disk*, available from Para Publishing, for actual subsidiary rights wording. See the Appendix.

— **Multimedia rights.** Your information may be turned into an electronic book and put on a CD-ROM disc.

> Remember: *A book not submitted is a book not chosen.*

Write to likely subsidiary rights prospects well before publication and ask if they would like to see photocopies of the manuscript. Then follow with a telephone call. Mail out a lot of inquiries simultaneously, don't go at them one at a time. There isn't enough time for this luxury.

Co-publishing is a way for two firms to spread the risk and reward in a new book. Usually one publisher is large and the other small, or the two concentrate on different markets. Usually the larger publisher handles the bookstores and libraries, while the smaller publisher sells direct to user groups and handles the individual mail order sales.

Selling out. Many new author-publishers have published their first book and then sold out to a large publisher. Many sell too cheap. Editors from major houses make the rounds of the booths at bookfairs, such as the American Booksellers Association Book Fair in the spring. These acquisition editors are hunting for good books to add to their lines. Small publishers are usually thrilled to be courted by a big house and often make the mistake of selling for the same 10% (or less) royalty an author gets for a manuscript.

Ten percent of the cover price is small reward after expending so much time and money to package and promote a book as well as to test the market. The big publisher is exploiting the little publisher at 10%, because all the risk has been removed. Successful books should cost more. The large publisher must understand the book is coming from another publisher; this is not just an untested manuscript from an author. A fee should be paid to the small publisher for packaging and market exploration as well as a royalty to the author.

When a large publisher buys a book from a small publisher, the price should be two or three times the production costs, plus 10% of projected sales. They should pay for all your time, work and financial risk. The deal should be made "royalty inclusive," which means receiving your money up front—not waiting until months after their books are sold.

Sell only the *North American rights* to the *book trade*. Retain all rights, except to the bookstores and libraries in the U.S.

and Canada. Always keep the non-exclusive individual sale, mail order rights. The big publisher will not be interested in individual sales anyway. Make sure you can buy books for the printing cost plus ten percent. Normally you will be required to buy in lots of 500 or more, but this is a bargain for you because you do not have to invest in a large print run. Make sure all rights revert to you once the publisher lets the book go out of print. In evaluating a contract, consider the royalty, advance, when you will get paid, who gets what part of other subsidiary rights, the duration of the contract, and free copies to the author.

Small publishers and self-publishers would be better off to cut a distribution deal or co-publish with a larger publisher. In a distribution arrangement, the big publisher would buy several thousand books for 60% to 70% off list price on a non-returnable basis with payment in 30 days and would have an exclusive in the book trade: bookstores and libraries. Insist on a large quantity so the large publisher is in deep and has to promote the books. With the book trade covered, the author-publisher is now free to concentrate on the retail mail order sales and the nonbook markets. But be forewarned; if you do sell out, you will probably make less money while losing control of your book.

Exchange title promotion. Mail order customers interested in a certain subject tend to purchase every book which covers the area. Unfortunately, many small publishers do not have titles in any depth on any particular topic. When two or more publishers of like material handle each other's books, their customers get a wider range of choices and the publishers get an improved response rate to their advertising. This cross-distribution, formerly common only in other sales channels, is now becoming more familiar in mail order book marketing.

Approach publishers with books that complement yours. Trade cartons of books based on their list price, and add them to your brochure. If you do not wish to take on products from other publishers, at least make an agreement to stuff each other's brochures into outgoing packages.

Bookshelf books. Offering other books in the same line as the anchor product will spread costs and make you the *information center* for your interest area. For example, Para Publishing has six books on various areas of publishing, with *The Self-Publishing Manual* as our anchor product. We have special reports on very narrow publishing subjects, a newsletter, *Publishing Poynters*, a Fax-On-Demand information system, speeches, private consulting, and we host publishing workshops. But there are a lot of good books we did not write which will help publishers, so we buy them from their publishers and offer them to our book publishing customers. Request FOD Document 133. See the Appendix.

Keep your bookshelf focused on a particular topic. Most of your orders will be for your own books. The bookshelf books will sell well, but they will not approach the sales of your own books.

Recordings and Braille editions are published for the blind. If your book is well received, you may be approached by a library for permission to translate your book into Braille or to put it on tape. When you fill out the copyright form for your book, you will have the opportunity to give the Library of Congress a non-exclusive right to reproduce your book in recorded or Braille form.

The international market. Foreign sales of books exceeded $1.64 billion in 1992, with most going to Canada, Great Britain and Australia. English is the commercial language of the world, has always been the aviation language, has replaced German as the scientific language and has replaced French as the diplomatic language. More people in the world speak English as a second language than any other. People look to the U.S. for the latest information, and with the dollar low on world markets, our books are not expensive.

The most common way to cater to the international market is to fill and mail foreign orders in the same way you fill domestic ones. Most of your export sales will come with the daily mail. They will be just like your domestic orders except for their lighter-weight stationery, strange addresses and pretty stamps. Most of the foreign bookstores will get your address from Bowker's *Books In Print.*

Postal rates for foreign shipments may be higher or lower than domestic rates, depending on which rate has been raised most recently. There is a 5 kg (11 lb.) weight limit for books, but if you are shipping more than 15 lbs., you may qualify for "Direct Sacks of Prints" at $1.32 per pound. See Chapter Ten. Since it is so inexpensive to export, it makes little sense to print the book abroad in English unless the press run is huge.

Be advised that adding a country will not double your sales. For example, expanding from the U.S. to Canada may increase sales 7% to 10%. You must compare the sizes of the English-speaking populations.

Look for publishers that concentrate on your same type of book. Look them up in *International Literary Market Place.* Foreign bookstores and libraries may also be found in *International Literary Market Place.*

Sponsored books are those you are almost commissioned to write. There may be an institution which wants your book printed badly enough to give you a large advance order. For example, if you wrote a book on the Frisbee® disc and there were no others on the subject, the Wham-O™ Manufacturing Company, which makes flying discs, might want the book to be published because the publicity would help their sales. With this sponsorship, they might want some sort of cover credit, such as: "Published in association with Wham-O." Such an endorsement would be to your advantage, as it would lend credibility to the book.

Some industries need favorable publicity and find that sponsoring a book is much less expensive than placing full-page ads. A book is also much more effective promotion as it appears to be more objective.

See Para Publishing's Special Report *Exports/Foreign Rights, Selling U.S. Books Abroad.* See the Appendix.

Specialty shows, such as sport and boat exhibitions and trade shows, are rarely worthwhile for a small author-publisher with a single title. However, you can make sure that your book is carried and offered for sale by someone in the show. Find a booth with related merchandise and offer them some books on consignment. Give them a carton of books and an examination copy for the table. They get a piece of the action and you get the exposure while moving books.

Bookfairs provide important exposure to your book. The major national U.S. shows are sponsored by:

1. The American Booksellers Association, 560 White Plains Road, Tarrytown, NY 10591, Tel: (914) 631-7800; Fax: (914) 631-8391 (often in late May and attended primarily by bookstore managers)

2. The American Library Association, 50 East Huron Street, Chicago, IL 60611, Tel: (312) 944-6780; Fax: (312) 944-8741 (late June and attended primarily by librarians)

3. The National Association of College Stores (NACS), 528 East Lorain Street, Oberlin, OH 44074, Tel: (216) 775-7777; Fax: (216) 775-4769 (usually mid-spring and attended by college bookstore managers)

Write to the listed organizations regarding the fairs, and then attend a nearby one yourself to assess how you might fit in to your advantage. The big associations also sponsor regional and local bookfairs.

International bookfairs are held all over the world, with the most important being in London and Frankfurt. They can give good exposure and may lead to foreign rights but probably are not worth your own exhibiting effort.

Conventions and conferences of professional, academic and trade associations will present you with a "qualified" audience for your books, if you match your subject matter to the show. Educational books do well at educational exhibits, and these conferences are especially fun as they provide an opportunity to meet with authors as well as customers. For more ideas, consult *National Trade & Professional Associations of the U.S. and Canada Directory* and Gale's *Encyclopedia of Associations*, available in your library.

Exhibiting at a bookfair is often an inspiring experience; it will recharge your batteries. You will learn more about the industry, meet some great people, make valuable contacts, sell a few books, and perhaps even sell some subsidiary rights. Typically, the show's management provides a space measuring about 10' x 10', a draped table, curtained side and back panels, a sign, carpet, and a chair or two. Check their brochure closely. Get some book stands and take a good supply of books and brochures.

Shows cost money. Booth space at the big American Booksellers Association fair runs $2,000 and up. The American Library Association (ALA) is much higher. But they also have a small press section for less. In addition to booth expenses, you must consider your personal travel, book shipping, hotels, meals, etc. You can spend $4,000 exhibiting, and $6,000 is not unusual.

Exhibiting services will put your books on display with those of other publishers very inexpensively, and some do a very good job of representing your wares. Write to several of them to compare prices and see which fairs they plan to attend; some offer package deals if you sign up for the whole season.

For more information on bookfairs, read *Book Fairs, An Exhibiting Guide for Publishers* by the author. See the Appendix.

The secret to successful publishing is not to produce more books but to market effectively those books already published.

The best book is a collaboration between author and reader.
— Barbara Tuchman, *Practicing History*

Books are the main source of our knowledge, our reservoir of faith, memory, wisdom, morality, poetry, philosophy, history and science. — Daniel J. Boorstin, Librarian of Congress, 1984 report, "Books In Our Future"

Chapter Nine

Advertising Your Book

Direct Mail, Print, Broadcast

Advertising may be used to create an awareness of your new book, and even to stimulate interest in it, but advertising is expensive and must be approached cautiously. Nonproductive advertising will deplete your bank account fast. It is a cold, hard fact that most advertising doesn't pay, often because the approach is wrong. Feel out each of the many areas and test them before you jump in with lots of money.

It is said that advertising will make a good book sell better, but it can't turn a poor one into a success. We will have to assume that more people besides just you see some value in your book.

First we will talk about advertising in general, and then we will discuss the details of your brochure, direct mail advertising, classifieds, space ads and radio/TV. Much of the information is overlapping and may be applied to more than one area of advertising, so it is advisable to read the entire chapter.

The success of your advertising campaign will depend upon the sales potential of your book, whether you contact the right market and whether your ad is effective. You must select your markets (buyers) and then find the least-expensive way to reach them. Target your primary market, but do not overlook the secondary ones. Concentrate on one medium of advertising (e.g., direct mail), but do not dismiss the others (e.g., space ads).

Remember that we do not recommend spending money on advertising until all the free publicity is exhausted. Advertising is just too expensive and rarely pays when selling books. When in doubt, do not advertise.

In each ad campaign, run a small test and then figure the cost of the campaign "per sale" (how many books did this ad sell?). The cost "per contact" is interesting, but it is the cost per sale that tells you if you are winning or losing. Ads placed in magazines that will send buyers to bookstores must generate more sales than ads directing the orders to you (mail order). The difference is that you are giving your distributor 65% of the list (cover) price, whereas the mail sales come directly to you at full price. Do not run unprofitable ads! They waste money and make you work for nothing.

Determining an ad's potential profitability is not the place for wishful thinking. You have to calculate all the possibilities, the types of advertising and the places it might be put; this comparison will help you to choose where to place your money.

The people selling advertising talk about the "number of impressions" and "accumulative impact" when they try to get you to spend more on promotion (or try to explain why your ad wasn't successful). A series of good, consistent ads

---

It is easier to promote one book twice than to write a second book.

may be of some help, as a prospect may remember that he has heard of the book before, but remember that you are selling a $20 or $30 book, not a $20,000 or $30,000 automobile. You have to sell a lot more product to pay for the ad and you can't even justify as much need.

If you have a good method, don't deviate. Creativity for creativity's sake is dumb. Whatever worked before will almost certainly work again. All marketing methods must be tested, not just direct mail advertising. Once you find a good system, stick with it.

The most-recommended book in this area is *Successful Direct Marketing Methods,* by Bob Stone. See the Appendix.

Direct response marketing is any promotion or advertising that provokes a measurable response or order from the individual to whom it was targeted. In book publishing, direct marketing consists of order blanks in books, catalogs, package inserts, radio, television and direct mail.

Creating ad copy. You will need a good, basic description of the book that will appeal to the consumer; this material, altered as required, will then be used over and over. Come up with a very few words to describe the book. This becomes its "handle" and might even be the subtitle for the book. This handle will be expanded for brochures and catalogs, while it is directed toward the intended audience. Some small ads will only have space for the handle and a small amount of hard-hitting copy. Once this is done, the future copy writing is easier, as you are not starting from scratch each time.

Direct mail advertising. Most people like to receive mail, and one book out of four is sold via direct mail advertising. Most of this volume goes to book clubs, but they don't get all the business; there is over a half billion dollars left. Direct mail offers the small publisher an opportunity to

---

I know half my advertising is wasted but I do not know which half. — William Wrigley

sell the customer without competing with the big publishers. Mail provides equal treatment.

Every household in the U.S. receives 84 pounds of direct (bulk) mail each year. We use three working days to sort and decide what to do with it. There are ways for publishers to stand out from the clutter.

> Don't confuse *direct mail* with *mail order*. Direct mail is a form of advertising which competes with space ads and television spots, while mail order is a delivery method or form of distribution which competes with storefronts.

— **This is the age of** *specialization*, of target marketing, of the narrow focus. As consumers, we have the advantage of buying only those products that are specific to our wants and needs. As entrepreneurs, we *tailor* our products to special segments of the population and then *tailor* our pitch to bring the product to their attention.

Direct mail advertising allows you to pinpoint your target market with a specialized pitch. For example, the people you target with your mailing might be skydiving instructors. Skydiving instructors have different needs and desires than skydiving students, or jump pilots, or parachute riggers, or drop zone owners. Each is involved in skydiving in general, but each requires a different pitch.

— **Target marketing.** Direct mail advertising is another targeted shot at the customer. This is not a shotgun blast at every household in the neighborhood, hoping to find a couple of people interested in your books. It is (hopefully) a mailing only to those who have expressed a past (recent) interest in your type of merchandise. They have expressed not only an interest in books, but in your type of books, and have responded before by sitting down, writing out a check and sending for something.

> *What can be more fun than going to the Post Office and finding 500 envelopes, each with a check in it, from people who want to buy what you have created?*
> — Jameson Campaigne, Jameson Books

Unless you have several related titles, priced over $35 each, to share your brochure, you won't make money regularly in direct mail advertising. The smaller and newer publisher will only be successful using direct mail for pre-publication offers and occasional mailings to (often smaller) highly targeted lists.

— **Think long term.** Very few mailings make a killing from outright sales the first time out. With each mailing, you are trying to add qualified buyers to your house list for future orders. A *qualified buyer* is someone who has sent money to you before; this person is more likely to respond again and again. The objective is to develop a customer, not just to make a sale.

Your house list also becomes a valuable asset and a new profit center, as you will be able to rent it to other firms. More on renting your own list later.

Direct mail advertising is one very effective way to contact potential buyers for your book. The mailing usually includes a cover letter, brochure, order form and reply envelope, but it may also direct the addressee to a nearby store.

— **The economics of direct mail.** One must understand the economics to put direct mail advertising of books into perspective. If you tell enough people about your book, a certain percentage will buy it. The challenge is to keep costs down by telling just that certain buying percentage. A general-interest book advertised to a general consumer audience is lucky to generate a return of 1.5% to 2%. That is just 15 to 20 orders per 1,000 pieces mailed. In fact, only 10% of the recipients will even remember the mailing piece.

The cost, on the other hand, may be quite high (probably around $450 per thousand or 45 cents per piece). The amount depends upon the price of the list (the more selective ones cost more), the postage, the type and number of inserts and other expenses, such as mailing house stuffing fees. A high response rate is required just to break even. So, it is tough to make a living selling a single title through direct mail. But now you have a customer who may buy again. And that means you need more than one product.

The direct marketing formula. What makes direct marketing successful is the offer of the right products via the right medium with the most enticing propositions, presented in the most effective formats, proved successful as a result of the right tests. The successful direct mail campaign is made up of planning, list selection, copy, layout, timing and testing.

— **Repetition.** One rule of direct mail is that if you remail to the same list any time after a couple of months, the response will be almost as great as the results from the first try. Many marketing people use a list four times a year, and if it fails to break even or better each time, it is time to change the list. They say that repetitive mailings have a cumulative effect and the message is strengthened. Good lists have a certain amount of turnover. Names are continually being added and deleted.

— **Timing.** The best time for your mail to arrive is on a Tuesday, Wednesday or Thursday. A lot of mail arrives on Mondays and the day after holidays, and your piece could be lost in the clutter. Friday's mail is often put aside as the recipient is about to leave for the weekend. Unfortunately, it is difficult, if not impossible, to time delivery of mailing pieces to a day of the week when using bulk rate.

The best times of year for offers to arrive, according to some experts, are after the new year and after Labor Day. The Direct Marketing Association compares the months for response (assuming your book is not season-related, such as a Christmas book or a year-end holiday gift offer) as follows:

January 100%	July 73.3%
February 96.3%	August 87%
March 71%	September 79%
April 71.5%	October 89.9%
May 71.5%	November 81%
June 67%	December 79%

Best months based on January

Other months are compared with January, the best month. Some say that March to April (income tax time?) and

May to June are the worst months. Other experts warn against the summer months, when people are away and the mail piles up. Most agree December is bad because the post office is jammed and the potential customer is busy with family and holiday activities. Late December is a good time to mail as the piece will arrive in January.

The subject of your books will determine the best months. For example, if your books are on outdoor sports, the best months are January through May, with a peak in March, and September through November. During the summer, the prospects are out doing what they were reading about during the winter. The best time to mail to federal libraries is March and April, when they are preparing for their next fiscal year. May appears to be the best month for schools. Professional books seem to sell better in the first quarter of the year. The third quarter is second best. All factors must be considered in relation to your specialized subject and audience.

Many DM professionals like to test in September so they can roll out in January. And remember, what counts is when the mailing is delivered, not when it was posted.

— **Foreign mailings.** The United States is a culturally *influencing* country. The world consumes great quantities of U.S. information and thought. With the increase in both the standard of living and purchasing power in many other countries, the potential for book sales is increasingly good. There is a demand for books on leading edge subjects.

English has become a world language in this century. In fact, while 3,000 languages are spoken in the world, over 40% of the knowledge base is in the English language. English has replaced German as the scientific and technical language, replaced French as the diplomatic language and is the international language of aviation. English is also the world language of business. Business books from the U.S. have

---

A good test of the worth of a book is the number of times we can read it with profit.

done very well in the last few years, with the surge of worldwide interest in U.S. management thought.

Naturally, books in English should be promoted with brochures in English, and prices should be quoted in dollars, as it is customary to settle international accounts in U.S. currency.

The problems in mailing outside the U.S. aren't any greater; they are simply different. Check the postal regulations for foreign mailings. Send for a copy of the Postal Service's *International Mail Manual.*

Foreign mailing lists are available, though generally they aren't as sophisticated as those in the U.S. When renting foreign lists, specify one-inch Cheshire format, or you may receive a printout you can't use.

In the book industry, direct mail to foreign potential buyers is the most underused marketing technique. It has great potential and is waiting to be properly exploited.

— **Bulk rate.** Any serious direct mail campaign will use the Postal Service's third class bulk rate. The annual bulk mailing fee is $50. Once this is paid, you may mail for .198 cents per piece up to 3.3667 ounces each, as long as you are mailing 200 pieces or more. See the Postal Service's *Domestic Mail Manual.*

— **Line of books.** One way to increase your return on a mailing list is to promote more than one book, but don't confuse the customer with a cluttered brochure. Concentrate your books in a single interest area. Don't bury the gems in garbage; the recipients may not take the time to dig out the books they need.

Publishers should concentrate on a single line of books, such as aviation, regional subjects or wastewater treatment. Then all the books in your brochure or catalog will relate to each other. There is no need to make up a separate brochure

---

When you are ready to draft an ad, stimulate your creative juices by reading a couple of articles or a couple of chapters on copy writing.

for each book. Think like a specialized book club and define your audience.

— **Order blank in book.** Every book should have an order blank for the same and/or other books on the last page— facing out. Turn to the last page in this book as an example. It is important to ask for an order, and that is what order blanks are designed to do. It is not enough to hope a potential buyer might find your address on the copyright page, because he or she still won't know how much to include for shipping and sales tax. The order blank says: *Yes, we accept orders, will take your check or credit card and here is exactly what the book will cost.*

> Why would anyone buy a book they already have? For a friend! At Para Publishing, we receive more orders on our back-of-the-book order blank than from any other direct response effort we make. We have over a million books out there, and each is selling more books for us.

— **800 numbers.** It is generally accepted that a toll-free 800 order number will increase the response to an offer. Another benefit of the 800 number to publishers is to raise the level of customer service.

800 numbers work best when paired with credit card charge arrangements. Today, people are prepared to place a call and charge a product to a credit card.

— **Charge cards** make buying much easier and will bring both more and larger sales. They are particularly handy for telephone orders. See the discussion of credit cards in Chapter Ten.

— **Lettershops** have machinery so they can do your envelope stuffing and mailing faster and cheaper than you can. Check the *Yellow Pages* and call a few for prices. Save your time, and let the lettershop do the licking, sticking, stuffing, sorting, sacking and posting.

> *If you want a response, you have to ask for it.*
> — John Huenefeld

If you deal with a mailing house, they will deliver the stuffed and addressed envelopes to the post office. The post office will send you their receiving form, detailing the quantity delivered, with your bill.

Always give the lettershop a folded and stuffed example of your mailing piece. You want to make sure the envelopes go out with the inserts in a certain order and facing the right direction.

— **Book pricing.** Direct mail advertising is expensive, so, generally speaking, the book must be priced at $35 or more to make the project viable. The price of the book may be lower if it will appeal to a highly targeted group that is easy to reach. Professional books tend to carry a higher price. Law, medical and many engineering books are over $80. Lower-priced popular books positioned for trade distribution are rarely profitable to advertise by mail.

— **Piggyback offers.** One way to reduce costs is to place more than one offer in an envelope. Direct mail advertising is the most obvious place to co-op. You want to be sure the extras don't detract from, and dilute, the main offer. Many publishers piggyback by simply including a brief backlist of other related books rather than another fancy brochure.

— **Bookshelf.** The additional books you offer may be yours, or they may be from other publishers. You should be able to buy books wholesale from other publishers at 50% off through their Special Sales department. To learn all about how to carry complementary books, see the Special Report *Bookshelf, Selling Books From Other Publishers.* See the Appendix.

— **Sell nonbook items.** Ray Teagarden has a very successful book in his *The Muffler Shop Manual*, but it is his first and only book. So he drafted another flier for specialized muffler tools, many of which he designed himself. Now he is the source for muffler information *and* tools. Every book he sells establishes his credibility and leads to sales of other products.

— **Weight limits.** You can get a #10 envelope, four sheets of paper, a stamp and a label under the one-ounce, first class mail limit, and you can send more if you are using the 3.3667-ounce bulk rate. Be careful; staples and stamps add to the weight, too. But you can get twelve or thirteen 3.625" x 8.5" slips into the envelope. They provide the recipient with an easy reading/sorting format similar to a card deck. He or she is more likely to look over each offer when it is presented separately, than to inspect a page with several offers jumbled together.

For a more accurate measure and to get the maximum out of your postage, weigh up several stuffed envelopes at the same time. Ten should weigh just barely under ten ounces on the scale, for example. That is cutting it close!

To calibrate your scale, use nine unworn, *solid* copper pennies (not the new sandwiched ones). Nine pennies weigh one ounce. Calibrating a scale to zero without weight is not accurate.

— **Sales tax on printing.** Some states, such as California, do not charge sales tax on the printing of direct mail packages. Direct mail brochures, letters and envelopes must be delivered directly to the mailing house by the printer to qualify. This can be quite a saving, so it is worth checking the laws in your own state.

California also does not charge sales tax on shipping supplies, such as cartons, bags and tape. Presumably the purpose of the exemption is to create jobs and promote exports.

— **Response formulas** are used to speed testing. They are also useful when the orders are coming in and you want to know what can be expected over the next few weeks.

If you mail **first class**, you can assume that within two weeks of receiving your first response, you will have received 50% of the total responses you will receive. So plot mail receipt on your calendar. Two weeks after the first or-

> *A book should not just be something to read, it should be something to possess.* — Lee Collins

der arrives, double the orders received so far, and that is the number you may expect over several months.

If you mail bulk rate, you will receive half your responses within four weeks of your first response. Ninety-eight percent of the responses to a mailing will come within 13 weeks.

The heaviest day for responses should be the second Monday after the first order arrives. Mondays are always a heavy mail day because you are receiving three days' worth. Tuesdays are always light because few people mail over the weekend. In fact, Tuesdays often have a higher percentage of foreign mail (which was mailed the previous week).

With an ad or book review in a *daily newspaper*, you can expect 80% of your orders within a week.

The response formulas mentioned above are generalities. Direct mail is an art, not a science. There is no substitute for your experience in your own field. Keep response analysis records so you can develop your own response rates.

— **Echo effect.** Every promotion campaign you wage for a book will bring in some sales that are not directly attributable to that campaign. Some people find it easier or faster to buy your product somewhere else, such as dropping by a retailer. There are many ways people can get the book besides returning the order form. Professors who receive interesting mailings often request their libraries to order the book. Echo effect is difficult to measure, but some direct marketers claim it often exceeds the direct orders.

Since over 75% of libraries deal with wholesalers, most of the orders from a mailing to libraries will come to you through Baker & Taylor. Sometimes, publishers even help the potential customer in this direction and, in effect, give him a choice of purchasing by mail or visiting a bookstore. The brochure might say: *Available at your local Walden Bookstore or direct from the publisher*. Some publishers imprint circulars for bookstores, to be mailed to the bookstore's mailing list.

— **White mail.** Orders not traceable to any promotional effort or source are called "white mail." The longer you are in business, the more orders you will receive that are not traceable to any specific promotion.

— **Profit analysis.** Direct mail marketing is a process of looking where you have been, seeing how you got there and deciding where to go next. Past mailings and testing are the tools for future decisions. Profit (or loss) may be determined by taking your book sales, less returns, less your cost of books and fulfillment and less your direct mail costs of postage, printing and lettershop fees. A P/L sheet might look like this:

Direct Mail Profit/Loss

Gross sales	$_____	
Less returns	$_____	
Net sales		$_____
Less cost of sales		
Product (production cost x units sold)	$_____	
Royalty	$_____	
Cost of fulfillment (wrapping and postage)	$_____	
Total cost of sales		($_____)
Less promotion costs		
Mailing list rental	$_____	
Printing	$_____	
Lettershop fees	$_____	
Your time	$_____	
Total promotion costs		($_____)
Profit (or loss): (Net sales less total cost of sales and less total promotion costs)		$_____

— **Follow the rules.** Finally, direct mail advertising is no place to be innovative. The margin for error is slim; you cannot afford mistakes. Read the books and magazines and do what everyone else is doing. Advance into direct mail advertising slowly by testing small numbers. Direct mail advertising works for books only when the book is specific and the list is highly targeted.

— **Mailing lists.** While many elements are required for a successful direct mail package, the list is the most important part. The best package mailed to the wrong list can't do well. Conversely, the worst package mailed to the best list often does acceptably well. Obviously, the goal is to mail a good package to a good list.

Mailing lists make the difference between success and failure in direct mail marketing. The list must target the appropriate group and be up-to-date. Posting your offer to the wrong person is a waste you cannot afford; the margin is just too slim. You want quality, not quantity. People get new jobs, move, die, lose interest in certain fads and trends, forget hobbies, etc. Yesterday's prime prospect may have other interests today, or may have moved.

In late 1987, the author wrote and published *The Expert Witness Handbook*. He rented the list of *expert witnesses* from the National Forensic Center. The 4,400 names came from an expert witness directory where each person listed had filled out a questionnaire to be listed. The response was a whopping 11%, and there were very few nixies (bad addresses). Based on these heady results, he rented another list of 22,500 *experts and consultants* from another organization. The result was a disappointing 1%, and there were hundreds of nixies. When selecting lists, you need perfect matches and the list must be clean.

> *Most small press publishers lack an understanding of mailing lists. So many firms waste so much money on lousy lists. They buy "mail order" lists not knowing what those people bought, how much they paid, what their profile is, how many times the list has been rented, when they bought, and on, and on.*
> — Galen Stilson

— **List categories.** The real purpose of direct mail advertising is to build a list of qualified buyers. These are people who have ordered books by mail and have ordered from you.

Direct mail mailing lists fall into three categories, sometimes called *yours, theirs* and *compiled*:

1. **House** lists
   a. Sales. Past buyers.
      1. Premier list. Multiple-order past buyers
   b. Prospects
2. Mail **response** lists. Lists of people who have responded to offers similar to yours. These are lists you rent from list owners or list brokers.
3. **Compiled** lists. These lists are developed from membership lists, directories, etc. These are lists you rent from list owners or list brokers.

— **House list.** The highest-quality list is normally your own. This is your list of customers—those who have contacted you. Your house list should pull two to ten times better than any you might rent. The people on your list know you and your product; they look to you as an old friend; they feel comfortable doing business with you and have done business with you before.

The people who were your best customers last month are most likely to be your best customers this month. They should be contacted repeatedly. These customers will buy from you again and again as they experience changes in their needs, mood and financial condition. You may not change (with something new to sell them), but they may change.

Think of using your house list in three ways:

1. Identifying the best customers on your house list.
2. Finding more customers for your house list by using outside lists.

3. Selling books to your house list at a maximum profit with minimum waste.

You should maintain two house lists: a *sales* list (those who have bought something) and an *inquiries* list (those who have contacted you for information but have not sent money). All other lists from other people contain only *prospects*.

Your sales list is by far the most important. The only people who should be added to it are those who have paid to get on it by buying something.

There are several ways to build your house list. The common way is to rent another list, make a mailing and then add the names of those who respond to your own list. Names of good prospects may be found in various directories, depending on the subject of your book. Some firms have used contests to generate interest and more inquiries, while others have sold merchandise at a loss to attract attention. Just be sure to segregate all responses into the sales or inquiries lists, as appropriate. Do not corrupt your lists with untested names.

You may begin compiling your own retail prospect mailing list by going through your Christmas card list. Include all family, friends and acquaintances. Include anyone who might conceivably purchase your book.

Also start your **commercial lists**: bookstores, libraries, wholesalers, big nonbook accounts, people and companies in your industry.

And work on your **promotion mailing lists**: magazines, newspapers, radio and TV stations. Check reference books, such as *Literary Market Place*.

Keep your lists for your next book, so you will be prepared when it comes time to send out pre-publication announcements, review copies and other promotion.

> *New customers have to be bought (through list rental); existing customers are free.*

— List maintenance. Lists must be kept up-to-date if they are to maintain pace with our mobile society and remain valid. This means keeping the list in mind and continually being alert for address changes and returned mail.

Some publishers just "flush" the list, except for recent buyers, every couple of years. Even though a name was well qualified as a former customer, if he hasn't responded again in the last year, he probably never will.

Your house list should contain computer fields to indicate recentness, frequency and amount of purchase for each customer.

If you mail via first class, the letter will be forwarded, and if it can't be delivered, it will be returned. The problems are that first class costs more than bulk rate and you won't get a new address to update your file.

There are several endorsements you may place on the envelope. Each will solicit different treatment from the Postal Service. Some, which may be used alone or in combination, are:

1. Address Correction Requested
2. Address Correction and Forwarding Requested
3. Forwarding and Return Postage Guaranteed
4. Do Not Forward, Address Correction Requested, Return Postage Guaranteed

Read the excerpt from the *Domestic Mail Manual*. It is important to understand the services and prices before you mail. Do not use *Address Correction Requested* on a rented list. Do not clean someone else's list.

A certain percentage of bulk rate mail never gets delivered. Some estimate the amount to be as high as 10% to 20%. Five percent of the bulk rate mail is undeliverable due to the lack of a room number in large buildings. In a big

---

It costs more to sell a book to a new customer than to an existing customer.

city, 25% of the bulk rate mail may be discarded rather than delivered. Print the whole mailing address.

In one delivery test by Doubleday, a first class re-mail was made of 1,948 pieces of returned third class bulk rate mail. Eighty percent of the so-called nixies were either delivered or forwarded. First class mail gets better treatment.

— **Recency.** Lists, whether yours, theirs or compiled, must be recent. Any list not mailed within the last three months will not be *recent*. Since 20% of our population (over 50 million people) moves every year, there will be too many nixies. When renting, ask when the list was last *cleaned*.

— **Guarantee.** Most lists are guaranteed to be 90% deliverable. That means the owner or broker will send you a refund for all undeliverables *over* 10% of the list rented. Let us say you rented 10,000 names, mailed first class at 29 cents, and 1,020 pieces are returned as undeliverable. You get a refund of $5.80, or 29 cents each for 20 pieces—not much when you spent $290 to mail to the other 1,000 bad addresses.

— **Turned down?** Sometimes we approach a magazine or association to rent a list only to be turned down. We are told they are protecting their subscribers or members from junk mail. Any list can be rented if you can provide a sufficient *benefit* to the list owner. Try this approach: Tell the list owner that if he will give you the list on labels, you will pay all the mailing costs and will stuff his brochure for nothing. You get the list (free), and the list owner gets a mailing free. A win-win situation.

— **List brokers.** List brokers specialize in bringing list owners and list renters together. The broker receives his fee (usually 20%) from the list owner. Brokers can be a good source of direct mail advice.

Lists and list brokers can be found in *Direct Marketing* magazine, *Direct Marketing List Sources*, *Klein's Directory* and your local *Yellow Pages*, and several are listed in the Appendix of this book. Send to all the brokers in the Appendix for their catalogs.

One thing you will find is that the same lists are handled by many different brokers. You will see the same list in catalog after catalog. Many lists are small and brokers will have a minimum. And, since the broker is obtaining different lists from several different sources, they cannot be merged or totaled to meet minimums.

— **Copying lists.** Copying lists violates the rental agreement, normal business ethics, is against the law and is a waste of money. List *rentals* are for one-time use only, and you are obligated not to add the names to your file. The list owner guards against second usage by sprinkling the list with decoy names. Stealing an unproven name from a list will only dilute the quality of your own house list. You are, however, authorized to add a name to your list once you have qualified it, once it has resulted in an order.

Lists go out of date fast because people move. Over 20% of our gypsylike population moves each year, and younger people move even more often. Almost 47% of the population is not living in the same home they occupied five years ago. In the western U.S., the figure is over 56%.

Since you probably won't rent the same list more often than every six months, it is cheaper and more accurate to rent the list again than to copy *and* maintain it.

— **Hotline names** are new additions to the list. If you are selling books on beginning skydiving, why rent the whole membership list from the U.S. Parachute Association when you can rent names of just the new members? Hotline lists tend to be 60 to 90 days old.

— **Rent parts of lists.** You don't have to rent the entire list. Why send to all libraries when you are likely to get a better return from those with a higher book acquisition budget?

One co-op mailing operated by the Publishers Marketing Association is made to 2,500 public libraries with purchasing budgets of $25,000 or more. They could mail to 6,600 libraries with purchasing budgets of $1,000 or more, but most of those libraries cannot afford to buy. Be selective.

— **Testing a list**. The big direct mailers must be successful or they would not continue to mail. The main reason they are successful is that they test before investing large sums of money in a mailing.

Testing is a preliminary mailing or distribution intended as a preview or pilot before a major campaign. Test mailings are used to determine probable acceptance of a product or service and are usually made to a specially selected list.

Unless the list is very small or you are very sure of it, test it first. This is done by renting just part of the list and sending your mailing to every *nth* (e.g., tenth) name. Nth name testing provides a better sample than renting names from A through D or Zips from 0000 through 03000. A safer variation to Nth name rental is *last digit Zip* or *last two-digit Zip* selection. Just ask for names with Zips ending in a specified number. These variations stop list owners from slipping in *hot* names to enrich the tested list (in the hope you will be back to rent the entire list). Another advantage to Zip selection testing is that you can eliminate the tested names when mailing to the entire list.

A minimum sample should be 3,000 names (some experts say 5,000), and remember that you are testing the mailing package as well as the list; they both affect the results. Since you will need 30 to 50 responses for your test to be statistically valid, you may have to mail to 3,000 to 5,000 names (if you can realistically project a 1% response).

If a mailing to a sample group produces a 2% response, statistics show that a mailing to the entire list will result in a 1.4% to 2.6% response, and it is usually just under 2%. Realizing these probability limits will help you to evaluate a list and make the decision whether to risk a big mailing.

A lot of things can go wrong after a test mailing. A list can be non-representative or out-of-date, or your book could be bad, and the word may have circulated between the test and the big mailing. Keep good records; only with statistics can you effectively evaluate a mailing. Note all your costs. If a test is inconclusive, run another test. Most tests fail; expect it. When one fails, be thankful you didn't mail to the whole list. Then drop that list and don't try it again.

Roll-out mailings to the entire list do not always reflect your test results. There are just too many variables: time lapse, season, change in economics, weather, consumer behavior and many more. The test mailing benefits from pass-along readership. Some recipients who are not buying send the brochure on to a friend they know has an interest in this book. When you mail to the entire list, you also hit the pass-along readership, and they have already seen your offer.

If you are committed to marketing your book by direct mail, you will need a continuous program, one that can be constantly adjusted as needed. When a test list works, expand its use. When it fails, get rid of it.

It is a good idea to remain flexible by continually testing your mailing piece with small changes. Never make two significant changes at once in the same package, or you won't know which one is responsible for the change in response.

— **Address format.** Should you address your labels to the individual or the company? This depends upon the product and your approach. The question is whether you want the offer to go to the individual or the person in that particular job. People change jobs quite often these days.

The Postal Service now likes to have the *attention* part of the address on the first, rather than the last, line. On the other hand, you should decide if you are mailing to a company with an employee or to an individual who wants to receive mail at work rather than home.

> PERSON'S NAME
> COMPANY NAME
> STREET ADDRESS
> P.O. BOX ADDRESS
> CITY STATE ZIP CODE + 4

The automatic sorting machinery likes all caps and no punctuation.

The Postal Service delivers mail to the address on the line immediately above the city-state-zip line. If the customer provides both a street address and P.O. Box, use the street address for UPS shipments and the P.O. Box for postal shipments. If you use both, put the street address above the P.O. Box.

Some people have more than one address or get mail at work addressed different ways. You might be sending two pieces to *Richard Stands, Zeller Mfg. Co.,* and *Zeller Mfg. Co., Attn: Richard Stands.*

— **Finding lists.** As a small publisher, you are probably also the author. You are a *participant* in the subject you write about. While a book is just a product to a large New York publisher, you have a mission and are closer to the book's subject matter. If, for example, your book is on skydiving, you know there are two magazines, one national organization and one national championship catering to your group. You know how to reach your readers because you are one of them. Associations have direct lines to people interested in their mission. Most have a membership list, magazine, annual function, etc. Contact associations.

Direct Marketing List Source lists 80,000 mailing lists. Ask for it at the reference desk of your public library.

If a space ad in a magazine has pulled well, consider renting their subscription list for an expanded offer. Compare list rental costs with the cost to buy space advertising in the magazine. Consider renting select portions of the list or the hotline (just recent subscribers).

Your competitors may not be interested in renting you their house list, but they may be willing to trade for your house list on a name-for-name basis.

— **Costs of lists.** Most lists run between $40 and $100 per thousand or four to ten cents per name. Cleaner, more highly targeted lists tend to cost more.

— **Sell your mailing list.** If you maintain your mailing list by noting which book (subject area) the customer purchased, it becomes very selective and quite valuable. These are people who have taken the time to sit down, get out the checkbook and send away for a book. They are very good prospects for similar offers.

You may handle your own list or work through a broker. To contact a broker, see the lists in the Appendix. Most brokers will be interested in handling your list when you reach 20,000 names; some want 50,000.

Start by getting listed in *Direct Marketing List Source*. This directory provides the details on over 80,000 lists. For a listing form, write to the Standard Rate and Data Service, Inc., *Direct Marketing List Sources*, 3004 Glenview Road, Wilmette, IL 60091, Tel: (708) 258-6067, (800) 851-7737.

Your brochure lies at the heart of your promotional campaign, and it may be produced long before your book is off the press. The brochure should describe the book, tell something about you, and answer most of the recipient's potential questions. The basics are the book's measurements, number of pages, type and number of illustrations, binding and price. The contents should be summarized to provide a clear understanding of the book's coverage. Do not use too much detail, or the buyer may find too much material he or she does not want—sell the sizzle, not the steak. Excerpts from reviews will demonstrate that others like your book, too. Follow the proven, standard formats.

The brochure will be stuffed into most of the letters you send out daily to friends, associates and relatives, used with your other pre- and post-publication mailings, and sent to those who respond to your ads inviting them to "send for a free descriptive brochure." Yes, your brochure is more important than a business card and has a lot more information.

The best way to answer inquiries is with your brochure. If the writer asks particular questions, the simplest way to answer is by circling the appropriate parts of the mailing piece. Many publishers like to return the inquiry letter with the brochure to remind the writer that he asked for this advertising matter. If you aren't over the postage limit yet, it is nice to stuff in other related information. For example, if the inquiry is about hang gliding, enclose a membership application from the hang gliding association. You will build valuable good will, and you received an *implied* endorsement from the association.

Brochures provide you with an opportunity to say nice things about yourself that you can't say in face-to-face selling. It is almost as though someone else wrote the copy. Be direct and clear, and give the reader as much information as possible.

Your local instant printshop can give you the best deal on black-and-white 8.5" x 11" brochures. If you need more space, they can handle 8.5" x 14" and you can fold it four times to fit a standard #10 envelope.

Every pass through the press costs more money, so some people like to use colored paper and another color ink. This gives the appearance of a lot of color but is still a one-color print job. Use good materials and make the brochure slick. If you send out a photocopied brochure, people may assume you are selling a photocopied book.

Some publishers have produced very nice brochures by printing their ad copy on the back of book cover or jacket overruns. Ask your printer for any "overs," and ask him to print a few hundred extra covers.

People like to see what they are buying, so a photo of the book should appear in the brochure. You don't have to wait for your book to be printed to take a photograph of it, however. Photograph the cover art and have the print blown up to book size (e.g., 5.5" x 8.5"). Then make a dummy by wrapping the print around another book. Take several photos with different settings and from several angles. Then select the best print and have some "4 x 6's" made up. At this point, you may not know exactly how many pages the book will have, but you can estimate and then use a description like: "over 180 jam-packed pages."

Once the brochures arrive, use them everywhere. Stuff them in every package, letter, news release, mailing, etc. Carry some in the car; leave them at the barbershop, in the seat back pocket on the airplane, at the dentist's office, etc., and carry some with you at all times. Pack one in with every book you mail out. A brochure has to be distributed to do any good.

Pre-publication offers are often in black and white, as time is of the essence. For short press runs, you may be better off going with a black-and-white flier and dealing with your local quick printer for quality, price and quick delivery. Over 10,000, it pays to go color, and at 25,000, the price drops again significantly.

Printers specialize, and a number do nothing but four-color *catalog sheets*. These catalog sheets may be called a *flier* if flat and a *brochure* if folded. These specialists buy large quantities of the same type of paper at a lower price and have all their equipment set up in–line for greater operating efficiency. They are standardized at 8.5" x 11" on 70- pound or 80-pound white, slick paper, with four colors on one side and one color on the other, or four colors on both sides. You may also use 11" x 17" stock, folded.

Here are some typical 1995 prices from Econocolor for a flier 8.5" x 11", four-color on one side, one-color on back:

> 5,000: 25 cents each
>
> 10,000: 15 cents each
>
> 15,000: 11 cents each
>
> 25,000: 7 cents each (enough for web press)
>
> 50,000: 5 cents each

When you are ready to work on your brochure, see the Special Report *Brochures for Book Publishers.* See the Appendix.

In a direct mail piece, the circular, flier or brochure is always introduced by your cover letter, and all pieces work together. Until you get into big mailings with specially designed packages, you may use your *regular* brochure, with a cover letter tailored to the list to be used. In a very large mailing, it won't cost any more to print up a specific circular for that mailing, and it will bring greater results.

Tell not what the recipient can do for you, tell what you can do for the recipient.

— **Benefit copy.** State your primary benefit in your headline. Capture the reader's attention by promising something the reader wants and can relate to.

Features or benefits? People do not buy what you sell, they buy what your book will do for them. They buy happiness—which comes in the form of making more money, keeping up with the Joneses, being sexier, more "with it," more of everything that makes them feel good about themselves. Features are the number of pages, the size of the book and how many years it took you to write it (boring). Stress benefits.

Make the benefits believable. Readers will be skeptical. Make the benefits specific. The reader must be able to relate to your offer. Use *you* copy. There should be at least twice as many *you's* as *I's*.

— **The "AIDA formula"** is the oldest and most widely used method of reader motivation. It is designed to lead the recipient to the offer and impel him to take action. AIDA stands for: get ATTENTION, arouse INTEREST, stimulate DESIRE, ask for ACTION. Some people have modified AIDA to: ATTENTION, INVOLVEMENT, DECISION and ACTION. AIDA is just as effective today as it has always been.

— **Drafting the brochure.** Follow these steps when drafting your brochure. To lay out the circular, start with a blank folded dummy, and plot the location of each part of it: the teaser copy, order form, photos, etc. Set up the brochure and then write the copy to fit. If you do this on your computer screen, parts will be easy to move around.

The circular should have big, compelling headlines that give the recipient a chance to see himself in the mailing. He will respond favorably if he identifies subconsciously with the product. Always include a photo of the book, so he can see how big and nice it looks. Make the copy easy to read: one thought to a sentence, short words, short paragraphs and don't overdo it. Make the type big and bold, and use the layout to lead the reader from start to finish in one logical, flowing sequence. Special emphasis may be given to the more important paragraphs by setting them in italics, bold-face or by indenting them. Use subheads. Use all the information necessary and end with an order form. Look over the slick promotions you receive in the mail every day and analyze them.

Most mailings succeed or fail within about ten seconds after they are opened. If they don't catch the recipient's attention in that time, they go into the round file. We are bombarded with thousands of advertising messages from the mail, billboards, TV, etc., every day, and we tend to build up a defense toward them.

Little "grabbers" can also help. Words like *you* and *new* and *save* and *free* still work. Gimmicks like offering to pay postage if they order today from this form invite action, even though it may be your policy to ship all retail sales postpaid anyway.

Highlight the important aspects of the book in the rest of the copy. Relate to the reader and use testimonials, which are more objective, if you have them. Keep the message brief, or the reader will get lost in the copy and give up. He feels his time is valuable, so don't insult him by wasting it. Give details on the number of pages, illustrations, chapter titles, etc. Facts, not words, sell books.

If your brochure is mixed up and illogical, what will the recipient think you are capable of doing in a book? Be specific. If yours is a technical manual directed at a select audience, the package doesn't have to be terribly fancy, but it should be very detailed.

— **Self-mailers** are brochures mailed without envelopes. While less expensive to produce, they usually don't pull as well as offers arriving in envelopes. Self-mailers may not be used in international mail; letters going out of the U.S. must be in envelopes.

If you use a FREE offer, be sure there are no strings attached. People get mightily fed up with "free" offers that cost them money.

— **Consider a postcard** with a photo of you and your book as an inexpensive way to reach prospects. Postcards are not as expensive to print as a full mailing package, and they cost less to mail. Some publishers have cards printed when their covers are printed. The cards wind up being 12 pt. C1S cover stock with four colors and a plastic coating.

— **The direct mail package** has five main elements:

1. Graphics. What does it look like?
2. Offer. What is the deal?
3. Copy. How well have you described the product and offer?
4. List. Who is the offer being sent to?
5. Timing. When will the mail be received?

— **The offer or "order form."** While it usually comes last in the direct mail package, the order form should be written first, as it is the cornerstone around which the rest of the mailing is built. The purpose of your mailing may be to solicit an order or to request some descriptive literature, and you must guide the recipient to take the specific action you want. By preparing the order form first, you will assure co-ordination of all the parts of the mailing and keep all copy headed in the same direction. Make the offer simple, clear and easy.

Many people don't read the whole brochure; they are sold early in the package and turn straight to the order form. If you have more than one title, print a check-off list. Don't ask the customer to write the title in; he may lose interest or may write in the title of only one book because you have not prompted him with more titles. If you use the words, "I enclosed $_____ for:" you are making it easy for him. If the order form is printed on colored paper, it will be easier to locate.

> *It is a good rule to have your name and address on every piece of a mailing package. One piece alone sometimes makes the sale.*

Make the order form easily detachable or on a separate card. Note the deadline, shipping costs and sales tax, if any. Always include a money-back guarantee, an unconditional one. The form should have enough room for the customer to write in his or her name and address; make this area big so you will be able to read the handwriting. Make sure your name and address appear on the front, back or both. Pre-addressed envelopes are expensive, but they are probably worth sending to nonbusiness people (who may not have an envelope handy). Some advertisers like to call their order form a "trial order card." Refer to it in the text of your letter to remind the customer that it is there.

If you are offering airmail delivery for an additional charge, add a box where the customer may make a check mark. Note on the form that *book rate* may take three to four weeks, while an air shipment will be three to four days.

— **The cover letter.** Each mailing should start with a cover letter to personalize the message and to bring attention to your offer. The letter is your prime selling tool; it encourages the recipient to read the flier and to use the order card.

The direct mail letter should be interesting and easy to read. It has to grab the attention and relate to an interest of the reader in three to five seconds, or it will go straight into the round file. So, draft your letter to the type of person on the list.

As with any personal message, it should be friendly but not insincere or disrespectful. Sincerity is hard to define, but insincerity can be spotted instantly. Make sure the letter is clear and complete by having a friend read it both to himself and aloud. Write as you talk; don't search for big words. The letter may run one to four, or even more, pages, whatever it takes to make the pitch. Be concise, and don't use any more space than necessary. Keep the paragraphs short; five sentences should be the limit. Sentences should be short and simple; ten to twelve words are enough.

Your opening sentence has to be dramatic. It has to make the reader want to read more. Stress **benefits** to the reader. What can your book deliver to him or her? Change "We'll help . . ." to: "you will . . ." When you find yourself writing: "This book will help you . . .," stop and change it to: "You'll discover how easy it is to . . ." Change "if you" copy to "when you" copy. Do not give the reader a yes/no option. "If you order before the end of January, you will receive . . ." should be changed to: "When you order before the end of January, you will receive. . . ."

Do not make broad, generalized claims; be specific. "This could be the greatest book you will ever encounter" should be changed to: "With this book, you will be able to . . . ."

The ten words with the most magic in copy writing are: *Free, New, You, Now, Win, Easy, Introducing, Today, Save and Guarantee.*

The offer of a bonus will increase response. On a **prepublication mailing**, say: "And if you will order from this form, we will pay the postage and will send the book as soon as it comes off the press." On pre-publication offers, emphasize that the book is on the press, and assure them you won't cash the check until the book is shipped. Mention an expected shipping date, but give yourself an extra month to six weeks.

End your sales letter by telling the reader exactly what you want him or her to do. "Grab your pen and checkbook right now and fill in the order blank. We absolutely guarantee your satisfaction. The book must meet your expectations or your money back. You can't lose!"

Your letter should have a date so it will look like a letter. Use wide margins; the eye is trained to handle narrow newspaper columns. Small margins make a letter look too detailed, too much of a project to read. It is nice to address the recipient, such as "Dear Dr. Brock," but this requires time and some automatic equipment. A "Dear Colleague" or "Dear Fellow Skydiver" may be printed on. Some people like to use a headline to grab attention, even though it is much less personal. Important points may be set off from the body of the letter with indented paragraphs, underlining, or italicized type. But don't overdo it or the value becomes diluted. If your audience tends to be older (with poorer eyesight), be sure to use 12- or even 14-point type. If you run the letter in two colors, say black and blue, you may use the blue ink for your signature.

If you print on both sides of the letterhead, put "Please turn over" at the bottom. It is surprising how many people never think to turn the paper over. Don't end a sentence at the bottom of a page. Keep the reader hanging. Carry him over to the next page with some provocative copy.

The "second chance letter" increases sales. It is the one which says: "Don't read this unless you have decided not to order." You get mailings with second chance letters every day.

Fold the letter—printed headline side out so the recipient doesn't have to unfold it to start reading. Use a letter fold, not an accordion fold, or the stuffing machinery at the letter-shop may have trouble inserting the letter into the envelope.

Always include a letter in your direct mail advertising package. There is an old saying: "Let the flier do the telling and the letter do the selling."

Make your letter easy to read. Keep your words, sentences and paragraphs short. Use subheads or bolding to ease skimming. Many readers skim the letter first to see if it is worth reading. Break the copy into units. Do not put more than two commas in a sentence or more than six commas in a paragraph. Do not put two sentences with commas back to back. Include a personal P.S. Many feel the P.S. is second in importance only to the headline.

— **Letterhead.** Your letterhead is you. It is a matter of image, since most of your customers and suppliers never see you in the flesh. A nice design costs little more to print than a poor one, and you want to instill trust and confidence. If you wish to appear successful, you might like expensive paper with an engraved and/or embossed letterhead.

For everyday letters, you can lay out your letterhead with your computer and laser printer. Scan your logo and drop it

> *It takes hard writing to make easy reading.*
> — Robert Louis Stevenson

in with some distinctive type. Then try printing it on some expensive textured paper.

— **Envelope.** If the recipient does not open the envelope, then all your creativity, work and expense on the inside go to waste.

> Galen Stilson, the famous copywriter, has a research assignment for you: Take two or three hours on a slow day and visit the post office to observe people going through their mail. See how many people pick up their box mail and head straight for the wastebasket to sort out the pieces they don't want to carry home. After a couple of hours of seeing ad mail being quickly glanced at and discarded, unopened, you will gain a new appreciation for the importance of the envelope. In the future, you will spend more time trying to figure out how to make that envelope do what it is supposed to do for you—get opened.

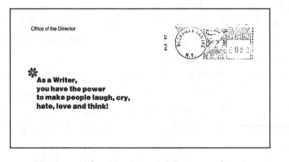

Doesn't this message make you curious?

The envelope is often used to arouse the recipient, inviting him to open it with some printing on the outside. This printing is called *teaser copy*.

Teaser copy by way of words, photos, etc., is used to suggest a strong and clear **relevance** to an immediate need. To be effective, the teaser must be directed to the type of people in the specific list. The teaser must relate to the recipient. Individual buyers want to know what the book can do for them, librarians want to know what it can do for their patrons and a bookstore owner wants to know if it will sell (as opposed to why it may be a good book).

The teaser copy is located on the outside of the envelope or self-mailer, but it should also be repeated on the inside to help the recipient find the place to start reading and to reassure him or her that you are going to deliver on your promise. Even if the recipient keeps the contents, he or she will surely discard the envelope, and you don't want them to lose the teaser.

If you are offering something free, say so on the envelope. Do not tell too much. The purpose of a teaser is to get the envelope opened. Do not try to sell the book on the envelope. Get the letter opened, so you can sell the book on the inside.

To get the recipient's attention, your envelope must stand out from all the rest. Many things affect whether the envelope will be opened, such as color, artwork, size, stock, etc. Go through the mail you receive and ask yourself what your reaction is to various possibilities.

Most smaller publishers do not have to be preoccupied with tricking recipients into opening their envelopes. Since they know this group of people (because they are one of them), they know the recipients are interested in their company and product. When you receive an envelope from someone in the book industry, don't you open and read it? Of course. You may not buy every time, but you are interested enough to read the contents because you are a publisher.

— **Business reply envelopes** (BRE) will increase response from individuals but will not significantly improve the response from businesses. Business people have less trouble finding envelopes and stamps. The cost of business reply service has increased so much, it probably is no longer worth the expense when selling low-priced books. A business reply mail permit is $75 per year. Each letter returned will cost you the first class postage plus 9 cents, for a total of 38 cents per piece (in 1994).

— **Testimonials.** People are overwhelmed with exaggerated claims and hype. Therefore, it is important to incorporate a confidence factor into your promotional copy. Testimonials will help justify your claims for the book and draw attention to your customer service. Testimonials help build the reader's perception of believability, stability, honesty, and value. Testimonials may be placed in the circular or on a separate sheet.

To be valuable, the endorsement must be from someone who has a *name* or *title* recognizable and important to the reader. For example, if you have a book on golf, you might want a few nice words signed by Arnold Palmer or a testimonial from (John Doe), Executive Director of the PGA.

There are two ways to gather testimonials: wait for them and ask for them. Collect the testimonials from your *happy letters* and book reviews. You may ask for testimonials with a letter or an evaluation form enclosed with the book.

Save your testimonials and use them when writing up your next mailing. Be sure to get permission.

— **The guarantee.** The guarantee card may be separate, part of the brochure or part of the order card, but the guarantee itself should be mentioned several times. Some publishers leave their address off the guarantee card to make it more difficult to find (the address is on the order card, and that was mailed). Some ask that books be returned via insured parcel post, which is more expensive than book rate and makes the customer go to the post office to mail the book back. A general "complete satisfaction guaranteed" is preferable. You want to build your customer list and are aiming for repeat customers, not just a single sale. Unless your book is worthless, you will experience few returns.

A money-back guarantee may boost a response as much as 25%. People are more likely to give the book a try if they feel they have nothing to lose.

At Para Publishing, we offer an unconditional money-back guarantee at any time, no questions asked. We want customers to be happy with their purchases. If they return a book, we are glad they took the time to look it over. The theory behind the *no-time-limit guarantee* is that without a deadline, such as ten days, a customer may never get around to making the return. Either the theory is valid or we have very good products, because we have very few returns.

— **The order of insertion.** The order of insertion will be the way you want the recipient to read the material. The most logical way is: cover letter, brochure, testimonial sheet, order card and return envelope. And remember, people open envelopes from the back, not the front. In foreign mailings, check the local custom. Do their envelopes normally close on the top or the end? Always make up an example of the mailing for the lettershop to follow.

— **Card decks.** There are several ways to get your message to potential customers, and one is with card decks. You may join another deck or start your own. If you join another deck, make sure the lists are well targeted to your book's audience.

Standard Rate and Data Service lists over 600 card decks in its *Business Publication Rates and Data Directory*. Ask the reference librarian for it at your local public library. You may find a deck going to a list well targeted for your book.

Decks are printed and packaged by special machinery. If you decide to run a card deck mailing yourself, a deck printer will give you a better price than a local job printer.

— **Co-op mailings.** One way to reduce mailing costs is through cooperative mailings. Several publishers may share a mailing by stuffing their fliers into one envelope. This system works when publishers of like books are approaching the same market. Co-op mailing is offered by a number of companies which combine your brochure with other related solicitations and mail them to a selected list in a single envelope. The postage savings can be considerable. Each firm operates differently and uses different lists, so you should write to them all and compare their deals.

Broadcast advertising. There are many ways to get time on radio and television. You can buy time, make a "Per Inquiry" deal, run an "Infomercial" and/or be interviewed.

— **Buying time.** Many of the principles to buying space advertising apply to buying broadcast time.

Revlon makes cosmetics in the factory and sells hope in the drugstore. — Charles Revson

— **Infomercials** can propel you to the big time, but they are expensive to make and many of them fail. Work with an infomercial producer.

— **Interviews.** Now that you are a published author, talk shows will want to interview you. See the discussion in Chapter Seven.

Magazine and newspaper advertising can be broken down into two subgroups: *classified* and *space* (display). Unless you are covering a strictly local subject, you probably won't consider newspapers. Their audience is general and the life of the paper is short.

Most publishers stick with the cheaper classified ads and only venture to display ads in highly targeted magazines. The problem is that a book is a low-priced item. You have to sell a bunch to make an ad pay.

Today there are a lot of highly specialized magazines which cater to particular groups. The ad costs are usually lower, the quality of the prospect better and the response ordinarily greater. If your book is on parachuting, you would want a monthly ad in *Parachutist* magazine. If your book is about left-handed people, advertise in their magazine. Since 10% to 12% of the population are "lefties," an ad in any other magazine will be wasted on 88% to 90% of the readers.

Be your own ad agency, and save over 15% on your space ads. Advertising firms make their money through the 15% commission on all the space they write for a magazine or newspaper. Normally commissions apply only to space ads, not to classifieds. If you place your own ads, you can get even more. For example:

Cost of ad	$100.00
Ad commission (15%)	-15.00
Cash with order (2%)	-1.70
Total ad cost	$83.30

Being a new account, the periodical probably won't extend credit anyway, so simply write up your ad insertion order like the following one, take the 2% deduction for cash

INSERTION ORDER

AGENCY:

A.M. FURMAN ASSOCIATES
527 Madison Avenue
New York City, NY 10022
(212) 421-3707

PRODUCT   DATE:
ADVERTISER: THIS ORDER APPLIES TO OUR CONTRACT
                           NO.

TO:

Dates of Insertion	Times	Caption	Key	Space Ordered	Position

Example of an advertising insertion order

Special Instructions:

RATE _____   LESS FREQ. DISC. _____ PERCENT
_____ LESS AGENCY COMMISSION _____ PERCENT OF GROSS
_____ LESS CASH DISCOUNT _____ PERCENT ON NET
                         NET AMOUNT THIS ORDER $ _____
BY: _____

and enclose your check. It is very unlikely that they will reject your terms.

Check to see if the magazine offers MasterCard or VISA. By charging your advertising, you won't be billed until the magazine appears. This can give you use of your money between then and when you placed the ad order.

To establish your own ad agency, there will be a small investment necessary to give the appearance of a completely separate entity. You will need a different firm name, letterhead, telephone number, checkbook, etc. Make sure that all are signed by people outside of your publishing company. Many publications, such as *The National Enquirer*, will not allow commissions to "in-house" ad agencies. Some will even spend quite a bit of time trying to match up telephone numbers, signatures, etc.

They all want the same thing—a magic button to push that will make them thinner, more beautiful, richer.

Per Inquiry ads require no investment and are a good way for you to try out new advertising media. Many smaller newspapers, magazines, radio and television stations will run your ad for a share of the results. The orders are sent to them with the checks made out to you, thus giving you both a check on each other. Their cut is usually 33% to 50% of the order, about what you would give any retailer. The reason they do this is to fill unused space or time, making blank areas generate some income.

Normally you have to prepare the ad. This means nice "camera-ready" artwork for newspapers and magazines or tapes for radio and television. A one-minute videotape may run $100 originally and about $25 for each duplicate. Many authors (and other entrepreneurs) prefer doing their own shows to hiring an actor at $100 or more. The author is very much a part of her book, and the personal touch can go a long way.

The best approach is to write the station, paper, etc., describing your book and asking if they accept Per Inquiry advertising. They want sure deals, so if you have done this before, recite your good track record.

If you have already tested a medium and experienced a good return, it may not be worth your while to offer them a PI deal. It is usually better to pay for your ads and get all the money, than to go PI and take only part. On the other hand, even free advertising is wasted if it fails to generate business; it is a waste of your time and energy.

Piggyback promotion consists of attaching information on additional books to your regular promotional work. While not a major part of your promotional effort, this element is worth constant consideration as it leads to bonus sales; it moves more books at little additional cost or effort.

The ad worked because it attracted the right audience . . . because it aroused curiosity and because it offered a reward.
— John Caples

Add brochures and fliers to your outgoing mail. Filling up the monthly statement envelopes may have less value. Some of these people are "slow pay," and it is questionable whether you want to encourage any more of their business. Secondly, the statements go to the business office, not to the buyers. Unless you have an office procedures-type book, the brochure may never get to the right person. Some accounts are with small firms where one person handles everything; here a stuffer will get to the right person. If they want your new book badly enough, they may be encouraged to pay the old bill.

Exchanging brochures with other firms works well. This mutual promotion operates on the theory that once you have sold a customer your book, you have nothing more to offer. But you and another small author-publisher with a similar book can pat each other on the back and give each other a hand by each stuffing the other's brochure. It is like exchanging mailing lists, except that it is easier and cheaper (no licking, postage or envelopes). When a brochure arrives in a mailing from another publisher, it is an implied endorsement of your book.

> Dustbooks (P. O. Box 100-P, Paradise, CA 95969) will pay you $3.40 for each copy of their *International Directory of Little Magazines and Small Presses* which is sold via their piggyback stuffer.

Bookstores are sometimes receptive to stuffing your brochures in their outgoing mail. They will want their address on the fliers.

Blank back matter pages may be used to announce your other titles. Book copy and signatures rarely come out even; there are usually a few blank pages at the end. These pages should be put to work rather than wasted. This principle is so common in Germany that the last section of many books looks like a catalog. When the book is being pasted up, be prepared to add some additional promotional copy to fill up the last signature. This will also add to your mailing list, since it will bring in sales from those who have purchased books before, not directly from you, but from bookstores and other indirect outlets.

"Pass along" approaches work well in large organizations such as libraries and schools, particularly when you aren't sure who you should be contacting or if more than one person is involved in the decision-making process. Just send two or three pieces of the same brochure (consider postage again) and ask the recipient to pass the others on to someone else.

Envelopes can be used for piggybacking by printing teaser ads on the outside. Some firms use their envelopes to promote "hot" forthcoming books with an exciting blurb. Then they use these envelopes for all their mail.

Remember that the piggyback principle is an "add on" to other promotion only. While it will generate more business from existing customers, it will not bring in new clients. Every time you make a contact with a potential customer, you want to show him everything you have to offer. Hopefully, at least one will appeal to him. But remember that stuffers cost money and must not be wasted. Send them only when there is a chance of an order.

Co-op advertising is a popular way the big publishers direct sales to bookstores with local space ads. Typically, the publisher pays 75% of the ad cost (but no more than 10% of the value of the books shipped to the store), and the bookstore pays 25%. If the store is a regular advertiser in the local papers, they usually get a slightly better rate. The procedure is to have the store place the ads, but the tear sheets and bills go to the publisher. Then the publisher credits the store with 75% of the bill toward book purchases.

To justify co-op advertising, you have to anticipate that the store will move a lot of books. And, while the stores may be the major outlet for the big publisher, they are usually a minor one for a small firm which concentrates on mail order sales.

The Federal Trade Commission (FTC) regulations insist that any deal offered to one dealer must be made available to all. A small publisher who tests co-op ads with one store could find himself in great financial difficulty, being obligated to advertise for everyone else.

Many small firms feel that co-op advertising is just too complicated and too time-consuming, and they routinely answer all inquiries in the negative. They save time, money and stay away from the FTC.

Point-of-purchase sales aids include bookmarks, dumps, posters, etc. Posters can be very useful in specialty shops and exhibits, but there just isn't any room for them in a bookstore. Librarians like posters, but they rarely buy more than one book. Free bookmarks with advertising are used 30% to 38% of the time by bookstores. Dumps are special shipping cartons/display units, which are used by 38% to 40% of the stores, depending on the available counter and floor space. Many larger stores suggest and request them. Some clever publishers have designed small dumps with directions for detecting counterfeit bills on the back. This assures premium display space on the counter near the cash register.

> Dumps can often be found in dumpsters behind bookstores. Many publishers ship their books in counter dumps, floor dumps and shippers (cartons). Bookstores do not need the dumps because they have shelves, so they toss both the dump and the shipper into the dumpster. You will find a variety of colors, sizes and shapes. Use the dumps for testing new (nontraditional) markets.

Catalogs. There are two types of catalogs: general book catalogs, which are not interesting, and special-interest catalogs, that are. Catalogs can move a lot of books and they are committed to you for the life of the catalog—usually one year.

Special merchandise catalogs are those which feature a line of merchandise but devote a page or two to related books. Since you are already in the field (having written about it), you probably know who they are. See the various catalog directories at your public library.

> *Show how your book solves problems and enhances the stature of the user among his or her contemporaries.*

Your catalog is probably a long way off. After you have published ten to twelve books, you will need a catalog just to maintain organization. A catalog is a good reference and public relations tool. With just a few books, a much cheaper brochure for each book is all you will need. Fliers on individual books will usually out-pull a catalog, which is too big and takes too much time to read through.

The big publishers separate their catalogs into two distinct sections: the new titles, or *frontlist,* and the *backlist.* The catalog may be titled "Books for Spring" and will feature all the current offerings up front. Last season's titles which are still available will be in the less-prominent backlist in back.

If you want to publish a catalog but have only a few titles, you might consider carrying related titles from other publishers.

Remainders are overstock books which are sold off to remainder dealers at greatly reduced prices. The big publishers are only interested in books while they are maintaining a certain level of sales. When the demand drops, out they go. Your situation is different, because you are storing the books at home, have a lower overhead, like the prestige of having a current book and can get by on the occasional sales. Initially, each book in your brochure adds to your size. You will have to have a number of titles before you will be interested in dropping any. You can always run off another 1,000 copies; there is no reason to go out of print. If it is a good how-to book and you have kept it up-to-date with revisions at each printing, it should continue to sell.

Typically, a remainder dealer will offer you 1% to 3% of the list (cover) price of the book. On a $19.95 book, that would be just 20 to 60 cents each. Do not remainder a book until the value of your storage space exceeds these amounts.

John Huenefeld offers this rule of thumb for determining when to dump a title: Multiply the quantity on hand by the

> *Good judgment comes from experience, and experience—well, that comes from poor judgment.*

list price. Then divide by 20 to get 5% of the list price value of the stock. Now compare this 5% figure with the net sales for the last 12 months. If the sales were not greater than this 5% figure, it's time to call the truck.

Remaindering is big business. Twenty thousand titles go out of print each year, and some 25 million copies are remaindered. A lot of big firms are in this business; many wholesalers carry remainders, and they may account for one-third of a bookstore's gross. Some books see their sales pick up once they have been remaindered. The new price and marketing effort has turned books completely around. Remaindered books have sold out and have gone back on the press.

Notify your distributor before remaindering a book and offer to take their stock back.

Lists of remainder dealers may be found in *Publishers Weekly, Literary Market Place* and the *American Book Trade Directory*, all at your library. Write to a number of remainder dealers, indicating the quantity, list price, title, hardbound or paperback, condition, location, whether they are prepackaged, and if so, in what increments. Enclose a copy of the book and your sales materials. Establish a closing date and announce that you will accept the best offer for any quantity. Shipping is FOB your warehouse, terms are net 30 days and the books are not returnable. Once you have selected the highest bidder, call him and make sure you have a deal.

Most remainder dealers will want 1,000 to 5,000 books, minimum, and they want your entire stock so as to have an exclusive. Some will take your slightly damaged stock— those scratched copies returned by bookstores.

For detailed information on remainder and other forms of inventory reduction, see the Special Report *Beyond Remainders*. See the Appendix. Hopefully, you won't have to deal in remainders.

Donate damaged returns to a charity. You may deduct the value of the book at its original acquisition cost plus the postage out. Prisons, foreign libraries and church bazaars will be very happy to accept your books. By donating your scuffed books, you recover your original investment in them.

For details and addresses for donating books and taking tax deductions, see our Special Report *Beyond Remainders*. See the Appendix.

Your book is a success when people who haven't read it pretend they have.

Chapter Ten

Fulfillment

Moving Your Book Out the Door

Book order *fulfillment* consists of invoicing, inventory storage, picking, packaging and shipping. These routines involve opening the mail, sorting it, keyboarding the invoices, wrapping the books, affixing the shipping label, applying postage to the package, making the trip to the post office (or other delivery system) and maintaining a record of the sale. *Inventory management* includes storage and stock monitoring so you will know when to order another printing.

Fulfillment is expensive. According to John Huenefeld, most small- to medium-sized publishers spend about 10.5% of their gross on fulfillment. All costs, including labor, storage and shipping materials, amount to $2.44 per order handled, or 66 cents per book. If your business is mostly wholesale (many copies of the same book to fewer customers), you should be able to drop your fulfillment percentage to six or seven.

Mail order selling offers you the opportunity to run a high-volume, worldwide business without a large cash investment in multiple facilities. To compete with larger companies, all you will need is a better product and more efficient promotion. Since we are far from most of our customers, book publishing is in the mail order business.

Mail order businesses are those which deal with their customers at a distance, without personal delivery. The product may not be delivered by the post office; a large shipment might go by truck. Mail order is particularly appropriate for the distribution of books. In fact, over half of the business and professional books are shipped directly from the publisher to the ultimate consumer.

Smaller publishers are attracted to mail order selling because it is easier than getting into bookstores. They ship to wholesalers and stores, but they don't spend the money on visiting them. In fact, there are many stories about books which had done poorly in the stores but which, when properly promoted, sold well through mail order.

Mail order buyers probably do not frequent bookstores, and it is likely they do not even think of themselves as *book buyers*. In a *Publishers Weekly* article about Bantam, it was noted that geographically, mail orders line up proportionally to population figures. Most orders come from the most populated states, California and New York, not from the states with fewer bookstores. Mail order purchasing is a habit. Many people prefer to buy informational books this way. Once they begin, they often collect everything they can find on the subject.

Order processing. Once your business grows to the point where you have numerous titles and several employees, you will require a more elaborate fulfillment system. Initially you will do it all yourself so you can keep it simple. One way to keep it simple is to streamline the workload to avoid any duplication of effort. For example, keyboarding an invoice and then typing a separate label is a waste of time and money (cost of label, etc.). Just print out three copies of each invoice and use one copy for the shipping label/packing slip. This *one-writing* avoids transposition errors in figures and addresses.

To enable you to visualize the distribution system, the fulfillment process will be discussed in sequence.

— **Postal orders.** Open the mail and check the contents, but do not take the orders and checks out of their envelopes. Sort the stuffed envelopes into piles according to whether they are individual retail sales, book dealers (stores or distributors), libraries or special accounts, such as associations, sport centers, etc. Make up a separate pile for inquiries—you will want to send these people a brochure. Other separate piles will be for accounts receivable, letters to be answered, etc.

When a retail order arrives without a check, make a note of the omission (such as "check not enclosed") on the envelope. Then send a brochure with a note requesting money in the correct amount. Occasionally, you will get a letter back saying that a check was enclosed with the original order, but you will have your note on that envelope to confirm your suspicions and jog your memory. Make a photocopy of the envelope with the notation, and request that the sender re-check his or her records and/or send you a photocopy of the canceled check.

— **Telephone orders.** More and more people are ordering by telephone. It is easier and faster than ordering by mail and not much more expensive.

Telephone contacts are important opportunities for sales and increased sales. They take place when you have the attention of the prospect and they are (usually) paying for the call. Consequently, telephone calls should not be handled by an untrained employee. Make sure everyone knows who is to take calls, except in case of overflow, or train every staff member to take calls. Have an order form ready, or route orders to the order-entry computer operator for direct punch-up. Order pads prompt questions, so that all information, such as the *ship to* address, is obtained.

As you grow, you might investigate credit card sales and accepting orders via toll-free (800) telephone numbers, but initially postal and regular telephone communication will be sufficient. For details and addresses, see the Special Reports *Book Fulfillment* and *Merchant Card Status*. See the Appendix.

— **Answering machines** are very useful in business, as they can take orders after business hours. They are a great convenience to both you and the customer. Buyers may order at any time, and it is nice when you return after a weekend away to find a number of orders waiting for you.

> Many people like our recording which says: "Para Publishing, this is Dan Poynter. If you would like an information kit on publishing or parachuting, please leave your name and address. If you would like to charge a book to your VISA, MasterCard, Discover or American Express card, please leave your name, address, telephone number, the name of the book, type of charge card, the card number and the expiration date. Thank you." *(beep)*

— **Telex** is useful for accepting international orders. If you have one now, keep it. If you don't, get a fax machine instead.

— **Fax.** Faster than Federal Express and cheaper than a stamp, the fax machine is replacing the Postal Service. You must have a fax machine—on a separate telephone line. List your fax number on your letterhead, business card and order blanks. Without a fax, people will wonder if you are really in business. Get a plain-paper model.

Facsimile transmissions do not replace the telephone; they replace the Postal Service for delivering letters, purchase orders and drawings. Many of your orders will come in by fax.

When you think about it, paying someone to hand-carry a letter across town or across the country is a waste of time and energy resources. If you can fax it, don't mail it.

Credit cards will increase sales and increase the size of the sale while cutting down on collection problems. People have become accustomed to telephoning an order and placing the charge on a credit card. VISA and MasterCard are

Why pay the Postal Service 32 cents to store your mail?

used the most in telephone orders, American Express is third, with Discover and the others used to a much lesser extent. While the bank will want 3% to 7% of each sale, depending upon the average size of the sale and your monthly volume, it credits your account immediately. Credit cards will increase your cash flow and may decrease your need for expensive short-term loans.

Credit card orders take more time to process because you must print out a charge slip and call in for approval. But the sale always comes out even, so there is no additional billing or difference to refund, and there are no accounts receivable collection problems.

The problem is in getting the Merchant Card privilege from the bank. Because of high losses to fly-by-night boiler room telephone operations, the banks have stopped offering Merchant Card privileges to mail order and telephone order businesses.

The Merchant Card Packets from most banks list the prohibitions (such as no telephone orders, no mail orders, no working from home), but they also have lists of exceptions. Get packets from several banks and compare. See our Special Report *Merchant Card Status* for details. See the Appendix.

Order-entry software. You may start with an inexpensive order-entry/accounting program such as *QuickBooks* (Intuit, P.O. Box 3014, Menlo Park, CA 94026, Tel: (800) 433-8810). With the computer you will be able to do much more with the collected information. Later you may invest in an even more sophisticated order entry computer program. See the Appendix.

Initially, you will use the invoice forms designed for your order-entry program. Later, you will graduate to your own custom-printed invoice.

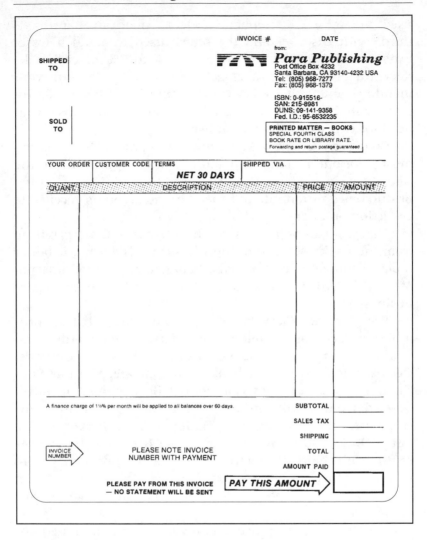

Example of an invoice

One copy of your invoice is folded in thirds and slipped into a 4.5" x 8.5" clear packing slip envelope (Stock #45-3-23, Associated Bag Co., Milwaukee, WI 53207). With the shipping instructions ("Printed Matter," etc.) printed on the top third of the invoice, you won't need to use a rubber stamp for this information.

Individual orders. Open the envelope and enter the order into your computer. Set the check aside for deposit or process the credit card number. Print out two copies of the invoice. One will be used as a shipping label/packing slip for the package, and the other will go into a three-ring binder as a permanent record. Normally, it is not necessary to send a separate record of the sale to the customer via first class mail.

— **Save the envelopes** with their enclosed orders. At the end of each week or month, rubber band the envelopes and date the pile. Save them for 12 to 18 months, in case a customer contacts you about the order or the package is returned as undeliverable. If a book is returned by the post office as undeliverable, check the postmark to determine when the shipment went out and then go through the envelopes to find the original order. The book may have been sent to the address on the check rather than the one on the envelope, numbers may have been transposed, etc.

If a customer complains that the wrong book was shipped, he or she did not order the book or a check was enclosed, a check of the original order will confirm or deny the claim. When replying, enclose a photocopy of the original order so the customer can see what he or she did.

— **Books not received.** Occasionally a customer will write complaining that he or she has not received the book. Check back through the original order envelope and label carbon or computer record to make sure you received the order, that the book was sent and when. Then write to the customer stating the date the book was shipped and that it was sent via slower, but cheaper, book rate, which can take up to 30 days in the U.S. and 120 days to foreign addresses. Remind him the package had a return address and mention that the parcel was not returned to you. Rarely does the post office lose books. Tell him that if the book does not arrive in a couple of weeks more "to return this letter and you will ship out another book."

When you ship the second book, write up the transaction on an invoice, make three copies and airmail one to him.

Note on it that if he receives two books to *refuse delivery* of the second one. This way the post office will return the book to you with only postage due. If the customer accepts delivery, he may never get around to sending the book back and you are out a book. Explain to him that you are sorry for the inconvenience and do not wish to inconvenience him further by having him rewrap and reship the (second) book. Once he receives a book, the chances are very good he will refuse delivery of the second one because he does not need two.

— **Ad codes.** At the end of each month, total up the orders responding to each address code and record the responses. See the discussion of address coding in Chapter Seven.

— **Short slips** may be used to collect small amounts. Some customers will not send enough to cover the book, shipping and sales tax. Sometimes the shortage is not worth the cost to collect it. Very small improper payments (high or low) are not worth haggling over. Just ship the book.

Short slips may be used to collect these small amounts, but set certain limits such as:

0 to 40 cents short: Forget it.

40 cents to $4.99: Enclose a short slip.

Over $5.00: Cut an invoice for the balance.

You must compare the costs of collecting small amounts with the amount that can be collected. Most people are good about short slips and will pay, but it is not worth badgering them for 30 cents if they must use first class postage to send it to you. Collect these small payments as they come in and bank them once a month. The small amounts add up and are worth collecting.

— **Overpayments.** If the customer sends a little too much, ship the book a faster way, such as UPS or Priority Mail. If he or she sends a lot too much, issue a refund check for the balance. Fortunately, credit card orders come out even.

Short Slip

Your order was short $ _____ .

We know you will appreciate our shipping the books now rather than holding up the shipment pending payment of this small amount.

Please return this slip when you next contact us—now OR with your next order or payment. THANK YOU.

Your name: _____

Check number: _____

Send to: Para Publishing
          Accounting Department
          P.O. Box 8206
          Santa Barbara, CA 93118-8206
          Tel: (805) 968-7277
          Fax: (805) 968-1379

Short slip

— **Bad checks.** Checks rarely bounce, and it is not worth the record keeping and loss of customer good will to delay shipments until a check clears the bank. When a check is returned, check the original order envelope to see if there is more than one address. Send off a photocopy of the returned check and the bank notice that came with it. Write across the photocopy *Please send another check,* and circle the bank charge and the new total amount. Most of these paperhangers will make the bad check good. You may always include a short, direct letter, but this photocopy technique is faster and simpler. Since books have a high markup, it probably is not worth your time to expend more effort trying to collect these few small debts.

— **Insurance.** Insuring book shipments is a waste of time and money. Books lost or damaged in the mails should be replaced by the shipper. Your only alternative is to insure each parcel. It is far cheaper to *self-insure* and replace the occasional lost or damaged book. There will not be many lost books, and the cost of replacement is small, compared to the price of insurance and the paperwork involved, to say nothing of the value of a happy customer.

— **Refunds** should be handled promptly. *The customer is always right.* A cheerful, fast refund will let him know he can trust you, and there is a good chance he will be back.

Set up as few barriers to ordering as possible. If your product is good, most customers will keep it. Since there is no limit on the free trial period, most unsatisfied customers will put off the return—forever.

Unlimited Guarantee

We guarantee your satisfaction. Order any book and look it over. You may return it at any time if you are not satisfied and your full purchase price will be refunded, no questions asked. There is no 10 day or 30 day limit; you may even return it after a year.

The customer usually pays the shipping on an order and on a return. This means that you refund or issue a credit only for the price of the book.

Dealer orders are those from your distributor, commercial wholesale customers and those individual retail customers, such as libraries and large companies, that must be billed.

For dealers, print out three copies of the invoice. Send one copy via first class mail by simply folding and slipping it into a windowed #10 envelope (or fax it). Include your brochure and other promotional information. The second copy goes to your shipping area, and the third copy is stapled to the purchase order, hole-punched and placed in your accounts receivable three-ring binder in invoice number order.

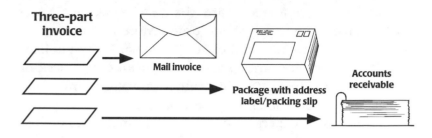

The invoice route

— **Accounts receivable.** When payment arrives, match the check with the invoice, and date-stamp the invoice to give you a record of the date payment was received. Then move the invoice to a binder of a different color for storage. Update your computer file.

Sales tax will have to be added onto the invoice on those *retail sales made within your state.* Do not collect sales tax on books sold *for resale* to bookstores and other firms in your state. When you sell to another reseller in your state, you must record their state *resale number.* The point is that the ultimate purchaser will pay the tax. You must either collect it or get a resale number to indicate who will collect it. In most states, libraries are not exempt from sales taxes; after all, they do not resell the books. Usually, the sales tax is not collected for any sales made out of your state. The sales tax is on the merchandise only, not the shipping charges. The time may come when we will have to collect sales taxes for all retail sales, because Congress periodically considers a national sales tax.

The bottom of the invoice may be used for any other pertinent information or even nice personal notes.

Credit. The customer may send a check, authorize you to charge his or her credit card, or you may extend credit (e.g., *Net 30 days*). Most publishers require a check or credit card from individuals and extend credit to bookstores, libraries, their distributor and wholesalers, but there are exceptions.

— **Individuals** usually send a check when ordering by mail and authorize a credit card charge to VISA or Master-Card when making a telephone order. More and more people are ordering by card and expect to do so. Many publishers follow the rule: *no credit sales to individuals.* Get a check or credit card or ship COD. This rule eliminates many small receivables and occasional uncollectibles.

— **Businesses** expect terms, but many small ones are using credit cards. Though the interest rate is high, cards offer convenience and simple credit to the small business.

For those businesses that insist on sending purchase orders without money, you may extend 30-day credit terms or send a *pro forma invoice.* This is a regular invoice listing the books, shipping charges, sales tax (if applicable) and the total. Once they pay the invoice, you ship the books. Most small publishers routinely extend credit to bookstores, libraries and businesses as long as the orders are not too large.

— **Wholesalers.** The book industry is not known for fast pay. Sixty-, 90- and even 120-day payments are not uncommon, and since books have to be sold on a return basis, they are, in effect, on consignment anyway. Some publishers have put the large wholesalers on a CWO (cash with order) basis. Even Baker & Taylor will pay up front if requested.

If a bookstore or wholesaler is slow or fails to pay, tighten up or cut them off. Many publishers follow this system: Any dealers over 60 days are put on a CWO (cash with order) basis until their accounts are brought up-to-date. In other words, they get credit until they abuse it, and then they pay in advance. Some publishers extend credit only to their distributor with whom they have a contract and college (tax-supported) bookstores. Everyone else pays in advance. Some publishers deal only through their distributor and direct any bookstore and library orders to that distributor.

— **Distributors.** Your relationship with your distributor will be governed by your contract. Many distributors pay 90 days after they ship the books. Most will send a monthly printout of sales so you will know what size checks to expect.

Shipping labels will be needed for non-invoiced shipments. Labels come in fanfold stacks with pin-feed holes on the sides for printer use. You may also use a typewriter for single labels. Here is an example of a 3" x 5" label:

Fanfold label

Fanfold, custom-printed labels are available from label manufacturers. One is Discount Label, P.O. Box 709, New Albany, IN 47151-0709, Tel: (800) 457-2400.

Do not order labels on slick stock. Addresses will smear and ink takes much longer to dry.

Back orders are those that cannot be completely filled when the order is received. Usually most of the order can be filled and is shipped, while the single out-of-stock book order is put aside until the book is received and can be shipped.

Most publishers use a common code of abbreviations to cover the most frequent back order problems: "OS" (out of stock), "TOS" (temporarily out of stock), "OP" (out of print), "TOP" (temporarily out of print), "NOP" (not our publication) and "FP" (future publication). If you use these abbreviations, make sure they are explained elsewhere on the invoice, such as on the back. Only librarians and bookstore buyers will understand the codes.

The Federal Trade Commission (FTC) has some strict rules for CWO (cash with order) mail order operations. If you receive money for books:

- You must ship the order within 30 days of receiving it (or charging their credit card), unless your offer clearly stated shipping would take longer.

- If it appears the order will not be shipped when promised, you must notify the customer before the promised date, giving a definite new date, if known, and offering the opportunity to cancel the order with a refund or consent to a definite delayed shipping date or an indefinite delay.

- Your notice must contain a self-addressed, stamped card or envelope with which to indicate a preference. If there is no response to this notice, you may assume agreement to the delay but must ship the order within 30 days of the original shipping date promised or required, or the order will be automatically canceled. A prompt refund must be made if the order is canceled.

- Even if the customer consented to an indefinite delay, he or she retains the right to cancel the order at any time before the item is shipped.

- If the customer cancels an order that has been paid for by check or money order, you must mail a refund within seven business days.

- If they cancel a credit card order, you must issue a credit within one billing cycle following the receipt of their request. The customer may stop payment pending settlement of the matter if the purchase is over $50 and he or she is within 100 miles or is within the same state.

All this FTC discussion regarding credit card rules may not count, as your contract with the credit card company probably says if the customer purchased by mail or telephone (without physically handing you the card) and later contests the bill, you must issue a credit.

- Credits toward future purchases are not acceptable.

- If the book ordered is unavailable, you may not send substitute merchandise without the customer's consent.

Send to the Federal Trade Commission, Washington, DC 20580, (202) 326-2000, for the following pamphlets:

1. *Shopping by Mail? You're Protected!*
2. *FTC Buyer's Guide No. 2*

As long as you guarantee satisfaction by offering to send a refund for any merchandise returned for any reason, you shouldn't have any run-ins with the FTC. Just treat your customers right and keep in touch with them.

Orders should be shipped as soon as possible after receipt, usually the next day. This involves a trip to the post office once each day to pick up the mail and to deliver the wrapped books from orders received the previous day. The sooner the orders are processed, the sooner the money will be deposited; this is the best incentive for speedy fulfillment.

Customers want their books as soon as possible. A few who are not familiar with mail order will even write two days later looking for their package, but this is rare. When business is slow, post office runs may be made every other day, say Monday, Wednesday and Friday. If you must be away from the business, you will find that only one or two inquiries will be received if you fail to ship for up to a month.

Unordered books. Customers receiving unordered merchandise may not be pressured to pay for it or return it.

They may use it or discard it as they see fit. So be careful where you ship books. See the *Postal Service Domestic Mail Manual.*

Quality control. One way to avoid shipping errors is to employ as few people as possible in the order-entry and packaging functions. Fewer people in the loop provides accountability. The second secret is cross-training so everyone understands the system (and can fill in during absences). If an error is made punching up an order, the packer may spot it, if he or she understands the system. Try to limit order handling to the mail opener/telephone operator who receives the orders, the order-entry computer operator who punches up the orders, and the shipper who picks, packs and posts. In very small companies, one person will perform all functions, but as you hire help, be sure to cross-train. If the same person handles mail opening or order entry and accounts receivable, he or she will remember the bad debts and other problems and will flag new orders.

Complaints must be viewed as an opportunity, not a problem. Complaints can be expensive if not handled quickly, and they mean a lost sale unless you can make a substitute or convince the customer you are worthy of a future order. Some mail order companies, such as Quill, the large office-supply company, enclose a return form with every order to emphasize how easy it is to do business with them.

Complaints should be answered promptly. Even if the book has probably arrived by the time you get the complaint, you should answer. You must maintain credibility.

Written complaints should be handled with a call, unless a lot of photocopied documentation is required. Customers can be cooled down more easily over the telephone.

When someone calls in a complaint, you have an opportunity to wrap up the problem on the telephone at their expense, so do not offer to get back to them. Remind the caller or writer that you guarantee satisfaction. You will try to work out the problem, but if you can't, you will refund the money. Most customers want the book, and the problem worked out.

Find out what the customer wants before suggesting a solution. Ask: "What do you want?" The answer is usually much easier and less expensive than you would have guessed.

A checklist form letter may be used to handle common small problems, but impersonal forms should not be used for major complaints.

Inventory and storage. Book storage cannot be taken lightly because books are not light. If your floor will not support a water bed, do not haul in a ton of books. The people downstairs will not like your books any better than the water. The best place to store your new product is in the garage, alongside the shipping table. This way, the books may be off-loaded in the driveway and stacked in the garage, wrapped as needed and placed back in the car for the post office run. All these operations will be done with a minimum of carrying. Hauling books down steep steps into a cellar, only to wrap them and haul them back up, gets very old very soon and makes no sense at all. This is heavy work.

Tell the printer you want the finished books shrink-wrapped in stacks of two books each. The plastic runs about ten cents per shrink. If you shrink-wrap them individually, stores and potential customers will not remove the plastic, so they will not check the contents and you will probably lose the sale.

The plastic wrap will keep the books clean, dry, and dust-free, and the books will not rub on the carton. Small publishers need shrink-wrapping and tightly packed cartons because they often store the books in places without climate control, such as in an unheated garage. If the cartons are not tightly packed (filled to the top), they will crush and tip, rather than stack well.

> *The fewer the people touching the orders, the faster, less expensively and more accurately the job will be completed.*

Do not stack cartons directly on top of each other. Stack them alternately like bricks. The alternating stack will be solid and will not tip over. Very little shelving is required, as books should be stored in their original cartons.

If your state has an inventory tax, you can avoid most of the bite by careful ordering, or by having your printing done in another state. Then, keeping an eye on the tax date, have the printer ship in a pallet of books as needed.

As noted above, the books should be shrink-wrapped, boxed and sealed. Then the cartons should be palletized, banded three ways and trucked to you as a unit. This keeps the books from shifting in the cartons, which scratches the covers. Palletized and banded (with straps or plastic wrap) cartons are less likely to be broken open en route, but always expect at least one carton to be torn, so that the spine of some books can be read. Books delivered to home addresses, as opposed to normal places of business, are sometimes porno books. Of course, if you are publishing pornography, expect some books to be missing from the shipment.

New titles may be drop shipped directly from the printer to your wholesale accounts. There is no reason to expend the time and money to route them, for example, from Michigan to the publisher in California and then back to Quality Books in Illinois.

Books must be kept in a cool, dry, dust-free place. Dampness may ripple or curl the pages, make them stick together and rust wire stitches (staples) in saddle stitched books. Depending upon your location, moisture and type of flooring, it may be wise to stack the cartons on pallets, so air can circulate under the stack. Always leave an air space between the stack and a wall. Sunlight will fade and yellow paper. Dust will scratch the covers and dirty the edges.

Fire is always a problem, and insuring the inventory in a noncommercial (hence non-fire-rated) area may be impossible. Ask your insurance agent.

If your books are damaged, slowly or quickly, you are out of business. Your inventory must be protected, and this means starting by leaving the books in their protective cartons and bags and opening only one carton at a time as needed. Unbelievably, some publishers unpack their books and place them on shelves, exposed to sun and dust.

If the pages of the books ripple due to dampness, they may straighten out when the humidity returns to normal.

Inventory control is simpler if all the books are stored in a single place. If you have cartons of books scattered around your garage, in the office, at the printer's, with friends, and in a mini-storage warehouse, some will disappear and you will never know how many you have. If you do not have a garage or spare room, try renting warehouse space. Mini-warehouses are quite common now; check the *Yellow Pages*. Then try to store books in one place, or no more than two: the bulk in the warehouse and a few cartons in the shipping area.

Visual physical inspection is the easiest way to get stock information; it is faster than going through the invoices. If you quickly count the books on hand monthly, you will be able to plot a good inventory chart. These figures will be a great help in your planning next year. Reorders must be scheduled so the reprints will arrive just before the previous supply is exhausted. Having to report a delay in filling an order costs in paperwork, and time is money. Decisions to reprint will be determined by rate of sale, stock level, seasonal sales expectations (outdoor books sell better in the spring), the time required to print and, in some states, the date of the inventory tax.

Dun & Bradstreet reports that 9.5% of all business failures are due to excessive inventory. Keep the inventory low and order more often.

The shipping area is where you do the picking, packing and posting. It should be arranged so as to require as little motion as possible; books, bags, cartons, and other materials must all be within easy reach. Position the faster-selling books closer to the shipping table.

Packing involves the placing of the books in a protective wrapper so that your customer receives the clean, unmutilated goods he or she is paying for. Books must be packaged well enough to arrive in good condition the first time. It costs too much to ship them twice.

— **Saddle stitched booklets.** Small wire-stitched (stapled) paperbacks may be safely shipped in a heavy Kraft envelope; make sure the size is correct. If the envelope is too large, the book will slide around inside and the cover will be scuffed.

Shipping bag

— **Hardcover and perfect-bound (square-back) paperbacks up to 6" x 9" require a padded bag.** Standard padded bags are heavy, dirty and can only be stapled closed. The plastic-bubble Mail-Lite® bag, on the other hand, is clean, light and waterproof when heat-sealed. Compared to other plastic-lined bags, the Mail-Lite is not as smooth inside, making it difficult to stuff large books, but it offers the best protection. We have postal-tested every type of plain and padded bag, light-weight and heavy-weight, and have found the Mail Lite bag to be the best.

Mail Lite bags cost more than fiber-filled Jiffy bags, but you will save on postage. A standard 6" x 9" hardcover book measures a half-inch wider and longer and is a quarter-inch thicker than its paperback edition. Both fit the #1 Mail-Lite bag when they have less than 200 pages.

— **Heat-sealers.** The shipping bags may be stapled closed (get the heavy, hand-grip type stapler) or heat-sealed. The sealing machines come in several sizes and provide a moisture-tight closure. Sealed Air runs heat-sealer promotions from time to time. If your Sealed Air distributor is not running a promotion on heat-sealers, contact the sealer manufacturer directly: Heat Sealing Equipment in Cleveland, Ohio, Tel: (216) 341-2022. Call for the number of the dealer nearest you.

Call Sealed Air for the name of the local paper dealer who handles their Mail-Lite bags: Sealed Air Corporation, Park 80 Plaza East, Saddle Brook, NJ 07662, Tel: (201) 791-7600.

Also contact Quill for a catalog and compare bag prices (P.O. Box 4700, Lincolnshire, IL 60197-4700, Tel: (708) 634-4800/East or (714) 988-3200/West). Remember to add in shipping charges when comparing prices.

Multiple book orders, up to three books, may be shipped in larger shipping bags, if immobilized against rubbing by plastic bagging and taping. Greater quantities of books should be boxed.

— **8.5" x 11" softcover books** require the rigidity of Vari-depth mailers due to their longer spine. Vari-depth mailers are die-cut, flat shippers that can be folded around one or more books. The mailers cost more than shipping bags but offer excellent protection when the books are first placed in a plastic bag. (See next page.)

Cartons. Check the *Yellow Pages* for nearby paper-goods dealers, and purchase standard 5.5" x 8.5" or 6" x 9" cartons (as applicable) of various depths, which ordinarily come 25 to the bundle.

Bookstores are a good source of shipping cartons. They usually get more than they can recycle and disposal is expensive. Ask the store owner and check the dumpster.

If you will standardize the trim size of all your books, you will minimize the carton and bag sizes required for shipping. The best measurements for books are 5.5" x 8.5" and 8.5" x 11," as they will stack together.

Vari-depth mailer

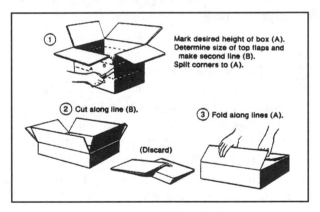

① Mark desired height of box (A). Determine size of top flaps and make second line (B). Split corners to (A).

② Cut along line (B).

(Discard)

③ Fold along lines (A).

How to cut down a box

Sealing a carton with nonreinforced paper tape

Incidentally, some states do not charge sales tax on shipping supplies, such as cartons and tape. This is probably to encourage exports. Check on this with your office-supply store or state taxing authority.

The least expensive way to seal cartons is with 3" nonreinforced brown paper tape. The reinforced tape is strong, but it is also dirty and hard to cut with inexpensive tape dispensers.

Tape dispensers. Fancy paper-tape machines cost several hundred dollars—quite a shock—so look around for a used one. Check *used* office equipment stores and swap meets. Also compare the prices at Quill. Call for a catalog: (708) 634-4800. They offer an electric model for about $265 which may be good. Also call Arrow Star for a catalog: (800) 645-2982.

The water will flow onto the paper tape more easily if you add a little vinegar to the reservoir in the tape machine. You may, alternatively, use a couple of drops of detergent, but detergent gums up the machine more quickly than vinegar.

Tape. Plastic sealing tape costs more than paper and is harder to use, but the handheld dispensers are less expensive. The lightest-weight plastic tape is sufficient; buy the cheapest, lowest-mil thickness available. Be very careful of the special sales on rolls of plastic sealing tape. The *rolls* vary in length and some offers are no bargain.

You will need half-inch reinforced glass strapping tape for large cartons, so you should also use it on the small ones. Do not waste money buying wider tape.

Do not use twine; UPS does not allow it anymore. String takes too long to put on and it catches in mail-handling machinery.

You will also need some cellophane tape to seal the packing list/address label envelope.

The machinery you will need includes tape dispensers, knife, stapler or heat-sealer, and a scale.

Plastic bags. Take a carton and 20 books to your paper-goods store. Pick up some large garbage can liner bags to line large cartons. Measure the bags against the carton. Then stack some books in one pile to fit the smaller cartons you are buying, and get some smaller plastic bag can liners to match. You have to run these packaging tests each time you buy, because the bag manufacturers are continually changing the measurements, mil thickness and gussets.

Knife. Get a common razor knife for opening cartons and keep it sharp. A sharpening stone will prolong the life of the blades. Be very careful when cutting open cartons. It is common to score the covers of the top books by cutting too deep.

AIR MAIL first class
SPECIAL
HANDLING
PRINTED MATTER – BOOKS
SPECIAL FOURTH CLASS
BOOK RATE OR LIBRARY RATE
Forwarding & Return Postage Guaranteed

Rubber stamps. The common rubber stamps you will need are here. Order them from your local office-supply store.

With the book rate notice printed on your mailing labels and invoices, you will need this rubber stamp just for occasional packages.

When shipping a package by AIR, stamp the notice *near* the address on the package so that it will be more noticeable to the mail sorters. A red AIR MAIL stamp over in one corner of the carton may be missed, resulting in a high-priced, slow delivery.

Turn your stamp pad over each night to make the ink flow to the top of the pad.

Ladder. Get a short, sturdy ladder or step stool so you will be able to stack cartons higher and retrieve them easily.

Scales fall into two categories and three general ranges. The categories are spring and electronic. The electronic scales should be more accurate.

The three categories are 0-2 lb. letter scale, 0-5 lb. (some go to 25 lbs.) small parcel scale and 0-50 lbs. (or more) large parcel scale. The larger scale need only read from 0-50 lbs. Packages heavier than 40 lbs. do not protect their contents well and should not be shipped.

Book publishers do not need fancy zone/rate-computing scales since books shipped at book rate are not zoned. A simple scale and a rate chart are all that are needed. Most small publishers will get by just fine with a 0-2 lb. letter scale and a 0-50 lb. large package scale.

The scale should be accurate, but do not be obsessed with its being perfect. The Postal Service rarely checks the postage on a package.

Packing. There are two important steps in successful book packaging: Keep the books clean and immobilize them. Start with cartons that are close to the size needed. If you have 5.5" x 8.5" books and can get 5.5" x 8.5" cartons in several depths, the fit will be perfect and there will not be any sliding and scuffing between books. Slip the books into a plastic bag and slide them into the carton. For the best fit, cut down the top of the carton rather than fill it with dunnage. The books will be kept clean by the plastic bag and immobilized by the perfect-fitting carton.

Plastic Styrofoam peanuts and discs are greasy, carry grit and will work their way between the pages of a book if not separated by a plastic bag. Reuse any peanuts sent to you, but do not buy them. The best shipping carton is a perfect fit or one that has been cut down to fit. The next best choice is to stuff with newspaper, but remember that newspaper is dirty, another reason to place the books in a plastic bag first.

Single orders may be prepackaged and stacked to wait for a label. Done in front of the TV set, the time passes quickly.

Labeling. Once the bag is stuffed or the carton is wrapped, it is time to apply the packing list/shipping label. This copy of the invoice is simply folded and inserted into a large, pressure-sensitive, adhesive-backed clear envelope and placed on the bag or carton. Now the person receiving the shipment will have exactly the same information as the person receiving the bill.

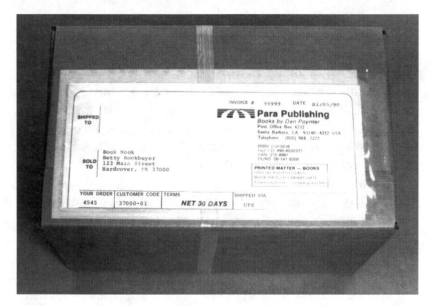

The wrapped and addressed carton

Occasionally, the person receiving the bill will not want the person receiving the books to know the prices and terms (such as in a drop shipment). In this case, simply use scissors to clip off the pricing information. When the *ship to* address is not the same as the invoiced address, cross out the latter and circle the former with a felt-tip pen, or use left-over one-across labels to cover the *sold to* address.

Taping. Using nonreinforced paper tape, seal the ends of the carton as well as the long flaps. Sealing the ends will make the carton far more sturdy. Place the address label/packing slip on top in its clear envelope and seal it with transparent tape. Place the packing slip envelope over the carton closure so the recipient will have to remove the envelope to open the carton. Then reinforce the carton by banding in at least two directions with reinforcing tape. Run the tape over the clear packing slip envelope to secure it to the carton. Then if another heavy package is skidded across this one, the label will not be spindled off.

When assembling cartons with paper tape, cut the tape long enough to hang over the carton by two to three inches on each end. Since folding down the four flaps and taping is a three-hand job, try this: Place the tape on the far long flap, close the carton by pulling the far side toward you and seal the near flap. Then push in the ends and seal the tape to them.

Shipping rates. Obtain both the domestic and international rate booklets from the post office, and make up postal charts for both the invoicing and wrapping areas. Inflate the figures on the chart for the invoicing area to allow for the price of the shipping bag, invoice, tape, envelope, the first class postage of the invoice and self-insurance (because you will replace any books which are lost or damaged in transit). It is cheaper to replace a lost book than to pay for postal insurance.

— **Book rate.** Most books are shipped by the post office at the special fourth class *book rate*. To qualify, books must have at least eight pages, contain no advertising and be permanently bound. Book rate is much cheaper than regular parcel post, and there are no postal zones to compute. The same low rate applies to any destination with a Zip code from Guam to the Virgin Islands, including APO's and FPO's.

Postal Rates
Surface Book Rate & Library Rate

Lbs.	U.S.	Canada	Foreign	Libraries
1	1.24	1.37	1.56	1.12
2	1.74	1.85	2.76	1.53
3	2.24	4.00	3.72	1.94
4	2.74	4.64	4.68	2.35
5	3.24	5.28	5.64	2.76
6	3.74	5.92	6.60	3.17
7	4.24	6.56	7.56	3.58
8	4.55	7.20	8.52	3.78
9	4.86	7.84	9.48	3.98
10	5.17	8.48	10.44	4.18
11	5.48	9.12	11.40	4.38
12	5.79	12 lbs. and over: Use		4.58
13	6.10	"Direct Sack of Prints"		4.78
14	6.41			4.98
15	6.72	Canada:	Rest:	5.18
16	7.03	.64/lb.	.79/lb	5.38
17	7.34	(9.60 min.)	(11.85 min.)	5.58
18	7.65			5.78
19	7.96			5.98
20	8.27			6.18
21	8.58			+.20/lb.
22	8.89			
23	9.20			
24	9.51			
25	9.82			
26	10.13			
27	10.44			
28	10.75			
29	11.06			
30	11.37			
31	11.68			
32	11.99			
33	12.30			
34	12.61			
35	12.92			
36	13.23			
37	13.54			
38	13.85			
39	14.16			
40	14.47			
41	14.78			
42	15.09			
43	15.40			
44	15.71			
45	16.02			
46	16.33			
47	16.64			
48	16.95			
49	17.26			
50	17.57			
	+.31/lb.			

First Class

Oz.	Rate
1	.32
2	.55
3	.78
4	1.01
5	1.24
6	1.47
7	1.70
8	1.93
9	2.16
10	2.39
11	2.62
12	2.85
13	Use Priority Mail

Priority Mail

Lbs.	Rate
2	3.00
(No wgt. limit on "flat rate" envelopes)	
3	4.00
4	5.00
5	6.00
6+	Zoned

Packages over 40 lbs. are difficult to handle & are subject to damage. Last changed January 1995. Check for current rates.

Rate chart

If, however, you are shipping a heavy parcel in the first few zones, compare the Postal Service's book rate and their regular parcel post rate along with UPS. Other rates may be lower. See Postal Manual DMM 711.2 & 711.22. For a free comparison chart, send a self-addressed, stamped envelope to Upper Access, P.O. Box 457-P, Hinesville, VT 05461. For a complete explanation, send $10 to Legacy Publishing, Dave Dunn, P.O. Box 968-D, Clinton, MA 01510-0968.

— **Library Rate.** Those packages going to public libraries, school libraries, museums, schools, colleges, universities, and even bookstores associated with academic institutions enjoy the even lower *library rate.* If the addressee has a school address and they have ordered the book, you may use the lower rate.

— **United Parcel Service** (UPS) provides excellent service, including daily pickup, but their prices for single books are not competitive with the post office, and their shipments require more paperwork. Daily pickup service costs only $7.00 per week. Contact your local UPS office for prices and details in the form of a *UPS Customer Materials Kit.*

By way of comparison, a one-pound parcel shipped coast to coast in the U.S. in 1995 would cost the following:

Postal Service		United Parcel Service	
Book rate (surface):	$1.24	Surface:	$3.46
Library rate (surface):	$1.12	Second Day Air:	$6.25
Parcel post (surface):	$2.95	Next Day Air:	$16.00
Priority Mail (air):	$3.00		
Express Mail (air):	$15.00	**Federal Express**	
		Second Day:	$13.00
		Overnight:	$16.50

Both the Postal Service and UPS will accept parcels up to 70 lbs. Over 40 lbs., however, cartons become unmanageable and are subject to damage.

— **Priority Mail.** "Flat rate" envelopes can be shipped for just $3.00, regardless of the weight. And, since you save 30 cents because the envelope is free, your cost is really just $2.70. You can get up to four books into the envelope, just over four pounds. Eighty-four percent of Priority Mail is delivered anywhere in the U.S. within two days. Whenever your customer orders two or more books, use Priority Mail; you will dazzle the customer.

— **Overnight delivery companies.** Some customers will want your books right away, so it is wise to offer overnight delivery. Federal Express is the largest of the overnight companies, followed by Airborne, Purolator and Emery. United Parcel Service, the U.S. Postal Service and Federal Express are the three largest second-day delivery services. Most offer pickup service, but charges are lower if you drop off the package at their office or drop box. Check the *Yellow Pages* and call all the overnight services listed for supply kits of envelopes, cartons and bills of lading.

Overnight and fast deliveries to foreign countries vary greatly in price. Always call for prices before selecting a carrier; prices vary widely. DHL is the oldest and largest international carrier.

— **International parcels** of printed matter are limited by the Postal Service to five kilograms (11 lbs.). Larger shipments must be broken down into 5 kg increments or wrapped in a larger carton weighing over 15 lbs., inserted into a mail sack and shipped as a *direct sack of prints* in *M bags*. Visit your post office for some No. 2 sacks and PS 158 tags. Also take some time to read section 225.953 of the *International Mail Manual.*

To ship in *direct sacks of prints*, line a carton with a heavy plastic bag and insert the books. Make sure the books are tightly packed, that they fit the cartons perfectly. Seal and reinforce the carton in all directions to guard against splitting. Then double-box by inserting the package into another carton and seal with paper tape. Xerox copier-paper cartons are slightly larger than the cartons holding four stacks of 5.5" x 8.5" books and work very well. Affix the shipping label with the added words: *Postage paid—direct sack of prints.* Then band with reinforcing tape in all three directions. Weigh the package at this point and affix postage to a PS 158 tag. (Postage is paid on the contents, not the weight of the bag.) Turn the carton on end and slip a No. 2 mail sack down over it. Attach a shipping label to the PS 158 tag, and attach the tag to the cinch clip on the mail sack. The Postal Service will pull the package out of the sack at the border, keep the sack and let the package continue by itself.

PS 158 tag

```
           M  (●) BAG
From(de):
     _____
     _____
     _____

To:  _____
(Pour)  (Name of Addressee)

        (Street and Number)

        (City, Province, Postal Code)

        (Country of Destination)


        M-BAG

   DIRECT SACK TO ONE ADDRESSEE
```

PS Form 2976

```
        CUSTOMS—DOUANE C 1
        May be Officially Opened
        (Peut être ouvert d'office)

     SEE INSTRUCTIONS ON BACK
   Contents in detail;
   Désignation détaillée
   du contenu: _____
   _____
   _____
   _____
   _____

   Mark X here if a gift . . . . . . . (  )
   Il s'agit d'un cadeau
   or a sample of merchandise . . . . .(  )
   d'un échantillon de marchandises

   Value: _____ Weight: _____
   Valeur           Poids
   PS Form 2976, Feb. 1989
```

Customs duty. As long as the carton is plainly marked *Printed Matter—Books*, and it is obvious the contents are books, no customs forms are necessary, but it never hurts to attach the small, green tag, PS Form 2976. Few countries charge duty on books.

Posting. You can drop the weighed and stamped packages off at the loading dock at the rear of the post office. Just drop them into a wheeled bin; do not wait in line at the counter. Most postal employees do not know much about classes and rates (just quiz one about library rate or direct sacks), so they aren't much help after a long wait in line.

Mail is usually sent from each post office to a centralized facility before being shipped out of town. If you drop the packages at this central mail-handling facility, they will move out faster and will be subjected to less handling. For these postal addresses, consult your telephone directory under *U.S. Government*.

> Some years ago, the author dropped off a load of packaged books at the branch post office where he has his postal box. Six days later he was dropping off another load at the central mail-handling facility and discovered the previous shipment. It had taken the books six days to travel ten miles.

If you like the large 1/4" x 3" rubber bands used by the Postal Service, you can get a box free. Just stop by the bulk mail office and tell them you are planning a large mailing. While there, pick up some mail trays, mail bins and some No. 2 mail bags. The trays are useful when processing and carrying large direct mailings of envelopes. The bins can be used to carry many small parcels to the post office, and the sacks will be used for direct sack shipments. Do not be bashful about asking for bins, sacks and trays. The Postal Service wants to lend them to you, as they make it easier for them to handle the mail.

Postage meters. Metered mail travels faster and is handled less, while the possible loss of stamps due to theft is eliminated. Stamped parcels are taken out of the bins at the post office, canceled and thrown back in. A heavy carton may come down on some of your single-book packets.

Whereas the postal clerks may compare stamps with weight, they rarely return metered mail for more postage. Once your firm has grown and you are afraid some employees might be walking off with stamps, you might consider a meter. You can never stop employees from running a few personal letters through the machine, but this is better than pinching a couple of one-dollar stamps every day. A meter imprint makes your publishing company appear more established, by eliminating that postage-stamped, *loving hands at home* look. The meter also allows you to print an advertising message on the outgoing mail.

On the other hand, postage meters cost time and money. It takes time to have the meter reloaded at the post office, there is no discount on postage, and the machine must be rented from the meter company.

Most postage meters come in two parts: the meter and the base unit. The base unit may be purchased outright, but the meter (the part holding the postage) may only be rented. Shop for a base unit that handles both envelopes and tapes for packages. Look for bases on the used market: at used business machine stores, swap meets and in the classified ads in local newspapers. Once you have purchased the base, contact the meter dealer for a matching meter. If you contract for your meter first, you will limit yourself in your choice of base units.

Pitney Bowes used to have a lock on the market, but now there are some other companies competing with them. Meters usually rent by the month on a yearly contract. Check prices for each model and make; they vary widely.

First class mail can be handled with a stamper machine filled with rolled stamps. Use the 100-stamp rolls; the rolls of 500 are too heavy to feed well. Stamper machines cost less than $25 at most office-supply stores.

Meter supplies. Buy regular, gummed paper meter tape; the pressure-sensitive labels are too expensive. Some rolls of meter tape have the gum on the outside, and some have it on the inside. Get the right one. Tape from sources other than the meter company is often less expensive but is sometimes a bit too narrow. Shop around. Do not use just any ink in the meter. The red ink supplied by the meter companies is fluorescent and is recognized by postal machinery to turn the envelopes face up. Do not use substitute ink.

Processing returns is not the best part of the book business. Any time you are feeling depressed over a return, remember that some large New York publishers get a lot of their books back. The industry considers 20%, or a little more, to be normal. In 1994, *Publishers Weekly* reported that publishers were experiencing 25% and more in returns. Smaller publishers rarely suffer such a high return rate.

When a book comes back, make out a receiving slip. This does not have to be a fancy form; a note on a scratch pad or your notation on the packing slip will do, but you will need some written record. Note the date received, the sender and the condition of the book. Determine whether any damage was caused in mailing, or before shipping, by the condition of the package.

Bookstore shipments almost always arrive damaged, because they just will not pack the books correctly. Bookstores will dump the books in a carton without a protective plastic bag or cushioning material, so they rattle around and become scuffed and bent, or they will place three books in an oversize Jiffy bag to rub against each other as they journey across the country.

On receipt, the good books should be returned to the storage area and the bad ones set aside in their box, pending settling up with the customer. Return the damaged books to the dealer with an invoice for the shipping and an explanation regarding the condition. Be sure to mark the books so they will be easy to spot if returned to you again. One publisher places a small black dot with a fine-tip felt marker on the bottom edge of the book near the spine.

One well-known eastern book wholesaler frequently orders books, and returns them from different departments on the same day.

The object is to get your books into the stores. If the store has tried your book on the shelf and it hasn't sold, they should not be penalized. If, on the other hand, the book is not shelf-worn but was obviously damaged in return transit due to poor packaging, the store or wholesaler should "eat" the book.

Books returned by the customer because they were received damaged should be replaced at once. This is a cost of doing business.

Damaged books may be offered to acquaintances as *selected seconds* and donated to institutions. Some publishers offer them to the walk-in traffic at a 50% discount with the explanation that *all books look like this after a week.*

When an individual retail order is returned by the post office marked *undeliverable,* check the original order to verify the address. If the address is wrong, slip the whole book *and* bag into another, larger bag so the addressee will see what happened and why the shipment took so long. If the address is correct, date the package and put the order and book aside and wait for his or her anxious letter or call.

Some publishers have different order addresses and shipping addresses. It is expensive and disruptive when cartons of books are delivered to the editorial offices. To avoid this problem, require that returns be made on your shipping labels. Add this requirement to your *Returns Policy.*

Alternatives. There are many ways to fulfill your orders besides filling them yourself. The alternatives are listed below.

Remember, however, that you will still need a small shipping facility for review copies and other mailings. Keeping your fulfillment in-house will provide better inventory control, faster shipping of orders, fewer shipping errors, fewer damaged books and lower fulfillment costs.

— **Joint representation** is where a large publisher accepts a smaller one with like titles. Commonly, the big firm takes over all the marketing, distribution and billing functions as well. The cost can be high: 20% or more of the net sale. Like the commission sales reps, the firm gets credit for all the sales no matter who generates them. Not only does the arrangement cost more than doing it yourself, you never learn the ropes. You become more dependent than ever. Unless you simply do not have the time or the will to do your own marketing and fulfillment, joint representation should not be considered until you have operated long enough to make an educated decision.

— **Fulfillment warehouses.** If you are unable to spend the time picking, packing and posting, lack the necessary space, or would rather concentrate on writing and marketing, there are commercial fulfillment firms which will do the job. Typically, they may charge per order for packaging, plus postage and packing materials. Additionally, they may charge per month per skid of books for storage. Figure roughly one cent per book per month for warehousing. You may send your invoices to the these fulfillment warehouses, or they will cut the invoices for you.

Fulfillment firms advertise in the classifieds in *Publishers Weekly,* and a large listing can be found in *Literary Market Place* under *Shipping Services;* consult your library. For more information on fulfillment, see the Special Report *Book Fulfillment.* See the Appendix.

Remember that fulfillment houses only store and ship, they do not *sell.* They will not get your books into bookstores or sell subsidiary rights. Moving books from your garage to someone's warehouse does not mean your books have been turned into cash.

You have all the ingredients for being a successful publisher. This book is your recipe.

Chapter Eleven

Technology and Publishing

Electronic Books, On-Line Services, Fax-On-Demand and Computers

D o not think of yourself as a book author or a book publisher. Think of yourself as an information provider. You are publishing your information in a book to achieve wide distribution, to establish a new profit center and because a book will bring you more credibility than any other format. Once the book is out, it is time to recycle your information into other formats for other customers.

People need more information in order to make critical decisions, and they want their information fast. You have the information some of them need, and you can get it to them faster electronically.

We are not just in the information age, we are in the electronic information age or, better yet, the communication age. Fortunately, publishers deal in products that can be communicated. The knowledge world is going from a paper culture to an electronic culture. It is only a question of how we want to package our information.

The costs of electronic delivery of information are decreasing, and the costs of storage and physical delivery are increasing. That is why the fax has become a common machine. We have learned it does not pay to give someone a letter and 32 cents to hand-carry the message across the country. Fax will do it faster and cheaper.

The electronic book. We are moving out of (printed) books. We are not talking about coffee table books—books as an art form. Fiction and poetry will be available in printed books for a long time. But *information* creation, storage, sale, retrieval and manipulation are going electronic.

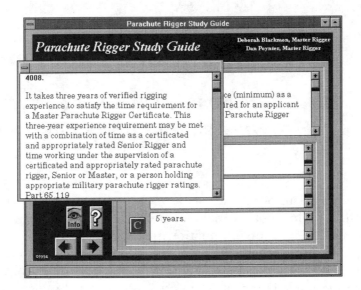

The electronic book

The concept is not that people will sit in front of their computers to read a book. The electronic book does not just

Some bound books will soon be as dead as the trees they are printed on.

replace the printed book; for some kinds of books it is better. No one would buy it if it did the same thing they already have in books. With the electronic book, you can read the text, listen to sound, watch animation, see video, and jump to other areas for more information. The electronic book is more useful, smaller, faster and cheaper to produce.

Electronic books will eliminate printing, binding, understocks, overstocks, freight, returns, shrinkage, warehouse space, damaged books, used books, the resale of review and "comp" copies, violation of copyright and deforestation.

The electronic book will save a lot of time, space and money. . . and trees.

The electronic version of your book will sell for less because you will have to invest less. Now your $20 book can sell for $10 and you will make more money. Your less-expensive book will reach more people.

"Authoring" software is used to format your information for the electronic book, to prepare it for CD-ROM. Authoring software is like *Pagemaker, Corel-Ventura* or *QuarkXpress* page layout programs. The difference is they are CD-book layout programs. Tomorrow, our books will move.

— **On floppy disk.** If your book is short enough, it may be published on computer disk. Then it can be read by anyone, not just those with CD-ROM drives. Many people will use a notebook computer to read your book.

One 3.5" high-density disk will hold 1.44 MB of material. You could publish straight text, but it is not too interesting to see. If you pour your material into an authoring program, some of the authoring software will have to be included on the disk to access your "book."

The electronic book of the future will be the size of a paperback book and will also contain a computer, a cellular

---

If book publishers can't see the writing on the wall, it is because the writing isn't on the wall. The writing is on a computer screen.

telephone and maybe even a global positioning system with a map. At last, you will know where you are.

— **On CD-ROM.** One CD holds 680 MB of material. Plenty of space for several books, line drawings, sound and even some video. It is estimated that in 1994, 90% of the computers sold had CD-ROM drives. See Fax-On-Demand Document 615, priced at $9.95.

Blockbuster Video has been renting CD-ROM disc titles since November 1993. Why not rent a couple and try them out?

Fax-On-Demand permits you to serve your customers while you sleep. What happens when a potential customer hears about one of your books and wants more information? They must wait to call between 9 and 5 in your time zone. You take the call, write down their name and request, type an envelope, find the appropriate brochures, stuff the envelope, apply (often) 78 cents postage and mail it. They don't receive your mailing for two to four days.

What if they could call your office in the middle of the night and get the information they want sent instantly and automatically to their fax machine?

A quick response to customer requests for information can mean the difference between making a sale and losing it, between building customer trust and risking it, or between superior customer service and business as usual. Now you can deliver accurate, timely documents into the hands of your customers when they need them. You can deliver product fliers, price lists and news releases at electronic speeds.

With Fax-On-Demand, you save on printing, envelopes, postage, storage, waste and staff time.

— **How Fax-On-Demand works.** You make up a menu, or table of contents, of all the brochures, free reports, short lists, news releases and other documents you are mailing free to customers now. Assign a number to each one.

> *The information highway is being built and we know: We can be part of the steamroller or part of the road.*

When a customer calls your FOD telephone number, they are prompted by your voice in digitally recorded messages. If they know the number of a document, they can punch in the number on their keypad. If they do not, they can request your complete menu. Once they punch in the numbers of the documents they want, they are asked to press the Start button. Then the requested documents come out of their machine and they may hang up the handset.

Your FOD telephone number and menu can be noted in your (small) ads, brochures, letterhead, answering machine recording, direct mail solicitations and other promotion. Existing and potential customers may call at any time for a current list of free documents.

For a demonstration of FOD, pick up the handset on your fax machine and call Para Publishing's FOD number: (805) 968-8947. Request Document 109 for a list of free documents on book marketing, promoting and distributing. For a complete two-page report on FOD for book publishers, request Document 874.

Fax-On-Demand saves you time and money. Now you can truly serve your customers while you sleep.

Computer. The computer has made self-publishing a more attractive, affordable and competitive option in today's market. This one invention is prompting an explosion in the number of authors deciding to accept the risks and rewards of publishing their own work.

All you need for book publishing are a good computer (486 or higher), a word processing program such as *Word For Windows* or *WordPerfect*, a page layout program such as *Page-Maker*, *Corel-Ventura* or *QuarkXpress* and a laser printer with 600 dpi or better output. Get a modem so you can do research and communicate on-line. You will also need a CD-ROM drive.

In-house laser typesetting saves money. But even more important, it provides the publisher with timeliness and control.

900 numbers are another way to sell your information electronically—and let the telephone company collect your payments. With "audio-text," "telemedia," or 900-number service, you might let callers listen to the author providing problem-solving tips, or you might give book updates. Take note of the 900 services you come across, and think of services you might offer.

There are a number of service bureaus that specialize in audio-text services. They know how to set it up, are familiar with the various service providers and have the specialized equipment. See the *Yellow Pages* under "Telephone."

900 Know-How is a great book on the subject, by Robert Mastin for $19.95. Order from Aegis Publishing Group, 796 Aquidneck Avenue, Newport, RI 02840, Tel: (401) 849-4200.

The New 900 Industry and Your Financial Freedom is a stimulating audiotape by Paul Hickey which may still be available (free) by calling (801) 377-0600 or (800) 782-0110.

Audiotape. You may record your speeches and put them on single cassettes for sale, or you may record your whole book and put it on several cassettes in an album. Contact Judy Byers at Audio/Video Cassette Producers, Tel: (303) 751-1198; Fax: (303) 751-5655. She can handle the recording, packaging and duplication.

Videotape. You may videotape your presentations, turn your book into a videotape or take short clips and add them to your electronic book. Again, contact Judy Byers.

On-Line services may be used to disseminate information (books) and they may be used to promote your books.

Electronic on-line books require no paper, no binding, no inventory and no traditional channels of distribution. There is no physical movement of heavy inventory.

Some on-line services can provide access to the Internet, the international connection of computer networks.

Contact the following on-line service providers for details and prices:

America Online (AOL), Tel: (800) 827-6364

CompuServe, Tel: (800) 848-8199

Prodigy, Tel: (800) 776-3449

The On-Line Bookstore and the Internet Bookstore will allow people to browse through books from their computers, or they can download the entire book. These are bookstores without shelves, selling books without paper. Selling your book on-line is an important subsidiary right.

For the very latest on all of the electronic media, as they relate to information publishing, call Para Publishing's Fax-On-Demand system from the handset of your fax machine: (805) 968-8947. Request Documents 109 and 601, which are menus of available documents.

The Internet and the World Wide Web offer publishers unlimited opportunities to do research for books, conduct business transactions, promote books and for selling books. If you like the library, you will love the Internet; it provides access to an incredible amount of information and makes it easy to find. You can do your banking and trace UPS and Fed Ex packages. Forget postage; you can blast information on your book to selected interested parties with the price of a local telephone call. And, it is inexpensive to set up a web site listing all your books and services. Customers can order your books with a credit card via e-mail. This is making money while you sleep.

You can get access to the Internet and the Web through CompuServe, America Online, Prodigy, Netcom, the Microsoft Network and many other services. For the latest details, get our Fax-On-Demand Document 627, priced at $9.95. Just call (805) 968-8947 from your fax machine and follow the voice prompts. An invoice will be sent for the 12-page report.

Check out the Para Publishing web site at http://www.parapublishing.com/books/para/890. It will lead you to more book publishing sites.

The Self-Publishing Manual (this book plus updates) is available on the web. Now you can read every page on the screen and even print out the pages. Try this system and think how it might work for your books. Since every page is a separate file, it is not likely anyone will print out more than a few pages.

Other sites with information on Para Publishing and Dan Poynter:

BookZone: http://ttx.com/poynter

BookPort: http://www.bookfair.com/publishers/para

Speakers On Line: http://speakers.com/spkr1108.html

> *Write and publish on a subject you love. Your profit center should also be your passion center.*

Chapter Twelve

Coping with Being Published

or What Do I Do Now?

Once you become a published author, your life will change. Being in the limelight may not always be as much fun as you used to dream about. This chapter discusses some of the interesting problems you will encounter and will provide some suggestions on how to deal with them.

Your status will change from that private person, the "writer," to a public person, the "expert." Your friends will treat you differently once you are published. Some will be very happy for you, and some will be jealous—jealous because they did not write the book. People new in your field will treat you like an idol, while those who have been around for years may feel threatened and be rather unkind.

Many new authors do not foresee their new popularity, their celebrity status. There is little you can do about your new treatment except to be prepared for it. Be nice, and in a few years your reputation will be so solid that no one will take swipes at you any more.

> Gary Glenn spent 27 years working as a fire investigator. When he and his wife Peggy wrote *Don't Get Burned! A Family Fire-Safety Guide*, life at work changed. The new fire fighters put him on a pedestal—they followed him around the firehouse, hoping he might drop a few pearls of wisdom—while some of his contemporaries in the very status-conscious fire fighting community were very cool toward him. This was not the only change. Peggy was known as a successful author-publisher, and Gary was not pleased at being referred to as "Mr. Peggy Glenn" at publishing functions. Now they are colleagues. The book project brought Gary and Peggy closer together, while Gary's in-laws suddenly saw him in a new light.

> Bob Johnson wrote a book on the triathlon. While some of the other ironman athletes were jealous and shunned him, he couldn't get rid of the groupies.

Autographing books is something you will be asked to do both in person and by mail. It is surprising how many prolific authors have never given much thought to how they might autograph a book. Confronted with an admiring fan, they are suddenly at a loss for words. Most authors simply sign: "To Kathy with best wishes," add their signature and sometimes the date. At times you want to be more personal, such as thanking a contributor for his or her help and support on the book. If there is something special about the buyer, include it in your autograph. Often, there is a question of time. On a mail order book, you can dream up something special, while at a well-attended autograph party it is difficult to think of a few well-chosen words while trying to give witty answers. And, by the way, especially when rushed, make sure you spell your buyer's name correctly. In all the hustle, it is easy to draw a blank and misspell the simplest name or word, ruining a book.

To autograph your book to a stranger is easy, to autograph for a friend is difficult. — Rex Alan Smith

Some authors autograph a number of books before an event so all they have to do is add the name of the individual.

Articles. Once your book is published and you become better known, editors will contact you for material. Usually they will ask you to write an article on your subject—something you probably will not have time to do. Additionally, once your book is in print, you will find new, pertinent information and will devise new, unique ways of explaining your program and methods. Your solution to these two problems is the "interview article."

As you think of a point you want to make, draft it in the form of a question and answer. Let these questions and answers build until you have several pages of them entered into your computer. Then when an editor calls, just say you are too busy to generate a specific piece, but that you have this Q&A article with all the very latest information. Say they may select the Q&A's most likely to be of interest to their readers, and to call if they need any more. Editors love this system and rarely can think of any more questions. Some editors run the Q&A's as is, while some reporters use them to generate an original article. What is important is that you have supplied an interview with written, well-thought-out answers. This system gets editors off your back, saves you a lot of time, fulfills your obligation to the media and generates a lot of publicity for your book.

Spin-off is an important concept. Repackaging the same information for various markets will bring in more money, while promoting the original book. Magazine articles may be extracted from the book, book chapters may be used as a basis for conference workshops, a series of magazine articles may be combined into a book, or the book may be rewritten and directed toward a new audience. With a computer, it is easy to pull out part of the book and add an introduction and a conclusion.

Always end your article with an "Editor's note," mentioning that the article was extracted from your book, and then give ordering information. Do not simply ask the editor to do this for you; place the words at the end of the article yourself.

Consulting. Many authors consult on their area of expertise. This author consults as a technical expert in parachute and skydiving legal cases. If you decide to sell your time, set your fee schedule early, so you will be ready with figures when you receive a call. Be advised that most beginning consultants price themselves too low. For guidance on legal consulting, see *The Expert Witness Handbook* by Dan Poynter. See the Appendix.

Speaking. As a published author, you will be asked to address all sorts of groups. Make sure the gathering will be large enough to make the trip worth your while. Even if they guarantee a large group where you may sell a number of books, you should require an honorarium.

Make sure your book can be sold in the back of the room. Do not try to handle the money yourself; you will be too busy handling questions. Try to get the organization sponsoring the event to sell the books, and give them a 20% commission on each one they sell. That way, you will gain their support and an implied endorsement for your books. If they do not wish to sell the books, draft an assistant to sell them for you. Compensate this helper with a free book.

Place photographic blowups of your books at the front of the room when you speak. They will act as *continuous communicators* because your audience will look at them all through the speech.

Provide handouts. The top sheet should have an outline of the speech and the back may contain a list of important contact addresses, resources and a listing of your other products. The outline will help the audience follow your presentation and will suppress questions during your speech. Staple this cover sheet to any supplementary materials and your brochures. This system assures that everyone will keep your promotional materials. For more on speaking, see Chapter Seven.

Promotion. Once your book is out, you will have to switch gears and put on your promotion hat. Your creativity will be redirected to brochures, sales letters and advertising copy. When sales slow down, you will have time to write another book. Remember that writing the book is just the tip of the publishing iceberg. The real work begins after you send the boards off to the printer.

Your will. Your book is a valuable asset. Draw up a will or have your current will amended. You will die, but you want your work to live on. Name an executor who understands publishing so that your books and papers will continue. The cost of a will is very little compared to the expenses of taxes and litigation, not to mention the time and the heartache a will could save your family and friends.

Stay in your field. It is nice to have your eggs in more than one basket, but you may spread your talents too thin. You are an expert in one field—that one in which you are a *participant*. You can stay in that field and become a super expert, or you can branch out into another field and run the risk of being unable to keep up with both of them adequately. Spin off your message into speeches, articles and more books. Do more of what you do best.

Publish more than one book. Distributors will be more interested in your publishing company if you have a line of books. Mailing and brochure printing will be more cost-effective if you can spread the costs over several titles—there is an economy of scale. With more books, you can pursue repeat business. It is much easier to sell to an existing customer than to find a new one. Spin off your information into several products.

Maintain consistent and appropriate packaging. If all your books look alike, you will have a recognizable product line. They will look as though they are members of the same family. Standardize your measurements to facilitate shipping. You want to stock as few shipping cartons and bags as possible.

Ship by the carton. It takes the same amount of time to process an order for a carton of books as it does for one book. Pursue wholesale sales, rather than retail, and you will save valuable time. Pursue nontraditional sales rather than bookstores, and you will ship in larger quantities, get paid sooner and will not receive returns.

Place your books in local stores. Then, when fans call up asking where they can purchase your book, you can send them to the store. This approach avoids the awkward situation where fans try to talk you into a free book, and it limits their late-hour visits. A one-hour visit for a one-book sale is not very cost-efficient. The store is a more objective sales rep. You don't have to try to talk the customer out of his or her money, while they don't have to decide against the purchase with you standing there.

Do not spend money on advertising until you have exhausted all the free publicity that is available to you. Use book reviews, news releases and, if appropriate to your book, a limited amount of highly targeted direct mail advertising.

Researching for revisions can bring a few surprises. Other books are likely to come out on the same subject after yours has been published. In reading them, you will find many interesting, though familiar, ideas. Many will be copied from your own work. Remember when you are writing that you are *committing history*—you will be quoted, or at least copied.

Your second book. Your big day arrives when someone calls to order a book and you get to ask, "Which one?"

Afterword

We *learn by doing,* and your first book will be your hardest. *We learn from our mistakes,* and hopefully, through the use of this book, your mistakes will be small ones. Learn the entire business by doing everything yourself before you begin to "farm out" some of the work. Doing it all yourself will provide you with a better understanding of publishing. I hope it introduces and guides you to a richer, more rewarding life.

The first step, the next one, is up to you. I hope you will take it. As you write, publish and market, refer to this manual. As you learn the business, make notes in it. Tell me your experiences. Let me know where this book may be improved. When you do get that first book into print, please send me a copy—autographed, of course.

Good luck,

Dan Poynter

Appendix

Your Book's Calendar

One of the biggest pitfalls in small publishing is the lack of sufficient planning, especially the first time around. You don't want to tie up funds by purchasing materials too soon, and you don't want to miss some important publicity because you missed a filing date.

This checklist will help to keep you on track. Follow this schedule for your first book. On your second, you will want to move some items up, while skipping some others.

Now

1. Send for five copyright forms. See Chapter Five.
2. Subscribe to *Writer's Digest* and *Publishers Weekly* (or read them at your library). See the Appendix.
3. Join the Publishers Marketing Association. See the Appendix.
4. Review the Appendix. Send for the books, magazines, brochures and catalogs which interest you. Join those associations which can help you.
5. Choose a company name. File a fictitious business name statement, if required.
6. Order some office supplies, such as letterhead stationery and envelopes. See Chapter Three and the Appendix.
7. Write to Bowker for ABI information and forms. See Chapter Five.
8. Apply for a post office box. See Chapter Three.
9. Read this book completely and highlight important areas.

10. Visit the library and study *Literary Market Place*. Order a copy now or wait until you are finished with your manuscript.

11. Contact the Small Business Administration for its publications. Write to the SBA, Washington, DC 20416, and request a *Directory of Business Development Publications*.

12. Apply for any local business licenses. Check with the Chamber of Commerce for advice.

13. Write to Para Publishing for a copy of *Publishing Forms, Is There a Book Inside You?, Building a Profitable Business,* by Chickadel and Straughn and *The Business Planning Guide*, by David H. Bangs. See the Appendix.

14. Call Para Publishing's Fax-On-Demand system from the handset of your fax machine, (805) 968-8947. Request Documents 109 and 601.

15. Draft your back-cover copy. See Chapter Two. Decide on your audience and what you promise to give them.

While writing your book

1. Review Chapter Two.

2. Write the CIP Office of the Library of Congress for *Information for Participating Publishers* and some Publisher Response forms.

3. Send to Bowker for ISBN/SAN information. See Chapter Five.

4. Send to Para Publishing for *Write Right!*, by Jan Venolia, and *A Business Guide to Copyright Law*, by Woody Young.

When your manuscript is nearly complete

1. Send *Requests For Quotations* to 40+ printers. See Chapter Four.
2. Purchase set of ISBNs from Bowker. See Chapter Five.
3. Design the book covers. Hire a cover designer.
4. Fill out the ABI form. See Chapter Five.
5. Write the Library of Congress for your LCCC number. See Chapter Five.
6. Send a photocopy of your ABI form to Baker & Taylor Co., Academic Library Services Selection Dept., P. O. Box 6920, Bridgewater, NJ 08807.
7. Send to Bowker for your own copy of *Literary Market Place*.
8. Research your title to make sure it is not being used.
9. Get any needed permissions.
10. Send manuscript out for peer review and copy editing.
11. Contact Para Publishing for *Book Production, Publishing Short-Run Books,* and *The Complete Guide to Paste-up,* by Walter B. Graham.
12. Select a distributor. See Special Report *Book Marketing* for a discussion of distributors and lists of what categories of books they want.

When the manuscript is ready to be delivered to the typesetter (or when you are about to typeset it)

1. Set the publication date. It will be at least four months in the future. See Chapter Seven.
2. Assign the ISBN(s). See Chapter Five.
3. Prepare a news release. See Chapter Seven.
4. Contact book clubs. See Chapter Eight.
5. Apply for a resale permit. See Chapter Three.

6. Contact Para Publishing for a copy of *Pocket Pal,* by International Paper.

7. Prepare a CIP data block. Contact Quality Books. See Chapter Five.

While the book is being typeset

1. Set up storage and shipping areas. See Chapter Ten. Send for Para Publishing's Special Report *Book Fulfillment, Order Entry, Picking, Packing and Shipping.*

2. If you are subcontracting the typesetting, maintain a good proofreading schedule. Don't hold up your typesetter.

3. Write *Contemporary Authors* for information. See Chapter Five.

4. Prepare mailing lists. See Chapter Nine.

5. Order shipping supplies and the rest of your office supplies. See Chapter Ten and the Appendix.

6. Send galleys to certain review magazines. See "Pre-publication Reviews" in Chapter Seven.

7. Prepare ads for specialty magazines. See Chapter Nine.

8. Send a book announcement to all wholesalers.

9. Prepare brochure. See Chapter Nine.

10. Write to the *International Directory of Little Magazines and Small Presses* for an application form. See Chapter Five.

11. Prepare your pre-publication offer. See Chapter Eight.

12. Print book review slips and order rubber stamps. See Chapter Seven.

13. Pursue subsidiary rights. See Chapter Eight.

14. Order reply postcards. See Chapter Seven.

15. Write to *Book Publishers of the United States and Canada* for an application form. See Chapter Five.

16. Write to *Publisher's International Directory* for an application form. See Chapter Five.

17. Contact Para Publishing for Special Reports titled *Book Marketing, A New Approach, Book Reviews, News Releases and Book Publicity* and *Direct Mail for Publishers, Export/Foreign Rights.*

18. Develop your marketing plan using the *Book Marketing* Special Report.

19. Order bar code.

20. Select a book printer. See the Special Report *Buying Book Printing.*

While the books are being printed

1. Proof the bluelines carefully.

2. Prepare review-copy materials. Stuff and label the bags, then put aside until books arrive.

3. Mail your pre-publication offer to individuals.

When the books arrive (3+ months prior to the official publication date)

1. Check the quality of the books. Make a count for your inventory.

2. Fill orders.

3. Make promotional mailing. See "Copyrights, listings and early reviews" in Chapter Seven.

4. Photograph book and order prints.

5. Print brochure. See Chapter Nine.

6. Pursue dealer sales. You want the books to be in the stores when all the promotion hits on the publication date.

7. Draft magazine articles. See Chapter Seven.

8. File copyright form. See Chapter Five.

9. Pursue book reviews. See "Book reviews" in Chapter Seven.

10. Pursue promotional possibilities per Chapter Eight.
11. Send copy of book to CIP Office. See Chapter Seven.
12. Contact Para Publishing for the Special Report *Brochures for Book Publishers*.
13. Visit bookstores in your area.

Publication date

Ninety percent of your initial promotional effort will be done before your official publication date. Your consumer advertising/promotion should be concentrated in the first few weeks after the publication date.

1. Pursue consumer-oriented promotion, such as autograph parties, talk shows, author tours, etc. See Chapter Seven.
2. Outline your continuing promotional program.

Ongoing promotion

Never give up. You have given birth to your book; now you have an obligation to raise it. Review what has worked and do more of it. Review what has not worked and cut your losses.

1. Contact Para Publishing for the promotion and marketing books that will be most useful to you. If radio and TV are working for you, get *Publicity for Books and Authors,* by Peggy Glenn, *On The Air,* by Al Parinello, and *Book Publicity for Authors and Publishers*, by Larry Rochester. If direct mail brings you a good return, get *Successful Direct Marketing Methods,* by Bob Stone.
2. Work on nontraditional or special sales.
3. Implement your continuing review program.
4. Consider radio and TV interviews.

5. Consider more direct mail solicitations.

6. Look for spin-off ideas. Repackage your information: audiotapes, electronic books, etc. Consider consulting in your area of expertise.

7. Make up a review/testimonial sheet. Paste up good reviews and reproduce them.

Resources
Books/Bibliography

Most of these reference books may be found in your local library. In addition, there are many good books on writing, publishing, printing, marketing, distribution and other aspects of book publishing. The best are listed here. As noted, some are available from Para Publishing. Use the order blank. For the rest, you should check your library, ask the Reference Librarian and visit a nearby bookstore. Then write to the publishers for latest price and delivery information.

Be advised the R.R. Bowker Co. is a large firm with numerous functions, products and services. While they have several offices, most of them are at the same New York and New Jersey addresses. Each office should be treated separately.

Here are several lists of contacts. Remember that over 20% of our population moves every year. If you find an address that is no longer valid, see *Literary Market Place* or call Directory Assistance for the new telephone number.

Documents from Para Publishing by Fax-On-Demand. The following reports and lists are **free** and are available to you instantly via your fax machine. Just go to your fax, lift the handset, call **(805) 968-8947** and follow the voice prompts to order the documents you want. Your fax machine will retrieve the documents from our system and print them out for you instantly; there is no waiting. This new system works 24 hours a day, seven days a week, even when our office is closed.

☐ 109: Menu of free documents of interest to book publishers. 4 pages.

☐ 601: Menu of *Instant Reports* of interest to publishers which are available for a small charge. 1 page.

☐ 112: *Poynter's Secret List of Book Promotion Contacts.* Names and numbers for ABI, LC, CIP, ISBN and more; list of pre-publication reviewers; list of directories you should be listed in and over 50 places to send your book for review. 8 pages.

☐ 113: List of attorneys who specialize in book publishing. Names and numbers. 1 page.

☐ 114: *Inside Book Writing. An Instant Report* of little-known and rarely understood secrets every author should know. 6 pages.

☐ 115: *Inside Book Publishing. An Instant Report* of little-known and rarely understood secrets every publisher should know. 8 pages.

☐ 120: *Bar Coding Books.* An *Instant Report* on what the bar code is all about, where to put it, how to get it, and a list of suppliers. 2 pages.

☐ 130: Para Publishing book brochure *Book Publishing Resources.* A brochure describing all of the book publishing, products and services offered by Para Publishing with ordering information. 4 pages.

☐ 131: Audio Tapes on Book Writing and Publishing. A brochure describing single- and multiple-cassette tapes on book creation and promotion with ordering information. 1 page.

☐ 132: Special Reports on Book Publishing. A brochure describing 19 detailed reports on book marketing/promoting and distributing with ordering information. 4 pages.

☐ 133: The Publisher's Bookshelf. A brochure describing 35 books for publishers on marketing, print promotion, radio/TV interviews, contracts, paste-up, product development, printing and more. With ordering information. 4 pages.

☐ 137: Consulting with Dan Poynter. You may speak with Dan Poynter one-on-one over the telephone or in person at your office or his. Descriptive brochure with rates. 2 pages.

☐ 138: Dealer Bulletin. Discounts offered to dealers for quantity purchases of books and disks on book publishing. 1 page.

☐ 139: Note to renters of mailing lists. 1 page.

☐ 140: *Resources on Writing and Publishing Specific Types of Books.* An *Instant Report* listing books, magazines, newsletters, pamphlets and associations dealing with specific areas of book writing and publishing. For example, there are three books on how to write, produce and market cookbooks, four on travel, eight on life stories, etc. 8 pages.

☐ 142: Mailing lists for promoting books. A brochure describing more than 80 lists of reviewers who want to write about your books. 2 pages.

☐ 250: A list of suppliers of services to the publishing industry with addresses and numbers. 1 page.

☐ 136: Dan Poynter speaking on book publishing. Descriptions of the presentations he makes on book publishing: marketing, promoting and distributing. 3 pages.

☐ 164: Calendar of Dan Poynter's presentations on book writing and publishing. 1 page.

☐ 167: Publishing workshops in Santa Barbara. A two-day marketing/promoting/distributing seminar at Dan Poynter's home/office. Description, rates and an application. 7 pages.

☐ 874: Fax-On-Demand article for publishers. 2 pages.

Brochures on books of interest to publishers are available from the following.

Publisher's Bookshelf
P. O. Box 8206-890
Santa Barbara, CA 93118-8206
Tel: (800) PARAPUB;
Fax-On-Demand:
  (805) 968-8947,
  Documents 109 and 133

R.R. Bowker Catalog
249 West 17th Street
New York, NY 10011

Direct Marketing Association
6 East 43rd Street
New York, NY 10017

Dustbooks
P.O. Box 100-P
Paradise, CA 95967

Gale Research Co.
Penobscot Building
Detroit, MI 48226

Towers Book Store
P.O. Box 2038-P
Vancouver, WA 98661

Writer's Digest Books
1507 Dana Avenue
Cincinnati, OH 45207

The Writer, Inc.
120 Boylston Street
Boston, MA 02116

J. Whitaker & Sons, Ltd.
12 Dyott Street
London WC1A 1DF
Great Britain

Reference books and directories may be used and previewed at the reference desk in your public library. Write to the publishers for ordering details.

— From R.R. Bowker, 121 Chanlon Road, New Providence, NJ 07974, Tel: (800) 521-8110; Fax: (908) 665-6688.

Literary Market Place. Very important. Lists agents, artists, associations, book clubs, reviewers, exporters, magazines, newspapers, news services, radio and TV, and many other services. Annual.

International Literary Market Place. Lists sources outside the U.S. and Canada.

Publishers' Trade List Annual. A compilation of 1,500 publishers' catalogs.

Publishers, Distributors & Wholesalers of the United States. A directory.

Ulrich's International Periodicals Directory. Lists 120,000 newsletters and magazines.

Irregular Serials and Annuals.

Translation and Translators: An International Directory and Guide.

American Book Trade Directory. Lists 29,000 booksellers, wholesalers, etc.

American Library Directory. Lists 35,000 U.S. and Canadian libraries.

International Publishers Imprints, Agents and Distributors Directory.

Books in Print. Lists all books currently available by subject, title and author. Annual.

Forthcoming Books. Books that will appear in the next edition of *Books in Print.*

— From K.G. Saur Publishing, Inc., 121 Chanlon Road, New Providence, NJ 07974, Tel: (800) 521-8110; Fax: (908) 771-7792.

American Publishers Directory
International Books in Print
International Directory of Book-sellers
World Guide to Libraries
Publishers International Directory

— **From B. Klein Publications,** P.O. Box 8503, Coral Springs, FL 33075, Tel: (305) 752-1708; Fax: (305) 752-2547.

Guide to American Directories. 8,000 directories.

Mail Order Business Directory. Over 10,000 mail order and catalog houses.

Directory of Mailing List Houses

— **From Dustbooks,** P.O. Box 100-P, Paradise, CA 95967, Tel: (800) 477-6110; Fax: (916) 877-0222.

International Directory of Magazines and Small Presses. A comprehensive listing of smaller publishers.

Small Press Record of Books in Print

Directory of Small Magazine/Press Editors and *Publishers International Yearbook*

— **From Editor and Publisher,** 11 West 19th Street, New York, NY 10011, Tel: (212) 675-4380; Fax: (212) 929-1259.

Market Guide

International Yearbook

Directory of Syndicated Features

— **From Gale Research Co.,** 835 Penobscot Building, Detroit, MI 48226, Tel: (800) 877-4253; Fax: (313) 961-6083. Send for catalog.

Encyclopedia of Associations. 22,000 associations.

International Organizations. 11,000 groups.

National Directory of Non-Profit Organizations. 273,000 associations.

Directory of Publications (Formerly Ayer Directory of Publications)

Newsletters in Print

International Directories in Print

Directories in Print

Association Periodicals
Publishers Directory
Business, Organizations, Agencies, and Publications Directory
Standard Periodical Directory (Oxbridge)
Directory of Special Libraries
Contemporary Authors
European Book World
National Fax Directory

— **From Writer's Digest Books,** 1507 Dana Avenue, Cincinnati, OH 45207, Tel: (800) 289-0963; Fax: (513) 531-4744.

Writer's Market

Writers Yearbook

Writer's Digest Books also publishes many specific publishing books such as how to publish cookbooks, children's books, etc.

— **From Oxbridge Communications, Inc.,** 150 Fifth Avenue, #302, New York, NY 10011, Tel: (800) 955-0231; Fax: (212) 633-2938.

Oxbridge Directory of Newsletters

College Media Directory

National Directory of Magazines. 21,000 magazines.

— **From American Booksellers Association,** 560 White Plains Road, Tarrytown, NY 10591, Tel: (914) 631-7800; Fax: (914) 631-8391.

Book Buyers Handbook

Directory of American Publishers. 20,000 U.S. and Canadian publishers.

— **From Columbia Books,** 1212 New York Avenue, NW, #330, Washington, DC 20005-3920, Tel: (202) 898-0662.

National Avocational Organizations

National Trade & Professional Associations of the U.S.

State & Regional Associations

— From Grey House Publishing, Pocket Knife Square, Lakeville, CT 06039, Tel: (800) 562-2139; Fax: (800) 248-0115.
Directory of Mail Order Catalogs. 7,300 catalogs.
Directory of Business to Business Catalogs. 5,700 catalogs.

— Books from publishers with one reference.

Bacon's Newspaper/Magazine Directory
Bacon's Information Service
332 South Michigan Avenue, #900
Chicago, IL 60604-4301
Tel: (800) 621-0561;
Fax: (312) 922-3127

Broadcasting/Cable Yearbook
1705 DeSales Street, NW
Washington, DC 20036

Dewey Decimal Classification and Relative Index
Forest Press, Inc.
85 Watervliet Avenue
Albany, NY 12206-2082

Direct Marketing List Source
SRDS
3004 Glenview Road
Wilmette, IL 60091
Tel: (708) 258-6067
Fax: (708) 441-2264

Freelance Editorial Assn. Yellow Pages
P.O. Box 835
Cambridge, MA 02238
Tel: (617) 729-8164

Gebbie Press All-In-One Directory
P.O. Box 1000
New Paltz, NY 12561
Tel: (914) 255-7560

Hudson's Newsletter Directory. 4,600 newsletters.
Howard Penn Hudson
44 West Market Street
Rhinebeck, NY 12572-1403
Tel: (914) 876-2081;
Fax: (914) 876-2561

Larimi Media Guides
5 West 37th Street
New York, NY 10018

Membership Directory
Marketing to Libraries Through Library Associations
American Library Association
50 East Huron Street
Chicago, IL 60611
Tel: (800) 545-2433;
Fax: (312) 944-8741

National Trade and Professional Associations of the U.S. and Canada
Columbia Books, Inc.
1350 New York Avenue NW #207
Washington, DC 20005

National Union Catalog
Library of Congress
Available in your local library.

Working Press of the Nation. Lists newspapers, magazines, radio, TV, feature writers and internal publications.
National Research Bureau
225 West Wacker Drive, #2275
Chicago, IL 60606
Tel: (800) 456-4555

Proofreading Manual and Reference Guide
Directory of Editorial Resources
Peggy Smith
Editorial Experts
66 Canal Center Plaza, #200
Alexandria, VA 22314-1538

Self-Publish Your Own Picture Book
Howard Gregory
640 The Village #209
Redondo Beach, CA 90277

Yearbook of Experts, Authorities & Spokespersons
Mitchell P. Davis
2233 Wisconsin Avenue NW #406-P
Washington, DC 20007-4104

Books on writing, printing, publishing, promotion, marketing and distribution

Publisher addresses can be found in *Books in Print*. Books may also be ordered from Publisher's Bookshelf, P.O. Box 8206-890, Santa Barbara, CA 93118-8206, Tel: (805) 968-7277. Shipping is $2.00 for the first book and $.75 for each additional book. The sales tax for books shipped to California addresses is 7.75%. Use the order blank on the last page. For the very latest list, call our Fax-On-Demand system and request Document 133.

Radio/TV Interviews

Publicity for Books and Authors by Peggy Glenn shows authors and publishers how to get free and effective publicity for their books. The author shares her own experiences on television talk shows, radio, with magazines and newspapers—what worked and what did not. Author-publisher Glenn knows the theory of promotion, practices it with success and teaches it well. Examples and ideas.
ISBN 0-936930-91-8   Softcover, 8.5 x 11   182 pages $12.95

Print Promotion

The Copy Writer's Handbook by Robert Bly. You will learn how to write stimulating, wallet-grabbing copy that makes readers respond with book orders. Bly reveals the copy-writing techniques that will help you draft brochures, ads, commercials and direct mail pieces—that get more attention and sell more books.
ISBN 0-8050-1194-3   Softcover, 5.5 x 8.25, 352 pages $12.95

Words That Sell by Richard Bayan is a thesaurus designed to be used to promote products, services and ideas. This unusual *advertising copy stimulator* provides a *short course* in writing advertisements and lists synonyms for the words you want to use. Useful and unique; worth every penny—ad copy writers cost a lot more. New lower price. One of our top sellers.
ISBN 0-87280-150-0   Softcover, 8.5 x 8.75, 128 pages $12.95

Book Publishing Resource Guide is a directory by Marie Kiefer that will help you find the many resources you need for book production and promotion. It also lists the top wholesalers, bookfairs, mailing list sources, books on publishing, fulfillment houses, marketing directories and much more. Essential reference.
ISBN 0-912411-28-7   Softcover, 8.5 x 11, 320 pages $24.95

Book Fairs, An Exhibiting Guide for Publishers by Dan Poynter, contains everything you need to successfully select, arrange and operate a booth at a bookfair. It contains inside tips on how to work a fair to your maximum advantage, whether you are staffing a booth or working the floor. Required reading for first-time exhibitors and a valuable reminder/checklist for the seasoned veteran. Don't leave for an exhibit without it.
ISBN 0-915516-43-8   Softcover, 5.5 x 8.5, 96 pages $7.95

Marketing

Book Marketing Made Easier, a Do-it-Yourself Marketing Kit for Book Publishers by John Kremer. How to work with wholesalers/distributors, get into bookstores, sell to catalogs, and approach all the nontraditional book markets. This is a gold mine of step-by-step book-marketing procedures and ideas. Examples, resources and more.
ISBN 0-912411-34-1 Softcover, 6 x 9, 384 pages $19.95

Mail Order Selling Made Easier, A Step-By-Step Guide to Organizing and Carrying Out a Successful Direct Marketing Program by John Kremer. A hands-on working guide with worksheets, sample letters, charts, checklists and the procedures you need to use direct marketing in your business. Kremer shows you how to design your direct mail package, select mailing lists, design and place ads in magazines, newspapers, radio and TV, while he discusses telemarketing, card decks, response formulas, and catalogs. Large resource section.
ISBN 0-912411-29-5   Hardcover, 6.25 x 9.25, 288 pages $19.95

1001 Ways to Market Your Books by John Kremer is simply a most creative, informational and useful manual on book marketing. Kremer writes from detailed research and hard-earned experience. He covers advertising, promotion, distributors, bookstores, book design, libraries, spin-offs, and much more. In fact, there is little he does not cover and cover well. This is not a *basic* book.
ISBN 0-912411-42-2 Softcover, 6 x 9, 384 pages $19.95

Paste-up and Layout

Book Design & Production for the Small Publisher by Malcolm E. Barker shows you how to *design* your book to achieve total harmony: Working with type, laying out the pages, photographs/halftones, and cover design. Part Two deals with production: finding help, dealing with typesetters and printers, and materials. If you are responsible for book design, you need the only book on the subject. Outstanding.
ISBN 0-930235-08-8   Softcover, 8.5 x 11, 233 pages $24.95

Complete Guide to Paste-up by Walter B. Graham is a definitive course in preparing camera-ready copy for printing. Graham reveals numerous time-saving and money-saving paste-up secrets and shortcuts. Clear step-by-step procedures for books and brochures; generously illustrated. If you perform paste-up functions or supervise paste-up, you need this book. Illustrated glossary.
ISBN 0-912920-40-8   Softcover, 8.5 x 11, 216 pages $19.95

Publishing Short–Run Books, How-to Paste up and Reproduce Books Instantly Using Your Quick Print Shop by Dan Poynter, is a revolutionary concept in *short–run book manufacture.* This is the ideal production system for educators needing just a few copies for a class, business managers needing a special look for a presentation, authors who are trying to get the attention of a publisher (it is easier to sell a book than a manuscript), poets who desire a small private printing, and anyone who is in a hurry to break into print. Full of inside paste-up tips and techniques.
ISBN 0-915516-61-6   Softcover, 5.5 x 8.5, 144 pages $5.95

Paperless Publishing by Colin Haynes shows you how to publish on CDs as well as over online services, networks and bulletin boards. Now you can publish multimedia electronic books and you can sell your books on the Internet. Haynes covers intellectual property rights, protecting your material, packaging and much more. There are over 80 pages just on marketing and distributing. Floppy disk included.
ISBN 0-07-911895-X   Softcover, 7.5 x 9.25, 370 pages $27.95

Contracts

Business & Legal Forms for Authors & Self-Publishers by Tad Crawford provides *actual tear-out forms and contracts*, explains each one and offers negotiation check-off lists. Some of the contracts are: Author-agent, author-publisher, collaboration, licensing of audio rights, lecture contract, privacy release, permission form, nondisclosure agreement, publisher-book designer, publisher-printer, sales representative, book distributor, copyright transfer, invoice and confirmation of assignment. Essential.
ISBN 0-927629-03-8 Softcover, 8.5 x 11, 176 pages $15.95

Publishing Agreements by Charles Clark provides several sample book contracts, with explanations of each paragraph. Contracts range from those for general books to academic books, to paperback rights, translator's agreements, a book club contract and much more. Out of print for eight months, we now have a stock of the new, revised third edition.
ISBN 0-941533-56-5 Hardcover, 6 x 9, 238 pages $29.95

Handbook of Publishing Law by Jonathan Kirsch, Esquire. You will find the answers to the most often asked legal questions: idea protection, co-authorship and copyright, the role of agents and packagers, a book publishing contract is discussed clause-by-clause, copyright infringement, defamation, invasion of privacy, trademarks, subsidiary rights, electronic rights, etc. With resources, sample contracts and forms. This book is a valuable reference.
ISBN 0-918226-33-3 Softcover, 6 x 9, 277 pages $21.95

Business

Financial Feasibility in Book Publishing by Robert Follett presents a step-by-step method for evaluating the financial future of new book projects. Worksheets, guidelines, projection methods, rules of thumb and estimating methods with explanations help you decide whether your book will make money. Highly recommended.
ISBN 0-931712-07-6 Softcover, 8.5 x 11, 64 pages $12.95

Small Time Operator, How to Start Your Own Small Business, Keep the Books, Pay Your Taxes & Stay Out of Trouble! by Bernard Kamoroff, C.P.A. Kamoroff covers licenses, permits, business setup, bookkeeping, accounting, business expansion, taxes, deductions and more. This is *the* book on accounting, written and published by a small publisher. 35th printing, over 330,000 in print!
ISBN 0-917510-10-0 Softcover, 8.5 x 11, 192 pages $14.95

Internet Success with Fred by Fred Klopfer, Ph.D., is absolutely the best book on the Internet and the World Wide Web. You will learn how to do electronic research from home, how to sell books on the Net, how to turn your print products into electronic products and avoid print bills and inventory and much, much more.
ISBN 0-9638715-4-4 Softcover, 193 pages $19.95

Product Development and Editing

Is There a Book Inside You?, A Step-By-Step Plan for Writing Your Book by Dan Poynter and Mindy Bingham is a step-by-step plan for writing your book. Now available in a completely revised third edition. You will learn: how to pick your topic, how to break it down into easy-to-attack projects, how and where to do research, a process that makes writing (almost) easy, how to improve your material, how to manage writing partnerships, how to evaluate your publishing options, as well as how to develop an individualized and workable plan. They will show you how to write your book, get the help you need and publish or get it published. With self-paced quizzes and resources. A Writer's Digest Book Club main selection.
ISBN 1-56860-019-4 Softcover, 236 pages $14.95

Is There a Book Inside You? (audiotapes and book) by Dan Poynter and Mindy Bingham is a step-by-step plan for writing your book. Complete and unabridged, an album containing six one-hour cassettes and a copy of the new, third edition of the book. Now, you may listen while driving and have a book to refer back to.
ISBN 0-915516-73-X (Tape P-102 and book) $69.95

How to Make a Whole Lot More Than $1,000,000.00 Writing, Commissioning, Publishing and Selling "How-To" Information by Jeffrey Lant is an exhaustive, absolute last word on information creation and selling. This book says it all and is the best there is. Highly recommended to nonfiction book publishers.
ISBN 0-940374-26-9 Softcover, 6 x 9, 552 pages $39.95

Publishing to Niche Markets by Gordon Burgett describes the T-C-E approach to successful publishing. Burgett shows you how to Target your market, Customize your material for it and then Expand by spinning off material into other formats. An eye-opener and very good advice. New. ISBN 0-910167-27-3 Softcover, 6 x 9, 200 pages $14.95

Write Right! by Jan Venolia. This desk-drawer digest of punctuation, grammar and style is an important reference which should be next to your dictionary. Demonstrating proper usage with quotes from literature and politics, *Write Right!* makes editing reports and books easy and fun. This style manual is essential when copy editing. Over 200,000 sold. ISBN 0-89815-061-2 Softcover, 5.5 x 7, 127 pages $5.95

A Business Guide to Copyright Law by Woody Young explains the new copyright law. The authors show you how much research material you may legally use and how to protect your work from others. They cover fair use, permissions, licensing, foreign protection, registration procedures and much more. Examples of forms. Glossary. ISBN 0-939513-51-X Softcover, 8.5 x 11, 98 pages $14.95

Book Writing and Publishing (audiotape). Dan Poynter on how to write and publish books. Reasons to write a book, what to write, how to write, publishing options, how to self-publish and the secrets of successful self-publishing. One 76-minute cassette with workbook and resources. ISBN 0-915516-75-6 (Tape P-101) $14.95

Let Your Ideas Speak Out, A Guide to Preparing and Marketing Spoken Words on Audiotape and CD by Eugene Wheeler and Rennie Mau.

Turn your books into audiotapes. Resources, contracts, release forms and sample budgets. NEW! ISBN 0-934793-33-6 Softcover, 5.5 x 8.5, 96 pages $8.95

Publishing

How to Get Happily Published by Judith Appelbaum. How to write, find a publisher, locate an agent or publish yourself, by an author with years of varied experience in New York publishing. Learn how the book publishing industry works. This is a gold mine of publishing information with a lengthy resource section. All new third edition. ISBN 0-06-273133-5 Softcover, 5.25 x 8, 317 pages $10.95

The Self-Publishing Manual, How to Write, Print & Sell Your Own Book by Dan Poynter is a complete course in writing, publishing, marketing, promoting and distributing books. It takes the reader step by step from idea through manuscript, printing, promotion and sales. Along with an in-depth study of the book publishing industry, the book explains in detail numerous innovative book marketing techniques. *The Manual* is a *Bible* for writers and a constant reference for publishers. ISBN 1-56860-018-6 Softcover, 5.5 x 8.5, 416 pages $19.95

Your Book Publishing Choices (audiotape). Dan Poynter will give you the tools to make an educated decision between sending your manuscript to a large (New York) publisher, a medium-

sized specialized publisher, a vanity or subsidy publisher, a book packager or producer, an agent or self-publishing—doing it yourself. He discusses your choices, tells the four things you must do if you sell out to a big publisher and shares the seven secrets to successful self-publishing. One 60-minute cassette with workbook and resources.
ISBN 0-915516-76-4 (Tape P-103) $14.95

The Huenefeld Guide to Book Publishing by John Huenefeld is the only book on all aspects of publishing-company management. You will learn how to successfully start, organize and manage your company, as Huenefeld takes you through editorial, marketing, production, fulfillment and financial. This is the book with financial guidelines, projection methods and ratios. Now revised and in softcover at a lower price. An indispensable reference.
ISBN 0-938179-33-0 Softcover, 6 x 9, 394 pages $34.95

Printing

Pocket Pal, A Graphic Arts Production Handbook, from International Paper. This is the best basic reference on pre-press and printing. It provides specifications and descriptions for paper (weight, comparisons, etc.), inks, copy preparation, film imposition, the mechanics of printing, binding and much, much more. Invaluable reference; you will always look it up in *Pocket Pal* first.

Order #91838 Softcover, 4.25 x 7.5, 216 pages $9.95

Special Reports

on various aspects of publishing by Dan Poynter. For the latest list, call our Fax-On-Demand system and request Document 132.

Book Marketing: A New Approach is a low-cost marketing plan for your book. It leads you through the three-step plan for selling direct to the buyer, the five-step plan for selling to bookstores, the seven-step plan for libraries, all the subsidiary rights and our specialty: the more lucrative nontraditional markets. This step-by-step plan will make sure you have completely covered every possible market. An absolute gold mine of book-promotion references and sources. Start your book promotion with this Special Report.
ISBN 0-915516-58-6   71 pages $14.95

Book Reviews shows you in detail how to take advantage of the free publicity available to books from the pre-publication galleys to a continuing review program. Book reviews are your least expensive and most effective form of book promotion. Reviews are not hard to get if you follow the unwritten (until now) rules. This Report provides paint-by-the-numbers instructions for making galleys and describes in a detailed action plan how to set up a review program so your books will be reviewed again and again. It covers pre-publication reviews, early re-

views, retail reviews and continuing reviews, with examples of the packages for each. The Report even tells you what to do with the reviews after you receive them. Complete with lists of major reviewers and sources for the rest. Examples and resources.
ISBN 0-915516-56-X   53 pages
$19.95

News Releases and Book Publicity shows you how to draft news releases and other publicity for your books. After book reviews, news releases are your most effective and least expensive form of book promotion and you may send one out every month. Yet, few publishers use or even know about news releases. Newspaper and magazine editors want to pass on interesting information to their readers. The trick is to draft an interesting news release (tied into your book) that the editor will want to use. Editorial matter is believed; advertising is viewed with skepticism. Do not spend money on advertising when you can use the same effort and less money to send off a news release. If you are not sending out a news release on each book every 30 days, get this Report. Step-by-step instructions, paint-by-the-numbers format outlines, many examples and resources are included.
ISBN 0-915516-52-7   47 pages
$19.95

Direct Mail for Book Publishers shows how you can compete with the larger publishers by taking your message direct to the reader. Study the rules of direct mail, such as repetition, timing, response formulas and profit analysis. Learn to find and evaluate lists. Follow the plan for drafting your brochure and cover letter; assemble a direct mail package that brings results. This Report also shows you how to assemble your own lists to rent to others—providing you with a new profit center. If you have a nonfiction book with an identifiable audience (and can find or assemble a mailing list for it), you may use direct mail successfully to sell books.
ISBN 0-915516-59-4   55 pages
$19.95

Exports/Foreign Rights: Selling U.S. Books Abroad shows you how to expand your markets by selling direct to foreign readers, using an exporter in the U.S., contracting with a foreign distributor, and selling subsidiary rights to foreign publishers, with variations such as international book packaging, co-production and format rights. Special sections cover options, taxes, shipping, agents, the Frankfurt Book Fair and more. Exports expand your market, while foreign rights are frosting on your publishing cake; they bring in revenue, while the sale amounts to a significant endorsement of your book. These endorsements help to sell more books at home. Complete with sample contracts, postal rate charts, sample letters and instructions for locating compatible foreign publishers. Glossary and an Appendix full of resources.
ISBN 0-915516-57-8   57 pages
$19.95

Buying Book Printing answers the question we hear most: how to find the best and least-expensive printer for your particular book. Each printer is set up to manufacture certain kinds of books. Specialties vary depending on type of binding, book measurements, print run, etc. This Report shows you how to make up a *Request for Quotation* and provides a mailing list of printers who specialize in book manufacture. A section on color printing describes how to contact local representatives of Hong Kong and other foreign printers. This Report tells you how to decide how many books to print, how to select the appropriate binding, what to look for when checking bluelines, whether you should use a printing broker, how to evaluate quotations, what kind of a printing job you can expect, how to inspect the final product, and even how to resolve disputes. This Report will save you thousands of dollars in printing, binding and trucking costs. Includes an action plan, forms, sample letters and an Appendix full of resources.
ISBN 0-915516-55-1   57 pages $14.95

Book Production: Composition, Layout, Editing, Design, Getting it Ready for Printing shows you how to prepare your manuscript for the printer. Good packaging sells breakfast food, pantyhose and hair spray; it should be used to sell books. Now that you have poured your heart and soul into the manuscript, you must package the information well to encourage people to buy it. This Report describes good book packaging and shows you how to lay out the inside (the text) as well as the outside (the cover). The text should go through several drafts, for content, peer review and copy editing. The front matter and back matter must be in the proper order. The Report shows you how to select a title that will not only describe but sell the book. It shows you how to lay out your back-cover copy with a paint-by-the-numbers form. Tells you where to get bar codes and discusses appropriate binding methods. If you do not have the time or expertise to do the jobs yourself, this Report tells you where to get help. Complete with a production schedule, an action plan and an Appendix full of resources.
ISBN 0-915516-62-4   42 pages $19.95

Book Fulfillment: Order Entry, Picking, Packing and Shipping explains in detail how to set up and run your shipping department. The Report covers order taking (letter openers, credit cards, card terminals, 800 numbers, fax, order services, order forms, and discount structures); order processing (computer hardware and software, shipping labels, short slips, bad checks, overpayments, invoices, back orders, the Federal Trade Commission rules, complaints, book return policy, statements and collections); inventory and storage (shipping instructions to printer, book receiving, book returns, inventory control, stacking, and shipping room layout) and book packaging (how to wrap, where to get and how to use ship-

ping bags and cartons, machinery such as tape dispensers, scales, postage meters and bag sealers with sources, using UPS, direct sacks and various postal rates, foreign shipping and customs duty). Then the Report covers the alternatives to in-house fulfillment: using wholesalers, distributors, joint representation and fulfillment warehouses, with a list of those to contact. Complete with forms and shipping rate charts, an action plan and an Appendix full of resources.
ISBN 0-915516-64-0 86 pages $19.95

Publishing Contracts, Sample Agreements for Book Publishers on Disk is a collection of the 22 most needed legal documents covering every facet of the book publishing business, including: an author-publisher contract for a trade book, a publisher-illustrator agreement, a foreign rights agreement and 19 more. Just slip the disk into your computer, call the appropriate contract to the screen, fill in the names and check the suggested percentages. Then print out these 12-page contracts. You do not have to draft the agreements, you do not even have to type them. Available for the IBM PC and workalikes (specify), and virtually any word processing program, such as Microsoft *Word, WordPerfect, Wordstar* and many more (specify) and the Apple Macintosh with Microsoft *Word* or *MacWrite*
ISBN 0-915516-46-2 (disk) $29.95

Business Letters for Publishers, Creative Correspondence Outlines is a collection of 75 letters drafted especially for publishers. They save time for the older firm and enable the newer publisher to establish company policy which conforms to current, sometimes peculiar, publishing industry standards. Available on disk for the IBM PC and workalikes (specify) and virtually any word processing program, such as Microsoft *Word, WordPerfect, Wordstar* and many more (specify) and the Mac with *Word* or *MacWrite.* Now you not only do not have to draft the letters, you do not have to type them.
ISBN 0-915516-47-0   Computer disk $29.95

Publishing Forms, A Collection of Applications and Information for the Beginning Publisher. Get your new book listed in all the right directories easily and registered with appropriate agencies correctly. Included are applications for ABI, LC, copyright, and more. Important reviewer, wholesaler and other contacts are supplied.
ISBN 0-915516-38-1   50 pages $14.95

Brochures for Book Publishers shows you how to draft and print full-color brochures for less than you are currently paying for black and white locally. Imagine full-color brochures for less than four cents each! This Report covers everything from choosing the right photographer to money-saving tricks and even includes a sample request for quotation (RFQ) letter, a mailing list of specialized brochure printers and examples of color brochures. Complete with an action plan and an Appendix full of resources.
ISBN 0-915516-48-9   30⁺ pages
$19.95

To order these reports, see the order blank on the last page.

Here are several lists of contacts. Remember that over 20% of our population moves every year. If you find an address that is no longer valid, see *Literary Market Place* or call Directory Assistance for the new number.

Professional organizations

Write for an application and inquire about benefits and dues. Many associations publish a magazine or newsletter. For a list of writers' associations, see *Writer's Market*.

Publishers Marketing Association
Jan Nathan
2401 Pacific Coast Hwy. #102-A
Hermosa Beach, CA 90254
Tel: (310) 372-2732
Fax: (310) 374-3342

Association of American Publishers
220 East 23rd Street
New York, NY 10010
Tel: (212) 689-8920;
Fax: (212) 696-0131

COSMEP
P.O. Box 420703-P
San Francisco, CA 94142-0703
Tel: (415) 922-9490

New Age Publishing & Retailing
  Alliance
P.O. Box 9
Eastsound, WA 98245-0009
Tel: (206) 376-2702
Fax: (206) 376-2704

Colorado Independent Publishers
  Assn.
3031 Fifth Street
Boulder, CO 80304-2501
Tel: (303) 449-8474

Texas Publishers Association
2315 Briarwood Drive
San Antonio, TX 78209-4259
Publishers Association of the South
P.O. Box 43533
Birmingham, AL 35243-3533

Catholic Press Association
119 North Park Avenue
Rockville Center, NY 11570
Tel: (516) 766-3400

American Booksellers Association
560 White Plains Road
Tarrytown, NY 10591
Tel: (800) 637-0037

Christian Booksellers Association
P.O. Box 200
Colorado Springs, CO 80901
Tel: (719) 576-7880

Direct Marketing Association
6 East 43rd Street
New York, NY 10017

Book Publicists of Southern
  California
Irwin Zucker
6464 Sunset Blvd. #580
Hollywood, CA 90028
Tel: (213) 461-3921
Fax: (213) 461-0917

Marin Small Publishers Association
P.O. Box E
Corte Madera, CA 94976

American Library Association
50 East Huron Street
Chicago, IL 60611
Tel: (312) 944-6780

The Authors Guild, Inc.
234 West 44th Street
New York, NY 10036

National Assn. of Ind. Pubrs.
P.O. Box 430
Highland City, FL 33846

Society for Scholarly Publishing
10200 W. 44th Ave., #304
Wheat Ridge, CO 80033
Tel: (303) 422-3914

Book Industry Study Group
160 Fifth Avenue
New York, NY 10010
Tel: (212) 929-1393
Fax: (212) 989-7542

Canadian Book Marketing Centre
2 Gloucester Street, #301
Toronto, ON M4Y 1L5
Canada
Tel: (416) 413-4930
Fax: (416) 413-4920

Association of Canadian Publishers
260 King Street East
Toronto, ON M5A 1K3
Canada
Tel: (416) 413-4929
Fax: (416) 413-4920

Independent Publishers Guild
147-149 Gloucester Terrace
London W2 6DX, Great Britain

Midwest Independent Publishers
  Assn.
9561 Woodridge Circle
Eden Prarie, MN 55347
Tel: (612) 941-5053

Magazines for publishers.
Write for a sample copy and
current subscription rates.

Publishers Marketing Assn. Newsletter
Jan Nathan
2401 Pacific Coast Hwy. #102-A
Hermosa Beach, CA 90254
Tel: (310) 372-2732
Fax: (310) 374-3342

Publishers Weekly
249 West 17th Street
New York, NY 10011
Tel: (212) 645-0067

Library Journal
249 West 17th Street
New York, NY 10011
Tel: (212) 645-0067; (212) 337-6812

School Library Journal
249 West 17th Street

New York, NY 10011
Tel: (212) 645-0067

American Bookseller Magazine
560 White Plains Road
Tarrytown, NY 10591
Tel: (800) 637-0037

Small Press Magazine
Kymbolde Way
Wakefield, RI 02879
Tel: (401) 789-0074

Small Publisher
Nigel Maxey
P.O. Box 1620
Pineville, WV 24874

ALA Booklist
50 East Huron Street
Chicago, IL 60611
Tel: (312) 944-6780

Choice
Patricia E. Sabosik
100 Riverview Ctr.
Middletown, CT 06457
Tel: (203) 347-6933

Kirkus Reviews
Anne Larsen
200 Park Avenue South
New York, NY 10003
Tel: (212) 777-4554

Horn Book Magazine
(children's books)
Anita Silvey
11 Beacon Street, Suite 1000
Boston, MA 02108
Tel: (617) 227-1555
Tel: (800) 325-1170
Fax: (617) 523-0299

Canadian Author & Bookman
P.O. Box 120
Niagara-On-The-Lake, ON L0S 1J0
Canada

Publisher Notes
Melvett Chambers
P.O. Box 8475
Denver, CO 80202
Tel: (303) 321-2955

Newsletters

Author's Newsletter
P.O. Box 32008
Phoenix, AZ 85064

Editorial Eye
66 Canal Center Plaza, #200
Alexandria, VA 22314-4915

Huenefeld Report
John Huenefeld
41 North Road, #201-P
Bedford, MA 01730
Tel: (617) 275-1070

Direct Response Specialist
Galen Stilson
P.O. Box 1075
Tarpon Springs, FL 34688

Memo to Mailers (free)
U.S. Postal Service
P.O. Box 999
Springfield, VA 22150-0999

INFO Marketing Report
Jerry Buchanan
P.O. Box 2038-P
Vancouver, WA 98668

Publishing Poynters (free)
Dan Poynter
P.O. Box 8206-890
Santa Barbara, CA 93118-8206
Call our Fax-On Demand system
at (805) 968-8947 and request
Documents 189 and 109.

Multimedia Business Report
IDP Report
Electronic Directory & Classified
    Report
Online Service: Review, Trends &
    Forecast (report)
Directory World
BP Report
Trade Book Publishing (report)
Information Publishing (report)
Information Marketplace (directory)

Simba/Communication Trends
P.O. Box 7430
Wilton, CT 06897-7430
Tel: (203) 834-0033
Fax: (203) 834-1771

Book Reviewers

Here is a short list of reviewers. For
a longer list, see *Literary Market Place*.
For a complete list on labels, contact
ParaLists, P.O. Box 8206-890, Santa
Barbara, CA 93118-8206, Tel: (805)
968-7277. For more lists, call our
Fax-On-Demand system at (805)
968-8947 and request Document
142. See the discussion in Chapter
Seven.

John Barkham Reviews
Kobernick House
1951 North Honore Avenue
Sarasota, FL 34235

Frances Halpern
P.O. Box 5657-P
Montecito, CA 93150

United Features
Sidney Goldberg
200 Park Avenue, #602
New York, NY 10166

Millicent Braverman
1517 Schuyer Road #A
Beverly Hills, CA 90210

Book Talks
Marion Benasutti
1616 Huntington Pike, #403
Meadowbrook, PA 19046-8001

Alan Caruba
P.O. Box 40
Maplewood, NJ 07040

Roving Critic
Charles Lee
Presidential Apts. #D-1203
Philadelphia, PA 19131

Jerry Mack
P.O. Box 5200
San Angelo, TX 76902

San Francisco Review of Books
2909 McClure Street
Oakland, CA 94609

Literary Lantern
103 Carl Drive, Rt. #4
Chapel Hill, NC 27516

Curtis Casewit
P.O. Box 19039
Denver, CO 80219

Bloomsbury Reviews
Tom Auer
P.O. Box 8928
Denver, CO 80201

Book Talk
Dwight Myers
8632 Horacio Place NE
Albuquerque, NM 87111

Book World
Broox Sledge
P.O. Box 112
Macon, MS 39341

King Features Syndicate
235 East 45th Street
New York, NY 10017

New York Review of Books
Robert B. Silvers
250 West 57th Street
New York, NY 10107-0001

New York Times Book Review
Rebecca Sinkler
229 West 43rd Street
New York, NY 10036

Reviewing Books
Martin Kich
709 South Irving Avenue
Scranton, PA 18505

Book Report
Sheldon Tromberg
4200 River Road NW
Washington, DC 20016

Forrest J. Ackerman
2495 Glendower Avenue
Los Angeles, CA 90027

Sun Features
Joyce Lain Kennedy
2382-K Camino Vida Roble
Carlsbad, CA 92009

George H. Tweney
16660 Marine View Drive SW
Seattle, WA 98166

Small Press Book Review
Henry Berry
P.O. Box 176
Southport, CT 06909

Authors & Books
Gary Baranik
1272 Prospect Avenue
Brooklyn, NY 11215

New Pages
Casey Hill
4426 South Belsay Road
Grand Blanc, MI 48439

Rainbo Electronic Reviews
Maggie Ramirez
8 Duran Court
Pacifica, CA 94044

Bookwatch, Midwest Review of Books
Diane C. Donovan
166 Miramar Avenue
San Francisco, CA 94112

Reference and Research Book News
Jane Erskine
5606 NE Hassalo Street
Portland, OR 97213

Small Press Review
Len Fulton
P.O. Box 100
Paradise, CA 95967

Pamphlets, reports

and other help of interest to publishers. Write for latest prices.

Federal Trade Commission
Washington, DC 20580
Shopping By Mail? You're Protected!
FTC Buyer's Guide No. 2
Consumer Alert—The Vanity Press
News Release, dated July 19, 1959
Vanity Press Findings. Docket 7005
and 7489

P.E.N. American Center
568 Broadway
New York, NY 10012
Grants and Awards Available to
American Writers

National Endowment For The Arts
Literature Program
1100 Pennsylvania Avenue, NW, #722
Washington, DC 20506-0001
Tel: (202) 682-5451
Assistance, fellowships and residencies for writers

Poets & Writers
72 Spring Street
New York, NY 10012
Tel: (212) 226-3586
Awards List
Sponsors List
Literary Bookstores in the U.S.
Writer's Guide to Copyright
Directory of American Poets & Fiction Writers
Contracts and Royalties, Negotiating Your Own
Literary Agents, A Writer's Guide

Chicago Advertising Agency
28 East Jackson Blvd.
Chicago, IL 60604
Ad Guide (Circulation and ad prices for numerous magazines)

Copyright Office
Library of Congress
Washington, DC 20559
Circular 1, *Copyright Basics*
Circular 2, *Publications on Copyright*

Small Business Administration,
1441 L Street NW
Washington, DC 20416
General business guidance and booklets for the new publisher. Send for a list of available publications. They cover many subjects, and some are excellent.
Directory of Business Development Publications

Postal books and manuals.

The following Postal Service publications should be consulted for more information.

Domestic Mail Manual. Complete rules, regulations and postal rate information for all classes of mail sent and received in the U.S. $17.00 for four revisions, issued as needed. Superintendent of Documents, U.S. Government Printing Office, Washington, DC 20402-0001. It is also available on disk.

International Mail Manual. Complete rules, procedures, regulations and postal rate information for all classes of mail sent out of the U.S. $17.00 per loose-leaf edition, issued as needed. Superintendent of Documents.

Express Mail Service Handbook **DM201.** Policies, regulations and procedures for Express Mail Service. $1.00 subscription. U.S. Postal Service, Eastern Area Supply Center, Somerville, NJ 08877-0001.

Postal Bulletin. Weekly newsletter providing specific details on procedures, rates and regulations. $71.00 per year. Superintendent of Documents.

National Five-Digit ZIP Code and Post Office Directory (Publication 65A)—Order Form 4243. Call for prices: U.S. Postal Service, Tel: (800) 238-3150

Zip +4 State Directory—Order Form 4242. Call for prices: U.S. Postal Service Tel: (800) 238-3150

Postal Facts. Interesting folder with postal statistics. Free from U.S. Postal Service, News Division, Communications Department, Washington, DC 20260-3121

The following publications are available free from your local post office. Many deal with direct mail (bulk rate, presort, etc.) rather than parcel post, but as long as you are collecting information at the post office, you might as well get everything.

Basic Addressing, Notice 23A
Addressing for Automation, Notice 221
A Guide to Business Mail Preparation, Publication 25
Metered Better, Treated Better, Notice 125
On-site Meter Setting, Notice 112
Bar Code/FIM Pattern Locator Gauge, Model 005
Postage Rates, Fees and Information, Notice 59
Express Mail Rate Chart, Poster 189
International Postage Rates and Fees, Publication 51
Mailer's Guide, Publication 19
Information Guide on Presort First Class Mail, Publication 61
Computer Programming for Presort First-Class Mail, Notice 244
A Bottom Line Estimate of Your Presort Savings, Notice 243
How to Prepare Presort First-Class Mail, Poster 89
ZIP + 4 codes . . . Why They Add Up for Business Mailers, Notice 186
Directory of ZIP + 4 Coding Services, Publication 148
ZIP + 4: Helping You Help Your Business, Notice 189
Express Mail International Service Guide, Publication 273
International Surface Airlift (ISAL) Service Guide, Notice 82A
International Priority Airmail Mailer Guidelines, Publication 507
INTELPOST Service Directory and Users

Guide, Notice 82A
National Change of Address, Notice 47
Preparing Business and Courtesy Reply Mail, Publication 12

Book wholesalers

The most important are listed here. For more, see the *American Book Trade Directory* and *Literary Market Place*, available at your public library. You will also want a single distributor on an exclusive basis. For descriptions of the distributors with lists of the categories of books they want, see the Special Report *Book Marketing*.

Academic Book Center
5600 NE Hassalo Street
Portland, OR 97213

Airlift Books
12 Market Road #5-P
London N7 9PW
Great Britain

Ambassador Book Service
42 Chasner Street
Hempstead, NY 11550

Baker & Taylor Co.
P.O. Box 6920
Bridgewater, NJ 08807-0920

Ballen Booksellers International
125 Ricefield Lane
Hauppauge, NY 11788

Blackwell North America
1001 Fries Mill Road
Blackwood, NJ 08012

Blackwell North America
6024 SW Jean Road #G
Lake Oswego, OR 97035

Book House, Inc.
208 West Chicago Street
Jonesville, MI 49250

Bookazine Co.
75 Hook Road
Bayonne, NJ 07002

Bookpeople
7900 Edgewater Drive
Oakland, CA 94621

Bookslinger, Inc.
2402 University Avenue W, #507
St. Paul, MN 55114

Brodart Company
500 Arch Street
Williamsport, PA 17705

Coutts Library Service
736 Cayuga Street
Lewiston, NY 14092

DeVorss and Company
P.O. Box 550
Marina del Rey, CA 90294

The Distributors
702 South Michigan
South Bend, IN 46601

Eastern Book Company
131 Middle Street
Portland, ME 04101

EBS Book Service
290 Broadway
Lynbrook, NY 11563

Emery-Pratt Co.
1966 West Main Street
Owosso, MI 48867

Ingram Book Company
P.O. Box 3006
LaVergne, TN 37086-1986

International Service Company
333 Fourth Avenue
Indialantic, FL 32903

Koen Book Distributors
10 Twosome Drive
Moorestown, NJ 08057

Midwest Library Service
11443 Charles Rock Road
Bridgeton, MO 63044

National Association of College
  Stores (NACS)
528 East Lorain Street
Oberlin, OH 44074

New England Mobile Book Fair
82 Needham Street
Newton Highlands, MA 02161

New Leaf Distributing
5425 Tulane
Atlanta, GA 30336-2323

Nutri-Books
P.O. Box 5793
Denver, CO 80217

Pacific Pipeline
8030 South 228th Street
Kent, WA 98032-2900

Spring Arbor Distributors
10885 Textile Road
Belleville, MI 48111

Sunbelt Publications
8630 Argent Street, #C
Santee, CA 92071-4172

Arthur J. Viders Co.
7906 Hopi Place
Tampa, FL 33634

Yankee Book Peddler
Maple Street
Contoocook, NH 03229

Chain bookstores

Here are the major chains. For smaller ones, see *The American Book Trade Directory*, available at your public library. Address the fiction or nonfiction, hardcover or paperback buyer. Also see our Special Report *Book Marketing*.

Walden Book Company
P.O. Box 10218
Stamford, CT 06904
Tel: (203) 352-2000

Barnes & Noble/B. Dalton
  Bookseller
122 Fifth Avenue
New York, NY 10011
Tel: (212) 633-3300

Crown Books
3300 75th Avenue
Landover, MD 20785
Tel: (301) 731-1260

Classic Bookshops
98 Carrier Drive
Rexdale, ON M9W 5R1
Canada
Tel: (416) 675-1962

Coles Book Stores Ltd.
Director of Marketing
90 Ronson Avenue
Etobicoke, ON M9W 1C1
Canada
Tel: (416) 243-3132

W.H. Smith Ltd.
Buying Manager
113 Merton Street
Toronto, ON M4S 1A8
Canada
Tel: (416) 485-6660

U.S. Government Procurement Offices

See the *Selling to the Government* discussion in Chapter Eight.

Department of the Army
Attn: DAAG-MSL
2461 Eisenhower Avenue #1
Alexandria, VA 22331-0512

Naval Education and Training
  Program
Management Support Activity
(Code 042)
Naval General Library Services
Pensacola, FL 32509-5100

Navy Resale & Services Support
  Office
Fort Wadsworth (CG4)
Staten Island, NY 10305-5097

Air Force Libraries Section
Acquisitions Librarian
AFPMPPB-3
USAF Military Personnel Center
Randolph AFB, TX 78148

Veteran's Administration Library
810 Vermont Avenue NW
Washington, DC 20402

U.S. Information Service
Attn: Resource Development Branch
301 Fourth Street SW #314 (E/CLD)
Washington, DC 20547

DoD Dependent Schools
(DGSC-PJ)
Education Supplies Division
Richmond, VA 23297

Army and Air Force Exchange
  Service
Public Affairs Div., Info. Serv. Br.
P.O. Box 222305
Dallas, TX 75268-02022

Commandant (G-FRS)
U.S. Coast Guard Hqs.
2100 Second Street, SW
Washington, DC 20593

Department of the Navy
HQ, Marine Corps (LFS-1)
Washington, DC 20380-0001

Pacific Stars and Stripes
Book Department
APO San Francisco, CA 96503-0110
Operates 31 bookstores and 500
  book departments in the Pacific

Stars and Stripes, Europe
Book Buyer
APO NY 09175

For the addresses of other government procurement offices, call your congressional representative's local office.

Send for the following government publications to:

Superintendent of Documents
U.S. Government Printing Office
Washington, DC 20402

U.S. Government Purchasing and Sales Directory, $5.50

Selling to the Government, $1.80

Selling to the Military, #008-000-00479-0, $8.00

Doing Business with the Federal Government, #022-003-01136-6, $2.50

Starting and Managing a Small Business of Your Own, Vol. 1, 045-000-00212-8, $4.75

Starting and Managing a Business From Your Home, Vol. 102, $2.00

Book designers and cover artists

Book producers or book packagers are graphic arts shops that specialize in the design, typesetting and layout of books. Send for brochures with prices. For more designers, call our Fax-On-Demand system at (805) 968-8947 and request Document 250.

Robert Howard Graphic Design
Robert Howard
631 Mansfield Drive
Fort Collins, CO 80525
Tel: (970) 225-0083

Cirrus Design *(Book Design Only)*
Christine Nolt
1326 Bath Street, #B
Santa Barbara, CA 93101
Tel: (805) 966-4239
Fax: (805) 965-0520

One-On-One Productions
Carolyn Porter
7944 Capistrano Avenue
West Hills, CA 91304
Tel: (818) 340-6620

Sara Patton
RR #1, Box 384-104
Wailuku, HI 96793
Tel: (800) 433-4804
Fax: (808) 242-7838

Lightbourne Images
Gaelyn Larrick
P.O. Box 3526
Ashland, OR 97520
Tel: (800) 697-9833
Fax: (503) 482-1730

Book printers

These printers specialize in manufacturing books. For more, see our Special Report *Buying Book Printing.*

Van Volumes Ltd.
Russell Tate
P.O. Box 449
Palmer, MA 01069
Tel: (413) 283-8556
Fax: (413) 283-7884

Courier-Westford
James F. Conway, III
Pleasant Street
Westford, MA 01886
Tel: (508) 692-6321

Book Press/Quebecor
Samuel Ratkewitch
Putney Rd.
Brattleboro, VT 05301
Tel: (802) 257-7701
Tel: (800) 732-7310
Fax: (802) 257-9439

Book Mart Press
Michelle S. Gluckow
2001 Forty Second St.
North Bergen, NJ 07047
Tel: (201) 864-1887
Tel: (212) 594-3344
Fax: (201) 864-7559

Maple-Vail
Sam W. Vail
P.O. Box 2695
York, PA 17405
Tel: (717) 764-5911
Fax: (717) 764-4702

Professional Press
P.O. Box 4371
Chapel Hill, NC 27515-4371
Tel: (800) 277-8960

Delmar Printing & Publishing
Frank Myers
P.O. Box 1013
Charlotte, NC 28201-1013
Tel: (800) 438-1504
Tel: (704) 847-9801
Fax: (704) 845-1218

Rose Printing
P.O. Box 5078
Tallahassee, FL 32314-5078
Tel: (904) 576-4151
Tel: (800) 227-3725
Fax: (904) 576-4153
Also specialize in minibooks
  (3.5 x 5.5)

Whitehall Company
Mike Hirsch
4244 Corporate Square
Naples, FL 33942-4753
Tel: (800) 321-9290
Fax: (813) 643-6439
Their short-run prices are hard
  to beat.

Donihe Graphics, Inc.
Cindy Pratt
766 Brookside Road
Kingsport, TN 37662
Tel: (800) 251-0337
Tel: (615) 246-2800
Fax: (615) 246-7297

BookMasters
Raymond Sevin
P.O. Box 159
Ashland, OH 44805-0159
Tel: (419) 289-6051
Tel: (800) 537-6727
Fax: (419) 281-1731

National Reproductions Corporation
James Williams
29400 Stephenson Hwy.
Madison Heights, MI 48071
Tel: (800) 628-2299
Tel: (313) 398-7900

Edwards Brothers
Mike Potter
2500 South State Street
Ann Arbor, MI 48106-1007
Tel: (313) 769-1000
Fax: (313) 769-0350

Malloy Lithographing
Will Upton
P.O. Box 1124
Ann Arbor, MI 48106-1124
Tel: (313) 665-6113
Tel: (800) 722-3231
Fax: (313) 665-2326

Braun-Brumfield
Lynn Hazelman
P.O. Box 1203
Ann Arbor, MI 48106-1203
Tel: (313) 662-3291
Fax: (313) 662-1667

Cushing-Malloy
Steven Kehoe
P.O. Box 8632
Ann Arbor, MI 48107-8632
Tel: (313) 663-8554
Fax: (313) 663-5731

Shear-Davis
Charlotte Ellison
715 West Ellsworth Road
Ann Arbor, MI 48108-3320
Tel: (313) 741-0123

Bookcrafters
Jeanne Atkinson
P.O. Box 370
Chelsea, MI 48118-0370
Tel: (313) 475-9145
Fax: (313) 475-7337

Thomson-Shore, Inc.
Mark Livesay
7300-P West Joy Road
Dexter, MI 48130-0305
Tel: (313) 426-3939
Fax: (313) 426-6219

McNaughton & Gunn
Ronald A. Mazzola
960 Woodland Drive
Saline, MI 48176
Tel: (313) 429-5411
Fax: (800) 677-BOOK

Harlo Press
Richard G. Heppard
50-P Victor Ave.
Detroit, MI 48203-3193
Tel: (313) 883-3600
Fax: (313) 883-0072

Data Reproductions Corporation
1480 North Rochester Road
Rochester Hills, MI 48307
Tel: (313) 652-7600
Fax: (313) 652-7605

Patterson Printing
Linda J. Seaman
1550 Territorial Road
Benton Harbor, MI 49022-1937
Tel: (616) 925-2177
Fax: (616) 925-6057

Eerdmans Printing Co.
Donald Miller
231 Jefferson Avenue SE
Grand Rapids, MI 49503-4569
Tel: (616) 451-0763
Fax: (616) 459-4356

Dickinson Press
Bob Worcester
5100 33rd Street SE
Grand Rapids, MI 49512
Tel: (616) 957-5100
Fax: (616) 957-1261
Specializes in light-weight papers
    (Bibles), 1 and 2 colors and
    minibooks (4.25 x 7 or smaller)

Bawden Printing, Inc.
Pete Bawden
400 South 14th Avenue
Eldridge, IA 52748
Tel: (319) 285-4800
Fax: (319) 285-4828

Omnipress
Robert G. Hamm
P.O. Box 7125
Madison, WI 53707-7125
Tel: (608) 246-2600
Tel: (608) 257-7275
Tel: (608) 828-0305 outside WI
Fax: (608) 246-4237

George Banta Co.
David Mead
Curtis Reed Plaza
Menasha, WI 54952
Tel: (414) 722-7771
Tel: (800) 722-3324
Fax: (414) 722-8541

Viking Press/Banta
Chip Fuhrmann
7000 Washington Avenue South
Eden Prairie, MN 55344
Tel: (800) 328-7327
Tel: (612) 941-8780
Fax: (612) 941-2154

Bang Printing
James Luker
18519 Twilight Trail
Eden Prairie, MN 55346
Tel: (800) 391-6662
Fax: (612) 975-9818

Adams Press
Joe Goodman
500 North Michigan Avenue, #1920
Chicago, IL 60611
Tel: (708) 676-3426
Tel: (312) 326-3838

R.R. Donnelley & Sons
Gary Davis
2223 Martin Luther King Drive
Chicago, IL 60616
Tel: (312) 326-8000
Tel: (800) 428-0832
Fax: (312) 333-7307

Walsworth Publishing Co.
Mark S. Anderson
306 North Kansas Avenue
Marceline, MO 64658
Tel: (816) 376-3543
Fax: (816) 258-7798
Also does unusual embossing and
  die-cutting

Gilliland Printing
Floyd Ferris
215 North Summit Street
Arkansas City, KS 67005
Tel: (800) 332-8200
Tel: (316) 442-0500
Fax: (316) 442-8504

Morgan Printing and Publishing
Ramsey Wiggins
900 Old Koenig Lane #135
Austin, TX 78756-1514
Tel: (512) 459-5194
Fax: (512) 451-0755
Specializes in very short runs

C&M Press
Beth Chapmon
850 East 73rd Avenue
Thornton, CO 80229
Tel: (303) 289-4757
Fax: (303) 289-3347
Specializes in very short runs

Publishers Press
Bruce Bracken
1900 West 2300 South
Salt Lake City, UT 84119
Tel: (801) 972-6600
Tel: (800) 456-6600
Fax: (801) 972-6601

Merrill Corporation
Linda Wexler
1926 East 14th Street
Los Angeles, CA 90021-2891
Tel: (213) 765-7000
Tel: (800) 334-7344

Griffin Printing and Lithograph Co.
544 West Colorado Street
Glendale, CA 91204-1102
Tel: (213) 245-3671
Tel: (818) 244-2128
Tel: (800) 826-4849
Tel: (800) 423-5789 (CA)
Fax: (818) 242-1172
Griffin also has a plant in
  Sacramento.

Alumni Graphics, Inc.
Ken Hoffman
13834 Del Sur Street
San Fernando, CA 91340
Tel: (818) 834-8283
Fax: (818) 896-8901

Delta Lithograph
Sonny Spencer
28210 North Avenue Stanford
Valencia, CA 91355-1111
Tel: (805) 257-0584
Tel: (800) 223-1478 (CA)
Tel: (800) 32D-ELTA
Fax: (805) 257-3867

Kimberly Press
Bill McNally
5390-P Overpass Road
Santa Barbara, CA 93111-2008
Tel: (805) 964-6469

Jostens Printing & Publishing
Dawn Willems
P.O. Box 991
Visalia, CA 93291
Tel: (209) 651-3300
Fax: (209) 651-0739

Griffin Printing
Dixie Robertson
4141 North Freeway Blvd.
Sacramento, CA 95834
Tel: (916) 448-3511
Tel: (800) 448-3511
Fax: (916) 448-3597
Griffin also has a plant in Glendale.

Canadian book printers

RBW Graphics
Ken Graves
515 Consumers Road, #200
Willowdale, ON M2J 4Z2
Tel: (416) 495-7244

Aprinco Book Manufacturers
Benjamin Chung
2220 Midland Avenue
Toronto, ON M1P 3E6
Tel: (406) 298-3265

Ashton-Potter Ltd.
Randy Davis
9010 Keele Street
Concord, ON L4K 2N2
Tel: (416) 736-4234

Hignell Printing Ltd.
Ray Hignell
488 Burnell Street
Winnipeg, MN R3G 2B4
Tel: (204) 783-7237

Gagne Printing
Jean-Pierre Gagne
80, St. Martin Avenue
Louisville, PQ J5V 1B4
Tel: (819) 228-2766

John Deyell Company
J. Denis Beaudin
2235 Sheppard Avenue East, #903
Willowdale, ON M2J 5B5
Tel: (416) 491-8811

T.H. Best Printing Co.
Douglas W. Best
33 Kern Road
Don Mills, ON M3B 1S9
Tel: (416) 447-7295

Mailing list brokers

For mailing list brokers and mailing services, see the *Yellow Pages* of your local telephone directory. Also see *Direct Marketing List Source* and *Literary Market Place* at your public library. Write for catalogs.

Advanced Publishing Systems
(college professors)
403 Grand Central Avenue
Lavallette, NJ 08735
Tel: (201) 793-5600

American Business Lists
(14 million businesses,
compiled from *Yellow Pages*)
P.O. Box 27347
Omaha, NE 68127
Tel: (402) 331-7169

American Direct Marketing Service
(compiler)
1261 Record Crossing
Dallas, TX 75235
Tel: (800) 527-5080
Tel: (214) 634-2361

American Library Association
(libraries)
50 East Huron Street
Chicago, IL 60611
Tel: (312) 944-6780

American List Counsel (book
buyers)
88 Orchard Road
Princeton, NJ 08540-8019
Tel: (800) 526-3973
Tel: (201) 874-4300

R.R. Bowker Lists (publishing
industry)
John Panza
245 West 17th Street
New York, NY 10011
Tel: (212) 337-7164

Ed Burnett Consultants (general)
99 West Sheffield Avenue
Englewood, NJ 07631
Tel: (800) 223-7777
Tel: (201) 871-1100

CMG Information Services
(academic-general)
187 Ballardsville St. #B-110
Wilmington, MA 01887
Tel: (800) 677-7959

Consolidated Mailing Service
(academic)
Max Bradbard
P.O. Box 495
St. James, NY 11780
Tel: (516) 584-7283

Dunhill International (executives)
2430 West Oakland Park Blvd.
Ft. Lauderdale, FL 33311

Dustbooks
Len Fulton
P.O. Box 100-P
Paradise, CA 95967
Tel: (800) 477-6110

Educational Lists Co.
500 North Broadway
Jericho, NY 11753
Tel: (516) 931-2442
Tel: (800) 331-8102

Educational Mailings Clearing
House (academic)
601 East Marshall Street
Sweet Springs, MO 65351
Tel: (816) 335-6373

Hugo Dunhill Lists (general)
630 Third Avenue
New York, NY 10017
Tel: (800) 223-6454
Tel: (212) 682-8030

Educational Directory (academic)
One Park Avenue
New York, NY 10016

Educational Lists Company
(schools)
161 Glen Head Road
Glen Head, NY 11545
Tel: (516) 671-5011

Executive Services Companies
(buyers by age)
Response+
901 North International Parkway
Richardson, TX 75081
Tel: (800) 527-3933
Tel: (214) 699-1271

IBIS Information Services (foreign)
152 Madison Avenue
New York, NY 10016
Tel: (212) 779-1344
Tel: (800) 433-6226

Market Data Retrieval (libraries
and schools)
16 Progress Drive
Shelton, CT 06484
Tel: (800) 435-3742 (CT)
Tel: (800) 243-5538

New Pages Lists (libraries and
bookstores)
4426 South Belsay Road
Grand Blanc, MI 48439
Tel: (313) 743-8055

ParaLists
P.O. Box 8206-890
Santa Barbara, CA 93118-8206
Tel: (805) 968-7277
Fax-On-Demand:
Tel: (805) 968-8947,
Document 142

Patterson's Mailing Lists (schools)
P.O. Box 199
Mount Prospect, IL 60056

PCS Mailing Lists (compiler/broker)
125 Main Street
Peabody, MA 01960
Tel: (800) 532-5478
Tel: (617) 532-1600

Quality Education Data (schools)
1500 Logan Street
Denver, CO 80203
Tel: (800) 525-5811

R.L. Polk & Company (general)
6400 Monroe Blvd.
Taylor, MI 48180
Tel: (313) 292-3200

Research Projects (compilers)
50 Clinton Street
Hempstead, NY 11550
Tel: (800) 645-2980
Tel: (212) 895-1048
Tel: (718) 481-4410

Resources (alternative America)
P.O. Box 134
Cambridge, MA 02238

Edith Roman Lists
   (compiler/broker)
875 Avenue of the Americas
New York, NY 10001
Tel: (800) 223-2194
Tel: (212) 695-3836

School Lists Mailing (schools)
1710 Hwy. 35
Oakhurst, NJ 07755
Tel: (201) 531-2212

Southam Direct Marketing
   (Canadian schools, libraries,
   bookstores, doctors and
   businesses)
12 Nantucket Blvd.
Scarborough, ON M1P 4W7
Canada

SpeciaLISTS
120 East 16th Street
New York, NY 10003-2150
Tel: (212) 260-5644

Willowood Lists (schools)
P.O. Box 1846
Minot, ND 58702

Mike Wilson List Counsel
   (institutional)
12120 Washington Blvd.
Los Angeles, CA 90066
Tel: (800) 445-2089
Tel: (213) 398-2754

Fred Woolf Lists (compiler/broker)
280 North Central Avenue
Hartsdale, NY 10530
Tel: (800) 431-1557
Tel: (914) 946-0336
Tel: (212) 679-4311

Woodruff-Stevens Lists
   (book buyers)
345 Park Avenue South
New York, NY 10010
Tel: (212) 685-4600

Worldata (general)
P.O. Box 443
Jericho, NY 11753
Tel: (516) 931-2442

Alvin B. Zeller, Inc. (general)
37 East 28th Street
New York, NY 10016
Tel: (212) 689-4900
Tel: (800) 223-0814

Zeller & Letica (book buyers)
15 East 26th Street
New York, NY 10010
Tel: (800) 221-4112
Tel: (212) 685-7512

Also see *The Encyclopedia of Associations* and other references. Most organizations rent their mailing lists.

Book Publicists

These professionals will schedule you for TV appearances, write your news releases and introduce you to other media contacts. For an expanded listing, see *Literary Market Place*.

Planned Television Arts
Rick Frishman
301 East 57th Street
New York, NY 10022
Tel: (212) 921-5111
Fax: (212) 715-1664

Promotion in Motion
Irwin Zucker
6464 Sunset Blvd.
Hollywood, CA 90028
Tel: (213) 461-3921

(list continues next page)

Sensible Solutions
Judith Appelbaum
271 Madison Avenue, #1007
New York, NY 10016
Tel: (212) 687-1761
Fax: (212) 867-8641

Allen Communications
Alice Allen
770 Lexington Avenue
New York, NY 10021
Tel: (212) 755-4545

KBS Promotions
Kate Bandos
55 Honey Creek NE
Ada, MI 49301
Tel: (616) 676-0758
Fax: (616) 676-0759

Gaughen Public Relations
Barbara Gaughen
226 East Canon Perdido
Santa Barbara, CA 93101
Tel: (805) 965-8482
Fax: (805) 965-6522
FOD: (805) 96-FAX-IT

Integrated Book Marketing
Sharon Castlen
P.O. Box 566
Huntington Station, NY 11746
Tel: (516) 427-7544

Bookfair exhibiting services

If you cannot attend the fair yourself, you might contract with an exhibiting service to show your books.
See the discussion in Chapter Nine
and read *Book Fairs.*

PMA Book Exhibits
2401 Pacific Coast Highway #102-A
Hermosa Beach, CA 90254
Tel: (310) 372-2732

COSMEP Book Exhibits
P.O. Box 420703-P
San Francisco, CA 94142-0703
Tel: (415) 922-9490

Association Book Exhibit
Mark Trocci

639 So. Washington St.
Alexandria, VA 22314
Tel: (703) 519-3909

Publishers Book Exhibit
179 White Street
Buchanan, NY 10511
Tel: (800) 462-7687

Office Supplies

Send for catalogs.

Chiswick Trading
33 Union Avenue
Sudbury, MA 01776-2267
Tel: (800) 225-8708

Grayarc
P.O. Box 2944
Hartford, CT 06104
Tel: (800) 243-5250

Robbins Container Corp.
222 Conover Street
Brooklyn, NY 11231
Tel: (718) 875-3204

Fidelity Products Co.
P.O. Box 155
Minneapolis, MN 55440
Tel: (800) 862-3765 U.S.
Tel: (612) 536-6500
Fax: (612) 536-6584

Paper Mart
5959 Corvette Street
Los Angeles, CA 90040
Tel: (800) 722-2204 (U.S.)
Tel: (800) 334-8800 (Southern
    California)
Tel: (800) 531-1778 (Northern
    California)

Drawing Board
P.O. Box 220505
Dallas, TX 75222

Quill Corporation
P.O. Box 94080
Palatine, IL 60094-4080
Tel: (708) 534-4800
Tel: (909) 988-3200

Fulfillment warehouses

Send for prices. Also see our Special Report *Book Fulfillment*.

Publishers Storage & Shipping
E.B. Quick
46 Development Road
Fitchburg, MA 01420
Tel: (508) 345-2121

Package Fulfillment Center, Inc.
Peter Norberto
1401 Lakeland Avenue
Bohemia, NY 11716
Tel: (516) 567-7000

Publishers Resources, Inc. (PRI)
Tom Scott
1224 Heil Quaker Blvd.
LeVergne, TN 37086
Tel: (615) 793-5090

BookMasters
Raymond Sevin
P.O. Box 159
Ashland, OH 44805-0159
Tel: (419) 289-6051
Tel: (800) 537-6727
Fax: (419) 281-1731

APEX, Inc.
Bret Butterfield
4931 South 900 East
Salt Lake City, UT 84117
Tel: (800) 654-8000,
Tel: (801) 265-3000

Thunderbird Fulfillment
Mark Field
4130 North Goldwater Blvd.
Scottsdale, AZ 85251
Tel: (602) 941-3937
Fax: (602) 941-3936

JV West
Ben Rose
P.O. Box 11950
Reno, NV 89510
Tel: (702) 359-9811

Order-entry software

Write for details and prices:

PIIGS
Upper Access Books
P.O. Box 457
Hinesburg, VT 05461
Tel: (800) 356-9315

Bookmaster
Harold G. Harvey
1000 Elwell Court
Palo Alto, CA 94303-4306
Tel: (415) 961-2600
Fax: (415) 961-4915

Cat's Pajamas
1253 North Hwy. 20
Anacortes, WA 98221
Tel: (206) 293-8372

QuickBooks
Quicken
Intuit
P.O. Box 3014
Menlo Park, CA 94026
Tel: (415) 858-6095

Courses, conferences and seminars

There are many educational programs of interest to publishers. Some of the most important are listed here. For more, see *Literary Market Place*.

Santa Barbara Publishing
   Workshops
Dan Poynter
P.O. Box 8206-890
Santa Barbara, CA 93118-8206
Tel: (805) 968-7277
Fax-On-Demand (805) 968-8947,
   Document 167

Huenefeld Seminars
P.O. Box 665-P
Bedford, MA 01730

Publishing Institute
University of Denver
2075 South University, #D-114
Denver, CO 80210

Stanford Conf. on Book Publishing
Stanford Alumni Association
Bowman Alumni House
Stanford, CA 93405

UC Berkeley Extension
University of California
Berkeley, CA 94720

New York University's Summer
   Publishing Institute
School of Continuing Education
Center for Publishing
48 Cooper Square
New York, NY 10211-0152

Chicago Book Clinic
100 East Ohio Street #630
Chicago, IL 60611

Publishing Program
University of Chicago
Office of Continuing Education
5835 South Kimbark Avenue
Chicago, IL 60637

Book Clubs

There are over 200 book clubs and most are very specialized. For more, see *Literary Market Place*.

The Literary Guild
1540 Broadway, 23rd Floor
New York, NY 10036

The Book-of-the-Month Club
1271 Avenue of the Americas
New York, NY 10020-2686

How-to Book Club
13311 Monterey Avenue
Blue Ridge Summit, PA 17294-0850

Newbridge Book Clubs
3000 Cindel Drive
Delran, NJ 08075

Quality Paperback Book Club
1271 Avenue of the Americas
New York, NY 10020

Glossary

AAP: Association of American Publishers.

AAUP: Association of American University Presses.

ABA: American Booksellers Association.

ABI: Advanced Book Information. Publishers supply information on their book to Bowker for inclusion in *Forthcoming Books* and *Books in Print*.

Accounts receivable: Money owed a company by credit customers.

Acquisitions editor: The person in a publishing firm who acquires new manuscripts.

Advance: An amount paid to the author on signing the contract. An advance is normally applied against royalties.

ALA: American Library Association.

American Booksellers Association: The trade association of non-chain retail bookstores in the U.S.

American Library Association: Largest library association in the U.S.

American National Standards Committee: Z39. The committee responsible for standard for libraries, information science and publishing.

Anthology: A collection of one or more authors published as a single work.

Antiquarian bookseller: One who specializes in selling old or rare books.

Artwork: Any illustrative matter other than straight text.

Association of American Publishers: The trade association of the largest book publishers in the U.S.

Association of American University Presses: The trade association of university presses.

Author's alterations: Changes made by an author after type has been set. See *printer's error.*

Back flap: The back inner flap of a dust jacket that often contains a biography of the author.

Back list: Previously published books that are still in print and available from a publisher. Not *frontlist* books which are recently published.

Back order: An order for books which are unavailable, which is held until the books become available.

Bar code: The identification and price marking in bar format on books. The bar code for books is called Bookland EAN.

Bastard title: Half title. Found on the page in front of the title page.

Belt press: A large printing press that prints many pages in one pass.

Benday: Various density screens printed on an adhesive-backed plastic sheet which may be pasted to artwork. The screening provides tonal qualities to artwork.

Best seller: A top-selling book. There are several best seller lists that draw sales figures from different markets.

Bibliography: That part of the back matter listing books and materials consulted by the author in preparing the book, or which the author wishes to bring to the reader's attention.

Binding: The processes following printing: folding, gathering, stitching, gluing, trimming and/or casing a book.

BISAC: Book Industry Systems Advisory Committee. A committee of the Book Industry Study Group.

Bleed: Ink printed over the edge of the paper. The edge is trimmed off.

Most magazines have covers with bleed.

Blueline: A proof sheet made by exposing a negative to a photosensitive paper. A blueprint.

Blurb: A promotional announcement, phrase or advertisement.

Boards: The camera-ready, pasted-up copy ready for the printer.

Body type: The majority of the type used in a book. Not a headline.

Boldface: Type which is heavier than the text type with which it is used.

Bond. A laid finish rag or sulphite paper used for stationery and forms.

Bookfair: An event where publishers display their books.

Book packager: A person or company who contracts with publishers to deliver contracted books.

Book post: The Postal Service's book rate.

Book: A publication of 49 or more pages which is not a serial or periodical.

Booklet: A small book, usually with less than 48 pages.

Bullets: Large black dots • used to set off items in a list.

C1S: Coated One Side. Usually refers to a book cover stock which is smooth on one side.

Camera-ready copy: A completely prepared paste-up which is ready for the camera or xerographic reproduction. No further graphic arts work is required.

Caption: The line of text accompanying an illustration.

Case binding: Hardcover.

Case-bound: Hardcover or edition binding.

Cataloging-in-Publication Data: Bibliographic information supplied by the Library of Congress which is printed on the copyright page. The CIP data helps libraries to shelve the book properly.

Chapbook: A small book or pamphlet of popular tales, ballads or poems.

Character: A letter, number, punctuation mark or space in printed matter.

Check Digit: A number used to validate the other numbers in the preceding numerical field. The last number in the ISBN is a *check digit*.

Clip art: Line drawings, screened pictures and illustrations designed to be cut out and pasted up.

Clipping service: A firm that collects articles of interest to the client from periodicals.

Coated stock: Paper manufactured with a variety of surfaces, which may be smooth, glossy or matte.

COD: Cash On Delivery. Where merchandise is paid for when delivered.

Cold type: Strike-on type, such as that produced by a typewriter or IBM Composer, or photocomposition type. Not hot metal type.

Collating: Gathering of printed sheets into proper order for binding.

Colophon: A listing of production details in the back matter.

Color separation: A camera technique using different-color lenses to draw out the three primary colors and black from a color illustration or photograph. The resulting negatives are used to make the printing plates.

Composition: Typeset material. Typeset text ready to be pasted up.

Content editing: Evaluating a manuscript for organization and style.

Continuity program: A standing order for succeeding volumes in a related program.

Contrast: The degree of difference between the lightest and darkest parts of a picture.

Co-op publishing: Where more than one person or company join to produce a book. Co-publishing.

Co-op advertising: Where the publisher and the bookstore share the cost of local book advertising. The publisher pays the larger share.

Copy editing: Technical editing of a manuscript for spelling, grammar and punctuation.

Copyright: The right to retain or sell copies of artistic works which you have produced.

Copyright notice: The words placed on the copyright page, such as "Copyright © 1989, Daniel F. Poynter."

COSMEP: The Committee of Small Magazine Editors and Publishers. A trade association based in San Francisco.

Credit memo: A statement showing money due a customer for returned merchandise.

Crop marks: The lines used to define the desired limits of the area of a photograph or illustration to be reproduced. See *trim marks*.

DBA: Doing business as. A sole proprietorship operated in another name.

Defamation: Libel (written) or slander (spoken) that injures a person.

Density: The relative darkness of an image area. In photography, the blackening or light-stopping ability of a photographic image, as numerically measured by a densiometer.

Direct mail advertising: Advertising matter mailed directly to a potential customer.

Display ad: A print advertisement using graphics.

Display type: Type which is larger than the text, as in a chapter headline.

Distributor: A company that acts as your marketing (usually to one market such as bookstores), warehousing and shipping department. Not a jobber or wholesaler.

Dummy: A preliminary mock-up of a book folded to the exact size of the finished job.

Dummy folio: "Working" page numbers added for identification purposes but changed before the book is printed.

Dump: A display for books, usually made of cardboard.

Dust jacket: The thin paper wrap on a hardcover book.

Editing: Changing, correcting or altering typed text into the required form.

Edition: All printings of a book from the same unaltered boards. Once changes are made, the book becomes a second edition.

El-hi: The elementary school/high school market.

Em dash: A dash—the width of an "M".

En dash: A dash–the width of an "N".

Endpapers: The heavy sheets that fasten the pages of a hardcover book to the cover.

Epilogue: The last part of the text that brings the reader up to date.

Errata: A loose sheet listing errors found in the printed book.

Exclusive: 1. A news or feature story printed by one media source substantially ahead of its competitors. 2. Sole distribution rights given to a distributor.

Fair use: The allowable and legal use of a limited amount of copyrighted material without getting permission.

First edition: The entire original printing from the same (unchanged) plates.

First serial rights: The exclusive

right to serialize a book in a periodical.

Flat: A printing term describing the assembling of negatives on a heavy paper sheet for platemaking. See *stripping.*

Flier: A printed announcement. A flier becomes a *brochure* when folded.

Flop: To flip over a photographic negative so that the image will be reversed.

Flush: To be even with, such as in "flush right."

FOB: Free On Board. "FOB origin" means the addressee pays the shipping. "FOB destination" means the shipper pays the shipping costs. "FOB Santa Barbara" means the goods are delivered free as far as Santa Barbara; the addressee pays for transportation, if any, from there.

F&Gs: Folded and gathered pages. The unbound signatures of a book sometimes sent to reviewers.

Folio: The number on the page of a book.

Font : The complete set of type in a single typeface, including characters, numbers and punctuation marks.

Foreign rights: Subsidiary rights allowing the book to be published in other countries.

Foreword: Introductory remarks about the book and its author found in the front matter. Not "forward."

Front matter: All the pages in a book before the main text.

Frontispiece: An illustration facing the title page.

FTC: Federal Trade Commission.

Fulfillment: The process of order processing, picking, packing and shipping.

Galleys: 1. Originally, a proof sheet run on the press to check the typesetting. 2. Later, the typeset pages prior to paste-up. 3. The pre-publication copies of the book sent to some reviewers.

Gang run (ganging): Putting numerous unrelated jobs together for printing by assembling them on a single printing plate. Provides lower costs by economizing on setup charges.

Ghostwriter: A professional writer who produces work for others. Work for hire.

Glossary: A list of definitions found in the back matter.

Glossy: A photograph with a shiny surface. Not matte.

Gripper margin: The unprintable edge of the sheet of paper where the printing press or photocopier clamps the sheet to pull it through the printing machine. Often on top of the sheet and usually .25".

Gutter: The space between columns of type, such as the inner margins in two facing pages of a book.

Hairline: A very finely ruled line.

Half title: Bastard title.

Halftone: A screened photograph. A tone pattern composed of dots of uniform density but varying in size. A reproduction of a photograph whereby the various tones (highlights and shadows) are translated into numerous tiny dots for printing.

Halftone screen: A screen placed in front of the negative material in the process camera to break up a continuous tone image into dots of black and white to produce a halftone. There are two types: ruled glass screens and contact screens.

Hardcover: A book bound in boards. Case-bound.

Headband: Reinforcing cloth at each end of the spine of a hardcover book.

Headline: A large bold caption at the top of an article or advertisement.

Hickey: A speck or blotch on a printed page.

Highlights: The lightest (or whitest) portions of a photograph or artwork.

Hot type: An older typesetting process using cast hot metal.

Hyperbole or hype: Exaggerated claims used in selling a product or person.

Illustration: Photographs and drawings. Artwork.

Image area: The printable area of a page surrounded by margins.

Imprint: The imprimata the publisher uses for a book. A publisher may have several imprints.

In print: Books that are currently available from publishers.

Index: An A to Z listing in the back matter giving the location of specific material.

Insertion order: A form used by advertising agencies to place advertising in various media.

International Standard Book Number: A unique number that identifies the binding, edition and publisher of a book. ISBNs are assigned by their publisher.

International Standard Serial Number: A number like an ISBN for serials—books published in a series. ISSNs are assigned by the Library of Congress.

Inventory: Books on hand available for sale.

Invoice: A bill.

Italics: Type with a *right-hand slant.* Used for quotations, titles and emphasis.

Jobber: One who buys books in large quantities for resale to retailers and libraries.

Justification: Composing lines of running text so that the left and right margins are even. Automatically performed by computerized typesetting machines.

Kerning: Removing space between letters.

Layout: A sketch or preliminary drawing of what is to be printed. A mockup.

Layout: A paste-up or mechanical.

Leading: The amount of vertical spacing, measured in points, between lines of typeset text. Rhymes with "heading."

Leaflet: A printed piece of paper folded in the center to produce four pages.

Letterpress: Printing from raised type rather than from photographic plates.

Libel: Written defamation.

Library edition: A book with a reinforced binding.

Library of Congress: The national library serving the U.S. Congress.

Library of Congress Catalog Card number: A unique title control number assigned by the Library of Congress to a given work.

Library rate: The special postal rate available for shipping books to or from libraries and educational institutions.

Line art: A black-and-white illustration that does not require screening.

Line shot: Any negative, print, copy or printing plate which is composed of solid image areas without halftone patterns.

Line drawing: A black-and-white drawing with no gray tones. Line art.

List price: The suggested retail selling price of merchandise.

Literary Market Place: The directory of the book publishing industry.

Logo: A symbol or illustration used as an identifying mark by a business. Like a trademark.

Lowercase: Small letters, not capitals.

Mail order: Fulfilling orders via the mail.

Make-ready: All the printing press setup in preparation for a print run.

Manuscript: The book (typed or handwritten) before it is typeset, pasted up and printed.

Margin: The white space around the copy on a page.

Marketing plan: A publisher's total promotional plan for a book, including reviews, subsidiary rights, advertising and other customer contact.

Mass-market paperback: The smaller, 4" x 7", cheaper editions usually sold next to magazines.

Matte: A non-shiny, dull surface.

Mechanical: See *paste-up.*

Media: Print, broadcast and other methods for delivering your message to the market.

Microfiche cards: A flat-surface film in card size. Many wholesalers send their inventory listings on microfiche to bookstores every couple of weeks.

Monograph: A short report on a single subject.

Negative: The image obtained from the original in the conventional photographic process. The tones are the reverse of those in the original subject. Positive prints are made from negatives.

News release: An announcement sent to a periodical.

Non-photo blue: A light blue pencil or ink which will not be picked up by a plate-making camera. Light blue pens and pencils are used to mark pasted-up sheets.

Nth name: Incrementally selected names from a mailing list, such as every 10th name. Used in testing lists.

OCR: Optical Character Recognition. A device that can recognize (read) typewritten characters and convert them to electronic impulses for translation to output media language. An OCR reader can read a printed page into a computer for editing and revised printout.

Offset lithography: Where the image is transferred from the printing plate to a rubber blanket and then to, or "offset" on, the paper. Practically all lithography is done by the offset method.

Opaque: Not admitting light. Painting out parts of negatives so they will not reproduce.

Out of print: A book is no longer available.

Overrun: The books over the ordered amount. Because there are so many parts to a book, printers are allowed overruns and underruns of up to 10%.

Packing slip: A document sent with a shipment of books itemizing the contents of the shipment.

Page proof: A layout of the pages as they will appear in the book.

Pagination: The numbering or order of pages in a book.

Paperback: A softcover book.

Paste-up: An array of reproduction-quality copy arranged in proper position on a paper prepared as line copy ready for the camera. Same as a mechanical.

Peer review: Manuscript editing by an expert in the subject field.

Pen name: A pseudonym.

Perfect binding: The standard glued-on cover seen on most softcover books. It has a squared-off spine on which the title and name of the author may be printed.

Periodical: A periodically issued publication such as a magazine.

Photocomposition: Setting type photographically by exposing a photosensitive paper or film to images of typed characters, in such a sequence as to create the desired text or copy.

Photodirect: Exposing an image directly to a light-sensitive offset plate material.

Photomechanical transfer, PMT, diffusion transfer: A process in which the paste-up is exposed to a sheet of sensitized paper, the paper is processed in contact with a receiver sheet, and the sheets are peeled apart to produce a usable image on the receiver.

Photostat or stat: A photographic reproduction—which can be negative or positive—made from film, artwork, other stats, etc., and used as line art for many art applications.

PI: Per inquiry advertising, where the media provide the space or time free and get a piece of each sale.

Pica: A printing industry unit of measure equal to approximately 1/16 of an inch. There are 12 points to the pica. Usually used to measure width.

Plagiarism: Copying the work of another and passing it off as one's own.

Plate, printing: Usually the master device bearing the image to be printed. May be paper, plastic or metal.

Plugging: A press condition whereby photographs appear muddy or characters fill in. Caused by poor plate burning, over-application of ink or incorrect ink/water balance.

PMS color: The Pantone Matching System for specifying specific shades of color.

Point: A vertical measurement used in typesetting. One point equals 1/72 of an inch.

Point of purchase display (POP): A dump or rack of books.

Positive: A photographic image in which the tones correspond to the original subject. A positive on paper is usually called a "print."

PPI: Pages per inch. Used to measure the thickness of paper.

Preface: Introductory remarks by the author in the front matter. The preface gives the reason for the book and defines its aims and scope.

Premium: A book given away as part of a promotion.

Press kit: A collection of publicity materials used to promote a book, usually presented in a cardboard folder with pockets.

Press release: See *news release.*

Printer's error: Mistakes made by the printer in preparing for the press. Not author's alterations.

Proof: A direct impression of type or plate showing what the printed page will look like.

Pseudonym: An assumed name used to conceal an author's identity. A pen name.

Public domain: Material not protected by copyright.

Publication date: The date on which a book's promotion is slated to peak and books are available for purchase. A *launch date* usually set three to four months after the book is printed.

Publicist: One who prepares promotional materials and/or schedules media appearances.

Publishers Marketing Association: A trade association that sponsors co-op promotions to help members sell books.

Purchase order: A request for the purchase of merchandise, describing the merchandise, shipping instructions and other conditions of sale. A PO generally represents a promise to pay. Acceptance by the supplier constitutes a contract to supply the merchandise under specified terms.

Quality paperback: A softcover or trade paper book.

Quick printing: Producing a printing plate or master directly from the original boards (paste-ups) to reproduce multiple copies.

Quote: 1. An endorsement for a book. 2. A price quotation for printing.

Ragged right: An uneven right-hand margin. Not justified.

Reduction: A photographic process creating a small image.

Register: The correct positioning of print on a page.

Remaindering: The selling off of the remaining stock of books after sales fall off.

Remnant space: Random advertising space in a periodical, which has not been sold and is available at a reduced rate. Occurs usually in regional editions of national magazines.

Reprint: 1. To go back to press on the same book. 2. Printing the book in another version, such as the paperback version of a hardcover book.

Reverse: To print an image white on black, rather than black on white.

Returns: Unsold books which are returned to a publisher for credit.

Review: An evaluation of a book, sometimes critical.

Review copy: A complimentary copy of a book sent to reviewers and potential quality purchasers.

Revised edition: The printing of a book after substantial changes to the contents. The ISBN should be different.

Rights: An agreement to allow someone else to use the book, usually in another form. Examples are foreign rights, first serial rights and film rights.

Royalties: Money paid to authors by publishers for the right to publish their work.

Runaround: Where text is typeset around an illustration.

Running heads. The book title or chapter title found at the top of the page in many books. See the top of this page.

Saddle stitch: See *stitch.*

Sales rep: An individual who presents books to stores and takes orders. A *book traveler.*

SASE: Self-addressed, stamped envelope.

Scaling: Using a proportion wheel to size an illustration for printing. Scaling determines how much to enlarge or reduce a photograph.

Scoring: Creasing or pressing a line into paper so that it will fold more readily and more accurately.

Screen: See *halftone screen.*

Serial: A publication issued in successive parts, usually at regular intervals.

Serif: The "tails" on a character that make it easier to read. The text in this book is set in a serif type. The headers at the top of the page are set in a sans serif (without serif) type.

Sheet: Two printed pages, one on each side of a leaf of paper. If the sheet is folded to create four printed pages, it is called a "leaflet."

Sheet-fed press: A printing press that prints on sheets of paper, not rolls.

Short discount: Less than 40%. Textbooks are often sold on a short discount.

Signature: A part of a book obtained by folding a large single sheet of paper into sections. A book signature may contain 8, 16, 32 or 64 pages.

Smyth sewn: Where signatures are

sewn together with thread prior to installing the cover on a book. Common with hardbound books.

Spine: The part of the book that connects the front to the back.

Spine out: Displaying books on a shelf so that the spine shows. Not "face out."

Spiral binding: Continuous wire binding.

Standard Address Number (SAN): A number assigned to all organizations involved in buying, selling and lending books. The numbers are assigned by the ISBN agency at Bowker.

Statement: A periodic (usually monthly) listing of invoices, credit memos and payments. Bookstores expect a monthly statement of account.

STOP orders: A cash with order, Single Title Order Plan used by bookstores.

Stet: A proofreading term to disregard editing notes and leave as is. From the Latin meaning "to stand."

Stitch: A staple. The staples seen in magazines and brochures are "saddle stitches."

Strike-on type: Cold type created with a typewriter, composer or computer character printer where the typeface makes an impression on paper through a carbon ribbon.

Stripping: The assembling of photographic negatives or positives and attaching them to the flat (a large sheet of heavy paper) for plate making.

Subsidiary rights: Additional rights to publish the book in other forms. Examples are book club rights, foreign rights and serial rights.

Subsidy press: A publisher who charges the author to publish a book. Subsidy presses have a bad reputation for editing, production and promotion. A "vanity press."

Tear sheets: Ads, stories, etc., torn from the magazine they appeared in.

Terms: Time, in days, allowed a customer for payment of an invoice. For example: Net 30 days.

Text: The main body of the page. Not the headlines.

Tipping-in: The pasting into a book of extra sheets such as foldout maps.

Title: 1. A book or stock of the same book. 2. The name of the book.

Trade paperback: A quality paperback or softcover book.

Trade publisher: One who publishes books primarily for the book trade: bookstores and libraries.

Transfer type: Sheets of characters, numerals, borders or symbols which may be burnished onto paper and added to the paste-up.

Traveler, book: A sales rep.

Trim marks: Lines made on the edges of a camera-ready board to indicate where the page will be cut (trimmed) after it is printed.

Trim size: The size of the page once trimmed to its final dimension.

Underrun: When a printer manufactures fewer copies than were ordered. See *overrun.*

Unit cost: The cost to print each book.

Vanity press: A subsidy press

Velox: A positive print of a photograph or line art ready for paste-up. Usually 65-, 85- or 100-line screen is used for photographs to produce "halftones."

Vendor: The supplier of goods or services.

Wax: An adhesive material used like rubber cement to attach elements to the paste-up board.

Web press: A fast printing press,

using paper on rolls as opposed to sheets.

Wholesaler: A company that buys books in quantities for resale to stores and libraries. "Wholesalers" handle books; "distributors" represent publishers.

White out: To remove unwanted parts of a paste-up by covering with an opaque liquid.

Window: A sheet of red, orange or black paper or acetate on a paste-up, to indicate where a photograph will be positioned. These colors photograph as black, creating a clear "window" in the black negative.

Work for hire: Writing in which the writer does not retain ownership. See *"ghostwriter."*

Working title: A preliminary title used during manuscript preparation before the book is named.

Index

Order Form

✳ Fax orders: (805) 968-1379

☎ Telephone orders: Call Toll Free: 1(800) PARAPUB. Have your AMEX, Optima, Discover, VISA or MasterCard ready.

💻 On-line orders: Orders@ParaPublishing.com

✉ Postal orders: Para Publishing, Dan Poynter, P.O. Box 8206-890, Santa Barbara, CA 93118-8206, USA
Tel: (805) 968-7277

Please send the following books:
I understand that I may return any books for a full refund—for any reason, no questions asked.

_____

_____

_____

❏ Please send the *Publishing Poynters* newsletter to me FREE.

Company name:_____

Name: _____

Address: _____

City: _____ State: _____ Zip: _____-_____

Telephone: (_____)_____

Sales tax:
Please add 7.75% for books shipped to California addresses.

Shipping:
$4.00 for the first book and $2.00 for each additional book.

Payment:
❏ Cheque
❏ Credit card: ❏ VISA, ❏ MasterCard, ❏ Optima, ❏ AMEX, ❏ Discover

Card number: _____

Name on card: _____ Exp. date: _____ /_____

Call *toll free* and order now

Order Form

✳ Fax orders: (805) 968-1379

☎ Telephone orders: Call Toll Free: 1(800) PARAPUB. Have your AMEX, Optima, Discover, VISA or MasterCard ready.

💻 On-line orders: Orders@ParaPublishing.com

✉ Postal orders: Para Publishing, Dan Poynter, P.O. Box 8206-890, Santa Barbara, CA 93118-8206, USA
Tel: (805) 968-7277

Please send the following books:
I understand that I may return any books for a full refund—for any reason, no questions asked.

_____

_____

_____

❑ Please send the *Publishing Poynters* newsletter to me FREE.

Company name:_____

Name: _____

Address: _____

City: _____ State: _____ Zip: _____-_____

Telephone: (____)_____

Sales tax:
Please add 7.75% for books shipped to California addresses.

Shipping:
$4.00 for the first book and $2.00 for each additional book.

Payment:
❑ Cheque
❑ Credit card: ❑ VISA, ❑ MasterCard, ❑ Optima, ❑ AMEX, ❑ Discover

Card number:_____

Name on card: _____ Exp. date: _____ /_____

Call *toll free* and order now

Order Form

✳ Fax orders: (805) 968-1379

☎ Telephone orders: Call Toll Free: 1(800) PARAPUB. Have your AMEX, Optima, Discover, VISA or MasterCard ready.

💻 On-line orders: Orders@ParaPublishing.com

✉ Postal orders: Para Publishing, Dan Poynter, P.O. Box 8206-890, Santa Barbara, CA 93118-8206, USA
Tel: (805) 968-7277

Please send the following books:
I understand that I may return any books for a full refund—for any reason, no questions asked.

_____

_____

_____

❏ Please send the *Publishing Poynters* newsletter to me FREE.

Company name:_____

Name: _____

Address: _____

City: _____ State: _____ Zip: _____-_____

Telephone: (____)_____

Sales tax:
Please add 7.75% for books shipped to California addresses.

Shipping:
$4.00 for the first book and $2.00 for each additional book.

Payment:
❏ Cheque
❏ Credit card: ❏ VISA, ❏ MasterCard, ❏ Optima, ❏ AMEX, ❏ Discover

Card number: _____

Name on card: _____ Exp. date: _____ /_____

Call *toll free* and order now